FEMINIST FILM THEORY

A READER

Edited and introduced by
Sue Thornham

EDINBURGH UNIVERSITY PRESS

© Selection and editorial material
 Sue Thornham, 1999

Edinburgh University Press
22 George Square, Edinburgh

Typeset in Gill Sans and Sabon
by Bibliocraft Ltd, Dundee, and
printed and bound in Great Britain
by the Cromwell Press, Trowbridge,
Wilts.

A CIP record for this book is available
from the British Library

ISBN 0 7486 0959 8 (hardback)
ISBN 0 7486 0890 7 (paperback)

The right of the contributors to be
identified as authors of this work has
been asserted in accordance with the
Copyright, Designs and Patents Act
1988

Feminist Film Theory

For Helen

CONTENTS

struggling 争斗/�'斗
avant-garde 先锋

INTRODUCTION

It is now over twenty-five years since the American journal *Women and Film* launched its passionate attack on behalf of the women's movement on 'women's image in film', and vowed to 'transform the derogatory and immoral attitudes the ruling class and their male lackys [*sic*] have towards women and other oppressed peoples' through the agency of feminist criticism and film-making (1972: 5). Its vocabulary now seems outdated and the terms of its argument no longer so clear. The women's movement has fragmented, no longer a political movement with a mass following. The relationship between a radical feminist politics and the academic feminism of film theory and criticism no longer seems self-evident; the two, indeed, often seem at odds. The assumption that the feminist theorist/critic speaks on behalf of all women can no longer be made. The category 'all women' has itself become suspect, as 'sisterhood' reveals itself to be fractured by power differences along lines of class, race and sexual orientation; and women can no longer line up so easily with 'other oppressed peoples'. Finally, of course, 'women's image in film' can no longer be seen as a simple matter of 'misrepresentation', to be corrected by the more 'realistic' portrayals to be produced by an emerging group of women film-makers.

We can no longer, then, assume a straightforward relationship between the film theorist and the political activist, between the theorist and the 'ordinary woman', between women and 'other oppressed peoples', and between the feminist theorist/critic and the feminist film-maker. Nor can we envisage a utopian moment when 'images of women' will 'reflect' the realities of women's lives: cinematic representations are far more complex than this. But questions about these relationships form the terms of the debates that are charted in this book. And because a vital part of feminism's project has been to 'transform women from an object of knowledge into a subject capable of appropriating knowledge' (Delmar 1986: 25), and because 'seeing' is so crucial to knowledge in Western culture, these debates have been central within feminist theory. As Judith Mayne comments:

> One of the most basic connections between women's experience in this culture and women's experience in film is precisely the relationship of spectator and spectacle. Since women are spectacles in their everyday lives, there's something about coming to terms with film from the perspective of what it means to be an object of spectacle and what it means to be a spectator that is really a coming to terms with how that relationship exists both up on the screen and in everyday life. (Citron et al. 1978: 86)

For the past twenty-five years, then, cinema has been, in Laura Mulvey's words, 'the crucial terrain' on which feminist debates about culture, representation and identity have been fought (1989: 77). This book seeks to chart the history of those debates, as feminist film theory has engaged both with theoretical currents from outside its own political borders – from structuralism and psychoanalysis in the 1970s to post-colonial theory, queer theory and postmodernism in the 1990s – and with its own internally generated conflicts.

Part I, then, introduces the debates of the 1970s about which theoretical tools will best serve the political ends of feminism and how we might best understand the relationship between oppressive images, representations, or structures of looking, and gendered structures of social and material power. The first three readings in this section date from 1972–4, and exemplify what B. Ruby Rich calls the 'two voices' of feminist film criticism during this period: the 'originally American, so-called sociological approach' and its British counterpart, the 'so-called theoretical approach'. The section closes with Rich's own 1978 overview of 1970s feminist film theory and criticism, in which she calls for a new theoretical language which might bring together the two approaches.

Part II represents what, following the work of Claire Johnston and Laura Mulvey in the 1970s, became the dominant strain in feminist film theory, one which, in Constance Penley's words, 'directly takes up the major issues of film theory as they were formulated in the theoretical ferment of the 1970s, generated and sustained by the interest in semiology, psychoanalysis, textual analysis, and theories of ideology' (1988: 1). Beginning with Laura Mulvey's (1975) 'Visual Pleasure and Narrative Cinema', it offers analyses of the spectator-screen relationship, of identificatory processes and pleasures in film, and of the relationship between narrative and desire. All draw on psychoanalytic theory to explore the ways in which cinematic pleasures operate for the male spectator, whilst the figure of 'woman' functions as fetishised object of desire or object of narrative punishment.

Discussion of the female spectator is the focus of Part III. A troubling issue already, as Mary Ann Doane's discussion of the 1940s 'woman's film' in Part II makes clear, the question of what happens when women engage in cinematic spectatorship is debated here. Two of the answers offered, those of Laura Mulvey and Mary Ann Doane, retain a psychoanalytic framework. The remaining two, however, offer a challenge to this perspective, returning us to a consideration of the woman viewer as socially as well as textually positioned spectator. Most notable in this respect is the final essay in this section, Annette Kuhn's 'Women's Genres'. Kuhn's insistence that we must consider context as well as text, the social audience as well as the textual spectator, in our analysis of the female viewer, shifts the analytic focus away from the purely textual and towards a perspective identified with a cultural studies analytic framework.

This framework is further developed in the essays that comprise Part IV. The explanatory model which Stuart Hall developed in his (1973) 'Encoding/ Decoding' paper is appropriated for a feminist analysis by Christine Gledhill. Like Hall, Gledhill argues that textual meaning 'is neither imposed, not passively imbibed, but arises out of a struggle or negotiation between competing frames of reference, motivation and experience'. Such negotiation takes place during processes of textual production, within the text itself, and in audience readings. Gledhill's focus is on the way in which popular texts may become the site of 'a struggle between male and female voices over the meaning of the symbol "woman" ' (1987: 37). Whilst Gledhill's analytic object remains the text itself, however, the remaining three essays in this section explore ways in which feminist film theory might be brought to bear on studies of film audiences, whether these are the family viewing audience of Valerie Walkerdine's study or the wider audiences considered in the work of Jackie Stacey and Janet Staiger.

Psychoanalytic theory has remained important within feminist film theory, however, and the essays that comprise Part V offer examples of more recent applications of psychoanalytic perspectives to popular film genres. All draw to some extent on psychoanalytic 'fantasy theory', which has its origins in the work of Laplanche and Pontalis. Their (1964) essay, 'Fantasy and the Origins of Sexuality', argues that fantasy is the staging of desire, its *mise-en-scène* rather than its object. Thus, whilst we are always present in our fantasies, our identification is shifting, not fixed along lines of sexual difference. Applications of this work to the cinematic 'fantasies' of the horror film, pornography and melodrama can be found in the three essays in this section. In the analyses by Carol J. Clover, Barbara Creed and Linda Williams of the pleasures, fears and desires at play in these contemporary 'body genres', 'fantasy theory' is combined with the work of Kaja Silverman on masochistic male fantasy, and of Julia Kristeva on designations of the fantasised 'impure' maternal body as 'abject', to offer insights which both extend and challenge earlier psychoanalytic feminist film theory.

The final section explores the limitations of earlier psychoanalytic feminist film theory when confronted by two groups of female spectators whose cinematic pleasures and identifications seem literally 'unthinkable' within its terms: black women and lesbian women. Like the writers in Part IV, these essays return us to issues of history, experience and political practice. Jane Gaines, then, points out the inadequacies of a psychoanalytically grounded theory of the 'male gaze' to deal with either the disabling of the black male gaze or the very different functioning of the image of the black woman to that of her white counterpart. These issues are also taken up in the essay by bell hooks, who argues that the gaze of the black female spectator functions as an oppositional or critical gaze. Offered no place within a visual economy which defines femininity as white femininity, she becomes a deconstructive spectator, her pleasures those of resistance, not only to the proffered feminine ideals but also to the structures of power which they embody.

The final two essays, by Tania Modleski and Judith Butler, return us to an engagement with psychoanalytic theory, though from the often critical perspectives of post-colonial and queer theory. Modleski draws on the work of Homi Bhabha on colonial stereotyping to examine the functioning in popular contemporary cinema of the relationship of white woman to black man and of the figure of the black woman. Like hooks, she argues that the functioning of the black woman in cinema as 'site of the displacement of white culture's (including white women's) fears and anxieties' demands a feminist theory that can embrace the binary opposition black/white as well as that of male/female, and insist on 'the "multiple and cross-cutting" nature of identity'. Finally, Judith Butler's analysis of the 1991 film, *Paris is Burning*, with its depiction of a black gay drag ball sub-culture, argues that all gender identity should properly be seen as performance. The self-conscious and parodic performance which is drag may then serve as a kind of 'talking back' to cultural gender norms, the almost-but-not-quite embodiment of the ideals of white femininity by its black male performers serving to draw attention both to the construct-edness of such ideals and to our own complicity in their endlessly reiterated performance.

It is a long way, then, from the heady optimism of the *Women and Film* editorial of 1972 to the complexities of these later analyses. Along the way, feminist film theory and criticism has become an academic subject and has become, perhaps, as Bergstrom and Doane suggest, 'cut off from its original sense of bold innovation and political purpose' (1989: 16). Nevertheless, the centrality of a feminist 'politics of vision' (Mulvey 1989: 77) unites all the readings in this book. If that politics has had more recently to recognise divisions and fragmentations in subjectivity other than those produced by the male/female opposition, and histories and experiences other than those of the white woman under Western patriarchy, such recognitions of the differences between women may be seen to signal the further development and not, as some have suggested,[1] a loss of direction in feminist film theory.

NOTES

1. See for example Mulvey (1989).

REFERENCES

Bergstrom, Janet and Doane, Mary Ann 1989: The Female Spectator: Contexts and Directions. *Camera Obscura* 20–1, pp. 5–27.

Citron, Michelle, Le Sage, Julia, Mayne, Judith, Rich, B. Ruby, Taylor, Anna Marie, and the editors of *New German Critique* 1978: Women and Film: A Discussion of Feminist Aesthetics. *New German Critique* 13, pp. 83–107.

Delmar, Rosalind 1986: What Is Feminism? In Mitchell, J. and Oakley A. (ed.), *What Is Feminism?* Oxford: Blackwell.

Gledhill, Christine 1987: The Melodramatic Field: An Investigation. In Gledhill, *Home is Where the Heart is: Studies in Melodrama and the Woman's Film*. London: BFI, pp. 5–39.

Mulvey, Laura 1989: British Feminist Film, Theory's Female Spectators: Presence and Absence. *Camera Obscura* 20/21, pp 68–81.

Penley, Constance 1988: Introduction – The Lady Doesn't Vanish: Feminism and Film Theory. In Penley, C. (ed.), *Feminism and Film Theory*. New York and London: Routledge/BFI, pp. 1–24.

Women and Film 1972: Overview. *Women and Film* 1, pp. 3–6.

PART I
TAKING UP THE STRUGGLE

INTRODUCTION

In 1972 the first issue of a shortlived American journal called *Women and Film* was published. Appearing just two years after the publication of Kate Millett's *Sexual Politics*, Shulamith Firestone's *The Dialectic of Sex*, Germaine Greer's *The Female Eunuch*, and Robin Morgan's anthology, *Sisterhood is Powerful*, it declares itself to be part of the 'second wave' feminism which these books heralded. It states:

> The women in this magazine, as part of the women's movement, are aware of the political, psychological, social and economic oppression of women. The struggle begins on all fronts and we are taking up the struggle with women's image in film and women's roles in the film industry – the ways in which we are exploited and the ways to transform the derogatory and immoral attitudes the ruling class and their male lackys [*sic*] have towards women and other oppressed peoples. (Editorial, *Women and Film* 1972: 5)

Women, the editors go on, are oppressed within the film industry (they are 'receptionists, secretaries, odd job girls, prop girls' etc.); they are oppressed by being packaged as images (sex objects, victims or vampires); and lastly they are oppressed within film theory, by male critics who celebrate *auteurs* like Sirk or Hitchcock for their complexity or irony or for in some way rising above their material – often the humble 'woman's picture' or 'weepie'. The editors' critical/theoretical project is therefore both an essential tool for an activist feminist politics and in itself a form of activism. Its desired outcome will be threefold: a transformation in film-making practice, an end to oppressive ideology and stereotyping, and the creation of a feminist critical aesthetics. The three are inseparable.

It is in this climate, then, that feminist film theory begins – as an urgent political act. Without theoretical tools, one cannot begin to transform existing myths and practices, and feminists from Simone de Beauvoir onwards had seen cinema as a key carrier of contemporary cultural myths. It is through these myths – found in 'religions, traditions, language, tales, songs, movies' argues de Beauvoir – that our material existences are viewed, and lived. And though '[r]epresentation of the world, like the world itself, is the work of men; they describe it from their own point of view, which they confuse with absolute truth' (1988: 175), women, too, must inevitably see themselves through these representations.

This sense of urgency, and of direct political engagement, is evident in all of the pieces in this opening section. But they also represent the opening of a number of debates. Which theoretical tools will best serve the ends envisaged by the editors of *Women and Film*? To what extent can non-feminist or pre-feminist thinking be appropriated in this process? What is the relationship between the different types of oppression which the editors describe? In particular, what is the precise relationship between oppressive images, representations, or structures of looking, and gendered structures of social and material power?

Sharon Smith's 'The Image of Women in Film: Some Suggestions for Future Research' appeared in the first issue of *Women and Film*. Like a number of American analyses of the time,[1] it employs a survey methodology, and takes as the focus of its attack the issue of 'sex-role stereotyping'. Smith's concern is to expose as both false and oppressive the limited range of images of women offered by film. In her account, films both reflect social structures and changes and misrepresent them according to the fantasies and fears of their male creators. The resultant stereotypes serve to reinforce and/or create the prejudices of their male audiences, and to damage the self-perceptions and limit the social aspirations of women. It is an account that is concerned to link the power of cinematic representations to the social context which produces and receives them, and to insist on women's collective power to instigate change. It is a powerful polemic, but its theoretical framework remains undeveloped. At times film representations appear to be the product of deliberate propaganda; at times they seem the result of unconscious fantasy. Film reflects social changes, but it also shapes cultural attitudes. Its stereotypes are the product of unconscious assumptions too deep-rooted to be changed simply by having more women in positions of power within the film industry, yet the 'vicious circle' of its cultural effects can be broken by a combination of rational persuasion and stereotype-correction. The way forward is for film to embrace 'a wider variety of roles' for women, but Smith recognises uneasily that for this to occur a completely new mode of thinking will be needed.

Molly Haskell's *From Reverence to Rape*, published in 1974, offers a more complex and developed version of Smith's position. 'The big lie perpetrated on

Western society is the idea of women's inferiority', her opening chapter begins, and the 'movie business', as the 'propaganda arm of the American Dream machine', is 'an industry dedicated for the most part to reinforcing the lie' (Haskell 1987: 1–2). Haskell's book charts the shifts in woman's image through the decades of the twentieth century: 'idealized as the "feminine principle incarnate" ', 'worshipped as "mother" ', 'venerated as "earth goddess" ', both 'celebrated and feared as separate-but-equal', and finally, in the backlash against feminism, excised altogether in the 1960s 'buddy-film' or subjected to the violence of Kubrick or Peckinpah. Like Smith, then, she sees images of women in film as 'the vehicle of male fantasies' and 'the scapegoat of men's fears' (1987: 39), but she also sees films as complex texts which may contain competing, even subversive voices.

It is in her chapter on 'The Woman's Film' of the 1930s and 1940s, reproduced here, that Haskell's most fully explores these issues. Here she departs from the chronological approach she employs elsewhere, in favour of a categorisation in terms of the genre's dominant themes. Pervading all categories, indeed virtually synonymous with the woman's film, is the theme of sacrifice. On the one hand, then, these films are politically conservative and masochistic. On the other, in this critically despised genre, 'the woman – a woman – is at the centre of the universe'. She may die at the film's close, but she dominates its narrative. Indeed, the tailoring of the genre for a female audience means that it must give voice not only to women's 'avowed obligations' but also to their 'unconscious resistance', the repressed anger and guilt which is the corollary of the insistence that a woman find fulfilment in institutions – marriage, mother-hood – which 'end her independent identity'.

Haskell, then, rejects an analysis that sees film merely as a 'rich field for the mining of female stereotypes' (1987: 30), arguing that it must be examined in all its complexities as film, and for all our complexities of response. Many of her points were to be taken up by later theorists, but, like Smith, she herself lacks a theoretical framework which might offer an adequate analysis of these elements, and her survey method militates against the development of theoretical complexity.

In 1973, *Notes on Women's Cinema*, edited by Claire Johnston, was published in Britain by the Society for Education in Film and Television. Its keynote article was Johnston's 'Women's Cinema as Counter-Cinema'. The pamphlet's opening seems to echo that of *Women and Film*:

> From the outset the Women's Movement has assumed without question the importance of film in the women's struggle ... The reason for this interest in the media is not difficult to locate: it has been at the level of the image that the violence of sexism and capitalism has been experienced. (1973: 2)

Johnston, however, goes on to attack what she terms the 'crude determinism' of the 'sociological perspective' exemplified by the American journal. Lacking an adequate theoretical framework, she argues, it provides neither a satisfactory critical analysis nor a way forward for feminist film-making. And '[i]f film criticism is to have any use, it is that it should provide a greater understanding of how film operates which will ultimately feed back into film-making itself' (1973: 3). Two years later she was to be equally dismissive of Haskell's book, and on the same grounds. In Britain, she was to add, feminist film criticism 'has taken a very different direction: here emphasis has been placed on the primacy of the film text itself, relating very directly to current developments in film theory as such' (1975: 122).

These developments drew on emergent theories within European structuralism and semiotics, Marxist concepts of ideology, and psychoanalytic theory. They insisted that film representations should not be viewed, as in the American approach, as reflections of reality, whether 'true' or 'distorted'. Films are 'texts' – complex structures of linguistic and visual codes organised to produce specific meanings. They are not merely collections of images or stereotypes. To evaluate cinematic images of women in terms of their greater or lesser 'truth' or their degrees of 'distortion' is therefore, argues Johnston, to miss the point. Films structure meaning through their organisation of visual and verbal signs. It is these textual structures that we must examine because it is here, rather than in any conscious manipulation by the individual film director, that meaning is produced. Films, in short, are bearers of ideology. Ideology is defined here as that representational system, or 'way of seeing',[2] which appears to us to be 'universal' or 'natural' but which is in fact the product of the specific power structures which constitute our society. The sign 'woman', then, has acquired its meaning within a sexist, or patriarchal, ideology. It has meaning only within that structure. It is thus pointless to compare film stereotypes of women with the reality of women's lives. What must be examined is how the sign 'woman' operates within the specific film text – what meanings it is made to bear and what desires and fantasies it carries. 'To disengage and place such ideologies', as Johnston argues elsewhere, is the primary task of feminist film criticism (1975: 123).

Similarly, Johnston argues that it will not be enough for cinema to offer more positive roles for women, or for women to operate collectively to produce more 'realistic' female images, for film-making to be transformed. Instead, within the Hollywood system women film-makers can operate to create disruptions in the ideological fabric of conventional films, and outside it they must seek to invest their film texts with women's desires and fantasies.

B. Ruby Rich's article, which closes this section, was written in 1978 and looks back over these early years of feminist film theory and criticism. Like many of the pieces written during this period, it is concerned to address issues in film practice as well as critical theory and to see both within the context of the Women's Movement, but it is the sections that deal with theoretical issues which are reproduced here. By 1978, the theoretical approach inaugurated in Britain by Claire Johnston and Laura Mulvey had become influential amongst American feminists via the journal *Camera Obscura*,[3] and Rich reflects on the 'two voices' of feminist criticism that had developed. She is unusual in her attempt both to bring the two together and to provide an analysis which encompasses both.

Characterising the two approaches as 'the language of experience' and 'the language of theory', she argues that, if the former, the 'originally American, so-called sociological approach', is unduly optimistic in its assumption that stereotypes can be simply 'corrected' by the conscious intervention of women, then the latter, the 'originally British, so-called theoretical approach' is unduly pessimistic. Reduced to a sign within a patriarchal ideology, woman in this account has no presence, no specific experience, and no possibility of active intervention at all. On the contrary, argues Rich, the female viewer interacts with both text and context. She is no passive recipient of ideological structures, but an active maker of meaning. In a highly suggestive formulation, whose resonances were to be picked up by later theorists, Rich argues that the female viewer within patriarchal culture is positioned both within and without its structures, the ultimate cultural dialectician. What is needed, she argues, is a theoretical language that can encompass these contradictions, and not become entrapped by either an activist optimism or a theoretical pessimism.

NOTES

1. See for example Marjorie Rosen's (1973) *Popcorn Venus*, as well as Molly Haskell's (1974) *From Reverence to Rape*.
2. The phrase is John Berger's. See Berger, *Ways of Seeing* (1972).
3. Issue 1 appeared in Fall 1976, with an editorial by Janet Bergstrom, Sandy Flitterman, Elisabeth Hart Lyon and Constance Penley, which declares that a 'feminist film analysis recognizes that film is a specific cultural product, and attempts to examine the way in which bourgeois and patriarchal ideology is inscribed in film' (1976: 3).

REFERENCES

Berger, John 1972: *Ways of Seeing*. London: BBC Books.
   Camera Obscura 1976: Feminism and Film: Critical Approaches. *Camera Obscura* 1, pp. 3–10.
De Beauvoir, Simone 1988 (1949): *The Second Sex*. London: Pan Books.
Firestone, Shulamith 1979 (1970): *The Dialectic of Sex: The Case for Feminist Revolution*. London: The Women's Press.
Greer, Germaine 1971 (1970): *The Female Eunuch*. St Albans: Granada Publishing.
Haskell, Molly 1987 (1974): *From Reverence to Rape: The Treatment of Women in the Movies* (second edition). Chicago and London: University of Chicago Press.
Johnston, Claire (ed.) 1973: *Notes on Women's Cinema*. London: Society for Education in Film and Television.
Johnston, Claire 1975: Feminist Politics and Film History. *Screen* 16, 3, pp. 115–25.
Millett, Kate 1977 (1970): *Sexual Politics*. London: Virago.
Morgan, Robin (ed.) 1970: *Sisterhood is Powerful: an Anthology of Writings from the Women's Liberation Movement*. New York: Vintage Books.
Rosen, Marjorie 1974 (1973): *Popcorn Venus*. New York: Avon Books.
   Women and Film 1972: Overview. *Women and Film* 1, pp. 3–6.

I

'THE IMAGE OF WOMEN IN FILM: SOME SUGGESTIONS FOR FUTURE RESEARCH'

Sharon Smith

Women, in any fully human form, have almost completely been left out of film. This is not surprising, since women were also left out of literature. That is, from its very beginning they were present, but not in characterizations any self-respecting person could identify with. Notable exceptions can be pointed to: *A Room of One's Own*, *The Doll's House*, etc., in literature, and a handful of films. Through history males have done almost all the writing and filmmaking, naturally from a male point of view. Of course that point of view has been molded or tempered by the culture each man lived in. However, in modern times, through the sudden (historically speaking) sophistication of the media and their uses, there exists a very large possibility that media now *shape* cultural attitudes, as well as reflect them. The attitudes of the (traditionally male) filmmakers towards women, and the roles they typically give them in films, must be evaluated in this light

The role of a woman in a film almost always revolves around her physical attraction and the mating games she plays with the male characters. On the other hand a man is not shown purely in relation to the female characters, but in a wide variety of roles – struggling against nature (*The Old Man and the Sea*; *Moby Dick*; *2001: A Space Odyssey*), or against militarism (*Dr Strangelove*; *Catch 22*), or proving his manhood on the range (any John Wayne Western). Women provide trouble or sexual interludes for the male characters, or are not present at all. Even when a woman is the central character she is generally shown as

* From *Women and Film* No. 1, 1972, pp. 13–21.

confused, or helpless and in danger, or passive, or as a purely sexual being) It just seems odd that these few images, and others like them, are all we see of women in almost every film. [...] Since very few filmmakers have given much thought to their habits of sex-role stereotyping, even a film which has one strong female character will revert to cliché motivations and actions for the rest.)

That last point is a very important one. (Filmmakers' *minds* must be changed, or this stereotyping will go on forever.) When a film is being made the emphasis is usually on the main theme, whether the film is about a spy ring or gangsters in the 1930s. Questions of modernizing sex-role stereotypes are rarely on the filmmakers' minds, even when the story is about a woman and man in love. In their desire to make the plot clear and get the message across, writers and directors often use shorthand expressions of characterization. Does a science fiction movie need sparking up? Bring in a female scientist and have a love scene (*The Forbin Project*). A woman who 'doesn't know her place' (that is, who has a career besides sex and motherhood) can bring a laugh and move the plot along. As John Simon put it, 'today's American actresses fall mainly into two categories ... those who in some way deflect, travesty, or blatantly overstate their womanliness and sensuality; and those who suppress it, or have nothing to suppress'.[1] Can you imagine the male hero confined to two categories, those who overstate their sensuality and those who suppress it? Men in films are judged on courage in war, loyalty to friends, faith in themselves – a thousand things. Who cares whether or not the hero of *The Confession* would be a good lay? By the way, I fully realize that the image of males in films is often stereotyped as well as that of women but in most cases this is the cliché of the virile and virulent macho male, which, though potentially destructive, is at least a symbol of power and authority [...]

Films express the fantasies and subconscious needs of their (mostly male) creators. How has the stereotype changed from the beginnings of film to the present? Here are some suggestions of the trend as I see it:

In the early 20th century, when women were just starting to have legal rights to money and possessions, Cecil B. DeMille produced *The Cheat* (1915), the story of a woman who has borrowed $10,000 from a Japanese man and tries to pay him back in cash instead of paying in sex. She is branded on her shoulder as one of his possessions for daring to presume a female could use cash instead of sex in the world of men. This was 'praised for the realism of its players' in its day.[2]

In the 1920s women were beginning to be employed in a number of fields. Men who confused business power with sexual potency were made insecure by the presence of women in jobs, even in jobs of an obviously servile nature. Clara Bow had such typical roles as manicurist, usherette, waitress, cigarette girl, taxi dancer, and lingerie saleswoman. All of these were roles in which a working woman's prime duties could be interpreted as flirting with the ever-changing male clientele (yea, even for lingerie). As time went on and women took themselves more seriously in jobs, any film about a working woman was at first funny – *The Lieutenant Wore Skirts* – later sexy – *The Stewardesses*. The message? Why take yourself seriously when all you have to do is be young and pretty to succeed where it really counts – with a man!

Moving into the thirties – research desperately needs to be done about censorship and Mae West. Suddenly there was a woman who simply *enjoyed* sex, didn't use it to hurt men, didn't suffer about it herself. As Lewis Jacobs put it, 'Mae West eyed a man from head to foot. All the time you knew she was evaluating him in terms of virility, as James Cagney eyed a woman.'[3] Six months after the release of *She Done Him Wrong* the Episcopal Committee on Motion Pictures was formed (1933) heralding the age of censorship. Was it the sex in her films that frightened the censors? Motion pictures had always been able to show naked or semi-nude women, in guise of historical or Biblical stories. And Mae left her clothes on, down to the last diamond. Or was it the obvious fact that she enjoyed every moment of her conquests, she, a female!

As she says in her autobiography, '*She Done Him Wrong* changed the fashions of two continents ... Women were trying to walk and talk like me ... Women became more sex conscious and this, for some men, was a big break; for others a bother. Sex was out in the open, and amusing.'[4] The film producers were getting enormous amounts of money from West's successful pictures, so they didn't try to stop her. But it would be very interesting to examine the motives of Will Hayes and the censors. Women expressing interest in sex was, for some men, 'a bother' ... It makes one wonder about the many films in which the woman 'naturally' is frigid and must be 'brought around' by the man. Generally a woman who actively likes sex, but on her own terms, seems to be cast as a 'castrating woman' by the men on whom she makes demands; or like Betty Field in *Of Mice and Men*, her sexuality brings death and destruction to the males.

It would also be very interesting to see research about the changing film image of women before and after the war. During the war, women worked at 'men's' jobs, went to college, supported themselves. Since the men were at war the women were naturally afraid they might never have love, homes and children. Then the GIs returned, and took back the jobs and the places in college. The fifties saw an enormous change as women immersed themselves in babies and housework. Was it partly the movies which made them feel that 'the cold dimension of loneliness which the war had added to their lives was the necessary price they had to pay for any interest outside the home'?[5] [...]

In serious dramas tragedy hits the career woman (or marriage does, for a happy ending). In 1950s sex comedies, the laughs are on her. She is assumed to be frigid, and the plot rolls along on the tricks a man plays on her, with liquor or words – until the very end of the film, when he suddenly gives in and marries her. With very few films available which provide a strong female character to identify with, women have learned to masochistically enjoy seeing women ridiculed on film. They murmur, 'of course, *I* would never be so foolish', or enjoy seeing a younger, more attractive woman 'put in her place'. And men have once more succeeded in dividing women's ranks.

It seems to me that the 'sexualization' of women in films started slowly but has been increasing at a tremendous rate, expecially in the last few years. *Ninotchka* (1939) merely made it clear that a female diplomat should not complete her mission to recover the jewels, but must make loving a man her mission. Current films, from *Lolita* to *1000 Convicts and a Woman*, show not only the sexual awakening, but (in ever more explicit details) the many physical acts the woman performs.

Naturally, it is possible for a woman to enjoy watching films of explicit sex acts. But out of bed the sex-star's role will be the usual: bitch, nymph, housewife, whore, essentially passive, nothing any sane woman would want to identify with. And it is the female star whose naked, silicone-stuffed body is plastered on billboards, not the male star. I don't think anyone will deny that when a female's body is the focus of attention the action is aimed at male viewers. The intent nowadays is not to give a mixed audience an interesting (humorous, tragic, etc.) study of male-female relationships, but to work out the neuroses of male filmmakers with an ever-increasing vengeance, aimed at tittilating male audiences who have the same neuroses. And in men and boys who do not already have these prejudices – it creates them.

What bothers me most about pornography is not the cubic inches of flesh displayed (which censors so misguidedly snip out) but the *image of women* in these films. Plenty of research has been done on the effect of violence on film and TV viewers. I imagine it is very rare that a person would see a murder on TV and immediately kill someone. But what about the persistence of attitudes learned from films? Many films persuade men that any and all women, walking down the street or sitting at home, day or night, are ripe for sex with any man who knows a few trick words, or is strong enough. I've never met a man who believed it, but it is a very unpleasant and frightening daily experience for a woman to walk down a street while men poke at her, make noises at her, and carry on monologues about her anatomy. But sex movies suggest that this is an effective way to excite a woman.

Films use all their powers of persuasion to reinforce – not the status quo, but some mythical Golden Age when men were men and women were girls. Traditionally the entire world is male. 'Man' means the whole human race, and 'woman' is just a part of it. But think 'in female' for a moment. Imagine:

That everything you have ever read uses only female pronouns, she, her, meaning both men and women. Recall that most of the voices on radio and faces on TV are female, especially when important events are in the news. Recall that you have only one male senator representing you in Washington (if you are tempted to laugh and say that would lead to catastrophe, ask yourself where we are now).

Imagine that women are the leaders, the power centers. Men are shown in films only in their natural roles as husband and father, or else as whores and very nasty persons. Men are shown only in their natural functions of trying to attract women and making the world a comfortable place for women. Film men who

17

rebel against this die very ugly deaths. Women star in all films of international excitement or adventure.

Imagine that countless films show men as simple-minded little sex objects, and you despair of finding a strong role-model for your little boy (for whom you see other futures than slut, bitch or house-husband).

Imagine that the women in charge of the film industry use their power to ridicule the men's liberation movement, presenting them in films as a bunch of frustrated studs, deluded into thinking they can be women, burning their jockstraps and waving signs – but always ending up in the boudoir of a condescending woman, always giving up the struggle and being happily subservient to her.

Then imagine that if you complain you are given the biological explanation: by design a female's genitals are compact and internal, protected by her body. A man's genitals are exposed and must be protected from attack. His vulnerability requires sheltering – thus, in films, men must not be shown in ungentle-manlike professions. Psychological films remind men of their childhood, when their sisters jeered at the primitive male genitals, which 'flap around foolishly' while the sisters could ride, climb and run unemcumbered. Men are passive, and must be shown that way in films, to reflect and protect reality. Anatomy is destiny.[6]

I hope by now it is obvious that women must be shown in a much wider variety of roles. Their characterizations must have heroism and human dignity – expressed in fields besides homemaking, loving a man, and bearing children. Women must be shown as active, not passive; strong women shouldn't constantly face ridicule and unhappy endings. Women should be shown in adventures which don't revolve around sexual attraction for a man; or working with other women without cattiness. *Men* will become more sensual in sex roles – how many films I have seen in which the hero somehow makes love without unzipping his fly! This does not mean that men and women's roles in films must be completely and irrevocably reversed. Women just want a chance to be heros; a chance to be shown as humanly (not just femininely) frail; and a chance to see men in some of the ungainly situations in which women have so commonly been shown. When you think 'in female' you will know that traditional themes, characterizations, and even, perhaps, standard approaches to tragedy and comedy, need to be translated 'into female.' [...]

This leads to a major question, which has been present in my constant use of the term 'male filmmakers' throughout the paper. Will all these problems change immediately for the better as the film industry is integrated by women?

Not necessarily. In the first place, it will be a long time before women will be represented in every aspect of the film industry. As a woman in the writer's guild put it, 'women are discriminated against in all aspects of the media. They are given the lower paying jobs, and have to fight twice as hard and be twice as good as males to get comparable jobs.'[7] And once in, they are traditionally kept from power. As an independent filmmaker (female) put it, 'behind every *"master-piece"* of male intelligence are hidden women, the editors, continuity girls, script girls, who are forgotten in that most incredible of all male film fantasies, the auteur theory.'[8]

In the second place, even with women fully represented in the film industry, men will continue to write, direct and produce films about women. Unless convinced otherwise, they will continue to produce the same old stereotypes.

Finally, many women, products of the same society that created the neurotic male filmmakers, are anti-woman. Simply having more females working in film will not change the films' content unless everyone working in films, male and female, starts rethinking the traditional sex role stereotypes.

(Culture influencing film content, in turn influencing culture – this need not continue to be a vicious circle.)I believe publication of research is the first step, to convince people a problem exists and what it consists of. Men, for example, might want to catalogue the types of role models provided by the classic sex role stereo-types of men. And I am presently researching women (some 350) who are working in film; their example might spur more people to hire women, and more women to enter filmmaking.

(Correcting the stereotypes will open up a new world of film themes. And new images of women and men in film will provide more constructive models for film viewers.)

NOTES

1. John Simon, *Private Screenings*, Macmillan, NY, 1967, p. 297.
2. Alexander Walker, *Sex in the Movies*, Penguin Books, 1966, p. 214.
3. Lewis Jacobs, *Rise of the American Film*, Columbia University Teachers College Press, 1939, p. 533.
4. Mae West, *Goodness Had Nothing To Do With It*, Macfadden-Bartell, 1959, p. 152.
5. Betty Friedan, *The Feminine Mystique*, W. W. Norton, 1963, p. 177.
6. Suggested by an article in *Everywoman* newspaper by Theodora Wells.
7. My own research.
8. My own research.

2

'THE WOMAN'S FILM'

Molly Haskell

What more damning comment on the relations between men and women in America than the very notion of something called the 'woman's film'? And what more telling sign of critical and sexual priorities than the low caste it has among the highbrows? Held at arm's length, it is, indeed, the untouchable of film genres [. . .]

Among the Anglo-American critical brotherhood (and a few of their sisters as well), the term 'woman's film' is used disparagingly to conjure up the image of the pinched-virgin or little-old-lady writer, spilling out her secret longings in wish fulfillment or glorious martyrdom, and transmitting these fantasies to the frustrated housewife. The final image is one of wet, wasted afternoons. And if strong men have also cried their share of tears over the weepies, that is all the more reason (goes the argument) we should be suspicious, be on our guard against the flood of 'unearned' feelings released by these assaults, unerringly accurate, on our emotional soft spots.

As a term of critical opprobrium, 'woman's film' carries the implication that women, and therefore women's emotional problems, are of minor significance. A film that focuses on male relationships is not pejoratively dubbed a 'man's film' (indeed, this term, when it is used, confers—like 'a man's man'—an image of brute strength), but a 'psychological drama.' European films, too, are automatically exempted from the 'woman's film' caste; thus, the critical status of *Mayerling* over *Love Affair*, *Le Carnet du Bal* over *Angel*, *Jules and Jim* over

* From Haskell, M. *From Reverence to Rape: the Treatment of Women in the Movies* (second edition). Chicago and London: University of Chicago Press, 1987 (1974), pp. 153–88.

Design for Living, *My Night at Maud's* over *Petulia*, and *The Passion of Anna* over Bergman's English-language *The Touch*. Also exempted are films with literary prestige, like *Carrie* or *Sunday, Bloody Sunday*.

In the thirties and forties, the heyday of the 'woman's film,' it was as regular an item in studio production as the crime melodrama or the Western. Like any routine genre, it was subject to its highs and lows, and ranged from films that adhered safely to the formulae of escapist fantasy, films that were subversive only 'between the lines' and in retrospect, and the rare few that used the conventions to undermine them. At the lowest level, as soap opera, the 'woman's film' fills a masturbatory need, it is soft-core emotional porn for the frustrated housewife. The weepies are founded on a mock-Aristotelian and politically conservative aesthetic whereby women spectators are moved, not by pity and fear but by self-pity and tears, to accept, rather than reject, their lot. That there should be a need and an audience for such an opiate suggests an unholy amount of real misery. And that a term like 'woman's film' can be summarily used to dismiss certain films, with no further need on the part of the critic to make distinctions and explore the genre, suggests some of the reasons for this misery.

In the woman's film, the woman—*a* woman—is at the center of the universe. Best friends and suitors, like Bette Davis' satellites (Geraldine Fitzgerald and George Brent) in *Dark Victory*, live only for her pleasure, talk about her constantly, and cease to exist when she dies. In the rare case where a man's point of view creeps in, as screenwriter Howard Koch's did in *No Sad Songs for Me*, it is generally reconciled with the woman's point of view. Thus, after Margaret Sullavan dies, the husband (Wendell Corey) will marry the woman (Viveca Lindfors) he almost had an affair with. But it is with the dead wife's blessing (she has actually chosen the woman who will replace her as wife and mother), and with the knowledge that when the chips were down, he preferred the wife to the 'other woman.' The result is the same as that of *Dark Victory*: The two loved ones—the remainders—may unite out of loneliness, but always with the shadow and memory of the 'great woman' (vivid and in her prime) between them. If woman hogs this universe unrelentingly, it is perhaps her compensation for all the male-dominated universes from which she has been excluded: the gangster film, the Western, the war film, the *policier*, the rodeo film, the adventure film. Basically, the woman's film is no more maudlin and self-pitying than the male adventure film (what British critic Raymond Durgnat calls the 'male weepies'), particularly in the male film's recent mood of bronco-busting buddies and bleary-eyed nostalgia. The well of self-pity in both types of films, though only hinted at, is bottomless, and in their sublimation or evasion of adult reality, they reveal, almost by accident, real attitudes toward marriage—disillusionment, frustration, and contempt—beneath the sunny-side up philosophy congealed in the happy ending.

The underlying mystique of the man's film is that these are (or were) the best of times, roaming the plains, or prowling the city, in old clothes and unshaven, the days before settling down or going home, days spent battling nature or the enemy. In such films, the woman becomes a kind of urban or frontier Xantippe with rather limited options. She can be a meddling moralist who wants the hero to leave off his wandering; or a last resort for him, after his buddies have died or departed; or an uptight socialite to whom the hero can never confess his criminal, or even just shadowy, past; or a nagging nice-girl wife, who pesters the hero to spend more time with her, instead of always working, working, working or killing, killing, killing. The most common pattern is probably the wife competing with her husband's other life—business, crime, or crime detection; and since these activities are the dramatic focus and lifeblood of the film, the wife becomes a killjoy, distracting not only the hero but the audience from the fun and danger.

Marriage becomes the heavy. The implication is clear: All the excitement of life—the passion, the risk—occurs outside marriage rather than within it. Marriage is a deadly bore, made to play the role of the spoilsport, the ugly cousin one has to dance with at the ball [. . .]

That love is woman's stuff is a hoary Anglo-Saxon idea, devolving from the (American) tough guy and (British) public school etiquette that to show emotion is bad form, a sign of effeminacy, and that being tender in love is the equivalent of doing the dishes or darning socks. The association takes. For the housewife, betrayed by her romantic ideals, the path of love leads to, becomes, the dead end of household drudgery. The domestic and the romantic are entwined, one redeeming the other, in the theme of self-sacrifice, which is the mainstay and oceanic force, high tide and low ebb, of the woman's film. The equation of time and Tide is not so risible as it seems, just as the emphasis in the women's movement on domestic arrangements is not a trivializing of 'larger issues.' Rather, it is an intuitive recognition that the essence of salvation is not in the single leap of the soul, but in the day-to-day struggle to keep the best of oneself afloat—the discovery that perdition is not the moment of Faustian sellout, but the gradual dribbling of self-esteem, and self, down the drain of meaningless activity.

To the view that women's concerns, and the films that depict them, are of minor significance in the drama of life and art, women themselves have acquiesced [. . .]

Central to the woman's film is the notion of middle-classness, not just as an economic status, but as a state of mind and a relatively rigid moral code. The circumscribed world of the housewife corresponds to the state of woman in general, confronted by a range of options so limited she might as well inhabit a cell. The persistent irony is that she is dependent for her well-being and 'fulfillment' on institutions—marriage, motherhood—that by translating the word 'woman' into 'wife' and 'mother,' end her independent identity. She then feels bound to adhere to a morality which demands that she stifle her own 'illicit' creative or sexual urges in support of a social code that tolerates considerably more deviation on the part of her husband. She is encouraged to follow the lead of her romantic dreams, but when they expire she is stuck.

Beyond this common plight of a generic nature, there are as many kinds of woman's film as there are kinds of women. One division, providing the greatest tension with conventions of the genre, is between the upper-middle-class elite and the rest of the world, between women as models and women as victims. There are the 'extraordinary' women—actresses like Marlene Dietrich, Katharine Hepburn, Rosalind Russell, Bette Davis, and characters like Scarlett O'Hara and Jezebel—who are the exceptions to the rule, the aristocrats of their sex. Their point of view is singular, and in calling the shots they transcend the limitations of their sexual identities. But their status as emancipated women, based as it is on the very quality of being exceptional, weakens their political value as demonstration-model victims and makes them, in their independence, unpopular with a majority of men and women.

Then there are the 'ordinary' women—women whose options have been foreclosed by marriage or income, by children or age, who are, properly speaking, the subject of women's films at their lowest and largest common denominator. As audience surrogates, their heroines are defined negatively and collectively by their mutual limitations rather than by their talents or aspirations. Their point of view is not singular but plural, political rather than personal. They embrace the audience as victims, through the common myths of rejection and self-sacrifice and martyrdom as purveyed by the mass media. These—the media—have changed over the years, from magazines like *Good Housekeeping, Cosmopolitan, The Saturday Evening Post,* and from novels like those of Fannie Hurst, Edna Ferber, and Kathleen Norris, through the movies of the twenties, thirties, and forties, to television soap opera today. But the myths have not changed, nor has the underlying assumption: that these women are stuck, and would rather be stuck than sorry. The purpose of these fables is not to encourage 'woman' to rebel or question her role, but to reconcile her to it, and thus preserve the status quo. The fictions are her defense not only against 'man,' but against the 'extraordinary woman.' For the average housewife, who has not quite gotten around to sex therapy or sensitivity training or group grope, prostitution, drugs, or even drink, these matinee myths are her alcoholic afternoons.

Between these two, there is a third category, one to which the better women's films aspire: It is the fiction of the 'ordinary woman who becomes extraordinary,' the woman who begins as a victim of discriminatory circumstances and rises, through pain, obsession, or defiance, to become mistress of her fate. Between the suds of soap opera we watch her scale the height of Stendhalian romance. Her ascent is given stature and conviction not through a discreet contempt for the female sensibility, but through an all-out belief in it, through the faith, expressed in directorial sympathy and style, that the swirling river of a woman's emotions is as important as anything on earth. The difference between the soap opera palliative and the great woman's film (*Angel, Letter from an Unknown Woman*) is like the difference between masturbatory relief and mutually demanding love.

All women begin as victims. Anna Karenina is a victim of the double standard no less than is Laura in *Brief Encounter*; Emma Bovary is as much a casualty of middle-class morality as is Ruby Gentry. Anna and Emma cease to be victims, cease to be easy identification figures, as they become increasingly complex and cruel, as they take fate into their own hands. As with all his characters, Tolstoy kept Anna at arm's length, in 'middle shot,' finding external correlatives to suggest her inner state. But movie heroines are in close-up; they have a narrower context in which to operate, and they must achieve stature in a different way. They cannot afford to alienate us (if the movie *Madame Bovary* had ended like the novel it would have been more catastrophic than courageous), because there is no wider field of vision, no social context or alternate major characters to claim our attention and absorb the shock. The movie of *Anna Karenina* is not, like the novel, about [Anna + Vronsky + Karenin + Levin + Kitty; country + city; society + art + religion] but about Garbo—or, in the later version, Vivien Leigh [. . .] But in the distinguished women's films, the combination of director and star serve the same function as the complex perspective of the novelist: They take the woman out of the plural into the singular, out of defeat and passivity and collective identity into the radical adventure of the solitary soul, out of the contrivances of puritanical thinking into enlightened self-interest.

It is this unique combination of actress plus director that makes, for example, one version of *Back Street* better or worse than another, even when the plot is identical. There are stars like Garbo and Marie Dressler and Joan Crawford who are their own genres. There are also distinctions to be made between one decade and another. Still, the bare bones remain remarkably similar, like grammatical models from which linguistical examples are formed. The themes of the woman's film can themselves be reduced to four categories, often found overlapping or in combination: sacrifice, affliction, choice, competition.

In the first, the woman must 'sacrifice' (1) herself for her children—e.g., *Madame X*, *The Sin of Madelon Claudet*; (2) her children for their own welfare—e.g., *The Old Maid*, *Stella Dallas*, *To Each His Own*; (3) marriage for her lover—e.g., *Back Street*; (4) her lover for marriage or for his own welfare—e.g., *Kitty Foyle* and *Intermezzo*, respectively; (5) her career for love—e.g., *Lady in the Dark*, *Together Again*; or (6) love for her career—e.g., *The Royal Family of Broadway*, *Morning Glory*. The sacrifice film may end happily, with the wife/mother reclaiming her husband/child when her rival dies, or tragically, as mother watches daughter's happiness from afar, or sees son or lover only to lose him once again. In either case, the purgative sensations—the joy of suffering, the pain of joy—are very close. But not identical. Indeed, most of the thirties' and forties' woman's films ended tragically, an indication perhaps of the vision women had of themselves.

In the second category, the heroine is struck by some 'affliction' which she keeps a secret and eventually either dies unblemished (*Dark Victory*), despite the efforts of her doctor-turned-lover, or is cured (*The Magnificent Obsession*), by the efforts of her lover-turned-doctor.

The third category, 'choice,' has the heroine pursued by at least two suitors who wait, with undivided attention, her decision; on it, their future happiness depends (*The Seventh Veil*, *Daisy Kenyon*, *Lydia*).

In the final category, 'competition,' the heroine meets and does battle with the woman whose husband (fiancé, lover) she loves (*The Great Lie*, *When Ladies Meet*, *Love Story*—the forties' English version; *Old Acquaintance*). While deciding the man's fate, the women will discover, without explicitly acknowledging it, that they prefer each other's company to his. The obtuseness of men generally is implied by their inability to perceive love or (in the case of the second category) disease.

As patently idiotic as these themes sound, how is one to explain the degree to which some of them enthrall us: the mesmerized absorption, the choking, the welling up of tears over some lugubrious rendition of a famous piano concerto that will haunt us forever afterward with the memory of James Mason rapping Ann Todd's knuckles or Margaret Lockwood banging away in Albert Hall?

The Mason-Todd scene comes, of course, from *The Seventh Veil*, coauthored by the husband-and-wife team of Muriel and Sydney Box, and directed by Compton Bennett. The title refers, in the pseudo-psychoanalytical idiom of the film, to that last 'wall' between a woman and her innermost thoughts. Along with *Daisy Kenyon*, this is a model of the 'choice' category, one of the most likable and yet most spurious, the pretense of suffering in a totally pleasurable situation being the height of hypocrisy. It is woman's understandable revenge, and reversal, of the state of affairs in which, as Byron said, 'Man's love is of man's life a thing apart/'Tis woman's whole existence.' The pattern of such films is to open with a period in which the heroine is spoiled and petted (metaphorically, of course) by several devoted males whose infatuation she either does not notice or is aggrieved by, after which she is given an ultimatum. She has to make a decision. At this point, a pretext will be found whereby the suitors are assembled, like characters in an Agatha Christie mystery—preferably at the bottom of a large staircase—to hear the 'solution.' This is, staircase and all, the arrangement that concludes *The Seventh Veil*. Ann Todd, resting upstairs, having been cured of her traumatic paralysis by psychiatrist Herbert Lom, will shortly descend and select either Hugh McDermott, the boorish American jazz musician whose wife has just divorced him, leaving him free to return to his first love; Albert Lieven, the world-weary Viennese artist who thought no woman could rekindle his dying passion; or James Mason, the witheringly sardonic guardian who trained and tyrannized her, poured his own pent-up talent into her, and couldn't let her go. (Although Lom, too, is undoubtedly in love with her, we can discount him as a contender, this being the modest era before mutual Oedipal transference and doctor-participation therapy.)

It isn't the list of players that tips us off—this is practically James Mason's first noteworthy movie. Nor is it the dime-store Freudianism that attaches to Mason's character (think of the penis envy potential in Todd's fingers and Mason's sadism). Nor is it just that he retains his dignity while those about him begin to fall apart. The choice has to be Mason, as any Anglo-American woman knows instinctively, because he, with his cultivated, misogynous manner, is the paragon of the English lover, the type most irresistible to the puritan woman. Father figure and mentor, Professor Higgins and Pygmalion, he exacts the best from her artistically, intellectually, spiritually, but makes no sexual demands. He never imposes on her; on the contrary, his indifference is the spur to her attraction. He is for most American women, the male ideal—cultured, genteel, refined, repressed, with a slight antagonism toward women that is not congenital but the result of an earlier wound or disillusionment, and therefore curable. But it is curable only by her. About all other women he continues to be cynical and disbelieving, and thus his fidelity is assured. He is, like the celibate clergyman or 'confirmed bachelor,' a challenge to a woman, and a relief from the sexually aggressive male.

The delicate, well-bred British hero (Mason, Herbert Marshall, the Howards—Trevor and Leslie) has had far more appeal than such matinee idol stock figures as John Boles, John Lund, George Brent, and all the other pretty profiles. Women's preference for the English gentleman—witty, overrefined, unsexual or apparently misogynous, paternal—is rooted in an instinct for self-preservation that expresses itself in the romantic drive. There is a split in a woman's sensibility, revealed over and over again in literature that expresses a woman's point of view, between her romantic interest—elevated, 'total' (that is, not total, but psychological, spiritual)—focusing on a hero who will look into her eyes and embrace her soul and demand nothing sexually, and her sexual drive, brute and impersonal, demanding to be ravished 'anonymously,' that is, taken without asking, almost unawares, so that she will neither be responsible for her surrender nor bound by it afterward. (Even today, studies show that an amazing number of modern women neglect to prepare themselves for intercourse with contra-ception, indicating that women still prefer to think of sex as a seduction rather than a partnership. The reluctance of women to take responsibility for sex would seem a prime factor in perpetuating the stereotypes of the dominant, active male and the submissive, passive female.) Hence Scarlett's bliss the morning after her 'rape' by Rhett Butler, although—and because—she will never love him the way she loves the unavailable, the undemanding Ashley. Her love for Ashley is passionate, but it is that of a tigress for a kitten; and his resistance and general effeteness assure us that even if he were to succumb she would have the upper hand. She is a diabolically strong woman—deceptively so, in the manner of the southern belle—and she fears the loss of her strength and selfhood that a total, 'animal' relationship with Rhett would entail [. . .]

Strictly speaking, the 'sacrifice' film constitutes a separate category, but in a broader sense it is, like the idea of 'middle-classness,' synonymous with the woman's film. The sacrifice film offers relief in, indeed thrives on, a contra-vention of its own morality: that 'you can't have your cake and eat it too.' The narrative impetus is based on an either/or ethic, on the universally accepted existence of fixed, life-and-death, in-or-out social rules which it is the film's precise purpose to circumvent. Doomed heroines, by not dying until the last moment, do not (as far as the experience of the film is concerned) really die. Women with fatal diseases receive all the attention and sympathy of an invalid without actually acting or looking sick. A heroine gets moral credit for not telling anyone of her illness . . . while only divulging it to an audience of millions.

Because the woman's film was designed for and tailored to a certain market, its recurrent themes represent the closest thing to an expression of the collective drives, conscious and unconscious, of American women, of their avowed obligations and their unconscious resistance. Children are an obsession in American movies—sacrifice of and for children, the use of children as justification for all manner of sacrifice—in marked contrast to European films about love and romantic intrigue, where children rarely appear at all and are almost never the instruments of judgment they are in American films. (To compare films made from almost-identical stories, Max Ophuls' *Letter from an Unknown Woman* introduces the illegitimate child only to kill him off shortly thereafter, while John Stahl's *Only Yesterday* makes his 'legitimization' the culmination of the film and the redemption of the mother.)

But in true having-your-cake-and-eating-it-too fashion, the underlying resentment will have its say. In films where the unmarried or poverty-stricken mother sacrifices her children for their advancement, the children are usually such little monsters that their departure provides secret relief. Where a mother holds on to the kids and sacrifices herself for them, they are even more thankless (*Mildred Pierce* is a good example).

The sacrifice of and for children—two sides of the same coin—is a disease passing for a national virtue, and a constant theme in films that preach one thing and, for anyone who is listening, say another. Whether the totem is challenged, as in the woman's films of European directors like Ophuls and Sirk (*Reckless Moment, There's Always Tomorrow, All That Heaven Allows*), or played straight and heartwarmingly, as in *Penny Serenade, Mildred Pierce, To Each His Own*, all three versions of *Madame X, The Old Maid*, and *That Certain Woman*, the spectacle of a woman owned by her children or consumed by her maternal zeal is as much the mainstay of the woman's film as it is of American culture and middle-class marriage.

Like all obsessions, this one betrays a fear of its opposite, of a hatred so intense it must be disguised as love. The obsession is composed of various related elements: a conviction that children are the reason for getting married (*Penny Serenade*) or the only thing holding marriage together (*The Great Lie, The Marrying Kind*), or woman's ultimate *raison d'être*, her only worth-confirming 'career.' The chain becomes a vicious circle. The woman without a job, without interests, without an absorbing marriage, invests her whole life, her erotic and emotional energy, in the child, who then becomes a divining rod, further drawing off the energy and electricity that should provide a constant current between husband and wife. The child that is seen as the means of shoring up a marriage becomes the wedge that drives a couple apart. But to admit this, to admit any reservations about having children or toward the children themselves, is to commit heresy. The only way to express this hostility is through a noble inversion: the act of sacrifice, of giving them up. Thus, the surrender of the children for their welfare (*Stella Dallas* and *The Old Maid*) is a maneuver for circumventing the sacred taboo, for getting rid of the children in the guise of advancing their welfare. (The sacrifice of oneself for one's children is a more subtle and metaphorical means to the same end: of venting hostility on the children through approved channels.) Both of these transactions represent beautifully masked wish fulfillments, suggesting that the myth of obsession—the love lavished, the attention paid to children, their constant inclusion in narratives where their presence is not required—is compensation for women's guilt, for the deep, inadmissible feelings of not wanting children, or not wanting them unreservedly, in the first place.

This goes some way toward explaining the plot contrivances and emotional excesses to be found in the 'sacrifice' film: Martyrdom must be proportionate to guilt, and the greater the aversion to having a child, the greater the sacrifices called for. The inconveniences the child will cause (to an unwed mother, for example) and which are the source of her aversion, become trials actively sought as tests of her mother-love [...]

The mother's excessive and covertly erotic attachment to her children leads to a sense of bereavement, of the mistress 'spurned,' when they grow up and away from her. Once again the 'woman's film' provides her with myths to support her sense of betrayal, to give her the sweet taste of revenge. Her sacrifice has spoiled them: When they leave home or 'outgrow' their parents, it is not from a child's natural desire to be on his or her own, but because they have adopted 'false values.' In the materialism with which mothers like Stella Dallas and Mildred Pierce smother their children (a figurative rendering of the cultural advantages, higher education, and 'quality' friends, in which the children go beyond their parents), in pushing them to want 'more,' they are creating monsters who will reject and be 'ashamed' of them; simultaneously, the children's heartlessness will vindicate and earn audience sympathy for the mothers.

Less riddled with ambivalence is the 'sacrifice-for-lover' film, although it carries a similar sense of pessimism and doom regarding marriage. Love is not lasting under the best of circumstances, such films suggest philosophically, but the best circumstances are not to be found in marriage. Hence the numerous stories of impossible, imaginary, or extramarital love [...]

The woman's film underwent a change between the thirties and forties, affecting—and affected by—the change in the image of women themselves. The forties were more emotional and neurotic, alternating between the self-denying passivity of the waiting war wife and the brittle aggressiveness of heroines like Davis and Crawford; thirties' heroines were spunkier and more stoical than their forties' sisters, the difference perhaps between a stiff and a quivering upper lip. Thirties' films unfolded against a normal society, whose set of standards the heroine automatically accepted. The social structure wavered in the forties, with women moving up the employment ladder and down from the pedestal, paying for one with their fall from the other. There is, as a result, a constant ambivalence in forties' films, a sensibility that is alternately hard and squishy, scathing and sentimental [...]

Women's films, particularly those of the thirties, have a stronger sense of social reality than their glossy-magazine or vacuum-sealed television equivalents. Aside from the portrait of American society they give as a matter of course, there are unconscious reflections of misery 'in passing,' like the image of a drunk or a prostitute reflected on the shiny surface of a parked limousine. The spectacle of perverted child-love is one such image, as are the American obsession with money, status, social climbing and its epiphenomenon, the *faux pas*. Who can forget the horror, and terrible humor, of the birthday party scene in King Vidor's *Stella Dallas*, when Stanwyck and daughter Anne Shirley wait at the place-marked and overdecorated table as first one, then another and another note of regret arrives.

A growing ambivalence and coyness in films began in the thirties and ran into the forties [...] Part of the silliness arose from the fact that sexual passion and desire could not be shown: compare the 1929 version of *The Letter*, in which Jeanne Eagels seems to disintegrate before our eyes with the force of her passion, and the 1941 remake, in which Bette Davis has to give a suppressed and largely psychological performance in conformance with code decorum. There was also a retrenchment from the feminism of the twenties and thirties. Women might have better jobs, largely as a result of the war and a shortage of male personnel, but they would pay more heavily for them in the movies. Naturally. They were more of a threat. Men were nervous not so much about women taking their jobs—the firing of women directly after the war and the reinstatement of protective legislation that had been temporarily suspended would take care of that—but about women leaving the home 'untended' as they crept back to work. For it was a fact that once women had savored the taste of work and independence, many didn't want to go back to being 'just housewives.' And so in films working women (who were statistically older than their prewar counterparts) were given a pseudo-toughness, a facade of steel wool that at a man's touch would turn into cotton candy [...]

The woman's film reaches its apotheosis under Ophuls and Douglas Sirk in the late forties and fifties, at a time when the genre was losing its mass audience to television soap opera. Eventually women-oriented films, like the women-oriented plays from which many of them were adapted, disappeared from the cultural scene. The derisive attitude of the eastern critical establishment won the day and drove them out of business. But at one time the 'matinee audience' had considerable influence on movie production and on the popularity of certain stars. This influence has waned to the point that the only films being made for women are the afternoon soaps, and there is very little attempt to appeal to women in either regular films or nighttime television.

Where are the romantic idols who made their reputations on their appeal to women, the John Barrymores and Leslie Howards to whom women offered themselves in marriage? To Robert Redford and Paul Newman, who might conceivably be thought of as their successors, women, when they bother, send only billet-doux. But like most of their colleagues, Redford and Newman would rather be 'real people' than actors, and would rather be 'real actors' than romantic leads. So instead of playing opposite beautiful women in love stories of civilized narratives, they play opposite each other in *Butch Cassidy and the Sundance Kid* and romance takes on a whole new twist. They are on their way to becoming the Myrna Loy–William Powell of the seventies [...]

The woman's film, its themes appropriated by the man's film, has died out, and with it a whole area of heterosexual feeling and fantasy. For the woman's film, like other art forms, pays tribute at its best (and at its worst) to the power of the imagination, to the mind's ability to picture a perfect love triumphing over the mortal and conditional [...] The lovers [...] are transfixed at the sublime moment of their love (denying yet improving on reality) by the power of the imagination, by the screen, and by their permanence in our memories.

3

'WOMEN'S CINEMA AS COUNTER-CINEMA'

Claire Johnston

1. MYTHS OF WOMEN IN THE CINEMA

There arose, identifiable by standard appearance, behaviour and attributes, the well-remembered types of the Vamp and the Straight Girl (perhaps the most convincing modern equivalents of the medieval personifications of the Vices and Virtues), the Family Man and the Villain, the latter marked by a black moustache and walking stick. Nocturnal scenes were printed on blue or green film. A checkered table-cloth meant, once for all, a 'poor but honest' milieu; a happy marriage, soon to be endangered by the shadows from the past symbolised by the young wife's pouring of the breakfast coffee for her husband; the first kiss was invariably announced by the lady's gently playing with her partner's necktie and was invariably accompanied by her kicking out with her left foot. The conduct of the characters was predetermined accordingly. (Erwin Panofsky in *Style and Medium in the Motion Pictures*, 1934 and in *Film: An Anthology*, D Talbot ed., New York, 1959.)

Panofsky's detection of the primitive stereotyping which characterised the early cinema could prove useful for discerning the way myths of women have operated in the cinema: why the image of man underwent rapid differentiation, while the primitive stereotyping of women remained with some modifications. Much writing on the stereotyping of women in the cinema takes as its starting point a monolithic view of the media as repressive and manipulative: in this way,

* From Johnston, C. (ed.), *Notes on Women's Cinema*. London: Society for Education in Film and Television, 1973, pp. 24–31.

Hollywood has been viewed as a dream factory producing an oppressive cultural product. This over-politicised view bears little relation to the ideas on art expressed either by Marx or Lenin, who both pointed to there being no direct connection between the development of art and the material basis of society. The idea of the intentionality of art which this view implies is extremely misleading and retrograde, and short-circuits the possibility of a critique which could prove useful for developing a strategy for women's cinema. If we accept that the developing of female stereotypes was not a conscious strategy of the Hollywood dream machine, what are we left with? Panofsky locates the origins of iconography and stereotype in the cinema in terms of practical necessity; he suggests that in the early cinema the audience had much difficulty deciphering what appeared on the screen. Fixed iconography, then, was introduced to aid understanding and provide the audience with basic facts with which to comprehend the narrative. Iconography as a specific kind of sign or cluster of signs based on certain conventions within the Hollywood genres has been partly responsible for the stereotyping of women within the commercial cinema in general, but the fact that there is a far greater differentiation of men's roles than of women's roles in the history of the cinema relates to sexist ideology itself, and the basic opposition which places man inside history, and woman as ahistoric and eternal. As the cinema developed, the stereotyping of man was increasingly interpreted as contravening the realisation of the notion of 'character'; in the case of woman, this was not the case; the dominant ideology presented her as eternal and unchanging, except for modifications in terms of fashion etc. In general, the myths governing the cinema are no different from those governing other cultural products: they relate to a standard value system informing all cultural systems in a given society. Myth uses icons, but the icon is its weakest point. Furthermore, it is possible to use icons, (i.e. conventional configurations) in the face of and against the mythology usually associated with them. In his magisterial work on myth (*Mythologies*, Jonathan Cape, London 1971), the critic Roland Barthes examines how myth, as the signifier of an ideology, operates, by analysing a whole range of items: a national dish, a society wedding, a photograph from *Paris Match*. In his book he analyses how a sign can be emptied of its original denotative meaning and a new connotative meaning superimposed on it. What was a complete sign consisting of a signifier plus a signified, becomes merely the signifier of a new signified, which subtly usurps the place of the original denotation. In this way, the new connotation is mistaken for the natural, obvious and evident denotation: this is what makes it the signifier of the ideology of the society in which it is used.

Myth then, as a form of speech or discourse, represents the major means in which women have been used in the cinema: myth transmits and transforms the ideology of sexism and renders it invisible – when it is made visible it evaporates – and therefore natural. This process puts the question of the stereotyping of women in a somewhat different light. In the first place, such a view of the way cinema operates challenges the notion that the commercial cinema is more manipulative of the image of woman than the art cinema. It could be argued that precisely because of the iconography of Hollywood, the system offers some resistance to the unconscious workings of myth. Sexist ideology is no less present in the European art cinema because stereotyping appears less obvious; it is in the nature of myth to drain the sign (the image of woman/ the function of woman in the narrative) of its meaning and superimpose another which thus appears natural: in fact, a strong argument could be made for the art film inviting a greater invasion from myth. This point assumes considerable importance when considering the emerging women's cinema. The conventional view about women working in Hollywood (Arzner, Weber, Lupino etc.) is that they had little opportunity for real expression within the dominant sexist ideology; they were token women and little more. In fact, because iconography offers in some ways a greater resistance to the realist characterisations, the mythic qualities of certain stereotypes become far more easily detachable and can be used as a short-hand for referring to an ideological tradition in order to provide a critique of it. It is possible to disengage the icons from the myth and thus bring about reverberations within the sexist ideology in which the film is made. Dorothy Arzner certainly made use of such techniques and the work of Nelly Kaplan is particularly important in this respect. As a European director she understands the dangers of myth invading the sign in the art film, and deliberately makes use of Hollywood iconography to counteract this. The use of crazy comedy by some women directors (e.g. Stephanie Rothman) also derives from this insight.

In rejecting a sociological analysis of woman in the cinema we reject any view in terms of realism, for this would involve an acceptance of the apparent natural denotation of the sign and would involve a denial of the reality of myth in operation. Within a sexist ideology and a male-dominated cinema, woman is presented as what she represents for man. Laura Mulvey in her most useful essay on the pop artist Allen Jones ('You Don't Know What You're Doing Do You, Mr Jones?', Laura Mulvey in *Spare Rib*, February 1973), points out that woman as woman is totally absent in Jones' work. The fetishistic image portrayed relates only to male narcissism: woman represents not herself, but by a process of displacement, the male phallus. It is probably true to say that despite the enormous emphasis placed on woman as spectacle in the cinema, woman as woman is largely absent. A sociological analysis based on the empirical study of recurring roles and motifs would lead to a critique in terms of an enumeration of the notion of career/home/motherhood/sexuality, an examination of women as the central figures in the narrative etc. If we view the image of woman as sign within the sexist ideology, we see that the portrayal of woman is merely one item subject to the law of verisimilitude, a law which directors worked with or reacted against. The law of verisimilitude (that which determines the impression of realism) in the cinema is precisely responsible for the repression of the image of woman as woman and the celebration of her non-existence.

This point becomes clearer when we look at a film which revolves around a woman entirely and the idea of the female star. In their analysis of Sternberg's

Morocco, the critics of *Cahiers du Cinema* delineate the system which is in operation: in order that the man remain within the centre of the universe in a text which focuses on the image of woman, the auteur is forced to repress the idea of woman as a social and sexual being (her Otherness) and to deny the opposition man/woman altogether. The woman as sign, then, becomes the pseudo-centre of the filmic discourse. The real opposition posed by the sign is male/non-male, which Sternberg establishes by his use of masculine clothing envelopping the image of Dietrich. This masquerade indicates the absence of man, an absence which is simultaneously negated and recuperated by man. The image of the woman becomes merely the trace of the exclusion and repression of Woman. All fetishism, as Freud has observed, is a phallic replacement, a projection of male narcissistic fantasy. The star system as a whole depended on the fetishisation of woman. Much of the work done on the star system concentrates on the star as the focus for false and alienating dreams. This empirical approach is essentially concerned with the effects of the star system and audience reaction. What the fetishisation of the star does indicate is the collective fantasy of phallocentrism. This is particularly interesting when we look at the persona of Mae West. Many women have read into her parody of the star system and her verbal aggression an attempt at the subversion of male domination in the cinema. If we look more closely there are many traces of phallic replacement in her persona which suggest quite the opposite. The voice itself is strongly masculine, suggesting the absence of the male, and establishes a male/non-male dichotomy. The characteristic phallic dress possesses elements of the fetish. The female element which is introduced, the mother image, expresses male oedipal fantasy. In other words, at the unconscious level, the persona of Mae West is entirely consistent with sexist ideology; it in no way subverts existing myths, but reinforces them.

In their first editorial, the editors of *Women and Film* attack the notion of auteur theory, describing it as 'an oppressive theory making the director a superstar as if film-making were a one-man show'. This is to miss the point. Quite clearly, some developments of the auteur theory have led to a tendency to deify the personality of the (male) director, and Andrew Sarris (the major target for attack in the editorial) is one of the worst offenders in this respect. His derogatory treatment of women directors in *The American Cinema* gives a clear indication of his sexism. Nevertheless, the development of the auteur theory marked an important intervention in film criticism: its polemics challenged the entrenched view of Hollywood as monolithic, and stripped of its normative aspects the classification of films by director has proved an extremely productive way of ordering our experience of the cinema. In demonstrating that Hollywood was at least as interesting as the art cinema, it marked an important step forward. The test of any theory should be the degree to which it produces new knowledge: the auteur theory has certainly achieved this. Further elaborations of the auteur theory (cf. Peter Wollen *Signs and Meanings in the Cinema*, Secker & Warburg, Cinema One Series, London 1972) have stressed the use of the theory to delineate the unconscious structure of the film. As Peter Wollen says, 'the structure is associated with a single director, an individual, not because he has played the role of artist, expressing himself or his vision in the film, but it is through the force of his preoccupations that an unconscious, unintended meaning can be decoded in the film, usually to the surprise of the individual concerned'. In this way, Wollen disengages both from the notion of creativity which dominates the notion of 'art', and from the idea of intentionality.

In briefly examining the myths of woman which underlie the work of two Hollywood directors, Ford and Hawks, making use of findings and insights derived from auteur analysis, it is possible to see that the image of woman assumes very different meanings within the different texts of each author's work. An analysis in terms of the presence or absence of 'positive' heroine figures within the same directors' *oeuvre* would produce a very different view. What Peter Wollen refers to as the 'force of the author's preoccupations', (including the obsessions about women) is generated by the psychoanalytic history of the author. This organised network of obsessions is outside the scope of the author's choice.

Hawks vs Ford

Hawks' films celebrate the solidarity and validity of the exclusive all-male group, dedicated to the life of action and adventure, and a rigid professional ethic. When women intrude into their world, they represent a threat to the very existence of the group. However, women appear to possess 'positive' qualities in Hawks' films: they are often career women and show signs of independence and aggression in the face of the male, particularly in his crazy comedies. Robin Wood has pointed out quite correctly that the crazy comedies portray an inverted version of Hawks' universe. The male is often humiliated or depicted as infantile or regressed. Such films as *Bringing Up Baby*, *His Girl Friday* and *Gentlemen Prefer Blondes* combine, as Robin Wood has said, 'farce and horror'; they are 'disturbing'. For Hawks, there is only the male and the non-male: in order to be accepted into the male universe, the woman must *become* a man; alternatively she becomes woman-as-phallus (Marilyn Monroe in *Gentlemen Prefer Blondes*). This disturbing quality in Hawks' films relates directly to the presence of woman; she is a traumatic presence which must be negated. Ford's is a very different universe, in which women play a pivotal role: it is around their presence that the tensions between the desire for the wandering existence and the desire for settlement/the idea of the wilderness and the idea of the garden revolve. For Ford woman represents the home, and with it the possibility of culture: she becomes a cipher onto which Ford projects his profoundly ambivalent attitude to the concepts of civilisation and psychological 'wholeness'.

While the depiction of women in Hawks involves a direct confrontation with the problematic (traumatic) presence of Woman, a confrontation which results in his need to repress her, Ford's use of woman as a symbol for civilisation considerably complicates the whole question of the repression of woman in his work and leaves room for more progressive elements to emerge (e.g. *Seven Women* and *Cheyenne Autumn*).

2. TOWARDS A COUNTER-CINEMA

There is no such thing as unmanipulated writing, filming or broadcasting. The question is therefore not whether the media are manipulated, but who manipulates them. A revolutionary plan should not require the manipulators to disappear; on the contrary, it must make everyone a manipulator. (Hans Magnus Enzensberger in *Constituents of a Theory of Media*, New Left Review No 64.)

Enzensberger suggests the major contradiction operating in the media is that between their present constitution and their revolutionary potential. Quite clearly, a strategic use of the media, and film in particular, is essential for disseminating our ideas. At the moment the possibility of feedback is low, though the potential already exists. In the light of such possibilities, it is particularly important to analyse what the nature of cinema is and what strategic use can be made of it in all its forms: the political film/the commercial entertainment film. Polemics for women's creativity are fine as long as we realise they are polemics. The notion of women's creativity *per se* is as limited as the notion of men's creativity. It is basically an idealist conception which elevates the idea of the 'artist' (involving the pitfall of elitism), and undermines any view of art as a material thing within a cultural context which forms it and is formed by it. All films or works of art are products: products of an existing system of economic relations, in the final analysis. This applies equally to experimental films, political films and commercial entertainment cinema. Film is also an ideological product – the product of bourgeois ideology. The idea that art is universal and thus potentially androgynous is basically an idealist notion: art can only be defined as a discourse within a particular conjuncture – for the purpose of women's cinema, the bourgeois, sexist ideology of male dominated capitalism. It is important to point out that the workings of ideology do not involve a process of deception/intentionality. For Marx, ideology is a reality, it is not a lie. Such a misapprehension can prove extremely misleading; there is no way in which we can eliminate ideology as if by an effort of will. This is extremely important when it comes to discussing women's cinema. The tools and techniques of cinema themselves, as part of reality, are an expression of the prevailing ideology: they are not neutral, as many 'revolutionary' film-makers appear to believe. It is idealist mystification to believe that 'truth' can be captured by the camera or that the conditions of a film's production (e.g. a film made collectively by women) can *of itself* reflect the conditions of its production. This is mere utopianism: new meaning has to *be manufactured* within the text of the film. The camera was developed in order to accurately reproduce reality and safeguard the bourgeois notion of realism which was being replaced in painting. An element of sexism governing the technical development of the camera can also be discerned. In fact, the lightweight camera was developed as early as the 1930s in Nazi Germany for propaganda purposes; the reason why it was not until the 1950s that it assumed common usage remains obscure.

Much of the emerging women's cinema has taken its aesthetics from television and cinema verite techniques (e.g. *Three Lives*, *Women Talking*); Shirley Clarke's *Portrait of Jason* has been cited as an important influence. These films largely depict images of women talking to camera about their experiences, with little or no intervention by the film-maker. Kate Millett sums up the approach in *Three Lives* by saying, 'I did not want to analyse any more, but to express' and 'film is a very powerful way to express oneself'.

Clearly, if we accept that cinema involves the production of signs, the idea of non-intervention is pure mystification. The sign is always a product. What the camera in fact grasps is the 'natural' world of the dominant ideology. Women's cinema cannot afford such idealism; the 'truth' of our oppression cannot be 'captured' on celluloid with the 'innocence' of the camera: it has to be constructed/manufactured. New meanings have to be created by disrupting the fabric of the male bourgeois cinema within the text of the film. As Peter Wollen points out, 'reality is always adaptive'. Eisenstein's method is instructive here. In his use of fragmentation as a revolutionary strategy, a concept is generated by the clash of two specific images, so that it serves as an abstract concept in the filmic discourse. This idea of fragmentation as an analytical tool is quite different from the use of fragmentation suggested by Barbara Martineau in her essay.[1] She sees fragmentation as the juxtaposition of disparate elements (cf. *Lion's Love*) to bring about emotional reverberations, but these reverberations do not provide a means of understanding within them. In the context of women's cinema such a strategy would be totally recuperable by the dominant ideology: indeed, in that it depends on emotionality and mystery, it invites the invasion of ideology. The ultimate logic of this method is automatic writing developed by the surrealists. Romanticism will not provide us with the necessary tools to construct a women's cinema: our objectification cannot be overcome simply by examining it artistically. It can only be challenged by developing the means to interrogate the male, bourgeois cinema. Furthermore, a desire for change can only come about by drawing on fantasy. The danger of developing a cinema of non-intervention is that it promotes a passive subjectivity at the expense of analysis. Any revolutionary strategy must challenge the depiction of reality; it is not enough to discuss the oppression of women within the text of the film; the language of the cinema/the depiction of reality must also be interrogated, so that a break between ideology and text is effected. In this respect, it is instructive to look at films made by women within the Hollywood system which attempted by formal means to bring about a dislocation between sexist ideology and the text of the film; such insights could provide useful guidelines for the emerging women's cinema to draw on.

Dorothy Arzner and Ida Lupino

Dorothy Arzner and Lois Weber were virtually the only women working in Hollywood during the 1920s and 30s who managed to build up a consistent body of work in the cinema: unfortunately, very little is known of their work, as yet. An analysis of one of Dorothy Arzner's later films, *Dance, Girl, Dance*, made in 1940 gives some idea of her approach to women's cinema within the sexist ideology of Hollywood. A conventional vaudeville story, *Dance, Girl, Dance* centres on the lives of a troupe of dancing girls down on their luck. The main characters, Bubbles and Judy are representative of the primitive iconographic depiction of women – vamp and straight-girl – described by Panofsky. Working from this crude stereotyping, Arzner succeeds in generating within the text of the film, an internal criticism of it. Bubbles manages to land a job, and Judy becomes the stooge in her act, performing ballet for the amusement of the all-male audience. Arzner's critique centres round the notion of woman as spectacle, as performer within the male universe. The central figures appear in a parody form of the performance, representing opposing poles of the myths of femininity – sexuality vs. grace & innocence. The central contradiction articulating their existence as performers for the pleasure of men is one with which most women would identify: the contradiction between the desire to please and self-expression: Bubbles needs to please the male, while Judy seeks self-expression as a ballet dancer. As the film progresses, a one-way process of the performance is firmly established, involving the humiliation of Judy as the stooge. Towards the end of the film Arzner brings about her tour de force, cracking open the entire fabric of the film and exposing the workings of ideology in the construction of the stereotype of woman. Judy, in a fit of anger, turns on her audience and tells them *how she sees them*. This return of scrutiny in what within the film is assumed as a one-way process constitutes a direct assault on the audience within the film and the audience of the film, and has the effect of directly challenging the entire notion of woman as spectacle.

Ida Lupino's approach to women's cinema is somewhat different. As an independent producer and director working in Hollywood in the 1950s, Lupino chose to work largely within the melodrama, a genre which, more than any other, has presented a less reified view of women, and as Sirk's work indicates, is adaptable for expressing rather than embodying the idea of the oppression of women. An analysis of *Not Wanted*, Lupino's first feature film gives some idea of the disturbing ambiguity of her films and their relationship to the sexist ideology. Unlike Arzner, Lupino is not concerned with employing purely formal means to obtain her objective; in fact, it is doubtful whether she operates at a conscious level at all in subverting the sexist ideology. The film tells the story of a young girl, Sally Kelton, and is told from her subjective viewpoint and filtered through her imagination. She has an illegitimate child which is eventually adopted; unable to come to terms with losing the child, she snatches one from a pram and ends up in the hands of the authorities. Finally, she finds a substitute for the child in the person of a crippled young man, who, through a process of symbolic castration – in which he is forced to chase her until he can no longer stand, whereupon she takes him up in her arms as he performs child-like gestures – provides the 'happy ending'. Though Lupino's films in no way explicitly attack or expose the workings of sexist ideology, reverberations within the narrative, produced by the convergence of two irreconcileable strands – Hollywood myths of woman vs. the female perspective – cause a series of distortions within the very structure of the narrative; the mark of disablement puts the film under the sign of disease and frustration. An example of this process is, for instance, the inverted 'happy ending' of the film.

The intention behind pointing to the interest of Hollywood directors like Dorothy Arzner and Ida Lupino is twofold. In the first place it is a polemical attempt to restore the interest of Hollywood from attacks that have been made on it. Secondly, an analysis of the workings of myth and the possibilities of subverting it in the Hollywood system could prove of use in determining a strategy for the subversion of ideology in general.

Perhaps something should be said about the European art film; undoubtedly, it is more open to the invasion of myth than the Hollywood film. This point becomes quite clear when we scrutinise the work of Riefenstahl, Companeez, Trintignant, Varda and others. The films of Agnes Varda are a particularly good example of an *oeuvre* which celebrates bourgeois myths of women, and with it the apparent innocence of the sign. *Le Bonheur* in particular, almost invites a Barthesian analysis! Varda's portrayal of female fantasy constitutes one of the nearest approximations to the facile day-dreams perpetuated by advertising that probably exists in the cinema. Her films appear totally innocent to the workings of myth; indeed, it is the purpose of myth to fabricate an impression of innocence, in which all becomes 'natural': Varda's concern for nature is a direct expression of this retreat from history: history is transmuted into nature, involving the elimination of all questions, because all appears 'natural'. There is no doubt that Varda's work is reactionary: in her rejection of culture and her placement of woman outside history her films mark a retrograde step in women's cinema.

3. CONCLUSION

What kind of strategy, then, is appropriate at this particular point in time? The development of collective work is obviously a major step forward; as a means of acquiring and sharing skills it constitutes a formidable challenge to male privilege in the film industry: as an expression of sisterhood, it suggests a viable alternative to the rigid hierarchical structures of male-dominated cinema and offers real opportunities for a dialogue about the nature of women's cinema within it. At this point in time, a strategy should be developed which embraces both the notion of films as a political tool and film as entertainment. For too long these have been regarded as two opposing poles with little common ground. In order to counter our objectification in the cinema, our collective fantasies must be released: women's cinema must embody the working through of desire: such an objective demands the use of the entertainment film. Ideas derived from the entertainment film, then, should inform the political film, and political ideas should inform the entertainment cinema: a two way process. Finally, a repressive, moralistic assertion that women's cinema *is* collective film-making is misleading and unnecessary: we should seek to operate at all levels: within the male-dominated cinema and outside it. This essay has attempted to demonstrate the interest of women's films made within the system. Voluntarism and utopianism must be avoided if any revolutionary strategy is to emerge. A collective film *of itself* cannot reflect the conditions of its production. What collective methods do provide is the real possibility of examining how cinema works and how we can best interrogate and demystify the workings of ideology: it will be from these insights that a genuinely revolutionary conception of counter-cinema for the women's struggle will come.

Editor's Notes

1. See Martineau, 'Subjecting Her Objectification, *or* Communism Is Not Enough' in *Notes on Women's Cinema*, ed. Claire Johnston (London: Society for Education in Film and Television, 1973).

4

'THE CRISIS OF NAMING IN FEMINIST FILM CRITICISM'

B. Ruby Rich

Whatever is unnamed, undepicted in images, whatever is omitted from biography, censored in collections of letters, whatever is misnamed as something else, made difficult-to-come-by, whatever is buried in the memory by the collapse of meaning under an inadequate or lying language – this will become, not merely unspoken, but unspeakable. (Adrienne Rich)[1]

Adrienne Rich's remarks at the 1976 and 1977 Women's Commission panels of the Modern Language Association inspired this investigation into the nature of language in the field of feminist film criticism. The situation for women working in filmmaking and film criticism today is precarious. While our work is no longer invisible, and not yet unspeakable, it still goes dangerously unnamed. The extent of the problem was manifested in the very decision of a title to this paper, designed to analyze naming in terms of film and the women's movement but limited to the two unsatisfactory choices of 'feminist film' or 'films by women.' Both are vague and problematic names: the one disregarded or even denied by certain women filmmakers and writers, the other descriptive of nothing but a sex-determined ghetto of classification. I see the lack of a proper name here as symptomatic of a crisis in the ability of feminist film criticism thus far to come to terms with the work at hand. Similarly, it is symptomatic of a basic difference between the name 'feminist' and other cinematic names, such as 'structuralist' for certain avant-garde films or 'melodrama' for certain Hollywood films,[2]

* From *Jump Cut* No. 19, 1978, pp. 9–12.

which despite their deficiencies at least derive from an initial critical inspection of the work itself and constitute descriptions, however distortive, of the film text. Unfortunately, our only name, 'feminist,' is one with little critical attachment to the work, describing instead the context of social and political activity whence that work sprung more often than the actual text of any given film. The reason for such a difference is to be found in the intrinsic connection between theory and practice in the field which 'feminist' came to designate, a connection not found in other areas of film activity.

THE HISTORY

The connection between practice and theory in feminist cinema is so assumed that its origin and development are frequently taken for granted. The following chronology of feminist filmmaking and criticism sketches some major events of the Seventies in North America and Great Britain in order to chart the progression of activity to date.

1971 – Release of *Growing Up Female, Three Lives, The Woman's Film*, and *Janie's Janie*, all feminist documentaries.

1972 – Events: First new York International Festival of Women's Films and The Women's Event at the Edinburgh Film Festival. Publications: First issue of *Women & Film* magazine; special issues devoted to women and film in *Take One, Film Library Quarterly* and *The Velvet Light Trap*; women's filmography in *Film Comment*.

1973 – Events: Toronto Women and Film Festival and season of women's cinema at the National Film Theatre in London. Publications: Marjorie Rosen's *Popcorn Venus*, first book on image of women in film, and *Notes on Women's Cinema*, BFI monograph edited by Claire Johnston, the first collection of feminist theory.

1974 – Events: Chicago Films by Women festival. Publications: first issue of *Jump Cut*; two more books on images of women in film, Molly Haskell's *From Reverence to Rape* and Joan Mellen's *Women and Their Sexuality in the New Film*.

1975 – *Women & Film* ceases publication after editorial board split.

1976 – Second New York International Festival of Women's Films (smaller, noncollective, less successful than the first) and Womanscene section of women's films within Toronto's Festival of Festivals: i.e., a less political replay of 1972.

1977 – First issue of *Camera Obscura* (journal of film theory founded by the dissident *Women & Film* members, initially in opposition to it); publication of Karyn Kay and Gerald Peary's *Women and the Cinema*, first anthology of criticism on women and film.

1978 – Period of normalization now fully underway.

This chronology is a selective one, but I believe that the major activities of the period are included, with two exceptions. Preceding the entire list was the publication in 1970 of a number of crucial feminist works, such as *Sexual Politics, Sisterhood is Powerful*, and *The Dialectic of Sex*, which must be seen as the backdrop to these film activities. Second, omitted from the chronology after 1971 are the hundreds of films by women made during the decade, a development presumably known to all of us and clearly another backdrop to this chronology as a whole.

The facts of the chronology suggest a number of observations and conclusions. It is immediately apparent that the 1972–3 period marks a cultural watershed that has not since been equalled and that the unity, discovery, energy, and general we're-here-to-stay spirit of the early days underwent a marked shift during 1975. Since then, the focus of the activity has changed, with new routes leading in the direction of increased specialization (such as *Camera Obscura*), institutionalization (such as classroom-aimed anthologies), the start of sectarianism, and most recently, a backlash emphasis on liberalization and 'human liberation.' Perhaps this discovery of increased fragmentation and decreased events comes as no surprise, yet the chronology helps remind us that memory is not playing tricks and that today presents a very different picture.

Another aspect of history made explicit by the chronology involves the initial crossfertilization between the energies of the women's movement and cinema, which took place in the area of practice rather than written criticism. The films came first. In fact, we find two different currents feeding into film work: one made up of women who were feminists and thereby led to film, the other made up of those of us already working in film and led therein to feminism. It was largely the first group of women who began making the films,[3] which were naturally named 'feminist', and largely the second group of women, often in university film studies departments, who began holding the film festivals, just as naturally named simply 'women and/in film.' Spadework has continued in both directions, creating a new women's cinema and rediscovering the antecedents, with the two currents feeding our film criticism, which has drawn from both kinds of knowledge and experience for its dual-purpose discourse.

Reviewing Adrienne Rich's statement of warning, we can take comfort in seeing that the past seven years of work have reduced some of the perils of which she speaks. No longer are women undepicted in images: even three years ago, Bonnie Dawson's *Women's Films in Print* could list over 800 available films by USA women alone, most depicting women in those images. No longer are women omitted from all biography, nor letters always censored: in this respect, most important is the ongoing work of the collective of four women engaged in The Legend of Maya Deren Project to document and demystify the life and work of a major, under-acknowledged figure in American independent cinema. No longer are women's films so hard to come by: the establishment of New Day Films (1972), Freude Bartlett's Serious Business Company, and the Iris Films collective (1975) ensure the continuing distribution of films by or about women, although the chances of seeing any features by women in a regular movie theatre are still slim (with *Antonia* and Claudia Weill's *Girl Friends* the only American films to succeed so far). Returning to the original warning, however, we reach the end of history's comforts and arrive at the nature of our present danger: 'whatever is unnamed ... buried in the memory by the collapse of meaning under an inadequate or lying language – this will become, not merely unspoken, but unspeakable.' Herein lies the crisis facing feminist film criticism today, for after seven years of film practice and theory, no new names have come into being. We still lack our proper names [...]

FEMINIST FILM CRITICISM: IN TWO VOICES

There have been two types of feminist film criticism,[4] motivated by different geographical and ideological contexts, each speaking in a very different voice.

> History of philosophy has an obvious, repressive function in philosophy; it is philosophy's very own Oedipus. 'All the same, you won't dare speak your own name as long as you have not read this and that, and that on this, and this on that ... To say something in one's own name is very strange. (Gilles Deleuze)[5]

Speaking in one's own name versus speaking in the name of history is a familiar problem to anyone who has ever pursued a course of study, become involved in an established discipline, and then tried to speak out of personal experience or nonprofessional/nonacademic knowledge without suddenly feeling quite schizophrenic. Obviously it is a schizophrenia especially familiar to feminists. The distinction between one's own voice and the voice of history is a handy one by which to distinguish the two types of feminist film criticism. At least initially, these two types could be characterized as either American or British: the one, American, seen as sociological or subjective, often a speaking out in one's own voice; the other, British, seen as methodological or more objective, often speaking in the voice of history. (The work of the past few years has blurred the original nationalist base of the categories: for example, the Parisian perspective of the California-based *Camera Obscura*.)

The originally American, so-called sociological approach is exemplified by early *Women & Film* articles and much of the catalogue writing from festivals of that same period. The emphasis on legitimizing women's own reactions and making women's contributions visible resulted in a tendency toward reviews, getting information out, a tendency to offer testimony as theory. Fruitful in this terrain, the weakness of the approach became the limits of its introspection, the boundaries established by the lack of a coherent methodology for moving out beyond the self. An example of this approach would be Barbara Halpern Martineau's very eccentric, subjective, and illuminating analyses of Nelly Kaplan and Agnes Varda films.[6] A dismaying example of the current decadent strain of this approach would be Joan Mellen's recent book *Big Bad Wolves*, which offers personal interpretations of male characters and actors in a move to shift attention to the reformist arena of 'human liberation.'

The originally British, so-called theoretical approach, is exemplified by the British Film Institute monograph on women and film (see above), by articles in *Screen*, and by the two issues of *Camera Obscura* (which, like the British writing, defers to the French authorities). Committed to using some of the most advanced tools of critical analysis, like semiology and psychoanalysis, this approach has tried to come to terms with *how* films mean – to move beyond regarding the image to analyzing the structure, codes, the general subtext of the works. Fruitful for its findings regarding signification, the weakness of the approach has been its suppression of the personal and a seeming belief in the neutrality of the analytic tools, so that the critic's feminist voice has often been muted by this methodology. Two of the most important products of this approach are pieces by Laura Mulvey and Claire Johnston.[7] Johnston has critiqued the image of woman in male cinema and finds her to be a signifier, not of woman, but of the absent phallus, a signifier of an absence rather than any presence. Similarly, Mulvey has analyzed the nature of the cinematic spectator and finds evidence in cinematic voyeurism, in the nature of the camera look, of the exclusively male spectator as a production assumption.

Another way of characterizing these two approaches would be to identify the American (sociological, or in one's own voice) as fundamentally phenomenological, and the British (theoretical, or the voice of history) as fundamentally analytical. Johnston and Mulvey's texts taken together, for example, pose a monumental absence that is unduly pessimistic. The misplaced pessimism stems from their overvaluation of the production aspect of cinema, a misassumption that cinematic values are irrevocably embedded at the level of production and, once there, remain pernicious and inviolable. Woman is absent on the screen and she is absent in the audience, their analysis argues. And yet here a bit of phenomenology would be helpful, a moment of speaking in one's own voice and wondering at the source in such a landscape of absence. As a woman sitting in the dark, watching that film made by and for men with drag queens on the screen, what is my experience? Don't I in fact interact with that text and that context, with a conspicuous absence of passivity? For a woman's experiencing of culture under patriarchy is dialectical in a way that a man's can never be: our experience is like that of the exile, whom Brecht once singled out as the ultimate dialectician for that daily working out of cultural oppositions within a single body. It is crucial to emphasize here the possibility for texts to be transformed at the level of reception and not to fall into a trap of condescension toward our own developed powers as active producers of meaning.

The differences implicit in these two attitudes lead to quite different positions and strategies, as the following selection of quotations helps to point up.[8] When interviewed regarding the reason for choosing her specific critical tools (auteurist, structuralist, psychoanalytic), Claire Johnston replied: 'As far as I'm concerned, it's a question of what is theoretically correct; these new theoretical developments cannot be ignored, just as feminists cannot ignore Marx or Freud, because they represent crucial scientific developments.' In contrast to this vision of science as ideologically neutral would be the reiteration by such theoreticians as Adrienne Rich and Mary Daly that 'you have to be constantly critiquing even the tools you use to explore and define what it is to be female.' In the same interview as Johnston, Pam Cook elaborated their aim as: 'Women are fixed in ideology in a particular way, which is definable in terms of the patriarchal system. I think we see our first need as primarily to define that place – that women are fixed in.' In marked contrast to such a sphere of activity, the *Womanifesto* of the 1975 New York Conference of Feminists in the Media stated: 'We do not accept the existing power structure and we are committed to changing it by the content and structure of our images and by the ways we relate to each other in our work and with our audience.' In her own article, Laura Mulvey identified the advantage of psychoanalytic critiques as their ability to 'advance our understanding of the status quo,' a limited and modest claim; yet she herself went beyond such a goal in making (with Peter Wollen) *The Riddles of the Sphinx*, a film which in its refusal of patriarchal codes and feminist concerns represents in fact a Part Two of her original theory. By moving beyond an analysis of the status quo to an action intervening in its codes, Mulvey thus made a start in the direction of synthesizing the values of the two approaches here delineated.

I have termed the British approach pessimistic, a quality which may be perceived by supporters as realistic or by detractors as colonized. I have termed the American approach optimistic, a quality which may be viewed by supporters as radical or by detractors as unrealistic, utopian. It is not surprising, however, that such a dualism of critical approach has evolved. In *Woman's Consciousness, Man's World*, Sheila Rowbotham points out: 'There is a long inchoate period during which the struggle between the language of experience and the language of theory becomes a kind of agony.'[9] It is a problem common to an oppressed people at the point of formulating a new language with which to name that oppression, for the history of oppression has prevented the development of any unified language among its subjects. It is crucial for those of us working in the area of feminist film criticism to mend this rift, confront the agony, and begin developing a synthesis of maximally effective critical practice. Without names, our work remains anonymous, insecure, our continued visibility questionable [...]

We are now in a period of normalization, a time that can offer feminists complacency as a mask for cooption. As long as we allow others to do our naming, we will go unnamed. It is tempting to be prescriptive, to say that feminist films should be anti-illusionist, or be made collectively, or offer positive role models, a good story or no story. Yet no prescription quite works, and the filmmakers themselves will continue to balk at such Procrustean beds that lop off their edges to fit the theoretical model. Likewise with critical practice, which suffers when fossilized into dogma at the expense of growth. Criticism is at its richest for us when it permits a largesse, a generosity of both sensibility and methodology, aimed at creating a critical practice of maximum use not only to ourselves but to all women making or viewing film. To name is to take possession, and the time is at hand to possess, finally, our own culture by name.[10]

NOTES

1. This statement is drawn from Adrienne Rich's presentation at the 1976 Modern Language Association, Evening Event sponsored by the Women's Commission and the Gay Caucus. See Adrienne Rich, 'It is the Lesbian In Us' in *Sinister Wisdom* #3, Spring 1977; and the section 'The Transformation of Silence Into Language and Action' in *Sinister Wisdom* #6, Summer 1978, which contains the papers from the 1977 Modern Language Association event. See also Mary Daly, *Beyond God the Father* (Boston: Beacon Press, 1973) for her pioneer analysis of naming as power.
2. 'Structuralist' and 'Melodrama' were the two names analyzed in papers presented by Bruce Jenkins and William Horrigan respectively, my co-panelists at the Purdue Conference on Film, April 1978, where an earlier version of this paper was read.
3. Women artists working in film continued, as before, to make avant-garde films, but these lie outside my present concerns. I am taking up only that area of intentionally feminist film activity.
4. Here I am considering only English-language feminist film criticism; there are other complex issues in French and German criticism, for example.
5. Gilles Deleuze, 'I have Nothing to Admit' in *Semiotexte*, No. 6 (Vol. 2, No. 3, 1977), p. 112.
6. See Barbara Halpern Martineau, 'Nelly Kaplan' and 'Subjecting Her Objectification, or Communism Is Not Enough' in *Notes On Women's Cinema*, ed. Claire Johnston (London: Society for Education in Film and Television, 1973).
7. See Claire Johnston, 'Women's Cinema as Counter-Cinema' in *Notes on Women's Cinema*, and Laura Mulvey, 'Visual Pleasure and Narrative Cinema' in *Women and the Cinema*, ed. Karyn Kay and Gerald Peary (New York: E.P. Dutton, 1977), pp. 412–28.
8. Quotations are taken from: E. Ann Kaplan, 'Interview with British Cine-Feminists' in *Women and the Cinema*, pp. 400–1; Barbara Charlesworth Gelpi and Albert Gelpi, *Adrienne Rich's Poetry* (New York: W.W. Norton, 1975), p. 115; Barbara Halpern Martineau, 'Paris/Chicago' in *Women & Film*, No. 7, p. 11; Laura Mulvey, 'Visual Pleasure and Narrative Cinema,' *Women and the Cinema*, p. 414, as well as personal communications. See also E. Ann Kaplan, 'Aspects of British Feminist Film Theory' in *Jump Cut*, No. 12/13, for an in-depth examination of the British theories and their implications.
9. Sheila Rowbotham, *Woman's Consciousness, Man's World* (London: Penguin, 1973), p. 33. See also her statement, p. 32, that language always is 'carefully guarded by the superior people because it is one of the means through which they conserve their supremacy.'
10. Many of the ideas in this article were first tested in a discussion in Chicago in February, 1978 which has been published as 'Women and Film: A Discussion of Feminist Aesthetics' in the *New German Critique*, No. 13; I am endebted to the three *NGC* editors and to my co-discussants Michelle Citron, Julia Lesage, Judith Mayne and Anna Marie Taylor for their feedback and support. Thanks also to my friends on the original Purdue panel, Bill Horrigan and Bruce Jenkins, for their reactions and intellectual generosity. Finally, the article has benefitted from the tough but sympathetic criticisms of the manuscript by Joan Braderman, Regina Cornwell, and Linda Williams.

PART I
FURTHER READING

Clough, Patricia Ticineto 1994: *Feminist Thought: Desire, Power and Academic Discourse*. Oxford: Blackwell.

Delmar, Rosalind 1986: What Is Feminism? In Mitchell, J. and Oakley A. (ed.), *What Is Feminism?* Oxford: Blackwell.

Doane, Mary Ann, Mellencamp, Patricia and Williams, Linda 1984: Feminist Film Criticism: An Introduction. In Doane, M. A., Mellencamp, P., and Williams, L. (eds), *Re-Vision: Essays in Film Criticism*. Los Angeles: American Film Institute, pp. 1–17.

Erens, Patricia 1979: *Sexual Strategems: The World of Women in Film*. New York: Horizon Press.

Erens, Patricia (ed.) 1990: *Issues in Feminist Film Criticism*. Bloomington and Indianapolis: Indiana University Press.

Gledhill, Christine 1978: Recent Developments in Feminist Criticism. *Quarterly Review of Film Studies* 3, 4, pp. 457–93.

Johnston, Claire (ed.) 1973: *Notes on Women's Cinema*. Screen Pamphlet 2. London: Society for Education in Film and Television.

Johnston, Claire 1975: Feminist Politics and Film History. *Screen* 16, 3, pp. 115–125.

Kaplan, E. Ann 1983: *Women and Film: Both Sides of the Camera*, New York and London: Methuen.

Kuhn, Annette 1982: *Women's Pictures: Feminism and Cinema*. London: Routledge & Kegan Paul.

Kuhn, Annette 1985: *The Power of the Image: Essays on Representation and Sexuality*. London: Routledge & Kegan Paul.

Macdonald, Myra 1995: *Representing Women: Myths of Femininity in the Popular Media*. London: Edward Arnold.

Nichols, Bill (ed.) 1976: *Movies and Methods*. Berkeley, Los Angeles and London: University of California Press.

Thornham, Sue 1997: Forerunners and Beginnings. In *Passionate Detachments: An Introduction to Feminist Film Theory*. London: Arnold, pp. 1–21.

Tong, Rosemarie 1989: *Feminist Thought: A Comprehensive Introduction*. London: Unwin Hyman.

Whelehan, Imelda 1995: *Modern Feminist Thought: From the Second Wave to 'Post-Feminism'*. Edinburgh: Edinburgh University Press.

PART II
THE LANGUAGE OF THEORY

INTRODUCTION

When B. Ruby Rich (Chapter 4) described the 'originally British, so-called theoretical approach' to feminist film criticism, she cited Claire Johnston and Laura Mulvey as its two most important figures. Mulvey's 1975 article, 'Visual Pleasure and Narrative Cinema', then, belongs chronologically with the articles which comprise Part I of this reader. But since it was to become the inaugural text for a feminist 'cine-psychoanalysis'[1] which would dominate feminist film theory during the 1980s, it is included in this section.

To Johnston's argument that the figure of 'woman' functions within film as a sign within a patriarchal discourse, not as a reflection of reality, Mulvey added an analysis of how cinema as an 'apparatus' creates a position for the film spectator, drawing on psychoanalytic theory to explain this positioning. In so doing, she also produced a shift in analytic focus, away from a purely textual analysis and towards a concern with the structures of identification and visual pleasure to be found in cinema: in other words, towards the spectator–screen relationship.

Mulvey's interest in psychoanalytic theory was one shared by a number of French film theorists in the early 1970s. Christian Metz and Jean-Louis Baudry, appropriating the theories of Freud and of French psychoanalyst Jacques Lacan, both compared the operation of the 'cinematic apparatus' upon the spectator to that of the dream. '[T]aking into account the darkness of the movie theater, the relative passivity of the situation, the forced immobility of the cine-subject, and the effects which result from the projection of images, moving images', argues Baudry, 'the cinematic apparatus brings about a state of artificial regression' (1976: 119). As with dreams and hallucinations, he continues, cinema offers us powerful but illusory perceptions (sound, images, movement) which give access to unconscious desires and fantasies, keeping at bay the 'reality principle' which would repress them. The spectator's entry to this realm of desire and fantasy, argues Metz, is via identification with the all-powerful gaze of the camera: 'At the cinema, it is always the other who is on the screen; as for me, I am there to look at him. I take no part in the perceived, on the contrary, I am *all-perceiving*' (1975: 51). Like theatre, cabaret or the strip-show, he continues, cinema offers its viewer a powerful and eroticised gaze. The cinematic gaze, however, is more fully a one-way process, lacking the element of reciprocity that characterises other modes of performance. Its object (the performance) is also doubly absent, since it is represented only by the cinema screen. Cinema's voyeuristic pleasures are therefore both more sadistic and more fetishised. Like the fetishist, the cinematic spectator both 'believes in' a presence (here the cinematic fiction) and knows it to be absence ('just a film').

The film spectator envisaged by both Baudry and Metz is male. The psychological mechanisms of voyeurism and fetishism, upon which their accounts depend, were both seen by Freud[2] as a means by which the male subject 'protects' himself against knowledge of sexual difference: of the female's 'castration'. In both their accounts, however, this 'masculinisation' of the spectator remains implicit, naturalised. Mulvey's appropriation of psycho-analytic theory, in contrast, places the issue of sexual difference at its centre. Her essay sets out to demonstrate 'the way the unconscious of patriarchal society has structured film form'. Like Johnston, she argues that the sign 'woman' in film is one constructed by and for a patriarchal culture, enabling man to 'live out his fantasies and obsessions ... by imposing them on the silent image of woman'. Cinema's pleasures include voyeurism, fetishism, and a return to the pleasures of infancy's 'mirror phase'. In this phase, as described by Jacques Lacan,[3] the child imagines itself to be a whole and powerful individual by identifying with its own more perfect mirror image, an image provided in film by the figure of the hero. But these are pleasures provided only for the male spectator. Women are objects, not subjects, of the gaze, their bodies eroticised and often fragmented. This division between active/male and passive/female, argues Mulvey, also structures film narrative. It is the film's hero who advances the story, controlling events, the woman, and the erotic gaze. Woman, in contrast, functions as erotic spectacle, interrupting rather than advancing the narrative.

Cinematic codes, then, construct meaning not only through visual images but also through film's ability to control the dimensions of time and space, through choice of shots, framing, editing and narrative pace. Its power and its pleasures come from the alignment of what Mulvey calls the 'three different looks' of cinema. What we see as spectators is determined by the gaze of the camera, and that in turn is aligned, through point-of-view shots, with the gaze of the film's characters at each other. In the latter, it is the look of the central male character which is privileged, so that we see events largely through his eyes and identify with his gaze. Thus the hero's narrative power – the power to control events –

coincides with the 'active power of the erotic look', the two together providing for the male spectator 'a satisfying sense of omnipotence'. Countering this will involve the destruction of conventional cinematic pleasure and the conceiving of 'a new language of desire'.

Mary Ann Doane's '*Caught* and *Rebecca*: The Inscription of Femininity as Absence', published in 1981, seeks to extend Mulvey's use of psychoanalytic theory to an analysis of the female spectator and, in particular, to the forms of identification offered her by a genre aimed specifically at a female audience: Hollywood's 'woman's film' of the 1940s. Films that address female spectators, she argues, cannot rely on the mechanisms of (male) voyeurism and fetishism which elsewhere establish the relationship between spectator and screen. Instead of an eroticised distance, then, they assume an overidentification of the spectator with the cinematic image – hence the term 'weepies' to designate this genre. The distinction between the subject of the gaze and its object is collapsed, and what the female spectator is offered is not an eroticisation of the female – or indeed of the male – image as spectacle, but instead an identification with herself as image, as object of desire. At the same time, however, the 'woman's film' centres both our narrative identification and its structures of looking on a female protagonist, so that its narratives claim, at least, to place female subjectivity, desire and agency at their centre. The result, argues Doane, is incoherence and instability. The female protagonist begins as active agent only to become passive object; the films begin with her voice-over only to erase it; they offer us identification with her gaze only to invest it not with desire but with anxiety and fear. Both of the films that Doane discusses in detail include a scene which demonstrates the 'impossibility' of female spectatorship. Both also include a sequence that literally erases the figure of the woman, replacing her by the camera which narrates her story in her absence.

Teresa de Lauretis' *Alice Doesn't: Feminism, Semiotics, Cinema*, published in 1984, also builds on the theoretical framework established by Laura Mulvey. She too deals with issues of identification, pleasure and desire as they relate to the positioning of the female spectator within a male-centred culture. Her primary focus, however, and her central concern in this extract, is on the working of desire in narrative. Narrative, she argues, is 'governed by an Oedipal logic'. Its paradigmatic structure, as both Mulvey and Doane suggest, is that of Freud's Oedipal journey. In the male-centred narrative this means the journey towards adult subjectivity and possession of the woman. In the female-centred narrative it means the relinquishing of desire, in favour of that state of passivity which for Freud characterised mature femininity, in which the woman accepts her role as object of desire for the man. In both, the female character represents the point of narrative closure. She is that portion of 'plot-space' which awaits the end of the hero's journey.

Although de Lauretis follows Mulvey thus far, however, she argues that the pleasures of cinematic identification cannot be explained simply by linking, as Mulvey does, 'identification-with-the-look' with masculinity and 'identification-with-the-image' with femininity. Both narrative and identification are processes. They involve movement.

To be swept up in the pleasures of narrative, women spectators must identify both with the image (the 'to-be-looked-at' female figure) and with the movement of the narrative, with the positions of both desired object and desiring subject. That women are – or have been – persistently 'seduced into femininity' by cinematic narratives that reinforce their positioning as passive/object does not mean that they cannot produce different narratives which will articulate their desire in terms that interrupt or reverse the Oedipal story.

The final chapter in this section comes from the opening chapter of Kaja Silverman's *The Acoustic Mirror: The Female Voice in Psychoanalysis and Cinema*, published in 1988. Like the others, it discusses cinema in psychoanalytic terms which link the processes of cinematic identification with the processes by which the individual human subject acquires his/her identity. It is this link, they argue, that accounts for the power and the pleasures of cinema. Like other theorists, Silverman sees cinema as offering an illusory 'plenitude' – a fullness and completion which seem to return us to that moment in infancy when we had no sense of separateness or of loss. She takes issue, however, with the psychoanalytic assumption underlying much film theory, that the subject's first experience of loss or lack is the Oedipal moment, when sexual difference is recognised and the female is seen (by both boy and girl) to be 'castrated'. In fact, she argues, the act of birth, the loss of the mother's breast, the splitting of the self that comes with the child's identification with its idealised image in the mirror phase, all precede the recognition of sexual difference. All apply to both the male and the female child. Freud's insistence on the primary importance of the moment of 'discovery' of sexual difference is no more than a displacement, a shifting on to the figure of woman the sense of 'lack' that the male subject himself feels.

Cinema, argues Silverman, re-enacts this process of displacement. If the spectator is offered an imaginary 'plenitude' by the cinematic screen, he must also confront the knowledge that it is imaginary, and that he himself has no power over/within the fantasy scenario that unfolds. It is 'spoken' from elsewhere. What mainstream cinema does, therefore, is transfer in narrative after narrative this sense of loss, failure and powerlessness on to the figure of woman – and punish her for it. She is no more than a mirror/screen for the male subject's own sense of lack.

NOTES

1. The term is Christine Gledhill's. See Gledhill (1988), and Chapter 13 of this volume.
2. For Freud's account of these mechanisms, see Freud (1977).
3. For a summary of Lacan's account of this phase, see Sarup (1992): 62–6 and 82–4.

REFERENCES

Baudry, Jean-Louis 1976: The Apparatus. *Camera Obscura* 1, pp. 104–26.
De Lauretis, Teresa 1984: *Alice Doesn't: Feminism, Semiotics, Cinema*. Basingstoke and London: Macmillan.

Freud, Sigmund 1977: *On Sexuality*. Pelican Freud Library Vol. 7. London: Penguin.

Gledhill, Christine 1988: Pleasurable Negotiations. In Pribram, E. D. (ed.), *Female Spectators: Looking at Film and Television*. London and New York: Verso, pp. 64–89.

Metz, Christian 1975: The Imaginary Signifier. *Screen* 16, 2, pp. 14–76.

Sarup, Madan 1992: *Jacques Lacan*. Hemel Hempstead: Harvester Wheatsheaf.

Silverman, Kaja 1988: *The Acoustic Mirror: The Female Voice in Psychoanalysis and Cinema*. Bloomington and Indianapolis: Indiana University Press.

5

'VISUAL PLEASURE AND NARRATIVE CINEMA'

Laura Mulvey

1. INTRODUCTION

(a) A Political Use of Psychoanalysis

This paper intends to use psychoanalysis to discover where and how the fascination of film is reinforced by pre-existing patterns of fascination already at work within the individual subject and the social formations that have moulded him. It takes as its starting-point the way film reflects, reveals and even plays on the straight, socially established interpretation of sexual difference which controls images, erotic ways of looking and spectacle. It is helpful to understand what the cinema has been, how its magic has worked in the past, while attempting a theory and a practice which will challenge this cinema of the past. Psychoanalytic theory is thus appropriated here as a political weapon, demonstrating the way the unconscious of patriarchal society has structured film form.

The paradox of phallocentrism in all its manifestations is that it depends on the image of the castrated women to give order and meaning to its world. An idea of woman stands as linchpin to the system: it is her lack that produces the phallus as a symbolic presence, it is her desire to make good the lack that the phallus signifies. Recent writing in *Screen* about psychoanalysis and the cinema has not sufficiently brought out the importance of the representation of the female form in a symbolic order in which, in the last resort, it speaks castration

* From *Screen* 16:3, 1975, pp. 6–18.

and nothing else. To summarise briefly: the function of woman in forming the patriarchal unconscious is twofold: she firstly symbolises the castration threat by her real lack of a penis and secondly thereby raises her child into the symbolic. Once this has been achieved, her meaning in the process is at an end. It does not last into the world of law and language except as a memory, which oscillates between memory of maternal plenitude and memory of lack. Both are posited on nature (or on anatomy in Freud's famous phrase). Woman's desire is subjugated to her image as bearer of the bleeding wound; she can exist only in relation to castration and cannot transcend it. She turns her child into the signifier of her own desire to possess a penis (the condition, she imagines, of entry into the symbolic). Either she must gracefully give way to the word, the name of the father and the law, or else struggle to keep her child down with her in the half-light of the imaginary. Woman then stands in patriarchal culture as a signifier for the male other, bound by a symbolic order in which man can live out his fantasies and obsessions through linguistic command by imposing them on the silent image of woman still tied to her place as bearer, not maker, of meaning.

There is an obvious interest in this analysis for feminists, a beauty in its exact rendering of the frustration experienced under the phallocentric order. It gets us nearer to the roots of our oppression, it brings closer an articulation of the problem, it faces us with the ultimate challenge: how to fight the unconscious structured like a language (formed critically at the moment of arrival of language) while still caught within the language of the patriarchy? There is no way in which we can produce an alternative out of the blue, but we can begin to make a break by examining patriarchy with the tools it provides, of which psychoanalysis is not the only but an important one. We are still separated by a great gap from important issues for the female unconscious which are scarcely relevant to phallocentric theory: the sexing of the female infant and her relationship to the symbolic, the sexually mature woman as non-mother, maternity outside the signification of the phallus, the vagina. But, at this point, psychoanalytic theory as it now stands can at least advance our understanding of the *status quo*, of the patriarchal order in which we are caught.

(b) Destruction of Pleasure as a Radical Weapon

As an advanced representation system, the cinema poses questions about the ways the unconscious (formed by the dominant order) structures ways of seeing and pleasure in looking. Cinema has changed over the last few decades. It is no longer the monolithic system based on large capital investment exemplified at its best by Hollywood in the 1930s, 1940s and 1950s. Technological advances (16mm and so on) have changed the economic conditions of cinematic production, which can now be artisanal as well as capitalist. Thus it has been possible for an alternative cinema to develop. However self-conscious and ironic Hollywood managed to be, it always restricted itself to a formal *mise en scène* reflecting the dominant ideological concept of the cinema. The alternative cinema provides a space for the birth of a cinema which is radical in both a political and an aesthetic sense and challenges the basic assumptions of the mainstream film. This is not to reject the latter moralistically, but to highlight the ways in which its formal preoccupations reflect the psychical obsessions of the society which produced it and, further, to stress that the alternative cinema must start specifically by reacting against these obsessions and assumptions. A politically and aesthetically avant-garde cinema is now possible, but it can still only exist as a counterpoint.

The magic of the Hollywood style at its best (and of all the cinema which fell within its sphere of influence) arose, not exclusively, but in one important aspect, from its skilled and satisfying manipulation of visual pleasure. Unchallenged, mainstream film coded the erotic into the language of the dominant patriarchal order. In the highly developed Hollywood cinema it was only through these codes that the alienated subject, torn in his imaginary memory by a sense of loss, by the terror of potential lack in fantasy, came near to finding a glimpse of satisfaction through its formal beauty and its play on his own formative obsessions. This article will discuss the interweaving of that erotic pleasure in film, its meaning and, in particular, the central place of the image of woman. It is said that analysing pleasure, or beauty, destroys it. That is the intention of this article. The satisfaction and reinforcement of the ego that represent the high point of film history hitherto must be attacked. Not in favour of a reconstructed new pleasure, which cannot exist in the abstract, nor of intellectualised unpleasure, but to make way for a total negation of the ease and plenitude of the narrative fiction film. The alternative is the thrill that comes from leaving the past behind without simply rejecting it, transcending outworn or oppressive forms, and daring to break with normal pleasurable expectations in order to conceive a new language of desire.

II PLEASURE IN LOOKING/FASCINATION WITH THE HUMAN FORM

A The cinema offers a number of possible pleasures. One is scopophilia (pleasure in looking). There are circumstances in which looking itself is a source of pleasure, just as, in the reverse formation, there is pleasure in being looked at. Originally, in his *Three Essays on Sexuality*, Freud isolated scopophilia as one of the component instincts of sexuality which exist as drives quite independently of the erotogenic zones. At this point he associated scopophilia with taking other people as objects, subjecting them to a controlling and curious gaze. His particular examples centre on the voyeuristic activities of children, their desire to see and make sure of the private and forbidden (curiosity about other people's genital and bodily functions, about the presence or absence of the penis and, retrospectively, about the primal scene). In this analysis scopophilia is essentially active. (Later, in 'Instincts and Their Vicissitudes', Freud, developed his theory of scopophilia further, attaching it initially to pre-genital auto-eroticism, after which, by analogy, the pleasure of the look is transferred to others. There is a close working here of the relationship between the active instinct and its further development in a narcissistic form.) Although the instinct is modified by other factors, in particular the constitution of the ego, it continues to exist as the erotic basis for pleasure in looking at another person as object. At the extreme, it can become fixated into a perversion, producing obsessive voyeurs and Peeping Toms whose only sexual satisfaction can come from watching, in an active controlling sense, an objectified other.

At first glance, the cinema would seem to be remote from the undercover world of the surreptitious observation of an unknowing and unwilling victim. What is seen on the screen is so manifestly shown. But the mass of mainstream film, and the conventions within which it has consciously evolved, portray a hermetically sealed world which unwinds magically, indifferent to the presence of the audience, producing for them a sense of separation and playing on their voyeuristic fantasy. Moreover the extreme contrast between the darkness in the auditorium (which also isolates the spectators from one another) and the brilliance of the shifting patterns of light and shade on the screen helps to promote the illusion of voyeuristic separation. Although the film is really being shown, is there to be seen, conditions of screening and narrative conventions give the spectator an illusion of looking in on a private world. Among other things, the position of the spectators in the cinema is blatantly one of repression of their exhibitionism and projection of the repressed desire onto the performer.

B The cinema satisfies a primordial wish for pleasurable looking, but it also goes further, developing scopophilia in its narcissistic aspect. The conventions of mainstream film focus attention on the human form. Scale, space, stories are all anthropomorphic. Here, curiosity and the wish to look intermingle with a fascination with likeness and recognition: the human face, the human body, the relationship between the human form and its surroundings, the visible presence of the person in the world. Jacques Lacan has described how the moment when a child recognises its own image in the mirror is crucial for the constitution of the ego. Several aspects of this analysis are relevant here. The mirror phase occurs at a time when children's physical ambitions outstrip their motor capacity, with the result that their recognition of themselves is joyous in that they imagine their mirror image to be more complete, more perfect than they experience in their own body. Recognition is thus overlaid with misrecognition: the image recognised is conceived as the reflected body of the self, but its misrecognition as superior projects this body outside itself as an ideal ego, the alienated subject which, re-introjected as an ego ideal, prepares the way for identification with others in the future. This mirror moment predates language for the child.

Important for this article is the fact that it is an image that constitutes the matrix of the imaginary, of recognition/misrecognition and identification, and hence of the first articulation of the I, of subjectivity. This is a moment when an older fascination with looking (at the mother's face, for an obvious example) collides with the initial inklings of self-awareness. Hence it is the birth of the long love affair/despair between image and self-image which has found such intensity of expression in film and such joyous recognition in the cinema audience. Quite apart from the extraneous similarities between screen and mirror (the framing of the human form in its surroundings, for instance), the cinema has structures of fascination strong enough to allow temporary loss of ego while simultaneously reinforcing it. The sense of forgetting the world as the ego has come to perceive it (I forgot who I am and where I was) is nostalgically reminiscent of that pre-subjective moment of image recognition. While at the same time, the cinema has distinguished itself in the production of ego ideals, through the star system for instance. Stars provide a focus or centre both to screen space and screen story where they act out a complex process of likeness and difference (the glamorous impersonates the ordinary).

C   Sections A and B have set out two contradictory aspects of the pleasurable structures of looking in the conventional cinematic situation. The first, scopophilic, arises from pleasure in using another person as an object of sexual stimulation through sight. The second, developed through narcissism and the constitution of the ego, comes from identification with the image seen. Thus, in film terms, one implies a separation of the erotic identity of the subject from the object on the screen (active scopophilia), the other demands identification of the ego with the object on the screen through the spectator's fascination with and recognition of his like. The first is a function of the sexual instincts, the second of ego libido. This dichotomy was crucial for Freud. Although he saw the two as interacting and overlaying each other, the tension between instinctual drives and self-preservation polarises in terms of pleasure. But both are formative structures, mechanisms without intrinsic meaning. In themselves they have no signification, unless attached to an idealisation. Both pursue aims in indifference to perceptual reality, and motivate eroticised phantasmagoria that affect the subject's perception of the world to make a mockery of empirical objectivity.

During its history, the cinema seems to have evolved a particular illusion of reality in which this contradiction between libido and ego has found a beautifully complementary fantasy world. In *reality* the fantasy world of the screen is subject to the law which produces it. Sexual instincts and identification processes have a meaning within the symbolic order which articulates desire. Desire, born with language, allows the possibility of transcending the instinctual and the imaginary, but its point of reference continually returns to the traumatic moment of its birth: the castration complex. Hence the look, pleasurable in form, can be threatening in content, and it is woman as representation/image that crystallises this paradox.

III Woman as Image, Man as Bearer of the Look

A   In a world ordered by sexual imbalance, pleasure in looking has been split between active/male and passive/female. The determining male gaze projects its fantasy onto the female figure, which is styled accordingly. In their traditional exhibitionist role women are simultaneously looked at and displayed, with their appearance coded for strong visual and erotic impact so that they can be said to connote *to-be-looked-at-ness*. Woman displayed as sexual object is the *leitmotif* of erotic spectacle: from pin-ups to strip-tease, from Ziegfeld to Busby Berkeley, she holds the look, and plays to and signifies male desire. Mainstream film neatly combines spectacle and narrative. (Note, however, how in the musical song-and-dance numbers interrupt the flow of the diegesis.) The presence of woman is an indispensable element of spectacle in normal narrative film, yet her visual presence tends to work against the development of a story-line, to freeze the flow of action in moments of erotic contemplation. This alien presence then has to be integrated into cohesion with the narrative. As Budd Boetticher has put it:

> What counts is what the heroine provokes, or rather what she represents. She is the one, or rather the love or fear she inspires in the hero, or else the concern he feels for her, who makes him act the way he does. In herself the woman has not the slightest importance.

(A recent tendency in narrative film has been to dispense with this problem altogether; hence the development of what Molly Haskell has called the 'buddy movie', in which the active homosexual eroticism of the central male figures can carry the story without distraction.) Traditionally, the woman displayed has functioned on two levels: as erotic object for the characters within the screen story, and as erotic object for the spectator within the auditorium, with a shifting tension between the looks on either side of the screen. For instance, the device of the show-girl allows the two looks to be unified technically without any apparent break in the diegesis. A woman performs within the narrative; the gaze of the spectator and that of the male characters in the film are neatly combined without breaking narrative verisimilitude. For a moment the sexual impact of the performing woman takes the film into a no man's land outside its own time and space. Thus Marilyn Monroe's first appearance in *The River of No Return* and Lauren Bacall's songs in *To Have and Have Not*. Similarly, conventional close-ups of legs (Dietrich, for instance) or a face (Garbo) integrate into the narrative a different mode of eroticism. One part of a fragmented body destroys the Renaissance space, the illusion of depth demanded by the narrative; it gives flatness, the quality of a cut-out or icon, rather than verisimilitude, to the screen.

B   An active/passive heterosexual division of labour has similarly controlled narrative structure. According to the principles of the ruling ideology and the psychical structures that back it up, the male figure cannot bear the burden of sexual objectification. Man is reluctant to gaze at his exhibitionist like. Hence the split between spectacle and narrative supports the man's role as the active one of advancing the story, making things happen. The man controls the film fantasy and also emerges as the representative of power in a further sense: as the bearer of the look of the spectator, transferring it behind the screen to neutralise the extra-diegetic tendencies represented by woman as spectacle. This is made possible through the processes set in motion by structuring the film around a main controlling figure with whom the spectator can identify. As the spectator identifies with the main male protagonist, he projects his look onto that of his like, his screen surrogate, so that the power of the male protagonist as he controls events coincides with the active power of the erotic look, both giving a satisfying sense of omnipotence. A male movie star's glamorous characteristics are thus not those of the erotic object of the gaze, but those of the more perfect, more complete, more powerful ideal ego conceived in the original moment of recognition in front of the mirror. The character in the story can make things happen and control events better than the subject/spectator, just as the image in the mirror was more in control of motor co-ordination.

In contrast to woman as icon, the active male figure (the ego ideal of the identification process) demands a three-dimensional space corresponding to that of the mirror recognition, in which the alienated subject internalised his own representation of his imaginary existence. He is a figure in a landscape. Here the function of film is to reproduce as accurately as possible the so-called natural conditions of human perception. Camera technology (as exemplified by deep focus in particular) and camera movements (determined by the action of the protagonist), combined with invisible editing (demanded by realism), all tend to blur the limits of screen space. The male protagonist is free to command the stage, a stage of spatial illusion in which he articulates the look and creates the action. (There are films with a woman as main protagonist, of course. To analyse this phenomenon seriously here would take me too far afield. Pam Cook and Claire Johnston's study of *The Revolt of Mamie Stover* in Phil Hardy (ed.), *Raoul Walsh* (Edinburgh, 1974), shows in a striking case how the strength of this female protagonist is more apparent than real.)

C1   Sections III A and B have set out a tension between a mode of representation of woman in film and conventions surrounding the diegesis. Each is associated with a look: that of the spectator in direct scopophilic contact with the female form displayed for his enjoyment (connoting male fantasy) and that of the spectator fascinated with the image of his like set in an illusion of natural space, and through him gaining control and possession of the woman within the diegesis. (This tension and the shift from one pole to the other can structure a single text. Thus both in *Only Angels Have Wings* and in *To Have and Have Not*, the film opens with the woman as object of the combined gaze of spectator and all the male protagonists in the film. She is isolated, glamorous, on display, sexualised. But as the narrative progresses she falls in love with the main male protagonist and becomes his property, losing her outward glamorous characteristics, her generalised sexuality, her show-girl connotations; her eroticism is subjected to the male star alone. By means of identification with him, through participation in his power, the spectator can indirectly possess her too.)

But in psychoanalytic terms, the female figure poses a deeper problem. She also connotes something that the look continually circles around but disavows: her lack of a penis, implying a threat of castration and hence unpleasure.

Ultimately, the meaning of woman is sexual difference, the visually ascertainable absence of the penis, the material evidence on which is based the castration complex essential for the organisation of entrance to the symbolic order and the law of the father. Thus the woman as icon, displayed for the gaze and enjoyment of men, the active controllers of the look, always threatens to evoke the anxiety it originally signified. The male unconscious has two avenues of escape from this castration anxiety: preoccupation with the re-enactment of the original trauma (investigating the woman, demystifying her mystery), counterbalanced by the devaluation, punishment or saving of the guilty object (an avenue typified by the concerns of the *film noir*); or else complete disavowal of castration by the substitution of a fetish object or turning the represented figure itself into a fetish so that it becomes reassuring rather than dangerous (hence overvaluation, the cult of the female star).

This second avenue, fetishistic scopophilia, builds up the physical beauty of the object, transforming it into something satisfying in itself. The first avenue, voyeurism, on the contrary, has associations with sadism: pleasure lies in ascertaining guilt (immediately associated with castration), asserting control and subjugating the guilty person through punishment or forgiveness. This sadistic side fits in well with narrative. Sadism demands a story, depends on making something happen, forcing a change in another person, a battle of will and strength, victory/defeat, all occurring in a linear time with a beginning and an end. Fetishistic scopophilia, on the other hand, can exist outside linear time as the erotic instinct is focused on the look alone. These contradictions and ambiguities can be illustrated more simply by using works by Hitchcock and Sternberg, both of whom take the look almost as the content or subject matter of many of their films. Hitchcock is the more complex, as he uses both mechanisms. Sternberg's work, on the other hand, provides many pure examples of fetishistic scopophilia.

C2   Sternberg once said he would welcome his films being projected upside-down so that story and character involvement would not interfere with the spectator's undiluted appreciation of the screen image. This statement is revealing but ingenuous: ingenuous in that his films do demand that the figure of the woman (Dietrich, in the cycle of films with her, as the ultimate example) should be identifiable; but revealing in that it emphasises the fact that for him the pictorial space enclosed by the frame is paramount, rather than narrative or identification processes. While Hitchcock goes into the investigative side of voyeurism, Sternberg produces the ultimate fetish, taking it to the point where the powerful look of the male protagonist (characteristic of traditional narrative film) is broken in favour of the image in direct erotic rapport with the spectator. The beauty of the woman as object and the screen space coalesce; she is no longer the bearer of guilt but a perfect product, whose body, stylised and fragmented by close-ups, is the content of the film and the direct recipient of the spectator's look.

Sternberg plays down the illusion of screen depth; his screen tends to be one-dimensional, as light and shade, lace, steam, foliage, net, streamers and so on reduce the visual field. There is little or no mediation of the look through the eyes of the main male protagonist. On the contrary, shadowy presences like La Bessière in *Morocco* act as surrogates for the director, detached as they are from audience identification. Despite Sternberg's insistence that his stories are irrelevant, it is significant that they are concerned with situation, not suspense, and cyclical rather than linear time, while plot complications revolve around misunderstanding rather than conflict. The most important absence is that of the controlling male gaze within the screen scene. The high point of emotional drama in the most typical Dietrich films, her supreme moments of erotic meaning, take place in the absence of the man she loves in the fiction. There are other witnesses, other spectators watching her on the screen, their gaze is one with, not standing in for, that of the audience. At the end of *Morocco*, Tom Brown has already disappeared into the desert when Amy Jolly kicks off her gold sandals and walks after him. At the end of *Dishonoured*, Kranau is indifferent to the fate of Magda. In both cases, the erotic impact, sanctified by death, is displayed as a spectacle for the audience. The male hero misunderstands and, above all, does not see.

In Hitchcock, by contrast, the male hero does see precisely what the audience sees. However, although fascination with an image through scopophilic eroticism can be the subject of the film, it is the role of the hero to portray the contradictions and tensions experienced by the spectator. In *Vertigo* in particular, but also in *Marnie* and *Rear Window*, the look is central to the plot, oscillating between voyeurism and fetishistic fascination. Hitchcock has never concealed his interest in voyeurism, cinematic and non-cinematic. His heroes are exemplary of the symbolic order and the law – a policeman (*Vertigo*), a dominant male possessing money and power (*Marnie*) – but their erotic drives lead them into compromised situations. The power to subject another person to the will sadistically or to the gaze voyeuristically is turned onto the woman as the object of both. Power is backed by a certainty of legal right and the established guilt of the woman (evoking castration, psychoanalytically speaking). True perversion is barely concealed under a shallow mask of ideological correctness – the man is on the right side of the law, the woman on the wrong. Hitchcock's skilful use of identification processes and liberal use of subjective camera from the point of view of the male protagonist draw the spectators deeply into his position, making them share his uneasy gaze. The spectator is absorbed into a voyeuristic situation within the screen scene and diegesis, which parodies his own in the cinema.

In an analysis of *Rear Window*, Douchet takes the film as a metaphor for the cinema. Jeffries is the audience, the events in the apartment block opposite correspond to the screen. As he watches, an erotic dimension is added to his look, a central image to the drama. His girlfriend Lisa had been of little sexual interest to him, more or less a drag, so long as she remained on the spectator side.

When she crosses the barrier between his room and the block opposite, their relationship is reborn erotically. He does not merely watch her through his lens, as a distant meaningful image, he also sees her as a guilty intruder exposed by a dangerous man threatening her with punishment, and thus finally giving him the opportunity to save her. Lisa's exhibitionism has already been established by her obsessive interest in dress and style, in being a passive image of visual perfection; Jeffries's voyeurism and activity have also been established through his work as a photo-journalist, a maker of stories and captor of images. However, his enforced inactivity, binding him to his seat as a spectator, puts him squarely in the fantasy position of the cinema audience.

In *Vertigo*, subjective camera predominates. Apart from one flashback from Judy's point of view, the narrative is woven around what Scottie sees or fails to see. The audience follows the growth of his erotic obsession and subsequent despair precisely from his point of view. Scottie's voyeurism is blatant: he falls in love with a woman he follows and spies on without speaking to. Its sadistic side is equally blatant: he has chosen (and freely chosen, for he had been a successful lawyer) to be a policeman, with all the attendant possibilities of pursuit and investigation. As a result, he follows, watches and falls in love with a perfect image of female beauty and mystery. Once he actually confronts her, his erotic drive is to break her down and force her *to tell* by persistent cross-questioning.

In the second part of the film, he re-enacts his obsessive involvement with the image he loved to watch secretly. He reconstructs Judy as Madeleine, forces her to conform in every detail to the actual physical appearance of his fetish. Her exhibitionism, her masochism, make her an ideal passive counterpart to Scottie's active sadistic voyeurism. She knows her part is to perform, and only by playing it through and then replaying it can she keep Scottie's erotic interest. But in the repetition he does break her down and succeeds in exposing her guilt. His curiosity wins through; she is punished.

Thus, in *Vertigo*, erotic involvement with the look boomerangs: the spectator's own fascination is revealed as illicit voyeurism as the narrative content enacts the processes and pleasures that he is himself exercising and enjoying. The Hitchcock hero here is firmly placed within the symbolic order, in narrative terms. He has all the attributes of the patriarchal superego. Hence the spectator, lulled into a false sense of security by the apparent legality of his surrogate, sees through his look and finds himself exposed as complicit, caught in the moral ambiguity of looking. Far from being simply an aside on the perversion of the police, *Vertigo* focuses on the implications of the active/looking, passive/looked-at split in terms of sexual difference and the power of the male symbolic encapsulated in the hero. Marnie, too, performs for Mark Rutland's gaze and masquerades as the perfect to-be-looked-at image. He, too, is on the side of the law until, drawn in by obsession with her guilt, her secret, he longs to see her in the act of committing a crime, make her confess and thus save her. So he, too, becomes complicit as he acts out the implications of his power. He controls money and words; he can have his cake and eat it.

IV SUMMARY

The psychoanalytic background that has been discussed in this article is relevant to the pleasure and unpleasure offered by traditional narrative film. The scopophilic instinct (pleasure in looking at another person as an erotic object) and, in contradistinction, ego libido (forming identification processes) act as formations, mechanisms, which mould this cinema's formal attributes. The actual image of woman as (passive) raw material for the (active) gaze of man takes the argument a step further into the content and structure of representation, adding a further layer of ideological significance demanded by the patriarchal order in its favourite cinematic form – illusionistic narrative film. The argument must return again to the psychoanalytic background: women in representation can signify castration, and activate voyeuristic or fetishistic mechanisms to circumvent this threat. Although none of these interacting layers is intrinsic to film, it is only in the film form that they can reach a perfect and beautiful contradiction, thanks to the possibility in the cinema of shifting the emphasis of the look. The place of the look defines cinema, the possibility of varying it and exposing it. This is what makes cinema quite different in its voyeuristic potential from, say, strip-tease, theatre, shows and so on. Going far beyond highlighting a woman's to-be-looked-at-ness, cinema builds the way she is to be looked at into the spectacle itself. Playing on the tension between film as controlling the dimension of time (editing, narrative) and film as controlling the dimension of space (changes in distance, editing), cinematic codes create a gaze, a world and an object, thereby producing an illusion cut to the measure of desire. It is these cinematic codes and their relationship to formative external structures that must be broken down before mainstream film and the pleasure it provides can be challenged.

To begin with (as an ending), the voyeuristic-scopophilic look that is a crucial part of traditional filmic pleasure can itself be broken down. There are three different looks associated with cinema: that of the camera as it records the pro-filmic event, that of the audience as it watches the final product, and that of the characters at each other within the screen illusion. The conventions of narrative film deny the first two and subordinate them to the third, the conscious aim being always to eliminate intrusive camera presence and prevent a distancing awareness in the audience. Without these two absences (the material existence of the recording process, the critical reading of the spectator), fictional drama cannot achieve reality, obviousness and truth. Nevertheless, as this article has argued, the structure of looking in narrative fiction film contains a contradiction in its own premises: the female image as a castration threat constantly endangers the unity of the diegesis and bursts through the world of illusion as an intrusive, static, one-dimensional fetish. Thus the two looks materially present in time and space are obsessively subordinated to the neurotic needs of the male ego. The camera becomes the mechanism for producing an illusion of Renaissance space, flowing movements compatible with the human eye, an ideology of representation that revolves around the perception of the subject; the camera's look is disavowed in order to create a convincing world in which the spectator's surrogate can perform with verisimilitude. Simultaneously, the look of the audience is denied an intrinsic force: as soon as fetishistic representation of the female image threatens to break the spell of illusion, and the erotic image on the screen appears directly (without mediation) to the spectator, the fact of fetishisation, concealing as it does castration fear, freezes the look, fixates the spectator and prevents him from achieving any distance from the image in front of him.

This complex interaction of looks is specific to film. The first blow against the monolithic accumulation of traditional film conventions (already undertaken by radical film-makers) is to free the look of the camera into its materiality in time and space and the look of the audience into dialectics and passionate detachment. There is no doubt that this destroys the satisfaction, pleasure and privilege of the 'invisible guest', and highlights the way film has depended on voyeuristic active/passive mechanisms. Women, whose image has continually been stolen and used for this end, cannot view the decline of the traditional film form with anything much more than sentimental regret.

6

'CAUGHT AND REBECCA: THE INSCRIPTION OF FEMININITY AS ABSENCE'

Mary Ann Doane

Historically, Hitchcock's *Rebecca* (1940) and Ophuls' *Caught* (1949) bracket a decade in which many films were aimed at a predominantly female audience. They are instances of a broad category of films frequently referred to as the 'woman film' or 'woman's picture.' This label implies that the films are in some sense the 'possession' of women and that their terms of address are dictated by the anticipated presence of the female spectator. Both presuppositions are problematic in light of contemporary film theory's investigation of positions offered by the film to the spectator – an investigation which stresses psychical mechanisms related primarily to the male spectator – voyeurism, fetishism, even identification. In this context, Hollywood narratives are analyzed as compensatory structures designed to defend the male psyche against the threat offered by the image of the woman. A crucial unresolved issue here is the very possibility of constructing a 'female spectator,' given the cinema's appeal to (male) voyeurism and fetishism.

Nevertheless, addressing themselves to the perhaps illusory female spectator, the 'women's films' are based on an idea of female fantasy which they themselves anticipate and in some sense construct. Interestingly, the problematic of female fantasy is most frequently compatible with that of persecution – by husband, family, or lover (both *Rebecca* and *Caught* can be aligned with this description). The films manifest an obsession with certain psychical mechanisms which have been associated with the female (chiefly masochism, hysteria, and paranoia). All

From *Enclitic* 5:2, 1981, pp. 75–89.

of them attempt in some way to trace female subjectivity and desire. Never-theless, because this attempt is made within the traditional forms and conven-tions of Hollywood narrative – forms which cannot sustain such an exploration – certain contradictions within patriarchal ideology become apparent. This makes the films particularly valuable for a feminist analysis of the way in which the 'woman's story' is told.

Caught and *Rebecca* are especially interesting, even exemplary, because each of them contains a scene in which the camera almost literally enacts the repression of the feminine – the woman's relegation to the status of a signifier within the male discourse. The camera movements in these scenes can be described as hysterical – frantically searching for, retracing the path of, the lost object, attempting to articulate what is, precisely, not there. As such, the camera movements have the status of symptoms. The symptom gives access to, makes readable, the work of repression and hence indicates the process of transition from one system in the apparatus to another. In a way, the symptom can be seen as manifesting the severity of the repression or the force of the energy attached to the repressed idea which 'breaks through' to the surface. In film theory and criticism, this scenario provides a means of accounting for perversion within the norm by positing the paradoxical possibility of the 'hysterical classical text.'[1] The hysteria frequently attributed to the female protagonist in the 'woman's film' proliferates, effecting a more general 'hystericization' of the text as body of signifiers.

It is quite appropriate that Laura Mulvey, in her influential essay on visual pleasure, limits her discussion to a Hollywood Cinema populated by male protagonists acting as relays in a complex process designed to insure the ego-fortification of the male spectator.[2] Yet there is a sense in which the 'woman's film' attempts to constitute itself as the mirror image of this dominant cinema, obsessively centering and re-centering a female protagonist. It thus offers resistance to an analysis which stresses the 'to-be-looked-at-ness' of the woman, her objectification as spectacle according to the masculine structure of the gaze. Hence it becomes crucial in an investigation of the 'woman's film' to trace the vicissitudes of the process of specularization. One assumption behind the positing of a female spectator (that is, one who does not assume a masculine position with respect to the reflected image of her own body) is that it is no longer necessary to invest the look with desire in quite the same way. A certain despecularization takes place in these films, a deflection of scopophilic energy in other directions. The aggressivity, which, as Jacqueline Rose has demonstrated,[3] is contained in the cinematic structuration of the look is released or, more accurately, transformed into a narrativized paranoia (most apparent in films tinged by the gothic such as *Rebecca*, *Gaslight*, and *Dragonwyck* where it is a question of the husband's murderous designs, but also evident in *Caught*). This sub-class of the 'woman's film' clearly activates the latent paranoia of the film system described by Rose.

Thus, the metaphor of paranoia may prove even more appropriate for a delineation of the 'woman's film' than that of hysteria. As Freud points out in his analysis of Dr Schreber, whose most striking symptom is his assumption of the position/body of the woman, paranoia is systematically disintegrative.[4] Hysteria condenses, paranoia decomposes. In this respect, both *Caught* and *Rebecca*, by privileging moments in which the cinematic apparatus itself undergoes a process of decomposition, situate themselves as paranoid texts. Both films contain scenes of projection in which the image as lure and trap is externalized in relation to the woman. The films dis-articulate the components of the apparatus which construct the woman as 'imagined' – camera, projector, and screen – and incorporate them within the diegesis as props. In this *mise-en-scène* of cinematic elements, camera, projector and screen are explicitly activated as agents of narrativity, as operators of the image.

Yet, this gesture of dis-articulation does not preclude an elaboration of the woman's relation to spectacle. In fact, the desire of the woman in both films is to duplicate a given image, to engage with and capture the male gaze. In *Caught*, the image is that of a woman in a mink coat; in *Rebecca*, that of 'a woman of thirty-six dressed in black satin with a string of pearls.' And in both films, movie projection scenes act to negate each of these appropriations of an image, to effect a separation on both literal and figurative levels between the woman and the image of her desire (always situated as a desire to be desired or desirable, hence as subordinate).

The background of the credit sequence in *Caught* is constituted by a series of pages in a fashion magazine, slowly flipped over in synchronization with credit changes to reveal women posing in front of monuments and art works, women posing in the latest fashions. Merging with the body proper of the film, this background becomes the first shot, its incorporation within the diegesis signalled by the addition of voices-over and pointing fingers, metonymic signifiers of female desire. The voices-over – 'I'll take this one,' 'That one,' 'This one's for me' – are the indexical actualizations of the female appetite for the image, an appetite sustained by the commodity fetishism which supports capitalism. And the ultimate commodity, as here, is the body adorned for the gaze. The logic of this economics of desire culminates in the final magazine image of the scene, a sketch of a woman modeling a fur coat, the unmediated signifier of wealth. The camera marks its significance by tracking back at this moment (accompanied by the voice-over, 'I'd rather have mink') to incorporate within its image the two women whose fantasies are complicit with the fashion industry. Signifier of economic success, the fur coat (which becomes mink, aligning itself with Leonora's desire) is the site of a certain semantic wealth in the text, re-surfacing again and again to mark the oscillations of female subjectivity. In the image, significantly, it is a sketch which replaces the human model as support of the coat. The fur coat overpowers the body, given only as trace.

This first scene initiates the narrative trajectory along the line of an investigation of the contradictions and convolutions of female spectatorship. Owners of the look in this instance, the woman can only exercise it within a narcissistic framework which collapses the opposition between the subject and the object of the gaze – 'This one's for me.' The woman's sexuality, as spectator, must undergo a constant process of transformation. She must look, as if she were a man with the phallic power of the gaze, at a woman who would attract that gaze, in order to be that woman. There is a necessary movement or oscillation between the periphery of the image to its center and back again. The convolutions involved here are analogous to those described by Julia Kristeva as 'the double or triple twists of what we commonly call female homosexuality': ' "I am looking, as a man would, for a woman"; or else, "I submit myself, as if I were a man who thought he was a woman, to a woman who thinks she is a man." '[5] For the female spectator exemplified by Maxine and Leonora in this scene, to possess the image through the gaze is to become it. The gap which strictly separates identification and desire for the male spectator (whose possession of the cinematic woman is at least partially dependent upon an identification with the male protagonist) is abolished in the case of the woman. Binding identification to desire (the basic strategy of narcissism), the teleological aim of the female look demands a becoming and hence, a dispossession. She must give up the image in order to become it – the image is *too* present for her.

And this is precisely the specular movement traced by *Caught*. Within the space of two scenes, the look is reversed – Leonora (Barbara Bel Geddes) dons the mink coat and adopts the pose of the model, soliciting the gaze of both male and female spectators. She now participates in the image, while her dispossession is signalled by the rhythmic chants which punctuate her turns, '$49.95 plus tax.' The economics of sexual exchange are on display, for it is not only the coat which is on the market. Leonora receives an invitation to the yacht party at which she will later meet millionaire Smith Ohlrig (Robert Ryan) and, as her friend Maxine points out in the face of Leonora's resistance to the invitation, 'How else do girls like us get to meet guys like Smith Ohlrig?' When Leonora actually marries Ohlrig, her transformation into the image is completed by the newspaper montage sequence announcing the wedding, framing and immobilizing her in the photograph.

These three moments of the narrative trajectory – defining the woman as, successively, agent, object and text of the look – would seem to be self-contained, to exhaust the potential variations of Leonora's relation to the image. Yet, the film recovers and re-writes its own beginning in the projection scene, situating Leonora once more in the place of the spectator. But this time she is explicitly located as a spectator who refuses to see, in a cinema delimited as male. By the time of the projection scene, Leonora is fully in place; she owns the mink coat and no longer has to model it. Her alienation from the cinematic apparatus is manifested by the fact of her exclusion, her positioning on the margins of the process of imaging. The cinema which Ohlrig forces her to attend is described only as the 'movies for my new project' and all of its spectators, except Leonora, are male (a situation which Leonora attempts to resist with the excuse she weakly presents to Ohlrig immediately preceding the screening. '... so many men.') [...]

The projection sequence as a whole marks an important turning point in the narrative. The interruption of the filmic flow of images within the diegesis, here as in *Rebecca*, is the metaphor for the disintegration of a short-lived family romance. Spectator of a cinema whose parameters are defined as masculine, Leonora is dispossessed of both look and voice. Yet, the trajectory which traces her dispossession in relation to the image is not completed until the end of the film. For, when Leonora leaves Ohlrig as a result of this scene, she takes a piece of the image with her – the mink coat, signifier of her continuing complicity in the process of imaging.

Hitchcock's *Rebecca* also contains a crucial scene in which the film effects a decomposition of the elements which collaborate in making the position of female spectatorship an impossible one. The home movie sequence depicts a process of projection constituted as an assault on the diegetic female spectator. This scene as well is preceded by the delineation of female desire in relation to the fixed image of the fashion magazine. A preface to the projection scene. the shot of the fashion magazine whose pages are slowly turned is here unlocalized. Unlike *Caught*, *Rebecca* elides the establishing shot which would identify the woman as viewer and, instead, dissolves immediately to her transformation into the image, an image she had previously promised Maxim (Laurence Olivier) she would never appropriate for herself – that of a woman 'dressed in black satin with a string of pearls'. The character played by Joan Fontaine (who is never given a proper name) enters the cinema in the hope of becoming a spectacle for Maxim but is relegated to the position of spectator – spectator of the images Maxim prefers to retain of her, those taken on their honeymoon [. . .]

It is as though in both *Caught* and *Rebecca*, the diegetic film's continuous unfolding guaranteed a rather fragile binding of the drives in the heterosexual unit of the harmonious couple. Its interruption, in each instance, signals the release of aggressive tendencies. In this way, the films play out the problematic of paranoia in its relation to the process of imaging, and, simultaneously, the institution of marriage. As Rose points out, paranoia is 'The aggressive corollary of the narcissistic structure of the ego-function.'[6] The 'woman's films' as a group appear to make a detour around or deflect the issue of spectacle and the woman's position (an obsession of the dominant cinema addressed to the male spectator), and hence avoid the problem of feminine narcissism. Yet, this narcissism returns and infiltrates the two texts by means of a paranoia which is linked to an obsession with the specular. The projection scenes in both films are preceded by the delineation of a narcissistic female desire – the desire to become the image which captures the male gaze. Nevertheless, it is as though the aggressivity which should be attendant on that structure were detached, in the projection scenes, and transferred to the specular system which insures and perpetuates female narcissism – the cinematic apparatus. Thus, the aggressivity attached to her own narcissism is stolen and used against the woman; she becomes the object rather than the subject of that aggression.

The desire to be looked at is thus transformed into a fear of being looked at, or a fear of the apparatus which systematizes or governs that process of looking. From this perspective, it is interesting to note that in the only case of female paranoia Freud treats, as described in 'A Case of Paranoia Running Counter to the Psychoanalytical Theory of the Disease,' the woman's delusion concerns being photographed. During lovemaking with a male friend, a young woman hears a noise – a knock or tick – which she interprets as the sound of a camera, photographing her in order to compromise her. Freud doubts the very existence of the noise: 'I do not believe that the clock ever ticked or that any noise was to be heard at all. The woman's situation justified a sensation of throbbing in the clitoris. This was what she subsequently projected as a perception of an external object.'[7] Female paranoia thus finds its psychoanalytic explanation in the projection of a bodily sensation from inside to outside, in a relocation in external reality.

Projection is a mechanism which Freud consistently associates with paranoia. Yet, he is reluctant to make it specific to paranoia, since it is present in more 'normal' provinces such as those of superstition, mythology and, finally, the activity of theorizing. For Freud, projection is instrumental in formulating the very condition of the opposition between internal and external reality, between subject and object. For projection enables flight (from the 'bad object') and the possibility of a refusal to recognize something in or about oneself.[8] The invocation of the opposition between subject and object in connection with the paranoid mechanism of projection indicates a precise difficulty in any conceptualization of female paranoia – one which Freud does not mention. For in his short case history, what the woman projects, what she throws away, is her sexual pleasure, a part of her bodily image. The sound of her own body throbbing becomes the click of the camera, the capture of her image. For the female spectator in the cinema, on the other hand, the spectator so carefully delineated in *Caught* and *Rebecca*, the problem is even more complex. In the cinematic situation, in the realm of the image, the distinction between subject and object effected by projection is not accessible to the female spectator in the same way as to the male. For Leonora and Maxine in *Caught* and the Joan Fontaine character in *Rebecca*, the pictures in fashion magazines demonstrate that to possess the image through the gaze is to become it. And becoming the image, the woman can no longer have it. For the female spectator, the image is *too* close – it cannot be projected far enough. The alternatives she is given are quite literally figured in the two films: (1) She can accept the image, full acceptance indicated by the attempts to duplicate it (by means of the mink coat or the black silk dress); or (2) She can repudiate the image (voluntarily in *Caught*, unwillingly in *Rebecca*). The absoluteness of the dilemma is manifested in the mutual exclusivity of its terms – a condition which does not mirror that of the male spectator, who, like Sean Connery in *Marnie* (as described by Mulvey), can 'have his cake and eat it too.' As a card-carrying fetishist, the male spectator does not have to choose between acceptance or rejection of the image; he can balance his belief and knowledge. Deprived of castration anxiety, the female spectator is also deprived of the possibility of fetishism – of the reassuring 'I know, but even so . . .'

To the extent that the projection scenes in *Caught* and *Rebecca* mobilize the elements of a specular system which has historically served the interests of male spectatorship, they are limit-texts, exposing the contradictions which inhabit the logic of their own terms of address as 'women's films.' The relation between the female body and the female look articulated by the two films (a relation which always threatens to collapse into the sameness of equivalence), together with the over-presence of the image, indicate a difficulty in the woman's relation to symbolization. Sexuality, disseminated in the classical representation across the body of the woman, is for her non-localizable. This is why psychoanalytic theory tells us she must be It rather than have It. As Parveen Adams points out, the woman does not represent lack; she lacks the means to represent lack.[9] According to the problematic elaborated by *Caught* and *Rebecca*, what the female viewer lacks is the very distance or gap which separates, must separate, the spectator from the image. What she lacks, in other words, is a 'good throw.'

Although the projection scenes in *Caught* and *Rebecca* do deconstruct, in some sense, the woman's position relative to the process of imaging, there is a missing piece in this *mise-en-scène* of cinematic elements – projector and screen are there but the camera is absent. In *Rebecca* the home-movie camera is briefly mentioned to justify the final shot, but in neither film is the camera visualized. The camera is, of course, an element whose acknowledgement would pose a more radical threat to the classicism which ultimately these texts fully embrace, particularly if the camera whose presence was acknowledged were non-diegetic. Yet, while it is true that indications of the presence of a camera are missing in the projection scenes, it is possible to argue that inscriptions of the camera are displaced, inserted later in the films to buttress a specifically male discourse about the woman. Paradoxically, in each of the films the camera demonstrates its own presence and potency through the very absence of an image of the woman. In a frantic, almost psychotic search for that image, the camera contributes its power to the hallucination of a woman.

In *Rebecca*, there is a scene late in the film which exemplifies the very felt presence of the woman who is absent throughout the movie, the woman whose initials continually surround and subdue the Joan Fontaine character – Rebecca. It is the scene in which Maxim narrates the story of Rebecca, despite his own claim that it is unnarratable ('She told me all about herself – everything – things I wouldn't tell a living soul.') The camera's very literal inscription of the absent woman's movements is preceded by a transfer of the look from narrator to narratee. Maxim, standing by the door, looks first at the sofa, then at Fontaine, then back at the sofa. Fontaine turns her glance from Maxim to the sofa, appropriating his gaze. From this point on, the camera's movements are very precisely synchronized with Maxim's words: when he tells Fontaine that Rebecca sat next to an ashtray brimming with cigarette stubs, there is a cut to the sofa, empty but for the ashtray; as he describes Rebecca rising from the sofa, the camera duplicates that movement and then pans to the left – purportedly following a woman who is not visible. In tracing Rebecca's path as Maxim narrates, the camera pans more than 180 degrees. In effect, what was marked very clearly as Maxim's point of view, simply transferred to Fontaine as narratee, comes to include him. The story of the woman culminates as the image of the man.

Caught makes appeal to a remarkably similar signifying strategy in a scene in which Leonora's absence from the image becomes the strongest signified – the scene in which her empty desk is used as a pivot as the camera swings back and forth between Dr Hoffman (Frank Ferguson) and Dr Quinada (James Mason) discussing her fate. The sequence begins with a high angle shot down on Leonora's desk, the camera moving down and to the left to frame Dr Hoffman, already framed in his doorway. Moving from Hoffman across the empty desk, the camera constructs a perfect symmetry by framing Dr Quinada in his doorway as well. The middle portion of the sequence is constituted by a sustained cross-cutting between Hoffman and Quinada, alternating both medium shots and close-ups. The end of the sequence echoes and repeats the beginning, the camera again pivoting around the absent woman's desk from Quinada to Hoffman and, as Hoffman suggests that Quinada 'forget' Leonora, back to the empty desk, closing the sequence with a kind of formal tautology. The sequence is a performance of one of the overdetermined meanings of the film's title – Leonora is 'caught,' spatially, between an obstetrician and a pediatrician (other potential readings include the theme of 'catching' a rich husband which initiates the film, the fact that Leonora is 'caught' in her marriage by her husband who wants to keep her child or that she is 'caught' between Smith Ohlrig and Larry Quinada).

In tracing the absence of the woman, the camera inscribes its own presence in the film as phallic substitute – the pen which writes the feminine body. The two scenes demonstrate the technical fluency of the camera in narrating the woman's story, extended to the point of ejecting her from the image. In its foreclosure of a signifier – here, the woman's body – from the symbolic universe, the camera enacts its paranoia as a psychosis. It is as though, in a pseudo-genre marked as the possession of the woman, the camera had to desperately reassert itself by means of its technical prowess – here embodied in the attribute of movement. The projection scenes discussed earlier effect a cleavage, a split between the image of the woman's desire (linked to stills – photographs or sketches without movement) and what is projected on the screen (in *Caught*, the machinery of industry, capitalist enterprise; in *Rebecca*, the images of Maxim's memory of her before the black satin dress). In each case, it is the man who has control of the projector and hence the moving image. Thus the films construct an opposition between different processes of imaging along the lines of sexual difference: female desire is linked to the fixation and stability of a spectacle refusing the temporal dimension, while male desire is more fully implicated with the defining characteristic of the cinematic image – movement. The two scenes in which the camera inscribes the absence of the woman thus accomplish a double negation of the feminine – through her absence and the camera's movement, its continual displacement of the fixed image of her desire. Invoking the specific attributes of the cinematic signifier (movement and absence of the object) around the figure of the woman, the films succeed in constructing a story about the woman which no longer requires even her physical presence.

Nevertheless, each of the films recovers the image of the woman, writing her back into the narrative. At the end of *Caught*, in a scene which echoes the earlier one pivoting on Leonora's empty desk, her image is returned to the diegesis. Inserted, almost accidentally it seems, between two shots of Dr Hoffman and Dr Quinada who are once more discussing her, is an image of Leonora in which the camera stares straight down at her lying in a hospital bed. In *Rebecca*, Joan Fontaine's full appropriation of Rebecca's position toward the end of the film coincides with the abolition of even the traces of Rebecca's absent presence. In the final shot of the film, the initial R which decorates the pillow of her bed is consumed by flames. This denial of the absent woman and the resultant recuperation of presence form the basis for the reunification and harmony of the couple which closes the film.

The closure in *Caught*, however, is less sure, the recuperation more problematic.[10] The oppressiveness of the *mise-en-scène* toward the end of the film is marked. This is particularly true of the scene inside an ambulance, in which sirens wail as Dr Quinada tells Leonora how free she can be if her child dies. The claustrophobic effect of the scene issues from the fact that there are two simultaneous movements toward Leonora – as the camera moves gradually closer and closer, framing her more tightly, Dr Quinada repeats its movement from another direction. By the end of the shot he appears to have nearly smothered her with his body. Leonora is caught in the pincers of his double movement as Quinada tells her, 'He (Smith Ohlrig) won't be able to hold you . . . Now you can be free.' The camera's movement explicitly repeats that of Dr Quinada in its domination, enclosure, and framing of the woman. In the next scene, in which the image of Leonora in a hospital bed is inserted between two shots of the doctors, the camera literally assumes Dr Quinada's position in the ambulance, aiming itself directly down at Leonora. Dr Quinada has just been informed by Dr Hoffman in the hallway that the baby has died and his reply, the same words he used in the ambulance – 'He can't hold her now – she's free' – constitutes the voice over Leonora's image.

But Leonora's ultimate 'freedom' in the last scene is granted to her by Dr Hoffman when he tells the nurse to take her mink coat away with the statement, 'If my diagnosis is correct, she won't want that anyway.' With the rejection of the mink coat comes the denial of the last trace of the image in its relation to Leonora. By means of the doctor's diagnosis, she becomes, instead of an image, an element in the discourse of medicine, a manuscript to be read for the symptoms which betray her story, her identity. It is appropriate that the final scene in *Caught* takes place in a hospital. For the doctor, as reader or interpreter of that manuscript, accomplishes the final de-specularization proposed by the text's own trajectory and the terms of its address. The final image of the film consists of the nurse slinging the mink coat over her shoulder and taking it away down the hospital corridor.

The movement of the narrative is thus from the representation of the mink coat which sparks desire to the rejection of the 'real thing' (a rejection really made 'on behalf' of the woman by the doctor). One could chart the elaboration of female subjectivity in the film according to the presence or absence of the mink coat. At the beginning of the film, Leonora's only desire is to meet a man rich enough to allow her to return to her home town with two mink coats – 'One for my mother and one for me.' A cut from Leonora at Dorothy Dale's School of Charm pretending that a cloth coat is mink to a tilt upwards along the mink coat she models in a department store in the next scene establishes her rise on the social scale. When she leaves Smith Ohlrig after the projection scene discussed earlier, she takes her mink coat with her and the coat immediately signals to Quinada her alliance with an upper class. Yet, when she briefly returns to Ohlrig after quitting her job as Quinada's receptionist, she realizes that he has not changed and, as she calls Dr Quinada on the phone, Leonora tells Franzi, 'I'm through with that coat.' Dr Quinada subsequently buys Leonora a cloth coat, an action which initiates their romance. The opposition cloth/mink governs the economic thematics of the text.

The mink coat is thus the means by which the specular is welded to the economic – it functions both as an economic landmark of Leonora's social position and as the articulation of the woman's relation to the spectacle and the male gaze. The textual meditations upon the sexed subject and the class subject merge imperceptibly. Leonora's desire to own the mink coat is both narcissistic and socially/economically ambitious. Yet, the text attempts to prove the desire itself to be 'wrong' or misguided since the man she marries in order to obtain the coat is dangerously psychotic. Dr Quinada, unlike Smith Ohlrig, is a member of her own class; hence, Leonora's understanding of her own sexuality is simultaneous with her understanding and acceptance of her class position.

In *Rebecca*, the situation is somewhat similar, with important deviations. Generic considerations are here much stronger since *Rebecca* belongs more clearly to a group of films infused by the gothic and defined by a plot in which the wife fears her husband is a murderer. In films like *Rebecca*, *Dragonwyck*, and *Undercurrent*, the woman marries, often hastily, *into* the upper class; her husband has money and a social position which she cannot match. The marriage thus constitutes a type of transgression (of class barriers) which does not remain unpunished. The woman often feels dwarfed or threatened by the house itself (*Rebecca*, *Dragonwyck*). A frequent reversal of the hierarchy of mistress and servant is symptomatic of the fact that the woman is 'out of place' in her rich surroundings. Nevertheless, in films of the same genre such as *Suspicion*, *Secret Beyond the Door*, and *Gaslight*, the economic sexual relationship is reversed. In each of these, there is at least a hint that the man marries the woman in order to obtain her money. Hence, it is not always the case that a woman from a lower class is punished for attempting to change her social and economic standing. Rather, the mixture effected by a marriage between two different classes produces horror and paranoia.

By making sexuality extremely difficult in a rich environment, both films – *Caught* and *Rebecca* – promote the illusion of separating the issue of sexuality from that of economics. What is really repressed in this scenario is the economics of sexual exchange. This repression is most evident in *Caught* whose explicit moral – 'Don't marry for money' – constitutes a negation of the economic factor in marriage. But negation, as Freud points out, is also affirmation; in *Caught* there is an unconscious acknowledgement of the economics of marriage as an institution. In the course of the film, the woman becomes the object of exchange, from Smith Ohlrig to Dr Quinada.[11] A by-product of this exchange is the relinquishing of the posited object of her desire – the expensive mink coat.

There is a sense, then, in which both films begin with a hypothesis of female subjectivity which is subsequently disproven by the textual project. The narrative of *Caught* is introduced by the attribution of the look at the image (the 'I' of seeing) to Leonora and her friend. The film ends by positioning Leonora as the helpless, bed-ridden object of the medical gaze. In the beginning of *Rebecca*, the presence of a female subjectivity as the source of the enunciation is marked. A female voice-over (belonging to the Fontaine character) accompanies a hazy, dream-like image: 'Last night I dreamed I went to Manderley again. It seems to me I stood by the iron gate leading to the drive. For a while I could not enter.' The voice goes on to relate how, like all dreamers, she was suddenly possessed by a supernatural power and passed through the gate. This statement is accompanied by a shot in which the camera assumes the position of the 'I' and, in a sustained subjective movement, tracks forward through the gate and along the path. Yet, the voice-over subsequently disappears entirely – it is not even resuscitated at the end of the film in order to provide closure through a symmetrical frame. Nevertheless, there *is* an extremely disconcerting re-emergence of a feminine 'I' later in the film. In the cottage scene in which Maxim narrates the 'unnarratable' story of the absent Rebecca to Joan Fontaine, he insists upon a continual use of direct quotes and hence the first person pronoun referring to Rebecca. His narrative is laced with these quotes from Rebecca which parallel on the soundtrack the moving image, itself adhering to the traces of an absent Rebecca. Maxim is therefore the one who pronounces the following statements: 'I'll play the part of a devoted wife' ... 'When I have a child, Max, no one will be able to say that it's not yours' ... 'I'll be the perfect mother just as I've been the perfect wife' ... 'Well, Max, what are you going to do about it? Aren't you going to kill me?' Just as the tracking subjective shot guarantees that the story of the woman literally culminates as the image of the man, the construction of the dialogue allows Maxim to appropriate Rebecca's 'I.'[12]

The films thus chronicle the emergence and disappearance of female subjectivity, the articulation of an 'I' which is subsequently negated. The pressure of the demand in the 'woman's film' for the depiction of female subjectivity is so strong, and often so contradictory, that it is not at all surprising that sections such as the projection scenes in *Caught* and *Rebecca* should dwell on the problem of female spectatorship. These scenes internalize the difficulties of the genre and in their concentration on the issue of the woman's relation to the gaze occupy an important place in the narrative. Paranoia is here the appropriate and logical obsession. For it effects a confusion between subjectivity and objectivity, between the internal and the external, thus disallowing the gap which separates the spectator from the image of his/her desire.

In many respects, the most disturbing images of the two films are those which evoke the absence of the woman. In both films these images follow projection scenes which delineate the impossibility of female spectatorship. It is as though each film adhered strictly to the logic which characterizes dream-work – establishing the image of an absent woman as the delayed mirror image of a female spectator who is herself only virtual.

NOTES

1. For an example of this use of the concept of hysteria in film analysis, see Geoffrey Nowell-Smith, 'Minnelli and Melodrama,' *Screen*, 18:2 (Summer 1977), pp. 113–18. I have discussed this idea of perversion within the norm more fully in 'The "Classical Hollywood Text" as Norm and Symptom,' paper presented at Clark/Luxembourg Film Conference, Luxembourg, May 1980.
2. Laura Mulvey, 'Visual Pleasure and Narrative Cinema,' *Screen*, 16:3 (Autumn 1975), pp. 6–18.
3. Jacqueline Rose, 'Paranoia and the Film System,' *Screen*, 17:4 (Winter 1976–7), pp. 85–104.
4. Sigmund Freud. *Three Case Histories* (New York: Collier Books, 1963), p. 149.
5. Julia Kristeva, *About Chinese Women*, trans. Anita Barrows (New York: Urizen Books, 1977), p. 29.
6. Rose, p. 86.
7. Freud, 'A Case of Paranoia Running Counter to the Psychoanalytical Theory of the Disease,' in *Sexuality and the Psychology of Love* (New York: Collier Books, 1963), p. 104.
8. See J. Laplanche and J.-B. Pontalis, *The Language of Psychoanalysis*, trans. Donald Nicholson-Smith (New York: Norton, 1973), pp. 349–56. Laplanche and Pontalis define projection as having a sense 'comparable to the cinematographic one: the subject sends out into the external world an image of something that exists in him in an unconscious way. Projection is here defined as a mode of *refusal to recognize (méconnaissance)* ...'.
9. 'Representation and Sexuality,' *m/f*. no. 1, pp. 66–7.
10. An acknowledgment of the difficulties with the ending of *Caught* can be found in Ophuls' remarks about the film: 'I worked for MGM. I made *Caught*, which I quite like. But I had difficulties with the production over the script, so that the film goes off the rails toward the end. Yes, the ending is really almost impossible, but up until the last ten minutes it's not bad.' Paul Willeman, ed. *Ophuls* (London: British Film Institute, 1978), p. 23.
11. In the generic sub-category to which *Rebecca* belongs, the 'paranoid' woman's film, there are frequently two major male characters, one evil or psychotic, the other good and heroic. The woman, as in Lévi-Strauss' fable of the constitution of society, is

exchanged from one to the other. In *Rebecca* this is not quite the case. Nevertheless, Maxim is a composite figure and therefore incorporates both character-types – both sane and insane, rich but with middle-class tastes (e.g. the Joan Fontaine character). At the end of the film, Fontaine finds a harmonious re-unification with the sane Maxim, whose strongest symbol of wealth – Manderley – burns to the ground.

12. The vicious quality of such a gesture is mitigated by the fact that Rebecca, in contradistinction to the Joan Fontaine character, is isolated as the evil, sexually active woman.

7

'OEDIPUS INTERRUPTUS'

Teresa de Lauretis

Suppose we were to ask the question: what became of the Sphinx after the encounter with Oedipus on his way to Thebes? Or, how did Medusa feel seeing herself in Perseus' mirror just before being slain? To be sure, an answer could be found by perusing a good textbook of classical mythology; but the point is, no-one knows offhand and, what is more, it seldom occurs to anyone to ask. Our culture, history, and science do not provide an answer; but neither do the modern mythologies, the fictions of our social imagination, the stories and the images produced by what may be called the psychotechnologies of our everyday life. Medusa and the Sphinx, like the other ancient monsters, have survived inscribed in hero narratives, in someone else's story, not their own; so they are figures or markers of positions—places and topoi—through which the hero and his story move to their destination and to accomplish meaning [...]

My question at the beginning of this chapter, what did Medusa feel seeing herself reflected in Perseus' shield just before being slain, was intended very much in the context of a politics of the unconscious. It is a rhetorical question, but one that nonetheless needs to be posed within the feminist discourse and urgently demands of it further theoretical attention. It is a rhetorical question in the sense that, I believe, some of us do know how Medusa felt, because we have seen it at the movies, from *Psycho* to *Blow Out*, be the film a *Love Story* or *Not a Love Story*. Yet our knowledge, and the experience of that feeling are discounted by film critics as subjective and idiosyncratic, and by film theorists as naive or

* From De Lauretis, T., Desire in Narrative. In *Alice Doesn't: Feminism, Semiotics, Cinema*. London: Macmillan, 1984, pp. 134–56.

untheoretical. Some, for example, would remind us that when we see Medusa being slain (daily) on the screen, as film and television spectators, we have a 'purely aesthetic' identification.[1]

Others—and probably you, too, reader—would object that my question about Medusa is tendentious, for I pretend to ignore that in the story Medusa was asleep when Perseus entered her 'cave'; she did not see, *she did not look*. Precisely. Doesn't an 'aesthetic' identification mean that, though we 'look at her looking' throughout the movie, we too, women spectators, are asleep when she is being slain? And only wake up, like Snow White and Sleeping Beauty, if the film ends with the kiss? Or you may remark that I am indeed naive in equating Perseus' shield with a movie screen. Yet, not only does that shield protect Perseus from Medusa's evil look, but later on, after her death (in his further adventures), it serves as frame and surface on which her head is pinned to petrify his enemies. It is thus, pinned up on the shield of Athena, that the slain Medusa continues to perform her deadly task within the institutions of law and war . . . and cinema (I would add), for which Cocteau (not I) devised the well-known definition, 'death at work.'

In an equally well-known paper of 1922, entitled 'Medusa's Head,' Freud reiterated his theory that 'the terror of castration . . . is linked to the sight of something,' the female genitals; and similarly 'the sight of Medusa's head makes the spectator stiff with terror, turns him to stone,' but at the same time offers him 'consolation . . . the stiffening reassures him.'[2] This is what Cixous parodies in 'The Laugh of the Medusa,' when she says: '[Men] need femininity to be associated with death; it's the jitters that give them a hard-on! for themselves!' (p. 255). 'What then of the look of the woman?' asks Heath. 'The reply given by psychoanalysis is from the phallus. If the woman looks, the spectacle provokes, castration is in the air, the Medusa's head is not far off; thus, she must not look, is absorbed herself on the side of the seen, seeing herself seeing herself, Lacan's femininity.' And he quotes the Lacanian analyst Eugénie Lemoine-Luccioni: 'In thus offering herself to the look, in giving herself for sight, according to the sequence: see, see oneself, give oneself to be seen, be seen, the girl—unless she falls into the complete alienation of the hysteric—provokes the Other to an encounter and a reply which give her pleasure.'[3] Cixous's anti-Lacanian response is certainly more encouraging, but only slightly more useful practically or theoretically: 'you only have to look at the Medusa straight on to see her. And she's not deadly. She's beautiful and she's laughing' (p. 255). The problem is that to look at the Medusa 'straight on' is not a simple matter, for women or for men; the whole question of representation is precisely there. A politics of the unconscious cannot ignore the real, historical, and material complicities, even as it must dare theoretical utopias.

Freud may not have known it, but in that two-page paper he put forth the definitive theory of pornographic cinema and, some have argued, of cinema *tout court*.[4] Death at work. But whose death is it, whose work, and what manner of death? My question then, how did Medusa feel looking at herself being slain and pinned up on screens, walls, billboards, and other shields of masculine identity, is really a political question that bears directly upon the issues of cinematic identification and spectatorship: the relation of female subjectivity to ideology in the representation of sexual difference and desire, the positions available to women in film, the conditions of vision and meaning production, for women.

To succeed, for a film, is to fulfill its contract, to please its audiences or at least induce them to buy the ticket, the popcorn, the magazines, and the various paraphernalia of movie promotion. But for a film to work, to be effective, it *has* to please. All films must offer their spectators some kind of pleasure, something of interest, be it a technical, artistic, critical interest, or the kind of pleasure that goes by the names of entertainment and escape; preferably both. These kinds of pleasure and interest, film theory has proposed, are closely related to the question of desire (desire to know, desire to see), and thus depend on a personal response, an engagement of the spectator's subjectivity, and the possibility of identification.

The fact that films, as the saying goes, speak to each one and to all, that they address spectators both individually and as members of a social group, a given culture, age, or country, implies that certain patterns or possibilities of identification for each and all spectators must be built into the film. This is undoubtedly one of the functions of genres, and their historical development throughout the century attests to the need for cinema to sustain and provide new modes of spectator identification in keeping with social changes. Because films address spectators as social subjects, then, the modalities of identification bear directly on the process of spectatorship, that is to say, the ways in which the subjectivity of the spectator is engaged in the process of viewing, understanding (making sense of), or even *seeing* the film.

If women spectators are to buy their tickets and their popcorn, the work of cinema, unlike 'the aim of biology,' may be said to require women's consent; and we may well suspect that narrative cinema in particular must be aimed, like desire, toward seducing women into femininity. What manner of seduction operates in cinema to procure that consent, to engage the female subject's identification in the narrative movement, and so fulfill the cinematic contract? What manner of seduction operates in cinema to solicit the complicity of women spectators in a desire whose terms are those of the Oedipus? In the following pages I will be concerned with female spectatorship, and in particular the kinds of identification available to women spectators and the nature of the process by which female subjectivity is engaged in narrative cinema; thus I will reconsider the terms or positionalities of desire as constituted in cinema by the relations of image and narrative.

The cinematic apparatus, in the totality of its operations and effects, produces not merely images but imaging. It binds affect and meaning to images by establishing terms of identification, orienting the movement of desire, and positioning the spectator in relation to them.

The film poses an image, not immediate or neutral, but posed, framed and centered. Perspective-system images bind the spectator in place, the suturing central position that is the sense of the image, that sets its scene (in place, the spectator *completes* the image as its subject). Film too, but it also moves in all sorts of ways and directions, flows with energies, is potentially a veritable festival of affects. Placed, that movement is all the value of film in its development and exploitation: reproduction of life and the engagement of the spectator in the process of that reproduction as articulation of coherence. What moves in film, finally, is the spectator, immobile in front of the screen. Film is the regulation of that movement, the individual as subject held in a shifting and placing of desire, energy, contradiction, in a perpetual retotalization of the imaginary (the set scene of image and subject).[5]

What Heath has called the 'passage' of the spectator-subject through the film (the movement of the spectator taken up as subject, performing the film) is modulated on the movement of the film, its 'regulation' of the flow of images, its 'placing' of desire. The process of regulation, in the classical economy of film, is narrativization; and narrative, the 'welding together' of space and spectator, is the form of that economy (p. 43). 'Narrativization is then the term of film's entertaining: process and process contained, subject bound in that process and its directions of meaning ... The spectator is *moved*, and *related* as subject in the process and images of that movement' (p. 62). The formulation is forceful and convincing, though not unambiguous. While anyone who has watched movies and reflected on the experience of spectatorship would agree that, indeed, to watch is to be moved and, at the same time, held in a coherence of meaning and vision; yet that very experience is what must make us question whether—or better, how—women spectators are 'related as subject' in the film's images and movement.

In the narrative film the spectator's movement or passage is subject to an orientation, a direction—a teleology, we might say, recalling Freud's word—that is the movement of narrative. Film narrative too, if Lotman's typology be credited, is a process by which the text-images distributed across the film (be they images of people, objects, or of movement itself) are finally regrouped in the two zones of sexual difference, from which they take their culturally preconstructed meaning: mythical subject and obstacle, maleness and femaleness. In cinema the process is accomplished in specific ways. The codes whereby cinema articulates and inscribes both the narrative movement and the subject's passage in the film, the codes which constitute the specificity of cinema as a semiotic practice, have been discussed elsewhere. But for the purposes of the present inquiry one crucial point may be usefully emphasized: the centrality of the system of the look in cinematic representation.

The look of the camera (at the profilmic), the look of the spectator (at the film projected on the screen), and the intradiegetic look of each character within the film (at other characters, objects, etc.) intersect, join, and relay one another in a complex system which structures vision and meaning and defines what Alberti would call the 'visible things' of cinema. Cinema 'turns' on this series of looks, writes Heath, and that series in turn provides the framework 'for a pattern of multiply relaying identifications'; within this framework occur both 'subject-identification' and 'subject-process.'[6] 'It is the place of the look that defines cinema,' specifies Mulvey, and governs its representation of woman. The possibility of shifting, varying, and exposing the look is employed both to set out and to contain the tension between a pure solicitation of the scopic drive and the demands of the diegesis; in other words, to integrate voyeurism into the conventions of storytelling, and thus combine visual and narrative pleasure. The following passage refers to two particular films, but could easily be read as paradigmatic of the narrative film in general:

> The film opens with the woman as object of the combined gaze of spectator and all the male protagonists in the film. She is isolated, glamorous, on display, sexualised. But as the narrative progresses she falls in love with the main male protagonist and becomes his property, losing her outward glamorous characteristics, her generalised sexuality, her show-girl con-notations; her eroticism is subjected to the male star alone.[7]

If the female position in narrative is fixed by the mythical mechanism in a certain portion of the plot-space, which the hero crosses or crosses to, a quite similar effect is produced in narrative cinema by the apparatus of looks converging on the female figure. The woman is framed by the look of the camera as icon, or object of the gaze: an image made to be looked at by the spectator, whose look is relayed by the look of the male character(s). The latter not only controls the events and narrative action but is 'the bearer' of the look of the spectator. The male protagonist is thus 'a figure in a landscape,' she adds, 'free to command the stage . . . of spatial illusion in which he articulates the look and creates the action' (p. 13). The metaphors could not be more appropriate.

In that landscape, stage, or portion of plot-space, the female character may be all along, throughout the film, representing and literally marking out the place (to) which the hero will cross. There she simply awaits his return like Darling Clementine; as she indeed does in countless Westerns, war, and adventure movies, providing the 'love interest,' which in the jargon of movie reviewers has come to denote, first, the singular function of the female character, and then, the character itself.[8] Or she may resist confinement in that symbolic space by disturbing it, perverting it, making trouble, seeking to exceed the boundary— visually as well as narratively—as in film noir. Or again, when the film narrative centers on a female protagonist, in melodrama, in the 'woman's film,' etc., the narrative is patterned on a journey, whether inward or outward, whose possible outcomes are those outlined by Freud's mythical story of femininity. In the best of cases, that is, in the 'happy' ending, the protagonist will reach the place (the space) where a modern Oedipus will find her and fulfill the promise of his (off-screen) journey. Not only, then, is the female position that of a given portion of the plot-space; more precisely, in cinema, it figures the (achieved) movement of the narrative toward that space. It represents narrative closure.

In this sense, Heath has suggested, narrative is a process of restoration that depends finally on the image of woman, generalized into what he calls the *narrative image*, a function of exchange within the terms of the film's contract. In *Touch of Evil*, specifically, 'the narrative must serve to restore the woman as good object (the narrative image depends on this); which obliges it to envisage her as bad object (the other side of the restoration that it seeks to accomplish).' Of narrative cinema in general he writes:

> Narrative contains a film's multiple articulations as a single articulation, its images as a single image (the 'narrative image', which is a film's presence, how it can be talked about, what it can be sold and bought on, itself represented as—in the production stills displayed outside a cinema, for example).[9]

If narrative is governed by an Oedipal logic, it is because it is situated within the system of exchange instituted by the incest prohibition, where woman functions as both a sign (representation) and a value (object) for that exchange. And if we remark Lea Melandri's observation that the woman as Mother (matter and matrix, body and womb) is the primary measure of value, 'an equivalent more universal than money,' then indeed we can see why the narrative image on which the film, any film, can be represented, sold, and bought is finally the woman.[10] What the promotion stills and posters outside the cinema display, to lure the passers-by, is not just an *image of woman* but the image of her narrative position, the *narrative image* of woman—a felicitous phrase suggestive of the join of image and story, the interlocking of visual and narrative registers effected by the cinematic apparatus of the look. In cinema as well, then, woman properly represents the fulfillment of the narrative promise (made, as we know, to the little boy), and that representation works to support the male status of the mythical subject. The female position, produced as the end result of narrativization, is the figure of narrative closure, the narrative image in which the film, as Heath says, 'comes together.'

With regard to women spectators, therefore, the notion of a passage or movement of the spectator through the narrative film seems strangely at odds with the theories of narrative presented so far. Or rather, it would seem so if we assumed—as is often done—that spectators naturally identify with one or the other group of text-images, one or the other textual zone, female or male, according to their gender. If we assumed a single, undivided identification of each spectator with either the male or the female figure, the passage through the film would simply instate or reconfirm male spectators in the position of the mythical subject, the human being; but it would only allow female spectators the position of the mythical obstacle, monster or landscape. How can the female spectator be entertained as subject of the very movement that places her as its object, that makes her the figure of its own closure?

Clearly, at least for women spectators, we cannot assume identification to be single or simple. For one thing, identification is itself a movement, a subject-process, a relation: the identification (of oneself) with something other (than oneself). In psychoanalytic terms, it is succinctly defined as the 'psychological process whereby *the subject* assimilates an aspect, property or attribute of the other and *is transformed*, wholly or partially, after the model the other provides. It is by means of a series of identifications that the personality is constituted and specified.'[11] This last point is crucial, and the resemblance of this formulation to the description of the apparatus of the look in cinema cannot escape us. The importance of the concept of identification, Laplanche and Pontalis insist, derives from its central role in the formation of subjectivity; identification is 'not simply one psychical mechanism among others, but the operation itself whereby the human subject is constituted' (p. 206). To identify, in short, is to be actively involved as subject in a process, a series of relations; a process that, it must be stressed, is materially supported by the specific practices—textual, discursive, behavioral—in which each relation is inscribed. Cinematic identification, in particular, is inscribed across the two registers articulated by the system of the look, the narrative and the visual (sound becoming a necessary third register in those films which intentionally use sound as an anti-narrative or de-narrativizing element).

Secondly, no one can really *see* oneself as an inert object or a sightless body; neither can one see oneself *altogether* as other. One has an ego, after all, even when one is a woman (as Virginia Woolf might say), and by definition the ego must be active or at least fantasize itself in an active manner.[12] Whence, Freud is led to postulate, the phallic phase in females: the striving of little girls to be masculine is due to the active aim of the libido, which then succumbs to the momentous process of repression when femininity 'sets in.' But, he adds, that masculine phase, with its libidinal activity, never totally lets up and frequently makes itself felt throughout a woman's life, in what he calls 'regressions to the fixations of the pre-Oedipus phases.' One can of course remark that the term 'regression' is a vector in the field of (Freud's) narrative discourse. It is governed by the same mythical mechanism that underlies his story of femininity, and oriented by the teleology of (its) narrative movement: progression is toward Oedipus, toward the Oedipal stage (which in his view marks the onset of womanhood, the initiation to femininity); regression is away from Oedipus, retarding or even impeding the female's sexual development, as Freud would have it, or as I see it, impeding the fulfillment of the male's desire, as well as narrative closure.

The point, however, is made—and it is relevant to the present discussion—that 'femininity' and 'masculinity' are never fully attained or fully relinquished: 'in the course of some women's lives there is a repeated alternation between periods in which femininity or masculinity gain the upper hand.'[13] The two terms, femininity and masculinity, do not refer so much to qualities or states of being inherent in a person, as to positions which she occupies in relation to desire. They are terms of identification. And the alternation between them, Freud seems to suggest, is a specific character of female subjectivity. Following through this view in relation to cinematic identification, could we say that identification in women spectators alternates between the two terms put in play by the apparatus: the look of the camera and the image on the screen, the subject and the object of the gaze? The word alternation conveys the sense of an either/or, either one or the other at any given time (which is presumably what Freud had in mind), not the two together. The problem with the notion of an alternation between image and gaze is that they are not commensurable terms: the gaze is a figure, not an image. We see the image; we do not see the gaze. To cite again an often-cited phrase, one can 'look at her looking,' but one cannot look at oneself looking. The analogy that links identification-with-the-look to masculinity and identification-with-the-image to femininity breaks down precisely when we think of a spectator alternating between the two. Neither can be abandoned for the other, even for a moment; no image can be identified, or identified with, apart from the look that inscribes it as image, and vice versa. If the female subject were indeed related to the film in this manner, its division would be irreparable, unsuturable; no identification or meaning would be possible. This difficulty has led film theorists, following Lacan and forgetting Freud, practically to disregard the problem of sexual differentiation *in the spectators* and to define cinematic identification as masculine, that is to say, as an identification with the gaze, which both historically and theoretically is the representation of the phallus and the figure of the male's desire.[14]

That Freud conceived of femininity and masculinity primarily in narrative rather than visual terms (although with an emphasis on sight—in the traumatic apprehension of castration as punishment—quite in keeping with his dramatic model) may help us to reconsider the problem of female identification. Femininity and masculinity, in his story, are positions occupied by the subject in relation to desire, corresponding respectively to the passive and the active aims of the libido.[15] They are positionalities within a movement that carries both the male child and the female child toward one and the same destination: Oedipus and the Oedipal stage. That movement, I have argued, is the movement of narrative discourse, which specifies and even produces the masculine position as that of mythical subject, and the feminine position as mythical obstacle or, simply, the space in which that movement occurs. Transferring this notion by analogy to cinema, we could say that the female spectator identifies with both the subject and the space of the narrative movement, with the figure of movement and the figure of its closure, the narrative image. Both are figural identifications, and both are possible at once; more, they are concurrently borne and mutually implicated by the process of narrativity. This manner of identification would uphold both positionalities of desire, both active and passive aims: desire for the other, and desire to be desired by the other. This, I think, is in fact the operation by which narrative and cinema solicit the spectators' consent and seduce women into femininity: by a double identification, a surplus of pleasure produced by the spectators themselves for cinema and for society's profit.

In other words, if women spectators are 'related as subject' in the film's images and movement, as Heath puts it, it is insofar as they are engaged in a twofold process of identification, sustaining two distinct sets of identifying relations. The first set is well known in film theory: the masculine, active, identification with the gaze (the looks of the camera and of the male characters) and the passive, feminine identification with the image (body, landscape). The second set, which has received much less attention, is implicit in the first as its effect and specification, for it is produced by the apparatus which is the very condition of vision (that is to say, the condition under which what is visible acquires meaning). It consists of the double identification with the figure of narrative movement, the mythical subject, and with the figure of narrative closure, the narrative image. Were it not for the possibility of this second, figural identification, the woman spectator would be stranded between two incommensurable entities, the gaze and the image. Identification, that is, would be either impossible, split beyond any act of suture, or entirely masculine. The figural narrative identification, on the contrary, is double; both figures can and in fact must be identified with at once, for they are inherent in narrativity itself. It is this narrative identification that assures 'the hold of the image,' the anchoring of the subject in the flow of the film's movement; rather than, as Metz proposes, the primary identification with the all-perceiving subject of the gaze.[16]

In fact, the order of priority borne by the words 'primary cinematic identification' might be reversed: if the spectator can identify 'with himself as look, as pure act of perception,' it is because such identification is supported by a prior, narrative identification with the figure of narrative movement. When the latter is weak, or undercut by a concomitant and stronger identification with the narrative image—as is the case with female spectators more often than not—the spectator will find it difficult to maintain the distance from the image implicit in the notion of a 'pure act of perception.' Metz's formulation of primary cinematic identification, which comes from Lacan's concept of the mirror stage, has been criticized precisely for the strictly chronological implication of the word 'primary.'[17] In the psychoanalytic discourse, primary identification refers to an early or primitive mode of identification with the Other (usually the mother) not dependent upon the establishment of an object-relationship, that is to say, prior to the subject's awareness of the Other's autonomous existence.[18]

Freud's other and more fundamental concept of primary and secondary processes, however, sheds doubt on the usefulness of the notion of a primary or primitive identification, at least insofar as adult spectators are concerned. Primary (unconscious) processes, one of the two modalities of the psychic apparatus, never exist alone after the formation of the ego, whose function is precisely that of inhibiting them. They do continue to exist, nevertheless, but only in interplay with or in opposition to the other modality, secondary (conscious-preconscious) processes, such as operate in waking thought, reasoning, judgment, etc. While Metz obviously recognizes that his analogy between the adult film spectator and the child at the mirror stage is no more than that: an analogy—he does not fully work out its limitations; a principal one being that if the child can be construed as not (yet) gendered, the adult spectator cannot. The basic hypothesis of psychoanalysis is that sexual differentiation occurs between 3 and 5 years of age, whereas the mirror phase is located between the ages of 6 and 18 months. But film spectators enter the movie theatre as either men or women, which is not to say that they are simply male or female but rather that each person goes to the movies with a semiotic history, personal and social, a series of previous identifications by which she or he has been somehow engendered. And because she and he are historical subjects, continuously engaged in a multiplicity of signifying practices which, like narrative and cinema, rest on and perpetuate the founding distinction of culture—sexual difference—the film's images for them are not neutral objects of a pure perception but already 'significant images,' as Pasolini observed; already significant by virtue of their relation to the viewer's subjectivity, coded with a certain potential for identification, placed in a certain position with respect to desire. They already bear, even as the film begins, a certain 'place of the look.'

This valence of images, the empirical fact of a certain 'impact' which certain images have on viewers, cannot be accounted for in terms of a simple notion of referentiality; but even the more sophisticated semiotic notion of image content as a cultural unit, proposed by Eco (and Gombrich), needs to be further articulated in relation to extratextual codes, such as narrative, which are nonspecific to the particular form and matter of expression of the iconic sign. And while narrative articulation in cinema has been examined, notably in Metz's early work, I have argued that the semiological definition of narrative was and remains inadequate, for it fails to address the working of desire in both the movement of narrativity and the critical discourse [...]

In the second part (the third reel) of *Vertigo*, after Madeleine's 'death,' Scottie essays to remake Judy in her image, to make her up, quite literally, to look like Madeleine. Ironically, it is exactly at the moment when he has achieved the transformation, and thus the identity of the two images (and just after a very long kiss sequence, ending in a fade, signals the moment of sexual consummation), that he discovered the hoax by which Judy had impersonated Madeleine; which renders both their images equally 'untrue.' But Judy has agreed to impersonate Madeleine *the second time* out of her love for Scottie; her desire is thus revealed at the same time as the hoax, concurrent and complicit with it. It is the same with Midge's portrait, only this time what is false is not merely the image (the portrait of Carlotta with Midge's face), but indeed the narrative image of the woman, for Judy-Madeleine turns out to be alive and real—and *thus* untrue. Unlike *Rebecca*, the different images and desires put in play by *Vertigo* are relayed through the male protagonist. Madeleine's desire for (and identification with) the dead Mother, mirroring Scottie's own desire, is impossible; the Mother is dead, and so does Madeleine die. Judy's and Midge's desires for Scottie are duplicitious. The film closes, appropriately, on the narrative image of Judy dead on the rooftop and Scottie looking.[19] Hitchcock says:

> I put myself in the place of a child whose mother is telling him a story. When there's a pause in her narration, the child always says, 'What comes next, Mommy?' Well, I felt that the second part of the novel was written as if nothing came next, whereas in my formula, the little boy, *knowing* that Madeleine and Judy are the same person, would then ask, 'And Stewart doesn't know it, does he? What will he do when he finds out about it?'[20]

This is the question the film addresses, as do so many other films and as Freud's exploration of the psyche does. No story perhaps can be written 'as if nothing came next.' But the question of desire is always cast in these terms: 'what will he do when he finds out?' the little boy asks of the man, or vice versa.

Such is the work of cinema as we know it: to represent the vicissitudes of his journey, fraught with false images (his blindness) but unerringly questing after the one true vision that will confirm the truth of his desire. So that even in the genre Molly Haskell aptly dubbed 'the woman's film,' which is supposed to represent a woman's fantasy, or, like *Rebecca*, actually sets in play the terms of female desire, dominant cinema works for Oedipus.[21] If it stoops to the 'old-fashioned psychological story,' the tear-jerker from the 'school of feminine literature,' as Hitchcock lamented of his script for *Rebecca*, it is to conquer women's consent and so fulfill its social contract, the promise made to the little man.[22] Alas, it is still for him that women must be seduced into femininity and be remade again and again as woman. Thus when a film accidentally or unwisely puts in play the terms of a divided or double desire (that of the person Judy-Madeleine who desires both Scottie and the Mother), it must display that desire as impossible or duplicitous (Madeleine's and Judy's, respectively, in *Vertigo*), finally contradictory (Judy-Madeleine is split into Judy/Madeleine *for* Scottie); and then proceed to resolve the contradiction much in the same way as myths and the mythologists do: by either the massive destruction or the territorialization of women.

This sounds harsh, I realize, but it is not hopeless. Women are resisting destruction and are learning the tricks of making and reading maps as well as films. And what I see now possible for women's cinema is to respond to the plea for 'a new language of desire' expressed in Mulvey's 1975 essay. I see it possible even without the stoic, brutal prescription of self-discipline, the destruction of visual pleasure, that seemed inevitable at the time. But if the project of feminist cinema—to construct the terms of reference of another measure of desire and the conditions of visibility for a different social subject—seems now more possible and indeed to a certain extent already actual, it is largely due to the work produced in response to that self-discipline and to the knowledge generated from the practice of feminism and film.

At the conclusion of her reading of *Story of O*, Silverman argues that only 'an extreme immersion' in discourse can alter the female subject's relationship to the current monopoly held by the male 'discursive fellowships,' and make her participate in the production of meaning. For the theory and the practice of women's cinema, this would entail a continued and sustained work with and against narrative, in order to represent not just the power of female desire but its duplicity and ambivalence; or, as Johnston has insisted since the early days of feminist film theory, 'women's cinema must embody the working through of desire.' This will not be accomplished by (paraphrasing Schafer) another normative narrative wrapped around a thematics of liberation. The real task is to enact the contradiction of female desire, and of women as social subjects, in the terms of narrative; to perform its figures of movement and closure, image and gaze, with the constant awareness that spectators are historically engendered in social practices, in the real world, and in cinema too.

NOTES

1. Seymour Chatman, 'What Novels Can Do That Films Can't (and Vice Versa),' *Critical Inquiry* 7, no. 1 (Autumn 1980): 139.
2. Sigmund Freud, 'Medusa's Head,' *Standard Edition of the Complete Psychological Works* ed. James Strachey (London: Hogarth Press, 1955), vol. 18, pp. 273–4.
3. Eugénie Lemoine-Luccioni, *Partage des femmes* (Paris, 1976), quoted by Stephen Heath, 'Difference,' *Screen* 19, no. 3 (Autumn 1978) p. 85.
4. For example Yann Lardeau, 'Le Sexe froid (du porno au dela),' *Cahiers du Cinéma* no. 289 (June 1978).
5. Stephen Heath, *Questions of Cinema* (Bloomington: Indiana University Press, 1981), p. 53.
6. Ibid., pp. 119–20. 'The shift between the first and second looks sets up the spectator's identification with the camera (rigorously constructed, placing heavy constraints, for example, on camera movement). The look at the film is an involvement in identifying relations of the spectator to the photographic image (the particular terms of position required by the fact of the photograph itself), to the human figure presented in image (the enticement and the necessity of a human presence 'on the screen'), to the narrative which gives the sense of the flow of photographic images (the guide-line for the spectator through the film, the ground that must be adopted for its intelligible reception). Finally, the looks of the characters allow for the establishment of the various 'point of view' identifications (the spectator looking with a character, from near to the position of his or her look, or as a character, the image marked in some way as "subjective")' (p. 120).
7. Mulvey, 'Visual Pleasure and Narrative Cinema,' *Screen* 16, no. 3 (Autumn 1975) p. 13. In this connection should be mentioned the notion of a 'fourth look' advanced by Willemen: a form of direct address to the viewer, an 'articulation of images and looks which brings into play the position and activity of the viewer ... When the scopic drive is brought into focus, then the viewer also runs the risk of becoming the object of the look, of being overlooked in the act of looking. The fourth look is the *possibility* of that look and is always present in the wings, so to speak.' (Paul Willemen, 'Letter to John,' *Screen* 21, no. 2 (Summer 1980): 56.)
8. See Claire Johnston, 'Women's Cinema as Counter-Cinema,' p. 27; and Pam Cook and Claire Johnston, 'The Place of Women in the Cinema of Raoul Walsh,' in *Raoul Walsh*, ed. Phil Hardy (Edinburgh: Edinburgh Film Festival, 1974).
9. Heath, *Questions of Cinema*, p. 121. The reference to *Touch of Evil* is on p. 140.
10. Lea Melandri, *L'infamia originaria* (Milan: Edizioni L'Erba Voglio, 1977).

11. J. Laplanche and J.-B. Pontalis, *The Language of Psycho-Analysis*, trans. Donald Nicholson-Smith (New York: Norton, 1973), p. 205; my emphasis.

12. This point is also made by Mulvey, 'Afterthoughts ... inspired by *Duel in the Sun*' (*Framework*, vols 15/16/17 (1981)), who, on the basis of Freud's view of femininity, proposes that female spectators have access to the (film's) fantasy of action 'through the metaphor of masculinity'; the character of Pearl (Jennifer Jones), by dramatizing the oscillation of female desire between 'passive' femininity and 'regressive masculinity,' encapsulates the position of the female spectator 'as she temporarily accepts "masculinization" in memory of her "active" phase.' However, Mulvey concludes, as Pearl's story illustrates, masculine identification for the female spectator is always 'at cross purposes with itself, restless in its transvestite clothes' (p. 15). Although my discussion will develop in rather different ways, I fully share her concern to displace the active-passive, gaze-image dichotomy in the theory of spectatorship and to rethink the possibilities of *narrative* identification as a subject-effect in women spectators, an effect that is persistently denied by the prevailing notion of women's narcissistic over-identification with the image. See Mary Ann Doane, 'Film and the Masquerade: Theorising the Female Spectator,' *Screen* 23, no. 3–4 (September/October 1982): 74–87.

13. Freud, 'Femininity,' *Standard Edition*, vol. 22, p. 131. It may be worth repeating, however, that Freud's view of the female's Oedipus situation underwent considerable transformation. In 'The Dissolution of the Oedipus Complex' (1924) he held that 'the girl's Oedipus complex is much simpler than that of the small bearer of the penis ... it seldom goes beyond the taking of her mother's place and the adopting of a feminine attitude towards her father.' In two subsequent papers, 'Some Psychical Consequences of the Anatomical Distinction Between the Sexes' (1925) and 'Female Sexuality' (1931), this situation became progressively more complex as Freud began to stress and to articulate the nature of the female's pre-Oedipal attachment to the mother. His last paper on 'Femininity' (1933) was further informed by analytical accounts of adult female patients provided by women analysts.

14. See Jacqueline Rose, 'The Cinematic Apparatus: Problems in Current Theory' in *The Cinematic Apparatus*, ed. Teresa de Lauretis and Stephen Heath (London: Macmillan and New York: St Martin's Press, 1980), pp. 172–86. See also Heath, 'Difference,' and note 3 above.

15. This is particularly clear in Freud's analysis of the beating fantasy in males and females. See 'A Child is Being Beaten,' *Standard Edition*, vol. 17, pp. 177–204.

16. C. Metz, *Imaginary Signifier*, trans. Ben Brewster et al. (Bloomington: Indiana University Press, 1981), p. 51.

17. See Mary Ann Doane, 'Misrecognition and Identity,' *Cine-Tracts*, no. 11 (Fall 1980), pp. 28–31.

18. Laplanche and Pontalis, p. 336. They also note, incidentally, that Freud differs from this recent view in that the other who serves as model for the subject is usually the father.

19. Actually, we do not *see* Judy's body on the rooftop, but rather we imagine it, seeing Scottie's look. More precisely, the film imagines it for us by calling up the visual memory of Madeleine's body on the rooftop in an earlier shot from the same camera position now occupied by Scottie. This is one example, among many that could be brought, of the working of narrativity in the filmic text to construct a memory, a vision, and a subject position for the spectator. It is an especially clear example of the distinction made earlier between image and figure. While Scottie is the image we spectators look at, and Judy is not in the image at all, what we see (envision and understand) is the object of his look; what we are seeing is not the woman but her narrative image. Scottie is the figure of narrative movement, his look and his desire define what is visible or can be seen; Judy/Madeleine is the figure of narrative closure, on whom look and desire and meaning converge and come to rest. Thus it is only by considering the narrative and figural dimension embedded in vision, in our

reading of an image, that the notion of 'woman as image' can be understood in its complexity.

20. François Truffaut, *Hitchcock* (New York: Simon & Schuster, 1967), pp. 184–5.

21. This is admirably demonstrated by Linda Williams in her extended review of *Personal Best*, Robert Towne's very popular film about two women pentathletes who are both friends and lovers, and competitors in the 1980 Olympics. While asserting a new ethic of support and cooperation among athletes who are female, the film denies or at least forcefully undercuts the significance of their lesbian relation and thus banishes one woman from its narrative conclusion in favor of reasserting the correct, adult heterosexuality of the other. Williams concludes: 'This allows the film to recuperate their (unnamed) sensual pleasure into its own regime of voyeurism. Ultimately, the many nude scenes and crotch-shots can be enjoyed much the way the lesbian turn-ons of traditional heterosexual pornography are enjoyed—as so much titillation before the penis makes its grand entrance.' Linda Williams, '*Personal Best*: Women in Love,' *Jump Cut*, no. 27 (July 1982), p. 12.

22. Despite the film's success and its winning an Oscar, Hitchcock himself does not like *Rebecca*. Asked by Truffaut whether he is satisfied with his first Hollywood film, the director answers: 'Well, it's not a Hitchcock picture; it's a novelette, really. The story is old-fashioned; there was a whole school of feminine literature at the period, and though I'm not against it, the fact is that the story is lacking in humor . . . [The film] has stood up quite well over the years. I don't know why.' (*Hitchcock*, pp. 91–3).

REFERENCES

Lotman, Jurij M. 1979: The Origin of Plot in the Light of Topology. Trans. Julian Graffy. *Poetics Today* 1, no. 1–2, pp. 161–84.

Silverman, Kaja 1983: *Histoire d'O*: The Story of a Disciplined and Punished Body. *Enclitic* 7, no. 2, pp. 63–81.

8

'LOST OBJECTS AND MISTAKEN SUBJECTS'

Kaja Silverman

[...] Castration, disavowal, fetishism: What are we to make of film theory's reliance upon psychoanalysis to account for the absence of the object within the cinematic experience, as well as the viewer's defenses against that absence? And why the constant return to concepts in psychoanalysis which derive their seeming value from the founding moment of sexual difference?

The first of these questions is more easily answered than the second. There is no problem of the object which is not simultaneously a problem of the subject, no loss within cinema which is not also a loss within the viewer. If crisis surrounds the discovery that filmic construction is organized around absence, that is because the spectating subject is organized around the same absence.

The history of the subject who rediscovers him- or herself within cinema unfolds through a series of 'splittings' or divisions, many of which turn on the object. Indeed, the case can be even more forcefully stated: These splittings or divisions produce both subject and object, constituting the one in opposition to the other. The child's entry into the symbolic order is made only at considerable cost, not merely through the loss of numerous 'parts' of itself, which are relegated to the status of objects, but through the sacrifice of its own being.

The first of these divisions occurs at the mirror stage, where the child arrives at an initial perception of self. That perception is induced through a culturally mediated image which remains irreducibly external, and which consequently implants in the child a sense of otherness at the very moment that identity is

* From Silverman, K. *The Acoustic Mirror: The Female Voice in Psychoanalysis and Cinema.* Bloomington and Indianapolis: Indiana University Press, 1988, pp. 6–32.

glimpsed. At least within the account Lacan offers in 'The Mirror Stage,'[1] in which the child catches sight of its actual reflection, that otherness would seem to be compounded by the fact that the child makes its self-discovery through a process of subtraction—through the understanding that it is what is left when a familiar object (e.g., the mother) has been removed. Subjectivity is thus from the very outset dependent upon the recognition of a distance separating self from other—on an object whose loss is simultaneous with its apprehension. (These losses are, of course, experienced only retroactively, from a position within the symbolic. Insofar as the mirror stage could be said to have any emotional 'content,' it would be that 'jubilation' of which Lacan speaks, a 'jubilation' which is itself based upon an illusory unity, or—as Jane Gallop encourages us to see it—upon an *anticipation* of self-mastery and a unified identity.)[2]

The child's as yet unsteady grasp of its own boundaries becomes firmer with the severance of various objects it previously experienced as parts of itself—the breast, the feces, the mother's voice, a loved blanket. However, these objects retain their aura of presence even after they have absented themselves, and are consequently described by Lacan as *objets petits autres* (objects with only a little 'otherness'). Since these objects are carved out of the subject's own flesh, they attest with unusual force to the terms under which the subject enters the symbolic—to the divisions through which it acquires its identity, divisions which constitute the world of objects out of the subject's own self. Although its full impact will not be felt until later, with the entry into language and the Oedipal matrix, the partitioning off of the part objects from the infant subject is experienced as a castration. Lacan stresses that the *objet (a)* is always 'bound to the orifices of the body.'[3] It is 'something from which the subject, in order to constitute itself, has separated itself off as organ,' and which consequently 'serves as a symbol of the lack.'[4]

The object thus acquires from the very beginning the value of that without which the subject can never be whole or complete, and for which it consequently yearns. At the same time, the cultural identity of the subject depends upon this separation. Indeed, it could almost be said that to the degree that the object has been lost, the subject has been found. Because at this point in the child's history, the object enjoys only a little 'otherness,' the subject enjoys only a little identity. Further divisions and losses will be necessary before the child can emerge as a coherent cultural subject.

The entry into language is the juncture at which the object is definitively and irretrievably lost, and the subject as definitively and almost as irretrievably found. It is also the occasion for a further sacrifice, that of the subject's own being. These losses are determined by the fact that although signification takes the place of the real, it is in no way motivated by or reflective of what it supplants. The signifier is a non-representative representation.[5]

When we say that language takes the place of the real, we mean that it takes the place of the real for the subject—that the child identifies with a signifier through which it is inserted into a closed field of signification. Within that field of signification, all elements—including the first-person pronoun which seems transparently to designate the subject—are defined exclusively through the play of codified differences. Not one of those elements is capable of reaching beyond itself to reestablish contact with the real. The door thus closes as finally upon the subject's being as upon the object. Lacan conveys the extremity of the opposition between language and the phenomenal realm when he describes it as a choice between meaning and life.[6]

It is this irrecoverability of object to subject, this irreducible distance separating representation from the real, that cinema has often seemed destined to overcome. Siegfried Kracauer describes the 'inveterate moviegoer' as someone alienated from the phenomenal world, who hopes to find in the darkened theater what he or she has lost elsewhere—the 'crude and unnegotiated presence of natural objects.'[7] This imaginary figure, who is a kind of distillate of not only Kracauer's but Bazin's realist aspirations, 'traces his suffering to his being out of touch with the breathing world about him, that stream of things and events which, were it flowing through him, would render his existence more exciting and significant. He misses "life." And he is attracted to cinema because it gives him the illusion of vicariously partaking of life in its fullness' (p. 169).

The life for which this spectator yearns is, of course, his or her own. Kracauer makes that clear not only through his emphasis upon the cinephile's self-alienation, but through the natal metaphor by means of which he articulates the ideal relationship between the cinematic apparatus and the profilmic event. Films, he writes, conform most rigorously to our dreams when the camera seems as if it has 'just now extricated [its objects] from the womb of physical existence and as if the umbilical cord between image and actuality [has] not yet been severed' (p. 164). Kracauer's viewer longs not only for the restoration of this 'actuality,' but for the return to a presubjective condition, as well. Significantly, the life line leading back to fusion and nondifferentiation is the indexical relation of the camera to its object.

The indexical relation of the camera to the profilmic event has always provided the most reliable guarantee that cinema is in fact capable of restoring the object to the subject. When Bazin celebrates the camera's ability to reproduce what is placed in front of it, and when he argues for the elimination of any human intervention, he leans with all his weight upon that guarantee:

> For the first time, between the originating object and its reproduction there intervenes only the instrumentality of a nonliving agent. For the first time an image of the world is formed automatically, without the intervention of man. All the arts are based on the presence of man, only photography derives an advantage from his absence. Photography affects us like a phenomenon in nature, like a flower or snowflake whose vegetable or earthly origins are an inseparable part of their beauty.
>
> This production by automatic means has radically affected our psychology of the image. The objective nature of photography confers upon it

a quality of credibility absent from other picture-making. In spite of any objections our critical spirit may offer, we are forced to accept as real the existence of the object reproduced.[8]

Despite its utopian fervor, this passage from 'The Ontology of the Photographic Image' reveals a complex understanding of the binary relation of subject to referent—of the fact that the presence of the one necessitates the absence of the other, since the former belongs to the symbolic order and the latter to the phenomenal realm. On this occasion Bazin opts for brute materiality over meaning; his nostalgia for the lost object is so intense that he is willing to sacrifice subjectivity in order to secure its restitution. However, lack returns via the route it invariably takes in Bazin—through the recollection that films are edited, and that shot-to-shot relationships usurp those which obtain between the camera and the profilmic event. He is obliged to conclude his essay-dream with the admission that 'cinema is also a language' (p. 916).

Cinema thus revives the primordial desire for the object only to disappoint that desire, and to reactivate the original trauma of its disappearance. Since the loss of the object always entails a loss of what was once part of the subject, it is—in the strictest sense of the word—a castration. Metz's use of that concept is consequently neither idiosyncratic nor hyperbolic. Indeed, Serge Leclaire maintains that *castration* is the only correct term with which to designate the break with the real induced by language, since it alone is equal to the task of marking 'the radicality of the division between the order of the letter (signifier) and the alterity of the object.'[9]

If *castration* is the only word which can properly he applied to the loss of the object induced by signification, and if film is (as even Bazin acknowledges) a language, then disavowal and fetishism would seem as accurately to name certain strategies deployed by classic cinema for concealing that loss. Metz's reliance upon those signifiers has the additional virtue of drawing attention to the fact that when a film covers over the absent real with a simulated or constructed reality, it also makes good the spectating subject's lack, restoring him or her to an imaginary wholeness [...]

Cinema challenges the imaginary plenitude of the viewing subject whenever it reveals the fantasmatic basis of its objects—whenever it re-enacts the foreclosure of the real from representation. I have indicated how fully this loss absorbs film theory, and the emphasis which is placed there upon the substitution of an 'impression of reality' for the absent real. Even more threatening to the subject's coherence is the disclosure of the cinematic signifier, since that disclosure not only finalizes the rupture with the phenomenal realm, but draws attention to the invisible enunciator—to the fact, that is, that films and their spectators are spoken by an unseen Other. Film theory has shown itself to be equally sensitive to this absence, and to the strategies developed by classic cinema to cover it over.

However, at no point in either of these extended theoretical discussions has it been noted that the lack which must somehow be disavowed not only structures male subjectivity as much as female subjectivity, but poses a far greater danger to the stability of the former than to that of the latter. Since the female subject is constructed through an identification with dispossession, her exposure to further castrations jeopardizes nothing. The male subject, on the contrary, is constructed through an identification with the phallus. That identification may be threatened by the disappearance of the object, but it is capsized by any reminder of the male subject's discursive limitations. It is impossible for a subject who knows himself to be excluded from authoritative vision, speech, and hearing to sustain a pleasurable relation to the phallus.

Nor has either of these theoretical explorations suggested that there might be an important connection between the losses which structure cinema and the representation of woman as lacking. This omission is particularly striking in the case of Oudart and Dayan, since the system of suture works precisely through the articulation of sexual difference. As I have argued elsewhere,[10] the most paradigmatic of all shot/reverse shot formations is that which aligns the female body with the male gaze. This two-shot not only covers over the absent site of production, but places the male subject on the side of vision, and the female subject on the side of spectacle. Moreover, insofar as the apparatus is anthropomorphized (insofar as the camera is associated with human sight and the tape recorder with human hearing), it assumes a paternal shape. The complex involvement of classic cinema in the articulation of sexual difference can best be demonstrated through a brief examination of yet another corpus of film theory preoccupied with the notion of lack.

Since the publication of Laura Mulvey's 'Visual Pleasure and Narrative Cinema' in 1975, feminist film theory has focused a good deal of attention on the coding of the female subject as inadequate or castrated within dominant cinema.[11] That theory has also looked closely at the potential for trauma contained within the spectacle of woman-as-lack, and at the defensive mechanisms made available to the viewer as a shield against that lack.

Curiously, the scenario described by Mulvey conforms much more rigorously to the original psychoanalytic paradigm of castration and crisis than do those of Metz and Comolli, or Oudart and Dayan. Like Freud's little boy, cinema's male viewer finds the vision of woman's lack threatening to his own coherence, and fears that he will become the victim of a similar deprivation. According to Mulvey, classic cinema offers two possible resolutions of this crisis: disavowal through fetishism, and avowal accompanied by disparagement. According to the first of these resolutions, an item of clothing or another part of the female anatomy becomes the locus of a compensatory investment, and substitutes for the organ which is assumed to be missing. The second of these resolutions has a very different end result, since instead of deflecting attention away from one part of the body to another, it shifts the focus from woman's 'outside' to her 'inside.' That transfer is effected through an investigation, which 'reveals' that the female subject has either committed a crime for which she has to be punished, or suffered from a crippling illness. Since in either case woman's castration can be traced back to her own interiority, this resolution of the male viewer's anxiety permits him to place a maximum distance between himself and the spectacle of lack—to indulge in an attitude of 'triumphant contempt' for the 'mutilated creature' who is his sexual other.

Its greater conformity to the Freudian formulation is not the only way in which Mulvey's account of cinematic castration deviates from those of the other theoreticians discussed here. An equally important and closely related deviation is that whereas Metz, Comolli, Oudart, and Dayan all emphasize the suturing effects of narrative—its capacity for covering over or making good cinema's various organizing absences—Mulvey locates the moment of loss inside the narrative. She displaces attention away from the extradiegetic castrations recounted by the others to one that occurs within the diegesis. Mulvey proposes, in other words, that the 'impression of reality' with which dominant cinema compensates for the absent real and effaces its own status as discourse relies upon a restaging of the drama of loss. What are we to make of this compulsion to repeat, this return of the repressed? And how are we to account for the paradoxical recourse to representations of lack with which to dispel the specter of an existential lack?

The first thing that must be said is that the narrative formulation is a repetition with a number of striking differences. The most important of these differences is that Mulvey's viewer, unlike that presumed by Metz, Comolli, Oudart, and Dayan, occupies a specifically masculine position. This viewer—whether in fact a man or a woman—identifies with the look of the male protagonist, experiencing with him the anxiety of castration and the pleasure of its neutralization.[12] Another difference within the narrative repetition is that whereas the spectator described by the other theoreticians disavows the loss of something which was earlier perceived as part of the self, whether it be the object or discursive potency, that described by Mulvey seems to disavow another's lack. The source of unpleasure is externalized in the form of the female body. It can be seen (and heard).

However, despite its apparent exteriority, this lack proves profoundly disturbing to the male viewer, in whom it inspires anxiety and fear. He experiences woman's wound as an assault upon his own subjectivity, a threat of like retribution. The violence of this reaction and the extremity of the measures which must be taken to neutralize it suggest that the image of woman reflects 'something which ought to have remained hidden but has come to light.' Far from exposing the male viewer to the 'new and alien,' that image would seem to confront him with 'something familiar and old-established [in his mind] ... which has become alienated from it through the process of repression.'[13]

We would seem to be face to face with another sexually differentiating projection—with an externalizing displacement of the kind unwittingly articulated by Freud's writings on the castration crisis. Here, as there, an unwanted part of the self is shifted to the outer register, where it can be mastered through vision. And here, as there, the projected image returns to trouble the male subject. However, the situation elaborated by Mulvey occurs well after the subject's entry into the symbolic, and is precipitated not only by the loss of the real and the renunciation of Oedipal desire, but by the 'encumbrance' of the phallus—by the weight of that signifier in relation to which the male subject can never be adequate.

Although the phallus is naturalized through its imaginary alignment with the penis, it is never more or less than a distillate of the positive values at the center of a historically circumscribed symbolic order. Those values stubbornly resist embodiment, designating a grammatical rather than an existential position—the place occupied by the name rather than the body of the father. Each of the dominant discourses which make up the larger symbolic order helps to define and localize the phallus by 'imagining' or 'fantasizing' a speaking subject—a subject authorized to command that discourse's power-knowledge. The phallus is in effect the sum of all such speaking subjects.

Like the phallus, the speaking subject is a symbolic figuration which always exceeds the individuals defined by it. That is particularly evident in the case of classic cinema, where enunciation is as much an effect of the ideological and technological apparatus as of any human intervention. Indeed, as I have already noted, the theoreticians of suture refer to classic cinema's enunciating agency not as the director but as the 'Absent One.'[14] The speaking subject—and so by implication the phallus—is here equivalent to this unseen enunciator, and to the attributes (transcendental vision, hearing, and speech) by which it is defined.

The exclusion of classic cinema's viewer from the point of discursive origin is thus simultaneously an isolation from the phallus. Every reminder of the foreclosed site of production draws attention to that isolation, revealing the gulf separating the male spectator from the paternal signifier upon which he relies for his cultural identity. Indeed, since every frame-line and cut constitute potential reminders of that hidden scene, the classic film poses a constant threat to the very subjectivity it wishes to consolidate.

I would argue that the castration crisis diagnosed by Mulvey can proceed only from this source—that in the final analysis it is the male viewer's own exclusion from the site of filmic production rather than the spectacle of woman's anatomical 'lack' which arouses such anxiety and fear in him. As with the foreclosed real, classic cinema musters numerous defences against this castration, both 'primary' and 'secondary.' (To the former category belong all those defences mounted directly against the male subject's lack. The second category contains all those defences which, like those discussed by Mulvey, seem to bear upon woman's lack, but which in fact bear indirectly upon male lack.)

Ideal representations play a key role here. The male subject is protected against the knowledge of his discursive insufficiency through the inscription into the diegesis of phallic characters with whom he is encouraged to identify—characters equipped with the phallic attributes of the 'Absent One' (i.e., with the capacity to look creatively, speak authoritatively, and capture and coerce the speech of others). However, projection plays an even more important part, since the male viewer can effect these pleasurable introjections only if he is able to disburden himself of the various losses which organize his subjectivity—if he is able to displace his discursive lack onto woman.

Once again, classic cinema engineers this projection for him. Through its endless renarrativization of the castration crisis, it transfers to the female subject the losses which afflict the male subject. It also arms him against the possible return of those losses by orchestrating a range of defensive operations to be used against the image of woman, from disavowal and fetishism to voyeurism and sadism. In this way the trauma which would otherwise capsize the male viewer is both elicited and contained.

But what does all of this entail for the female viewer, presuming that she, like the male viewer, is structured by secondary identification, and that secondary identification at least to some degree proceeds along lines of sexual difference? Above all, I want to stress that although woman's castration is always anatomically naturalized within Hollywood films, what this castration in fact entails is her exclusion from symbolic power and privilege. That exclusion is articulated as a passive relation to classic cinema's scopic and auditory regimes—as an incapacity for looking, speaking, or listening authoritatively, on the one hand, and with what might be called a 'receptivity' to the male gaze and voice, on the other. Thus, the female subject's gaze is depicted as partial, flawed, unreliable, and self-entrapping. She sees things that aren't there, bumps into walls, or loses control at the sight of the color red. And although her own look seldom hits its mark, woman is always on display before the male gaze. Indeed, she manifests so little resistance to that gaze that she often seems no more than an extension of it.

Woman's words are shown to be even less her own than are her 'looks.' They are scripted for her, extracted from her by an external agency, or uttered by her in a trancelike state. Her voice also reveals a remarkable facility for self-disparagement and self-incrimination—for putting the blame on Mame. Even when she speaks without apparent coercion, she is always spoken from the place of the sexual other.

Classic cinema's female subject is the site at which the viewer's discursive impotence is exhumed, exhibited, and contained. She is what might be called a synecdochic representation—the part for the whole—since she is obliged to absorb the male subject's lack as well as her own. The female subject's involuntary incorporation of the various losses which haunt cinema, from the foreclosed real to the invisible agency of enunciation, makes possible the male subject's identification with the symbolic father, and his imaginary alignment with creative vision, speech, and hearing. Indeed, not only is woman made to assume male lack as her own, but her obligatory receptivity to the male gaze is what establishes its superiority, just as her obedience to the male voice is what 'proves' its power.

The diegetic drama of castration described by Mulvey is thus a simulation of the crisis which occurs whenever the male viewer is reminded of his visual and verbal subordination to cinema's absent enunciator—a simulation which covers over that other scene of castration with its representations of phallic men and wounded women. Because it restages what happens elsewhere, in both the history of the subject and the production of the cinematic text, Hollywood's diegetic organization can perhaps best be characterized by a phrase from Bazin: it is 'a mirror with a delayed reflection, the tin foil of which retains the image' of earlier losses.[15] It is scarcely necessary to add that woman is the foil.

NOTES

1. Lacan's essay on the mirror stage is included in *Ecrits: A Selection*, trans. Alan Sheridan (New York: Norton, 1977), pp. 1–7.
2. See 'Where to Begin?' in *Reading Lacan* (Ithaca: Cornell University Press, 1985), pp. 74–92, for an excellent analysis of the ways in which anticipation and retroactivity organize the mirror stage.
3. Jacques Lacan, 'Seminar of 21 January 1975,' in *Feminine Sexuality*, ed. Juliet Mitchell and Jacqueline Rose (New York: Norton, 1983), p. 164.
4. Jacques Lacan, *The Four Fundamental Concepts of Psycho-analysis*, trans. Alan Sheridan (New York: Norton, 1978), p. 103.
5. Jacques Lacan, 'The Subject and the Other: Aphanisis,' in *Four Fundamental Concepts*, p. 218.
6. Ibid., pp. 211–13.
7. Siegfried Kracauer, *Theory of Film* (London: Oxford University Press, 1960), pp. 169 and 164.
8. Andre Bazin, *What is Cinema?* trans. Hugh Gray (Berkeley: University of California Press, 1967), vol. 1, p. 13.
9. Serge Leclaire, *Démasquer le réel: un essai sur l'objet en psychanalyse* (Paris: Editions du Seuil, 1971), p. 50.
10. K. Silverman, *The Subject of Semiotics*, (New York: Oxford University Press, 1983) pp. 222–5.
11. See Laura Mulvey, 'Visual Pleasure and Narrative Cinema,' *Screen* 16, no. 3 (1975): 8–18; Teresa de Lauretis, *Alice Doesn't: Feminism, Semiotics, Cinema* (Bloomington: Indiana University Press, 1984), pp. 1–36; Linda Williams, 'Film Body: An Implantation of Perversions,' *Ciné-Tracts* 3, no. 4 (1981): 19–35; Lucy Fischer, 'The Image of Woman as Image: The Optical Politics of *Dames*,' in *Genre: The Musical*, ed. Rick Altman (London: Routledge and Kegan Paul, 1981), pp. 70–84; and Sandy Flitterman, 'Woman, Desire, and the Look: Feminism and the Enunciative Apparatus in Cinema,' *Ciné-Tracts* 2, no. 1 (1978): 63–8.
12. Laura Mulvey provides an interesting discussion of the ways in which classic cinema facilitates the female viewer's identification with male as well as with female characters in 'Afterthoughts ... Inspired by *Duel in the Sun*,' *Framework* nos. 15/16/17 (1981): 12–15.
13. S. Freud, 'The Uncanny,' in *The Standard Edition of the Complete Psychological Works*, trans. James Strachey, (London: Hogarth Press, 1953), vol. 17, p. 241.
14. For a rather different account of authorship, see Silverman, *The Acoustic Mirror* (Bloomington and Indianapolis Indiana University Press), Chap. 4.
15. 'Theater and Cinema—Part Two,' in *What Is Cinema?* vol. 1, p. 97.

REFERENCES

Dayan, Daniel 1976: The Tutor Code of Classical Cinema. In Nichols, B. (ed.), *Movies and Methods*. Berkeley: University of California Press.
Oudart, Jean-Pierre 1977/78: Cinema and Suture. *Screen* 18, no. 4.

PART II
FURTHER READING

Bergstrom, Janet 1979: Rereading the Work of Claire Johnston. *Camera Obscura* 3/4, pp. 21–31.

Camera Obscura 1976: Feminism and Film: Critical Approaches. *Camera Obscura* 1 pp. 3–10.

De Lauretis, Teresa 1984: *Alice Doesn't: Feminism, Semiotics, Cinema*. Basingstoke and London: Macmillan.

De Lauretis, Teresa 1987: *Technologies of Gender: Essays on Theory, Film, and Fiction*. Basingstoke and London: Macmillan.

Doane, Mary Ann 1984: The 'woman's Film': Possession and Address. In Doane, M. A., Mellencamp, P., and Williams, L. (eds), *Re-Vision: Essays in Film Criticism*. Los Angeles: American Film Institute, pp. 67–82.

Doane, Mary Ann 1987: *The Desire to Desire: The Woman's Film of the 1940s*. Basingstoke and London: Macmillan.

Doane, Mary Ann 1991: *Femmes Fatales: Feminism, Film Theory, Psychoanalysis*. New York and London: Routledge.

Doane, Mary Ann, Mellencamp, Patricia and Williams, Linda (eds) 1984: *Re-Vision: Essays in Film Criticism*. Los Angeles: American Film Institute.

Erens, Patricia (ed.) 1990: *Issues in Feminist Film Criticism*. Bloomington and Indianapolis: Indiana University Press.

Flitterman-Lewis, Sandy 1992: Psychoanalysis, Film, and Television. In Allen, R. C. (ed.), *Channels of Discourse, Reassembled*. London: Routledge, pp. 203–247.

Heath, Stephen 1981: *Questions of Cinema*. Basingstoke and London: Macmillan.

Kaplan, E. Ann 1983: *Women and Film: Both Sides of the Camera*. New York and London: Methuen.

Kaplan, E. Ann (ed.) 1990: *Psychoanalysis and Cinema*. London: Routledge.

Kuhn, Annette 1982: *Women's Pictures: Feminism and Cinema*. London: Routledge & Kegan Paul.

Kuhn, Annette 1985: *The Power of the Image: Essays on Representation and Sexuality*. London: Routledge & Kegan Paul.

Lacan, Jacques 1982: *Feminine Sexuality* (ed. Mitchell, J. and Rose, J., trans. Rose). New York and London: W. W. Norton.

Mayne, Judith 1993: *Cinema and Spectatorship*. London and New York: Routledge.

Modleski, Tania 1988: *The Women who Knew too Much: Hitchcock and Feminist Theory*. New York and London: Methuen.

Mulvey, Laura 1989: *Visual and Other Pleasures*. Basingstoke and London: Macmillan.

Nichols, Bill (ed.) 1976: *Movies and Methods*. Berkeley, Los Angeles and London: University of California Press.

Penley, Constance (ed.) 1988: *Feminism and Film Theory*. New York and London: Routledge/BFI.

Penley, Constance 1989: *The Future of an Illusion: Film, Feminism and Psychoanalysis*. London: Routledge.

Rose, Jacqueline 1986: *Sexuality in the Field of Vision*. London: Verso.

Screen 1992: *The Sexual Subject: A* Screen *Reader in Sexuality*. London and New York: Routledge.

Silverman, Kaja 1983: *The Subject of Semiotics*. Oxford: Oxford University Press.

Silverman, Kaja 1988: *The Acoustic Mirror: The Female Voice in Psychoanalysis and Cinema*. Bloomington and Indianapolis: Indiana University Press.

Thornham, Sue 1997: Structures of Fascination: Ideology, Representation and the Unconscious. In *Passionate Detachments: An Introduction to Feminist Film Theory*. London: Arnold, pp. 23–44.

PART III
THE FEMALE SPECTATOR

INTRODUCTION

The figure of the female spectator has already made her appearance in this Reader, most notably in Mary Ann Doane's discussion of the 1940s 'woman's film'. But she has been a shadowy figure, more a position offered by/within the film text than an independent maker of meaning, and as such she has been singularly powerless. It is this powerlessness, which seems to be the inevitable result of an application of psychoanalytic theory to cinema, and which seems so at odds with a feminist politics, with which the participants in 'Women and Film: A Discussion of Feminist Aesthetics' take issue.

The discussion was published in 1978, and its participants were film-makers as well as critics and theorists. In it, a number of issues are raised which both return us to the emphasis on a politics of change that was so evident in the early pieces of feminist film criticism, and point towards new theoretical directions. Both Judith Mayne and B. Ruby Rich return us to the issue of women's experience as film viewers. Women, Mayne reminds us, are objects of spectacle in their everyday lives as well as in film, but they are also spectators. As spectators, women are caught up in relations of desire for, as well as identification with, the female figures in film. The relationship between female spectator and screen cannot therefore be a straightforward one, and cannot follow the active/male passive/female division proposed by psychoanalytic theory. It may be that the ideological structure of mainstream film works always to co-opt and/or punish these more complex – or subversive – responses. Nevertheless, as Julia Lesage points out, female figures in film may have a power for the woman spectator that exceeds, or runs counter to, the plot structure that reabsorbs them. Although the participants in this discussion vary in the extent to which they feel that psychonalysis can be useful as a tool for feminist film criticism, they agree in attributing to the female viewer and her representative, the feminist critic, a degree of power not afforded her in accounts dependent on psychoanalytic theory. As spectators who come to the film text already positioned as 'resistant' viewers, women will read it differently. It is the task of the feminist critic to find a language for this difference.

Laura Mulvey's 'Afterthoughts on "Visual Pleasure and Narrative Cinema" inspired by King Vidor's *Duel in the Sun*', published in 1981, is the 'follow-up piece' referred to in the 'Women and Film' discussion. Here Mulvey discusses the issues raised by both female spectator and female protagonist. Like the female viewer of the 'Women and Film' discussion, her female spectator is a resistant one. But to explain this 'resistance' she draws once more on Freudian theory. Pointing to the 'age-old cultural tradition' by which the female reader of popular narratives has been drawn into identification with a tale's hero, she argues that the pleasure of this identification comes from the fact that it allows the female reader to regress to the pre-Oedipal active phase of her development, before femininity imposed its straightjacket of passivity. The female spectator, then, habitually operates a 'trans-sex identification', an oscillating and uneasy 'trans-vestite' fantasy of masculinisation.

Like Teresa de Lauretis (Chapter 7), Mulvey sees the female-centred narrative as re-enacting this feminine version of the Oedipal narrative. In the example she chooses, *Duel in the Sun* (1946), the choice to be made by the female protagonist, Pearl, between an active, and regressive 'tomboy' relationship with the outlaw, Lewt, and the acceptance of a passive femininity in marriage to his respectable brother, Jesse, plays out for the female spectator her own uncomfortable Oedipal journey. But it is a doomed choice, for both protagonist and spectator: Pearl's '"tomboy" pleasures, her sexuality, are not fully accepted by Lewt, except in death. So, too, is the female spectator's fantasy of masculinisation at cross-purposes with itself, restless in its transvestite clothes'. Although Mulvey begins her article with a reference to the issue of the 'women in the audience', then, her use of a psychoanalytic framework allows these flesh-and-blood viewers no existence outside the Freudian positions replayed within the text itself. As a result, her analysis seems to permit no place for the actively resistant female reader; such a reader is only 'borrowing' masculinisation.

Mary Ann Doane's 'Film and the Masquerade: Theorising the Female Spectator' was published in 1982. As we have seen, Doane's analysis of the 'woman's film' of the 1940s (Chapter 6) seemed to offer the female spectator no way out of identification with its masochistic scenario. Yet her aim, as a feminist, is change – the production of a different spectatorship and subjectivity, and the creation of a different cinema. How then, she asks, might a different reading strategy be theorised for the female spectator, one resistant to the lure of 'overidentification'?

Her answer turns to the psychoanalytic concept of 'masquerade'[1] first theorised in 1929 by Joan Riviere. Riviere's analysis was of a successful 'intellectual woman' whose way of dealing with the threatening 'masculinity' of her position was to adopt an excessive pose of feminine flirtatiousness in her behaviour with men. 'Womanliness', argues Riviere, was 'assumed and worn as a mask, both to hide the possession of masculinity and to avert the reprisals expected if she was found to possess it' (Riviere 1986: 38). What is interesting about Riviere's account, however, is not only the fact that she sees such masquerade as a common strategy adopted by women, but that she sees it as a quality inherent in femininity itself: 'The reader may now ask how I define womanliness or where I draw the line between genuine womanliness and the "masquerade". My suggestion is not, however, that there is any such difference; whether radical or superficial, they are the same thing' (1986: 38). This wearing of femininity as a mask, argues Doane, can allow the female spectator to create a distance between herself and the image on the screen. Rather than overidentifying with it, she can play with the identifications offered by the film, manipulating them for her own pleasure and purposes. Whereas Mulvey's 'transvestite' spectator must fantasise masculinity in order to obtain cinematic pleasure, Doane's 'feminine' spectator can play at being a woman.

Both Laura Mulvey and Mary Ann Doane offer solutions to the 'problem' of the female spectator grounded in psychoanalytic theory. Both therefore focus on the spectator implied, imagined or constructed by the text rather than on the socially constructed 'woman in the audience'. Annette Kuhn's essay, 'Women's Genres', published in 1984, seeks to return us to the issue, raised by the participants in the 'Woman and Film' discussion, of how to bring together these two very different concepts of female spectatorship. Film theory, she argues, which has drawn on psychoanalytic accounts, has regarded the spectator as, in effect, constructed by the frameworks of the text. Its difficulty is that it cannot satisfactorily address issues of the historical specificity of particular films, their institutional or social contexts, or the ways in which actual audiences have understood them. If, however, we turn to the analyses of television viewing that have been produced within media studies, we find a very different focus. The concern here has been with the responses of actual audiences, so that the issue so central to film studies, of the ways in which the text itself can construct feminine positions for its viewers, remains relatively unaddressed. Yet feminists within both traditions have concerned themselves with 'women's genres' and the pleasures they offer to their female viewers. If, then, the concepts of 'spectator' and 'audience' seem distinct and irreducible the one to the other, how can the relationship between them be theorised?

We must distinguish analytically between the two concepts, argues Kuhn, but it is only if we can hold the two together that we can understand both the continuities and the dislocations between them, the ways in which 'women's genres' both address and construct their female/feminine spectators and the ways in which those spectators may be both formed by and resistant to those constructions. If text and context, spectator and social audience remain analytically distinct concepts, we cannot afford to ignore either. For if we do not take into account the wider social discourses[2] in which both films and their viewers are caught up, we cannot find a way of understanding the 'struggles over meaning' that may occur when 'women's genres' are viewed by the female spectator and/or the feminist critic.

NOTES

1. See also Doane's (1988–9) 'Masquerade Reconsidered: Further Thoughts on the Female Spectator', and Tania Modleski's response to Doane's first article, in *The Women who Knew Too Much: Hitchcock and Feminist Theory* (1988), pp. 25–7.
2. For a fuller account of the theoretical tradition on which Kuhn is drawing here, see Thornham (1997) pp. 81–3.

REFERENCES

Doane, Mary Ann 1991 (1988–9): Masquerade Reconsidered: Further Thoughts on the Female Spectator. In *Femmes Fatales: Feminism, Film Theory, Psychoanalysis*. New York and London: Routledge, pp. 33–43.

Modleski, Tania 1988: *The Women who Knew too Much: Hitchcock and Feminist Theory*. New York and London: Methuen.

Riviere, Joan 1986 (1929): Womanliness as a Masquerade. In Burgin, V., Donald, J. and Kaplan, C. (eds), *Formations of Fantasy*. London and New York: Routledge, pp. 35–44.

Thornham, Sue 1997: *Passionate Detachments: An Introduction to Feminist Film Theory*. London: Arnold.

9

'WOMEN AND FILM: A DISCUSSION OF FEMINIST AESTHETICS'

Michelle Citron, Julia Lesage, Judith Mayne, B. Ruby Rich, Anna Marie Taylor, and the editors of New German Critique

The following discussion, arranged by co-editor Renny Harrigan in Chicago at the start of 1978, took place among Michelle Citron, Julia Lesage, Judith Mayne, B. Ruby Rich and Anna Marie Taylor, plus co-editors Helen Fehervary and Nancy Vedder-Shults. For clarity we have designated all co-editors NGC.

The Editors

[. . .] MAYNE: One of the most basic connections between women's experience in this culture and women's experience in film is precisely the relationship of spectator and spectacle. Since women are spectacles in their everyday lives, there's something about coming to terms with film from the perspective of what it means to be an object of spectacle and what it means to be a spectator that is really a coming to terms with how that relationship exists both up on the screen and in everyday life. It is this phenomenon which speaks directly to women in their everyday lives. Women are *taught* to be objects of spectacle. And that means they have something in common with Marilyn Monroe since they both function as objects of spectacle. The cult figure is the extreme manifestation of that. But I think it's exactly the same phenomenon.

RICH: It occurs to me that the effect of this dichotomy you've described (spectacle versus spectator) is that, for a woman today, film is a dialectical experience in a way that it never was and never will be for a man under patriarchy. Brecht once

* From *New German Critique* 13, 1978, pp. 83–93.

described the exile as the ultimate dialectician in that the exile lives the tension of two different cultures. That's precisely the sense in which the woman spectator is an equally inevitable dialectician. The Mulvey and Johnston[1] articles are both 'positive' film criticism, yet what you are left with from each piece is very negative. According to Mulvey, the woman is not visible in the audience which is perceived as male; according to Johnston, the woman is not visible on the screen. She is merely a surrogate for the phallus, a signifier for something else, etc. As a woman going into the movie theater, you are faced with a context that is coded wholly for your invisibility, and yet, obviously, you are sitting there and bringing along a certain coding from life outside the theater. How does one enter into the experience of the film given that kind of structure? I think of Sheila Rowbotham's shock (in her book *Woman's Consciousness, Man's World*): she realized she has been identifying with the male character in Jack Kerouac novels! Likewise, the cinematic codes have structured our absence to such an extent that the only choice allowed to us is to identify either with Marilyn Monroe or with the man behind me hitting the back of my seat with his knees. How does one formulate an understanding of a structure that insists on our absence even in the face of our presence? What is there in a film with which a woman viewer identifies? How can the contradictions be used as a critique? And how do all these factors influence what one makes as a woman filmmaker, or specifically as a feminist filmmaker?

MAYNE: What you are suggesting is that Mulvey sets up a very one-dimensional identification with what goes on on the screen. In fact, male culture is not completely monolithic.

RICH: What Mulvey suggests is that since the films are made by men, for a male spectator's gratification, there is no point in discussing the woman in the audience because, in fact, there don't seem to be any women there. Perhaps to avoid any wishful thinking about a female presence, she uses only male pronouns throughout her article. In defense of her piece, she does show that psychoanalysis provides a useful tool primarily for analyzing the status quo, which is patriarchal. Whereas perhaps what one wants to say is: how can we now go *beyond* it rather than just analyzing it. And in fact she herself has begun that next step by making *Riddles of the Sphinx*.

TAYLOR: It's important to realize that the Freudian framework that both Mulvey and Johnston use cannot satisfactorily account for the position of female spectators. We sense that women have some kind of different relationship with what they see, and particularly with women they see on the movie screen. One of the points that the Freudian analysis makes is that the male filmmaker and male spectator fetishize the women as object. But the Freudian analysis doesn't take into account the fact that women spectators (something that Mulvey totally avoids) are also very attracted to these same visual objects. A good example which comes to mind is the film *Hustle* by Robert Aldrich which was recently shown on TV. Catherine Deneuve, the prostitute roommate of the police officer, is just so gorgeous throughout that you can hardly take your eyes off the TV set. I can't imagine a woman giving much of a damn for what's his name? – Burt Reynolds – while watching this film.

There's a point raised in the Freudian analysis, as Mulvey and other film theorists use it, which I believe can partially explain this phenomenon of visual pleasure on the part of female viewers. For the male, despite the strong voyeuristic attraction toward the image of a female body dressed and photographed according to certain fetishizing codes, this pleasure is always mixed with an attitude of degradation. Woman, according to the Oedipal system, represents a lack that is deeply and continuously threatening to man: the threat of not having a penis, the implied castration by the father, and so on. That element, that threat, that automatic degradation of what men see may not in fact be present for the woman spectator. Therefore, something different is going on between the female viewer and the female image which in fact women may find as attractive as men do. But that brings up another troublesome problem: have we as female viewers also been taken in by the way women have been filmed so that our own sexuality and therefore our very intense visual enjoyment regarding female stars is determined in advance elsewhere? This question finds its best response in the fact that a number of feminist filmmakers are attempting to construct alternative images, and to work with even very subtle cinematic effects, such as lighting and color, to de-code established cinematic practices in regard to the photographing of women's bodies and their relationship to the space around them.

NGC: There is also the question of the extent to which our sexuality has been formed by patriarchal and capitalist norms. In the Mulvey and Johnston articles, which have a Freudian perspective, sexuality is posited as an untouched force of energy, something not yet formed. In Freud, this energy is ultimately molded into heterosexuality. But sexuality itself is posited as authentic. It seems to me that sexuality, like any other form of human interaction, is formed by the dominant culture. I've reacted to female film stars as I'm sure a man would. But to decide if that is an 'authentic' sexual response in a world where no authenticity is allowed to a woman – whether in the sexual realm or otherwise – is an impossible task.

RICH: In other words, sexuality and psychoanalysis are considered to be ahistorical, eternal, outside ideology – exactly as women have been traditionally perceived.

LESAGE: Mulvey's article never positively articulated or defined women's desire and women's sexually. Although women's sexuality has been shaped under a dominant patriarchal culture, clearly women do not respond to women in film and the erotic element in film in quite the same way that men do, given that patriarchal film has the structure of a male fantasy. Even in a porn film, women respond to a lesbian scene somewhat differently from men for whom the scene is *just* a turn-on. I've often shown *Holding*, Constance Beeson's film of lesbian lovemaking, in my classes. While I think it suffers as a slick production, the film also offers a different order of experience for most women to think about in terms of lesbian lovemaking, and to see certain things which they might never have imagined before. Even in the context of a slick format, in a sense, the film is a liberating experience for them. That is why I am interested in Marlene Dietrich's underground reputation. She seems to represent for some women a kind of subcultural icon. She has a certain power in von Sternberg's films. If her portrayal doesn't escape completely from the totality of von Sternberg's male fantasy, the effect of her role is not locally explained in an analysis that sees women's desire primarily in terms of castration and lack.

NGC: How can the concepts of fetishization, castration (the threat posed by women) and voyeurism (the pleasure of the viewer as subject) be useful to us? I find Mulvey (whose film *Riddles of the Sphinx* is definitely feminist) provides a very useful analysis but can the analysis work if the assumptions (in this case Freudian) are false? Can we use Freudian concepts at all?

TAYLOR: Most psychoanalytic critics don't accept the Oedipal model as absolute truth but as a way to approach meaning in film which seems inaccessible to other analytical constructs. (Mulvey tries to make that explicit, but her analysis appears to many women to be too constrained within an Oedipal framework, perhaps because a follow-up piece was intended which hasn't yet appeared.) I agree with Mulvey, that since we live in a patriarchal culture we can use some of the theory that Freudians have developed. If it's not the truth about human social organization, it's the primary model by which the psychoanalytic institutions of the prevailing social organization itself explained the workings of the family and the law of the father carried to the entire social structure as patriarchal order. Freudian analysis can therefore be instrumental for understanding and therefore changing the representations of women as they are deeply established and repeated everywhere in the culture.

RICH: In conjunction with that, I find that Gilles Deleuze[2] has made a simple but useful point. He regards the function of 'history' within any discipline to be essentially repressive; for instance, the 'history' of philosophy acts to repress the voice of those currently studying/practicing philosophy. Deleuze talks about the way that history thus replaces one's individual voice, causing those best trained in a particular field often to feel incompetent about speaking out. You might say that we are educated to become so many marionettes for the great ventriloquist of 'history.' Deleuze urges the struggle to reclaim one's own voice. Now, a major legacy of the women's movement has been precisely its validation of subjective response, personal experience, the speaking out in a woman's own voice. To speak in the voice of history, in most cases, means speaking in a voice that has excluded women, or for a woman to speak in a voice which excludes her. Perhaps we could talk about the potential in feminist criticism or filmmaking for reconciling one's own voice with the voice of history, and how connections might be set up between various methodologies, histories and one's own experiences.

NGC: Perhaps this is the point to raise the question of analyzing female stereotypes, a study which would seem to have natural limitations within a male context in which woman is always treated as object, as 'Other.' Bovenschen talks about the 'kernel of truth' when 'the images, stereotypes are read against the grain' (p. 115),[3] Johnston talks about the need to show not only the oppression of women but also to interrogate the language of the cinema in order to challenge the depiction of reality, to effect a dislocation between (sexist) ideology and (film) text (p. 29). How can these suggestions be applied to make stereotype and image analysis in film more fruitful for women's films?

LESAGE: Dietrich, for example, fascinates women as a lesbian figure with whom they identify. Von Sternberg was pretty self-conscious in using her that way. In a sense she punishes men; she has romantic moments of dominance over them, such as when she is given a whip. She is used in von Sternberg's films to defy patriarchy even though she is reabsorbed into the male plot structure. As a female figure, she has many kinds of power in the film. For example, remember the scene in *Blonde Venus* when she sings in drag? I read that moment very lustfully; it gives me a really sexual feeling. Most women I know – gay or straight, but who are in tune to that kind of thing – feel the same way.

MAYNE: Many lesbians don't see it that way at all but rather as a parody of lesbianism and a male projection of what lesbians do when they are alone.

RICH: And one which can be possessed by the man ultimately. It's a version of lesbianism detoxified to offer the male a heightened erotic experience.

CITRON: But I think it can simultaneously be both: I'm attracted to what's going on because she's a very beautiful woman while I'm simultaneously appalled by it for the reasons you mention.

MAYNE: That relates to the two ways in which lesbianism or the relationship between women has been perceived in the film *Julia*. On the one hand, the only way lesbianism is consciously articulated within the film is in the character of the obnoxious man whom Lillian Hellman (Jane Fonda) slugs when he says that everyone thinks she and Julia (Vanessa Redgrave) are lesbians. On the other hand, all the scenes of sensuality between the two adult women are immediately connected visually in a very one-dimensional way with the childhood scenes, as if to suggest that this kind of sensuality is in fact just something that all little girls go through, a simple extension of adolescent experience. There is nothing threatening in this very contained, very male definition of what lesbianism is. I think that, even though there may be aspects of our own experience of watching a certain film that may transcend and deny a monolithic male phallic structure, at the same time we have to identify the ideological position of the film.

CITRON: The problem is even more obvious in *Looking For Mr Goodbar*. I know lesbians who have seen the film. They are the average audience who goes to films for entertainment and discussion. They feel that the film portrays the reality of what happens if you mess with men. The heroine is mixed up with heterosexual men who are just as vicious and sexually violent towards her as the homosexual man who murders her at the end. They see that as a realistic portrayal of the culture, and a warning to women even though they also recognize the homophobia of the final murder. Other viewers respond that women should think twice before they talk about liberation since the woman in the film is murdered simply by taking the same liberties men do who frequent the singles' bars.

LESAGE: In current films, there is a deliberate, industrially structured, response to ideological complexities. The industry wants to let everybody have their ideological cake and eat it, too. In other words, you'll see deliberate ambiguities structured into almost every film now to come out about strong women. Take *The Deep*, for example. In the opening sequence, Jacqueline Bisset is very strong. She is a much better scuba diver than Nick Nolte. She is the one who discovers the treasure. She dominates that whole first part. Even the gratuitous sexism of her wet tee-shirt with the nipples showing is pretty clear to a lot of people because it has nothing to do with the plot. In the middle of the film, Bisset loses the potential of being an active person. If you wanted to think of her as a strong person, you could only remember the opening sequences which established her. In *Julia*, everything is structured ambiguously throughout the film. We do not know whether Lillian and/or Julia were lesbians or not. When Lillian hits a drunken male friend in a restaurant, either she does so to prove that she and Julia were not lesbians or she does it because he was insulting lesbianism by dragging it down to the level of his own decadence. The movie *Saturday Night Fever* is fascinating. In so many ways the film is misogynous, but it is also attractive because the male lead is feminized: he's a very delicate dancer, wears colorful clothes and is sensitive. Different attitudes toward race are also structured into that film. A racist could use the film to reinforce racist attitudes: it's right to beat up everybody, it's right to get revenge. If you were a Latino, you could say, 'Yeah, look, the Latinos won the dance contest. It proves not only that Latinos are better dancers, but that the system won't let them get the reward they deserve.' It is cinema's new way of acknowledging that minorities and women are not going to go away. It is a clever ruse on the part of the people who want to keep the dominant ideology going. They build in the possibilities of all these subcultural responses and incorporate them into the whole. On the other hand, people do see the film in the way that Michelle said lesbians saw *Looking for Mr Goodbar*.

CITRON: The only people who are picking up on the subversive content of those ambiguities are the women who didn't need to pick up on them. The audience just selects the ideology it wants.

RICH: It's a strategy of dominant culture to coopt dissent. Instead of turning your back on the dominant culture and doing something else, you formulate a circuitous, subjective justification for it, which in the end is much more oppressive.

NGC: How can we support and reinforce the subcultural resistance that is already existent in the culture? Where are pockets of subcultural resistance? As filmmakers and film critics and as women in women's studies how can we reinforce and continue the struggle?

RICH: I think that relates to what was said about the dismissal of the female spectator in, e.g., the psychoanalytic criticism that's been done. The implication is that too much credit has been given to the notion of values being imbedded in production when, in fact, the values have been imbedded in the reception. If values are dependent on our reception, then the order is less immutable than supposed and, in that case, there's a lot more importance in criticism than we may have thought. This is of course an optimistic forecast.

NOTES

1. Laura Mulvey, 'Visual Pleasure and Narrative Cinema,' *Screen* (1974), 6–18, and Claire Johnston, 'Women's Cinema as Counter-Cinema,' in *Notes on Women's Cinema* (London, 1973).
2. 'I Have Nothing to Admit,' in *Anti-Oedipus* issue of *Semiotext(e)*, 2, No. 3 (1977), 110–16.
3. Silvia Bovenschen, 'Is There a Feminine Aesthetic?,' *New German Critique*, 10 (1977), 111–37.

10

'AFTERTHOUGHTS ON "VISUAL PLEASURE AND NARRATIVE CINEMA" INSPIRED BY KING VIDOR'S *DUEL IN THE SUN* (1946)'

Laura Mulvey

So many times over the years since my 'Visual Pleasure and Narrative Cinema' article was published in *Screen*, I have been asked why I only used the *male* third person singular to stand in for the spectator. At the time, I was interested in the relationship between the image of woman on the screen and the 'masculinisation' of the spectator position, regardless of the actual sex (or possible deviance) of any real live movie-goer. In-built patterns of pleasure and identification impose masculinity as 'point of view'; a point of view which is also manifest in the general use of the masculine third person. However, the persistent question 'what about the women in the audience?' and my own love of Hollywood melodrama (equally shelved as an issue in 'Visual Pleasure') combined to convince me that, however ironically it had been intended originally, the male third person closed off avenues of inquiry that should be followed up. Finally, *Duel in the Sun* and its heroine's crisis of sexual identity brought both areas together.

I still stand by my 'Visual Pleasure' argument, but would now like to pursue the other two lines of thought. First (the 'women in the audience' issue), whether the female spectator is carried along, as it were by the scruff of the text, or whether her pleasure can be more deep-rooted and complex. Second (the 'melodrama' issue), how the text and its attendant identifications are affected by a *female* character occupying the centre of the narrative arena. So far as the first issue is concerned, it is always possible that the female spectator may find herself so out of key with the pleasure on offer, with its 'masculinisation', that the spell of fascination is broken.

---

* From *Framework* 15–16–17 (summer 1981) pp. 12–15.

On the other hand, she may not. She may find herself secretly, unconsciously almost, enjoying the freedom of action and control over the diegetic world that identification with a hero provides. It is *this* female spectator that I want to consider here. So far as the second issue is concerned, I want to limit the area under consideration in a similar manner. Rather than discussing melodrama in general, I am concentrating on films in which a woman central protagonist is shown to be unable to achieve a stable sexual identity, torn between the deep blue sea of passive femininity and the devil of regressive masculinity.

There is an overlap between the two areas, between the unacknowledged dilemma faced in the auditorium and the dramatic double bind up there on the screen. Generally it is dangerous to elide these two separate worlds. In this case, the emotions of those women accepting 'masculinisation' while watching action movies with a male hero are illuminated by the emotions of a heroine of a melodrama whose resistance to a 'correct' feminine position is the critical issue at stake. Her oscillation, her inability to achieve stable sexual identity, is echoed by the woman spectator's masculine 'point of view'. Both create a sense of the difficulty of sexual difference in cinema that is missing in the undifferentiated spectator of 'Visual Pleasure'. The unstable, oscillating difference is thrown into relief by Freud's theory of femininity.

FREUD AND FEMININITY

For Freud, femininity is complicated by the fact that it emerges out of a crucial period of parallel development between the sexes; a period he sees as masculine, or phallic, for both boys and girls. The terms he uses to conceive of femininity are the same as those he has mapped out for the male, causing certain problems of language and boundaries to expression. These problems reflect, very accurately, the actual position of women in patriarchal society (suppressed, for instance, under the generalised male third person singular). One term gives rise to a second as its complementary opposite, the male to the female, in that order. Some quotations:

> In females, too, the striving to be masculine is ego-syntonic at a certain period – namely in the phallic phase, before the development of femininity sets in. But it then succumbs to the momentous process of repression, as so often has been shown, that determines the fortunes of a woman's femininity.[1]

> I will only emphasise here that the development of femininity remains exposed to disturbances by the residual phenomena of the early masculine period. Regressions to the pre-Oedipus phase very frequently occur; in the course of some women's lives there is a repeated alternation between periods in which femininity and masculinity gain the upper hand.[2]

> We have called the motive force of sexual life 'the libido'. Sexual life is dominated by the polarity of masculine-feminine; thus the notion suggests

itself of considering the relation of the libido to this antithesis. It would not be surprising if it were to turn out that each sexuality had its own special libido appropriated to it, so that one sort of libido would pursue the aims of a masculine sexual life and another sort those of a feminine one. But nothing of the kind is true. There is only one libido, which serves both the masculine and the feminine functions. To it itself we cannot assign any sex; if, following the conventional equation of activity and masculinity, we are inclined to describe it as masculine, we must not forget that it also covers trends with a passive aim. Nevertheless, the juxtaposition 'feminine libido' is without any justification. Furthermore, it is our impression that more constraint has been applied to the libido when it is pressed into the service of the feminine function, and that – to speak teleologically – Nature takes less careful account of its [that function's] demands than in the case of masculinity. And the reason for this may lie – thinking once again teleologically – in the fact that the accomplishment of the aim of biology has been entrusted to the aggressiveness of men and has been made to some extent independent of women's consent.[3]

One particular point of interest in the third passage is Freud's shift from the use of active/masculine as *metaphor* for the function of the libido to an invocation of Nature and biology that appears to leave the metaphoric usage behind. There are two problems here: Freud introduces the use of the word *masculine* as 'conventional', apparently simply following an established social-linguistic practice (but which, once again, confirms the masculine 'point of view'); however, secondly, and constituting a greater intellectual stumbling-block, the feminine cannot be conceptualised as different, but rather only as *opposition* (passivity) in an antinomic sense, or as *similarity* (the phallic phase). This is not to suggest that a hidden, as yet undiscovered femininity exists (as is perhaps implied by Freud's use of the word 'Nature') but that its structural relationship to masculinity under patriarchy cannot be defined or determined within the terms offered. This shifting process, this definition in terms of opposition or similarity, leaves women also shifting between the metaphoric opposition 'active' and 'passive'. The correct road, *femininity*, leads to increasing repression of 'the active' (the 'phallic phase' in Freud's terms). In this sense Hollywood genre films structured around masculine pleasure, offering an identification with the *active* point of view, allow a woman spectator to rediscover that lost aspect of her sexual identity, the never fully repressed bed-rock of feminine neurosis.

NARRATIVE GRAMMAR AND TRANS-SEX IDENTIFICATION

The 'convention' cited by Freud (active/masculine) structures most popular narratives, whether film, folk-tale or myth (as I argued in 'Visual Pleasure'), where his metaphoric usage is acted out literally in the story. Andromeda stays tied to the rock, a victim, in danger, until Perseus slays the monster and saves her. It is not my aim, here, to debate the rights and wrongs of this narrative division of labour or to demand positive heroines, but rather to point out that the 'grammar' of the story places the reader, listener or spectator *with* the hero. The woman spectator in the cinema can make use of an age-old cultural tradition adapting her to this convention, which eases a transition out of her own sex into another. In 'Visual Pleasure' my argument took as its axis a desire to identify a pleasure that was specific to cinema, that is the eroticism and cultural conventions surrounding the look. Now, on the contrary, I would rather emphasise the way that popular cinema inherited traditions of story-telling that are common to other forms of folk and mass culture, with attendant fascinations other than those of the look.

Freud points out that 'masculinity' is, at one stage, ego-syntonic for a woman. Leaving aside, for the moment, problems posed by his use of words, his general remarks on stories and day-dreams provide another angle of approach, this time giving a cultural rather than psychoanalytic insight into the dilemma. He emphasises the relationship between the ego and the narrative concept of the hero:

> It is the true heroic feeling, which one of our best writers has expressed in the inimitable phrase, 'Nothing can happen to me!' It seems, however, that through this revealing characteristic of invulnerability we can immediately recognise His Majesty the Ego, the hero of every day-dream and every story.[4]

Although a boy might know quite well that it is most *unlikely* that he will go out into the world, make his fortune through prowess or the assistance of helpers, and marry a princess, the stories describe the male fantasy of ambition, reflecting something of an experience and expectation of dominance (the active). For a girl, on the other hand, the cultural and social overlap is more confusing. Freud's argument that a young girl's day-dreams concentrate on the erotic ignores his own position on her early masculinity and the active day-dreams necessarily associated with this phase. In fact, all too often, the erotic function of the woman is represented by the passive, the waiting (Andromeda again), acting above all as a formal closure to the narrative structure. Three elements can thus be drawn together: Freud's concept of 'masculinity' in women, the identification triggered by the logic of a narrative grammar, and the ego's desire to fantasise itself in a certain, active, manner. All three suggest that, as desire is given cultural materiality in a text, for women (from childhood onwards) trans-sex identification is a *habit* that very easily becomes *second nature*. However, this Nature does not sit easily and shifts restlessly in its borrowed transvestite clothes.

THE WESTERN AND OEDIPAL PERSONIFICATIONS

Using a concept of character function based on V. Propp's *Morphology of the Folk-tale*, I want to argue for a chain of links and shifts in narrative pattern, showing up the changing function of 'woman'. The Western (allowing, of course, for as many deviations as one cares to enumerate) bears a residual imprint of the primitive narrative structure analysed by Vladimir Propp in folk-tales. Also, in the hero's traditional invulnerability, the Western ties in closely with Freud's remarks on day-dreaming. (As I am interested primarily in character function and narrative pattern, not in genre definition, many issues about the Western as such are being summarily side-stepped.) For present purposes, the Western genre provides a crucial node in a series of transforma-tions that *comment* on the function of 'woman' (as opposed to 'man') as a narrative signifier and sexual difference as personification of 'active' or 'passive' elements in a story.

In the Proppian tale, an important aspect of narrative closure is 'marriage', a function characterised by 'princess' or equivalent. This is the only function that is sex-specific, and thus essentially relates to the sex of the hero and his marriageability. This function is very commonly reproduced in the Western, where, once again, 'marriage' makes a crucial contribution to narrative closure. However, in the Western the function's presence has also come to allow a complication in the form of its opposite, 'not marriage'. Thus, while the social integration represented by marriage is an essential aspect of the folk-tale, in the Western it can be accepted . . . or not. A hero can gain in stature by refusing the princess and remaining alone (Randolph Scott in the Ranown series of movies). As the resolution of the Proppian tale can be seen to represent the resolution of the Oedipus complex (integration into the symbolic), the rejection of marriage personifies a nostalgic celebration of phallic, narcissistic omnipotence. Just as Freud's comments on the 'phallic' phase in girls seemed to belong in limbo, without a place in the chronology of sexual development, so, too, does this male phenomenon seem to belong to a phase of play and fantasy difficult to integrate exactly into the Oedipal trajectory.

The tension between two points of attraction, the symbolic (social integration and marriage) and nostalgic narcissism, generates a common splitting of the Western hero into two, something unknown in the Proppian tale. Here two functions emerge, one celebrating integration into society through marriage, the other celebrating resistance to social demands and responsibilities, above all those of marriage and the family, the sphere represented by woman. A story such as *The Man Who Shot Liberty Valance* juxtaposes these two points of attraction, and spectator fantasy can have its cake and eat it too. This particular tension between the double hero also brings out the underlying significance of the drama, its relation to the symbolic, with unusual clarity. A folk-tale story revolves around conflict between hero and villain. The flashback narration in *Liberty Valance* seems to follow these lines at first. The narrative is generated by an act of villainy (Liberty rampages, dragon-like, around the countryside). However the development of the story acquires a complication. The issue at stake is no longer how the villain will be defeated, but how the villain's defeat will be inscribed into history, whether the *upholder* of law as a symbolic system (Ranse) will be seen to be victorious or the *personification* of law in a more primitive manifestation (Tom), closer to the good or the right. *Liberty Valance*, as it uses a flashback structure, also brings out the poignancy of this tension. The 'present-tense' story is precipitated by a funeral, so that the story is shot through with nostalgia and sense of loss. Ranse Stoddart mourns Tom Doniphon.

This narrative structure is based on an opposition between two irreconcilables. The two paths cannot cross. On one side there is an encapsulation of power, and phallic attributes, in an individual who has to bow himself out of the way of history; on the other, an individual impotence rewarded by political and financial power, which, *in the long run*, in fact becomes history. Here the function 'marriage' is as crucial as it is in the folk-tale. It plays the same part in creating narrative resolution, but is even more important in that 'marriage' is an integral attribute of the upholder of the law. In this sense Hallie's choice between the two men is predetermined. Hallie equals princess equals Oedipal resolution rewarded, equals repression of narcissistic sexuality in marriage.

WOMAN AS SIGNIFIER OF SEXUALITY

In a Western working within these conventions, the function 'marriage' sublimates the erotic into a final, closing, social ritual. This ritual is, of course, sex-specific, and the main rationale for any female presence in this strand of the genre. This neat *narrative* function restates the propensity for 'woman' to signify 'the erotic' already familiar from *visual* representation (as, for instance, argued in 'Visual Pleasure'). Now I want to discuss the way in which introducing a woman as central to a story shifts its meanings, producing another kind of narrative discourse. *Duel in the Sun* provides the opportunity for this.

While the film remains visibly a 'Western', the generic space seems to shift. The landscape of action, although present, is not the dramatic core of the film's story, rather it is the interior drama of a girl caught between two conflicting desires. The conflicting desires, first of all, correspond closely with Freud's argument about female sexuality quoted above, that is: an oscillation between 'passive' femininity and regressive 'masculinity'. Thus, the symbolic equation, woman = sexuality, still persists, but now rather than being an image or a narrative function, the equation opens out a narrative area previously suppressed or repressed. Woman is no longer the signifier of sexuality (function 'marriage') in the 'Western' type of story. Now the female presence as centre allows the story to be actually, *overtly*, about sexuality: it becomes a melodrama. It is as though the narrational lens had zoomed in and opened up the neat function 'marriage' ('and they lived happily . . .') to ask 'what next?' and to focus on the figure of the princess, waiting in the wings for her one moment of importance, to ask 'what does *she* want?' Here we find the generic terrain for melodrama, in its woman-orientated strand. The second question ('what does *she* want?') takes on greater significance when the hero function is split, as described above in the case of *Liberty Valance*, where the heroine's choice puts the seal of married grace on the upholder of the law. *Duel in the Sun* opens up this question.

In *Duel in the Sun* the iconographical attributes of the two male (oppositional) characters, Lewt and Jesse, conform very closely to those of Tom and Ranse in

Liberty Valance. But now the opposition between Ranse and Tom (which represents an abstract and allegorical conflict over Law and history) is given a completely different twist of meaning. As Pearl is at the centre of the story, caught between the two men, their alternative attributes acquire meaning *from* her, and represent different sides of her desire and aspiration. They personify the split in *Pearl*, not a split in the concept of *hero*, as argued previously for *Liberty Valance*.

However, from a psychoanalytic point of view, a strikingly similar pattern emerges, Jesse (attributes: books, dark suit, legal skills, love of learning and culture, destined to be Governor of the State, money, and so on) signposts the 'correct' path for Pearl, towards learning a passive sexuality, learning to 'be a lady', above all sublimation into a concept of the feminine that is socially viable. Lewt (attributes: guns, horses, skill with horses, Western get-up, contempt for culture, destined to die an outlaw, personal strength and personal power) offers sexual passion, not based on maturity but on a regressive, boy/girl mixture of rivalry and play. With Lewt, Pearl can be a tomboy (riding, swimming, shooting). Thus the Oedipal dimension persists, but now illuminates the sexual ambivalence it represents for femininity.

In the last resort, there is no more room for Pearl in Lewt's world of misogynist machismo than there is room for her desires as Jesse's potential fiancée. The film consists of a series of oscillations in her sexual identity, between alternative paths of development, between different desperations. Whereas the regressive phallic male hero (Tom in *Liberty Vallance*) had a place (albeit a doomed one) that was stable and meaningful, Pearl is unable to settle or find a 'femininity' in which she and the male world can meet. In this sense, although the male characters personify Pearl's dilemma, it is their terms that make and finally break her. Once again, however, the narrative drama dooms the phallic, regressive resistance to the symbolic. Lewt, Pearl's masculine side, drops out of the social order. Pearl's masculinity gives her the 'wherewithal' to achieve heroism and kill the villain. The lovers shoot each other and die in each other's arms. Perhaps, in *Duel*, the erotic relationship between Pearl and Lewt also exposes a dyadic interdependence between hero and villain in the primitive tale, now threatened by the splitting of the hero with the coming of the Law.

In *Duel in the Sun*, Pearl's inability to become a 'lady' is highlighted by the fact that the perfect lady appears, like a phantasmagoria of Pearl's failed aspiration, as Jesse's perfect future wife. Pearl recognises her and her rights over Jesse, and sees that she represents the 'correct' road. In an earlier film by King Vidor, *Stella Dallas* (1937), narrative and iconographic structures similar to those outlined above make the dramatic meaning of the film although it is not a Western. Stella, as central character, is flanked on each side by a male personification of her instability, her inability to accept correct, married 'femininity' on the one hand, or find a place in a macho world on the other. Her husband, Stephen, demonstrates all the attributes associated with Jesse, with no problems of generic shift. Ed Munn, representing Stella's regressive 'masculine' side, is considerably emasculated by the loss of the Western's accoutrements and its terrain of violence. (The fact that Stella is a mother, and that her relationship to her child constitutes the central drama, undermines a possible sexual relationship with Ed.) He does retain residual traces of Western iconography. His attributes are mapped through associations with horses and betting, the racing scene. However, more importantly, his relationship with Stella is regressive, based on 'having fun', most explicitly in the episode in which they spread itching powder among the respectable occupants of a train carriage. In *Stella Dallas*, too, a perfect wife appears for Stephen, representing the 'correct' femininity that Stella rejects (very similar to Helen, Jesse's fiancée in *Duel in the Sun*).

I have been trying to suggest a series of transformations in narrative pattern that illuminate, but also show shifts in, Oedipal nostalgia. The 'personifications' and their iconographical attributes do not relate to parental figures or reactivate an actual Oedipal moment. On the contrary, they represent an internal oscillation of desire, which lies dormant, waiting to be 'pleasured' in stories of this kind. Perhaps the fascination of the classic Western, in particular, lies in its rather raw touching on this nerve. However, for the female spectator the situation is more complicated and goes beyond simple mourning for a lost fantasy of omnipotence. The masculine identification, in its phallic aspect, reactivates for her a fantasy of 'action' that correct femininity demands should be repressed. The fantasy 'action' finds expression through a metaphor of masculinity. Both in the language used by Freud and in the male personifications of desire flanking the female protagonist in the melodrama, this metaphor acts as a strait-jacket, becoming itself an indicator, a litmus paper, of the problems inevitably activated by any attempt to represent the feminine in patriarchal society. The memory of the 'masculine' phase has its own romantic attraction, a last-ditch resistance, in which the power of masculinity can be used as postponement against the power of patriarchy. Thus Freud's comments illuminate both the position of the female spectator and the image of oscillation represented by Pearl and Stella:

> ... in the course of some women's lives there is a repeated alternation between periods in which femininity and masculinity gain the upper hand.

> ... (the phallic phase) ... then succumbs to the momentous process of repression as has so often been shown, that determines the fortunes of women's femininity.

I have argued that Pearl's position in *Duel in the Sun* is similar to that of the female spectator as she temporarily accepts 'masculinisation' in memory of her 'active' phase. Rather than dramatising the success of masculine identification, Pearl brings out its sadness. Her 'tomboy' pleasures, her sexuality, are not fully accepted by Lewt, except in death. So, too, is the female spectator's fantasy of masculinisation at cross-purposes with itself, restless in its transvestite clothes.

NOTES

1. S. Freud, 'Analysis Terminable and Interminable', *Standard Edition*, vol. XXIII (London: The Hogarth Press, 1964).
2. S. Freud, 'Femininity', *Standard Edition*, vol. XXII (London: The Hogarth Press, 1964).
3. Ibid.
4. S. Freud, 'Creative Writers and Day Dreaming', *Standard Edition*, vol. IX (London: The Hogarth Press, 1964).

'FILM AND THE MASQUERADE: THEORISING THE FEMALE SPECTATOR'

Mary Ann Doane

1. HEADS IN HIEROGLYPHIC BONNETS

In his lecture on 'Femininity', Freud forcefully inscribes the absence of the female spectator of theory in his notorious statement, '... to those of you who are women this will not apply – you are yourselves the problem ...'[1] Simultaneous with this exclusion operated upon the female members of his audience, he invokes, as a rather strange prop, a poem by Heine. Introduced by Freud's claim concerning the importance and elusiveness of his topic – 'Throughout history people have knocked their heads against the riddle of the nature of femininity ...' – are four lines of Heine's poem:

> Heads in hieroglyphic bonnets,
> Heads in turbans and black birettas,
> Heads in wigs and thousand other
> Wretched, sweating heads of humans ...[2]

The effects of the appeal to this poem are subject to the work of over-determination Freud isolated in the text of the dream. The sheer proliferation of heads and hats (and hence, through a metonymic slippage, minds), which are presumed to have confronted this intimidating riddle before Freud, confers on his discourse the weight of an intellectual history, of a tradition of interrogation. Furthermore, the image of hieroglyphics strengthens the association made between femininity and the enigmatic, the undecipherable, that which is 'other'.

---

*From *Screen* 23: 3–4, 1982, pp. 74–87.

And yet Freud practises a slight deception here, concealing what is elided by removing the lines from their context, castrating, as it were, the stanza. For the question over which Heine's heads brood is not the same as Freud's – it is not 'What is Woman?', but instead, '... what signifies Man?' The quote is taken from the seventh section (entitled 'Questions') of the second cycle of *The North Sea*. The full stanza, presented as the words of 'a young man,/ His breast full of sorrow, his head full of doubt', reads as follows:

> O solve me the riddle of life,
> The teasingly time-old riddle,
> Over which many heads already have brooded,
> Heads in hats of hieroglyphics,
> Turbaned heads and heads in black skull-caps,
> Heads in perrukes and a thousand other
> Poor, perspiring human heads –
> Tell me, what signifies Man?
> Whence does he come? Whither does he go?
> Who lives up there upon golden stars?[3]

The question in Freud's text is thus a disguise and a displacement of that other question, which in the pre-text is both humanistic and theological. The claim to investigate an otherness is a pretense, haunted by the mirror-effect by means of which the question of the woman reflects only the man's own ontological doubts. Yet what interests me most in this intertextual mis-representation is that the riddle of femininity is initiated from the beginning in Freud's text as a question in masquerade. But I will return to the issue of masquerade later.

More pertinently, as far as the cinema is concerned, it is not accidental that Freud's eviction of the female spectator/auditor is co-present with the invocation of a hieroglyphic language. The woman, the enigma, the hieroglyphic, the picture, the image – the metonymic chain connects with another: the cinema, the theatre of pictures, a writing in images of the woman but not *for* her. For she *is* the problem. The semantic valence attributed to a hieroglyphic language is two-edged. In fact, there is a sense in which the term is inhabited by a contradiction. On the one hand, the hieroglyphic is summoned, particularly when it merges with a discourse on the woman, to connote an indecipherable language, a signifying system which denies its own function by failing to signify anything to the uninitiated, to those who do not hold the key. In this sense, the hieroglyphic, like the woman, harbours a mystery, an inaccessible though desirable otherness. On the other hand, the hieroglyphic is the most readable of languages. Its immediacy, its accessibility are functions of its status as a *pictorial* language, a writing in images. For the image is theorised in terms of a certain *closeness*, the lack of a distance or gap between sign and referent. Given its iconic character-istics, the relationship between signifier and signified is understood as less arbitrary in imagistic systems of representation than in language 'proper'. The intimacy of signifier and signified in the iconic sign negates the distance which defines phonetic language. And it is the absence of this crucial distance or gap which also, simultaneously, specifies both the hieroglyphic and the female. This is precisely why Freud evicted the woman from his lecture on femininity. Too close to herself, entangled in her own enigma, she could not step back, could not achieve the necessary distance of a second look.[4]

Thus, while the hieroglyphic is an indecipherable or at least enigmatic language, it is also and at the same time potentially the most universally understandable, comprehensible, appropriable of signs.[5] And the woman shares this contradictory status. But it is here that the analogy slips. For hieroglyphic languages are *not* perfectly iconic. They would not achieve the status of languages if they were – due to what Todorov and Ducrot refer to as as a certain non-generalisability of the iconic sign:

> Now it is the impossibility of generalizing this principle of representation that has introduced even into fundamentally morphemographic writing systems such as Chinese, Egyptian, and Sumerian, the phonographic principle. We might almost conclude that every logography [the graphic system of language notation] grows out of *the impossibility of a generalized iconic representation*; proper nouns and abstract notions (including inflections) are then the ones that will be noted phonetically.[6]

The iconic system of representation is inherently deficient – it cannot disengage itself from the 'real', from the concrete; it lacks the gap necessary for generalisability (for Saussure, this is the idea that, 'Signs which are arbitrary realise better than others the ideal of the semiotic process.'). The woman, too, is defined by such an insufficiency. My insistence upon the congruence between certain theories of the image and theories of femininity is an attempt to dissect the *episteme* which assigns to the woman a special place in cinematic representation while denying her access to that system.

The cinematic apparatus inherits a theory of the image which is not conceived outside of sexual specifications. And historically, there has always been a certain imbrication of the cinematic image and the representation of the woman. The woman's relation to the camera and the scopic regime is quite different from that of the male. As Noël Burch points out, the early silent cinema, through its insistent inscription of scenarios of voyeurism, conceives of its spectator's viewing pleasure in terms of that of the Peeping Tom, behind the screen, reduplicating the spectator's position in relation to the woman as screen.[7] Spectatorial desire, in contemporary film theory, is generally delineated as either voyeurism or fetishism, as precisely a pleasure in seeing what is prohibited in relation to the female body. The image orchestrates a gaze, a limit, and its pleasurable transgression. The woman's beauty, her very desirability, becomes a function of certain practices of imaging – framing, lighting, camera movement, angle. She is thus, as Laura Mulvey has pointed out, more closely associated with the surface of the image than its illusory depths, its constructed 3-dimensional space which the man is destined to inhabit and hence control.[8] In *Now Voyager*, for instance, a single image signals the momentous transformation of the Bette Davis character from ugly spinster aunt to glamorous single woman. Charles Affron describes the specifically cinematic aspect of this operation as a 'stroke of genius':

> The radical shadow bisecting the face in white/dark/white strata creates a visual phenomenon quite distinct from the makeup transformation of lipstick and plucked eyebrows ... This shot does not reveal what we commonly call acting, especially after the most recent exhibition of that activity, but the sense of face belongs to a plastique pertinent to the camera. The viewer is allowed a different perceptual referent, a chance to come down from the nerve-jarring, first sequence and to use his eyes anew.[9]

A 'plastique pertinent to the camera' constitutes the woman not only as the image of desire but as the desirous image – one which the devoted cinéphile can cherish and embrace. To 'have' the cinema is, in some sense, to 'have' the woman. But *Now Voyager* is, in Affron's terms, a 'tear-jerker', in others, a 'woman's picture', i.e. a film purportedly produced for a female audience. What, then, of the female spectator? What can one say about her desire in relation to this process of imaging? It would seem that what the cinematic institution has in common with Freud's gesture is the eviction of the female spectator from a discourse purportedly about her (the cinema, psychoanalysis) – one which, in fact, narrativises her again and again.

II. A LASS BUT NOT A LACK

Theories of female spectatorship are thus rare, and when they are produced, seem inevitably to confront certain blockages in conceptualisation. The difficulties in thinking female spectatorship demand consideration. After all, even if it is admitted that the woman is frequently the object of the voyeuristic or fetishistic gaze in the cinema, what is there to prevent her from reversing the relation and appropriating the gaze for her own pleasure? Precisely the fact that the reversal itself remains locked within the same logic. The male striptease, the gigolo – both inevitably signify the mechanism of reversal itself, constituting themselves as aberrations whose acknowledgment simply reinforces the dominant system of aligning sexual difference with a subject/object dichotomy. And an essential attribute of that dominant system is the matching of male subjectivity with the agency of the look.

The supportive binary opposition at work here is not only that utilised by Laura Mulvey – an opposition between passivity and activity, but perhaps more importantly, an opposition between proximity and distance in relation to the image.[10] It is in this sense that the very logic behind the structure of the gaze demands a sexual division. While the distance between image and signified (or even referent) is theorised as minimal, if not non-existent, that between the film and the spectator must be maintained, even measured. One need only think of Noël Burch's mapping of spectatorship as a perfect distance from the screen (two times the width of the image) – a point in space from which the filmic discourse is most accessible.[11]

But the most explicit representation of this opposition between proximity and distance is contained in Christian Metz's analysis of voyeuristic desire in terms of a kind of social hierarchy of the senses: 'It is no accident that the main socially acceptable arts are based on the senses at a distance, and that those which depend on the senses of contact are often regarded as 'minor' arts (= culinary arts, art of perfumes, etc.).'[12] The voyeur, according to Metz, must maintain a distance between himself and the image – the cinéphile *needs* the gap which represents for him the very distance between desire and its object. In this sense, voyeurism is theorised as a type of meta-desire:

> If it is true of all desire that it depends on the infinite pursuit of its absent object, voyeuristic desire, along with certain forms of sadism, is the only desire whose principle of distance symbolically and spatially evokes this fundamental rent.[13]

Yet even this status as meta-desire does not fully characterise the cinema for it is a feature shared by other arts as well (painting, theatre, opera, etc.). Metz thus adds another reinscription of this necessary distance. What specifies the cinema is a further re-duplication of the lack which prompts desire. The cinema is characterised by an illusory sensory plenitude (there is 'so much to see') and yet haunted by the absence of those very objects which are there to be seen. Absence is an absolute and irrecoverable distance. In other words, Noël Burch is quite right in aligning spectatorial desire with a certain spatial configuration. The viewer must not sit either too close or too far from the screen. The result of both would be the same – he would lose the image of his desire.

It is precisely this opposition between proximity and distance, control of the image and its loss, which locates the possibilities of spectatorship within the problematic of sexual difference. For the female spectator there is a certain over-presence of the image – she *is* the image. Given the closeness of this relationship, the female spectator's desire can be described only in terms of a kind of narcissism – the female look demands a becoming. It thus appears to negate the very distance or gap specified by Metz and Burch as the essential precondition for voyeurism. From this perspective, it is important to note the constant recurrence of the motif of proximity in feminist theories (especially those labelled 'new French feminisms') which purport to describe a feminine specificity. For Luce Irigaray, female anatomy is readable as a constant relation of the self to itself, as an autoeroticism based on the embrace of the two lips which allow the woman to touch herself without mediation. Furthermore, the very notion of property, and hence possession of something which can be constituted as other, is antithetical to the woman: '*Nearness* however, is not foreign to woman, a nearness so close that any identification of one or the other, and therefore any form of property, is impossible. Woman enjoys a closeness with the other that is *so near she cannot possess it any more than she can possess herself.*[14] Or, in the case of female madness or delirium, '... women do not manage to articulate their madness: they suffer it directly in their body ...'[15] The distance necessary to detach the signifiers of madness from the body in the construction of even a discourse which exceeds the boundaries of sense is lacking. In the words of Hélène Cixous, 'More so than men who are coaxed toward social success, toward sublimation, women are body.'[16]

This theme of the overwhelming presence-to-itself of the female body is elaborated by Sarah Kofman and Michèle Montrelay as well. Kofman describes how Freudian psychoanalysis outlines a scenario whereby the subject's passage from the mother to the father is simultaneous with a passage from the senses to reason, nostalgia for the mother henceforth signifying a longing for a different positioning in relation to the sensory or the somatic, and the degree of civilization measured by the very distance from the body.[17] Similarly, Montrelay argues that while the male has the possibility of displacing the first object of desire (the mother), the female must become that object of desire:

> Recovering herself as maternal body (and also as phallus), the woman can no longer repress, 'lose,' the first stake of representation ... From now on, anxiety, tied to the presence of this body, can only be insistent, continuous. This body, so close, which she has to occupy, is an object in excess which must be 'lost,' that is to say, repressed, in order to be symbolised.[18]

This body so close, so excessive, prevents the woman from assuming a position similar to the man's in relation to signifying systems. For she is haunted by the loss of a loss, the lack of that lack so essential for the realisation of the ideals of semiotic systems.

Female specificity is thus theorised in terms of spatial proximity. In opposition to this 'closeness' to the body, a spatial distance in the male's relation to his body rapidly becomes a temporal distance in the service of knowledge. This is presented quite explicitly in Freud's analysis of the construction of the 'subject supposed to know'. The knowledge involved here is a knowledge of sexual difference as it is organised in relation to the structure of the look, turning on the visibility of the penis. For the little girl in Freud's description seeing and knowing are simultaneous – there is no temporal gap between them. In 'Some Psychological Consequences of the Anatomical Distinction Between the Sexes', Freud claims that the girl, upon seeing the penis for the first time, 'makes her judgement and her decision in a flash. She has seen it and knows that she is without it and wants to have it.'[19] In the lecture on 'Femininity' Freud repeats this gesture, merging perception and intellection: 'They [girls] at once notice the difference and, it must be admitted, its significance too.'[20]

The little boy, on the other hand, does not share this immediacy of understanding. When he first sees the woman's genitals he 'begins by showing irresolution and lack of interest; he sees nothing or disowns what he has seen, he softens it down or looks about for expedients for bringing it into line with his expectations'.[21] A second event, the threat of castration, is necessary to prompt a rereading of the image, endowing it with a meaning in relation to the boy's own subjectivity. It is in the distance between the look and the threat that the boy's relation to knowledge of sexual difference is formulated. The boy, unlike the girl in Freud's description, is capable of a re-vision of earlier events, a retrospective understanding which invests the events with a significance which is in no way linked to an immediacy of sight. This gap between the visible and the knowable, the very possibility of disowning what is seen, prepares the ground for fetishism. In a sense, the male spectator is destined to be a fetishist, balancing knowledge and belief.

The female, on the other hand, must find it extremely difficult, if not impossible, to assume the position of fetishist. That body which is so close continually reminds her of the castration which cannot be 'fetishised away'. The lack of a distance between seeing and understanding, the mode of judging 'in a flash', is conducive to what might be termed as 'over-identification' with the image. The association of tears and 'wet wasted afternoons' (in Molly Haskell's words)[22] with genres specified as feminine (the soap opera, the 'woman's picture') points very precisely to this type of over-identification, this abolition of a distance, in short, this inability to fetishise. The woman is constructed differently in relation to processes of looking. For Irigaray, this dichotomy between distance and proximity is described as the fact that:

> The masculine can partly look at itself, speculate about itself, represent itself and describe itself for what it is, whilst the feminine can try to speak to itself through a new language, but cannot describe itself from outside or in formal terms, except by identifying itself with the masculine, thus by losing itself.[23]

Irigaray goes even further: the woman always has a problematic relation to the visible, to form, to structures of seeing. She is much more comfortable with, closer to, the sense of touch.

The pervasiveness, in theories of the feminine, of descriptions of such a claustrophobic closeness, a deficiency in relation to structures of seeing and the visible, must clearly have consequences for attempts to theorise female spectatorship. And, in fact, the result is a tendency to view the female spectator as the site of an oscillation between a feminine position and a masculine position, invoking the metaphor of the transvestite. Given the structures of cinematic narrative, the woman who identifies with a female character must adopt a passive or masochistic position, while identification with the active hero necessarily entails an acceptance of what Laura Mulvey refers to as a certain 'masculinisation' of spectatorship.

> ... as desire is given cultural materiality in a text, for women (from child-hood onwards) trans-sex identification is a *habit* that very easily becomes *second Nature*. However, this Nature does not sit easily and shifts restlessly in its borrowed transvestite clothes.[24]

The transvestite wears clothes which signify a different sexuality, a sexuality which, for the woman, allows a mastery over the image and the very possibility of attaching the gaze to desire. Clothes make the man, as they say. Perhaps this explains the ease with which women can slip into male clothing. As both Freud and Cixous point out, the woman seems to be *more* bisexual than the man. A scene from Cukor's *Adam's Rib* graphically demonstrates this ease of female transvestism. As Katherine Hepburn asks the jury to imagine the sex role reversal of the three major characters involved in the case, there are three dissolves linking each of the characters successively to shots in which they are dressed in the clothes of the opposite sex. What characterises the sequence is the marked facility of the transformation of the two women into men in contra-distinction to a certain resistance in the case of the man. The acceptability of the female reversal is quite distinctly opposed to the male reversal which seems capable of representation only in terms of farce. Male transvestism is an occasion for laughter; female transvestism only another occasion for desire.

Thus, while the male is locked into sexual identity, the female can at least pretend that she is other – in fact, sexual mobility would seem to be a dis-tinguishing feature of femininity in its cultural construction. Hence, transvest-ism would be fully recuperable. The idea seems to be this: it is understandable that women would want to be men, for everyone wants to be elsewhere than in the feminine position. What is not understandable within the given terms is why a woman might flaunt her femininity, produce herself as an excess of femininity, in other words, foreground the masquerade. Masquerade is not as recuperable as transvestism precisely because it constitutes an acknowledgement that it is femininity itself which is constructed as mask – as the decorative layer which conceals a non-identity. For Joan Riviere, the first to theorise the concept, the masquerade of femininity is a kind of reaction-formation against the woman's trans-sex identification, her transvestism. After assuming the position of the subject of discourse rather than its object, the intellectual woman whom Riviere analyses felt compelled to compensate for this theft of masculinity by over-doing the gestures of feminine flirtation.

> Womanliness therefore could be assumed and worn as a mask, both to hide the possession of masculinity and to avert the reprisals expected if she was found to possess it – much as a thief will turn out his pockets and ask to be searched to prove that he has not the stolen goods. The reader may now ask how I define womanliness or where I draw the line between genuine womanliness and the masquerade. My suggestion is not, however, that there is any such difference; whether radical or superficial, they are the same thing.[25]

The masquerade, in flaunting femininity, holds it at a distance. Womanliness is a mask which can be worn or removed. The masquerade's resistance to patriarchal positioning would therefore lie in its denial of the production of femininity as closeness, as presence-to-itself, as, precisely, imagistic. The transvestite adopts the sexuality of the other – the woman becomes a man in order to attain the necessary distance from the image. Masquerade, on the other hand, involves a realignment of femininity, the recovery, or more accurately, simulation, of the missing gap or distance. To masquerade is to manufacture a lack in the form of a certain distance between oneself and one's image. If, as Moustafa Safouan points out, '... to wish to include in oneself as an object the cause of the desire of the Other is a formula for the structure of hysteria',[26] then masquerade is anti-hysterical for it works to effect a separation between the cause of desire and oneself. In Montrelay's words, 'the woman uses her own body as a disguise.'[27]

The very fact that we can speak of a woman 'using' her sex or 'using' her body for particular gains is highly significant – it is not that a man cannot use his body in this way but that he doesn't have to. The masquerade doubles representation; it is constituted by a hyperbolisation of the accoutrements of femininity. *A propos* of a recent performance by Marlene Dietrich, Sylvia Bovenschen claims, '... we are watching a woman demonstrate the representation of a woman's body.'[28] This type of masquerade, an excess of femininity, is aligned with the *femme fatale* and, as Montrelay explains, is necessarily regarded by men as evil incarnate: 'It is this evil which scandalises whenever woman plays out her sex in order to evade the word and the law. Each time she subverts a law or a word which relies on the predominantly masculine structure of the look.'[29] By destabilising the image, the masquerade confounds this masculine structure of the look. It effects a defamiliarisation of female iconography. Nevertheless, the preceding account simply specifies masquerade as a type of representation which carries a threat, disarticulating male systems of viewing. Yet, it specifies nothing with respect to female spectatorship. What might it mean to masquerade as spectator? To assume the mask in order to see in a different way?

III. 'MEN SELDOM MAKE PASSES AT GIRLS WHO WEAR GLASSES'

The first scene in *Now Voyager* depicts the Bette Davis character as repressed, unattractive and undesirable or, in her own words, as the spinster aunt of the family. ('Every family has one.') She has heavy eyebrows, keeps her hair bound tightly in a bun, and wears glasses, a drab dress and heavy shoes. By the time of the shot discussed earlier, signalling her transformation into beauty, the glasses have disappeared, along with the other signifiers of unattractiveness. Between these two moments there is a scene in which the doctor who cures her actually confiscates her glasses (as a part of the cure). The woman who wears glasses constitutes one of the most intense visual clichés of the cinema. The image is a heavily marked condensation of motifs concerned with repressed sexuality, knowledge, visibility and vision, intellectuality, and desire. The woman with glasses signifies simultaneously intellectuality and undesirability; but the moment she removes her glasses (a moment which, it seems, must almost always be *shown* and which is itself linked with a certain sensual quality), she is transformed into spectacle, the very picture of desire. Now, it must be remembered that the cliché is a heavily loaded moment of signification, a social knot of meaning. It is characterised by an effect of ease and naturalness. Yet, the cliché has a binding power so strong that it indicates a precise moment of ideological danger or threat – in this case, the woman's appropriation of the gaze. Glasses worn by a woman in the cinema do not generally signify a deficiency in seeing but an active looking, or even simply the fact of seeing as opposed to being seen. The intellectual woman looks and analyses, and in usurping the gaze she poses a threat to an entire system of representation. It is as if the woman had forcefully moved to the other side of the specular. The overdetermination of the image of the woman with glasses, its status as a cliché, is a crucial aspect of the cinematic alignment of structures of seeing and being seen with sexual difference. The cliché, in assuming an immediacy of understanding, acts as a mechanism for the naturalisation of sexual difference.

But the figure of the woman with glasses is only an extreme moment of a more generalised logic. There is always a certain excessiveness, a difficulty associated with women who appropriate the gaze, who insist upon looking. Linda Williams has demonstrated how, in the genre of the horror film, the woman's active looking is ultimately punished. And what she sees, the monster, is only a mirror of herself – both woman and monster are freakish in their difference – defined by either 'too much' or 'too little'.[30] Just as the dominant narrative cinema repetitively inscribes scenarios of voyeurism, internalising or narrativising the film-spectator relationship (in films like *Psycho*, *Rear Window*, *Peeping Tom*), taboos in seeing are insistently formulated in relation to the female spectator as well. The man with binoculars is countered by the woman with glasses. The gaze must be dissociated from mastery. In *Leave Her to Heaven* (John Stahl, 1945), the female protagonist's (Gene Tierney's) excessive desire and over-possessiveness are signalled from the very beginning of the film by her intense and sustained stare at the major male character, a stranger she first encounters on a train. The discomfort her look causes is graphically depicted. The Gene Tierney character is ultimately revealed to be the epitome of evil – killing her husband's crippled younger brother, her unborn child and ultimately herself in an attempt to brand her cousin as a murderess in order to insure her husband's future fidelity. In *Humoresque* (Jean Negulesco, 1946), Joan Crawford's problematic status is a result of her continual attempts to assume the position of spectator – fixing John Garfield with her gaze. Her transformation from spectator to spectacle is signified repetitively by the gesture of removing her glasses. Rosa, the character played by Bette Davis in *Beyond the Forest* (King Vidor, 1949) walks to the station every day simply to *watch* the train departing for Chicago. Her fascination with the train is a fascination with its phallic power to transport her to 'another place'. This character is also specified as having a 'good eye'– she can shoot, both pool and guns. In all three films the woman is constructed as the site of an excessive and dangerous desire. This desire mobilises extreme efforts of containment and unveils the sadistic aspect of narrative. In all three films the woman dies. As Claire Johnston points out, death is the 'location of all impossible signs',[31] and the films demonstrate that the woman as subject of the gaze is clearly an impossible sign. There is a perverse rewriting of this logic of the gaze in *Dark Victory* (Edmund Goulding, 1939), where the woman's story achieves heroic and tragic proportions not only in blindness, but in a blindness which mimes sight – when the woman pretends to be able to see.

IV. OUT OF THE CINEMA AND INTO THE STREETS: THE CENSORSHIP OF THE FEMALE GAZE

This process of narrativising the negation of the female gaze in the classical Hollywood cinema finds its perfect encapsulation in a still photograph taken in 1948 by Robert Doisneau, '*Un Regard Oblique*'. Just as the Hollywood narratives discussed above purport to centre a female protagonist, the photograph appears to give a certain prominence to a woman's look. Yet, both the title of the photograph and its organisation of space indicate that the real site of scopophiliac power is on the margins of the frame. The man is not centred; in fact, he occupies a very narrow space on the extreme right of the picture. Nevertheless it is his gaze which defines the problematic of the photograph; it is his gaze which effectively erases that of the woman. Indeed, as subject of the gaze, the woman looks intently. But not only is the object of her look concealed from the spectator, her gaze is encased by the two poles defining the masculine axis of vision. Fascinated by nothing visible – a blankness or void for the spectator – unanchored by a 'sight' (there is nothing 'proper' to her vision – save, perhaps, the mirror), the female gaze is left free-floating, vulnerable to subjection. The faint reflection in the shop window of only the frame of the picture at which she is looking serves merely to rearticulate, *en abŷme*, the emptiness of her gaze, the absence of her desire in representation.

On the other hand, the object of the male gaze is fully present, *there* for the spectator. The fetishistic representation of the nude female body, fully in view, insures a masculinisation of the spectatorial position. The woman's look is literally outside the triangle which traces a complicity between the man, the nude, and the spectator. The feminine presence in the photograph, despite a diegetic centring of the female subject of the gaze, is taken over by the picture as object. And, as if to doubly 'frame' her in the act of looking, the painting situates its female figure as a spectator (although it is not clear whether she is looking at herself in a mirror or peering through a door or window). While this drama of seeing is played out at the surface of the photograph, its deep space is activated by several young boys, out-of-focus, in front of a belt shop. The opposition out-of-focus/in-focus reinforces the supposed clarity accorded to the representation of the woman's 'non-vision'. Furthermore, since this out-of-focus area constitutes the precise literal centre of the image, it also demonstrates how the photograph makes figurative the operation of centring – draining the actual centre point of significance in order to deposit meaning on the margins. The male gaze is centred, in control – although it is exercised from the periphery.

The spectator's pleasure is thus produced through the framing/negation of the female gaze. The woman is there as the butt of a joke – a 'dirty joke' which, as Freud has demonstrated, is always constructed at the expense of a woman. In order for a dirty joke to emerge in its specificity in Freud's description, the object of desire – the woman – must be absent and a third person (another man) must be present as witness to the joke – 'so that gradually, in place of the woman, the onlooker, now the listener, becomes the person to whom the smut is addressed ...'.[32] The terms of the photograph's address as joke once again insure a masculinisation of the place of the spectator. The operation of the dirty joke is also inextricably linked by Freud to scopophilia and the exposure of the female body:

> Smut is like an exposure of the sexually different person to whom it is directed. By the utterance of the obscene words it compels the person who is assailed to imagine the part of the body or the procedure in question and shows her that the assailant is himself imagining it. It cannot be doubted that the desire to see what is sexual exposed is the original motive of smut.[33]

From this perspective, the photograph lays bare the very mechanics of the joke through its depiction of sexual exposure and a surreptitious act of seeing (and desiring). Freud's description of the joke-work appears to constitute a perfect analysis of the photograph's orchestration of the gaze. There is a 'voice-off' of the photographic discourse, however – a component of the image which is beyond the frame of this little scenario of voyeurism. On the far left-hand side of the photograph, behind the wall holding the painting of the nude, is the barely detectable painting of a woman imaged differently, in darkness – *out of sight* for the male, blocked by his fetish. Yet, to point to this almost invisible alternative in imaging is also only to reveal once again the analyst's own perpetual desire to find a not-seen that might break the hold of representation. Or to laugh last.

There is a sense in which the photograph's delineation of a sexual politics of looking is almost uncanny. But, to counteract the very possibility of such a perception, the language of the art critic effects a naturalisation of this joke on the woman. The art-critical reception of the picture emphasises a natural but at the same time 'imaginative' relation between photography and life, ultimately subordinating any formal relations to a referential ground: 'Doisneau's lines move from right to left, directed by the man's glance; the woman's gaze creates a line of energy like a hole in space ... The creation of these relationships from life itself is imagination in photography.'[34] 'Life itself', then, presents the material for an 'artistic' organisation of vision along the lines of sexual difference. Furthermore, the critic would have us believe that chance events and arbitrary clicks of the shutter cannot be the agents of a generalised sexism because they are particular, unique – 'Keitesz and Doisneau depend entirely upon our recognition that they were present at the instant of the unique intersection of events.'[35] Realism seems always to reside in the streets and, indeed, the out-of-focus boy across the street, at the centre of the photograph, appears to act as a guarantee of the 'chance nature of the event, its arbitrariness, in short – its realism. Thus, in the discourse of the art critic the photograph, in capturing a moment, does not construct it; the camera finds a naturally given series of subject and object positions. What the critic does not consider are the conditions of reception of photography as an art form, its situation within a much larger network of representation. What is it that makes the photograph not only readable but pleasurable – at the expense of the women? The critic does not ask what makes the photograph a negotiable item in a market of signification.

V. THE MISSING LOOK

The photograph displays insistently, in microcosm, the structure of the cinematic inscription of a sexual differentiation in modes of looking. Its process of framing the female gaze repeats that of the cinematic narratives described above, from *Leave Her to Heaven* to *Dark Victory*. Films play out scenarios of looking in order to outline the terms of their own understanding. And given the divergence between masculine and feminine scenarios, those terms would seem to be explicitly negotiated as markers of sexual difference. Both the theory of the image and its apparatus, the cinema, produce a position for the female spectator – a position which is ultimately untenable because it lacks the attribute of distance so necessary for an adequate reading of the image. The entire elaboration of femininity as a closeness, a nearness, as present-to-itself is not the definition of an essence but the delineation of a *place* culturally assigned to the woman. Above and beyond a simple adoption of the masculine position in relation to the cinematic sign, the female spectator is given two options: the masochism of over-identification or the narcissism entailed in becoming one's own object of desire, in assuming the image in the most radical way. The effectivity of masquerade lies precisely in its potential to manufacture a distance from the image, to generate a problematic within which the image is manipul-able, producible, and readable by the woman. Doisneau's photograph is not readable by the female spectator – it can give her pleasure only in masochism. In order to 'get' the joke, she must once again assume the position of transvestite.

It is quite tempting to foreclose entirely the possibility of female spectatorship, to repeat at the level of theory the gesture of the photograph, given the history of a cinema which relies so heavily on voyeurism, fetishism, and identification with an ego ideal conceivable only in masculine terms. And, in fact, there has been a tendency to theorise femininity and hence the feminine gaze as repressed, and in its repression somehow irretrievable, the enigma constituted by Freud's question. Yet, as Michel Foucault has demonstrated, the repressive hypothesis on its own entails a very limited and simplistic notion of the working of power.[36] The 'no' of the father, the prohibition, is its only technique. In theories of repression there is no sense of the productiveness and positivity of power. Femininity is produced very precisely as a position within a network of power relations. And the growing insistence upon the elaboration of a theory of female spectatorship is indicative of the crucial necessity of understanding that position in order to dislocate it.

NOTES

1. Sigmund Freud, 'Femininity', *The Standard Edition of the Complete Psychological Works of Sigmund Freud*, ed. James Strachey. London, The Hogarth Press and the Institute of Psycho-analysis, 1964, p. 113.
2. This is the translation given in a footnote in *The Standard Edition*, p. 113.
3. Heinrich Heine, *The North Sea*, trans. Vernon Watkins, New York, New Direction Books. 1951, p. 77.
4. In other words, the woman can never ask her own ontological question. The absurdity of such a situation within traditional discursive conventions can be demonstrated by substituting a 'young woman' for the 'young man' of Heine's poem.
5. As Oswald Ducrot and Tzvetan Todorov point out in *Encyclopedic Dictionary of the Sciences of Language*, trans. Catherine Porter, Baltimore and London, Johns Hopkins University Press, 1979, p. 195, the potentially universal understandability of the hieroglyphic is highly theoretical and can only be thought as the unattainable ideal of an imagistic system: 'It is important of course not to exaggerate either the resemblance of the image with the object – the design is stylized very rapidly – or the 'natural' and 'universal' character of the signs: Sumerian, Chinese, Egyptian and Hittite hieroglyphics for the same object have nothing in common.'
6. Ibid, p. 194. Emphasis mine.
7. See Noël Burch's film, *Correction Please, or How We Got Into Pictures*.
8. Laura Mulvey, 'Visual Pleasure and Narrative Cinema', *Screen*, Autumn 1975, vol. 16 no. 3, pp. 12–13.
9. Charles Affron, *Star Acting: Gish, Garbo, Davis*, New York, E.P. Dutton, 1977, pp. 281–2.
10. This argument focuses on the image to the exclusion of any consideration of the soundtrack primarily because it is the process of imaging which seems to constitute the major difficulty in theorising female spectatorship. The image is also popularly understood as metonymic signifier for the cinema as a whole and for good reason: historically, sound has been subordinate to the image within the dominant classical system. For more on the image/sound distinction in relation to sexual difference see my article, 'The Voice in the Cinema: The Articulation of Body and Space', *Yale French Studies*, no. 60, pp. 33–50.
11. Noël Burch, *Theory of Film Practice*, trans. Helen R. Lane, New York and Washington, Praeger Publishers, 1973, p. 35.
12. Christian Metz, 'The Imaginary Signifier', *Screen*, Summer 1975, vol. 16 no. 2, p. 60.
13. Ibid, p. 61.
14. Luce Irigaray, 'This Sex Which Is Not One', *New French Feminisms*, ed. Elaine Marks and Isabelle de Courtivron, Amherst, The University of Massachusetts Press, 1980, pp. 104–5.
15. Irigaray, 'Women's Exile', *Ideology and Consciousness*, no. 1 (May 1977), p. 74.
16. Hélène Cixous, 'The Laugh of the Medusa', *New French Feminisms*, p. 257.
17. Sarah Kofman, 'Ex: The Woman's Enigma', *Enclitic*, vol. IV no. 2 (Fall 1980), p. 20.
18. Michèle Montrelay, 'Inquiry into Femininity', *m/f*, no. 1 (1978), pp. 91–2.
19. Freud, 'Some Psychological Consequences of the Anatomical Distinction Between the Sexes', *Sexuality and the Psychology of Love*, ed. Philip Rieff, New York, Collier Books, 1963, pp. 187–8.
20. Freud, 'Femininity', op. cit., p. 125.
21. Freud, 'Some Psychological Consequences . . .', op. cit., p. 187.
22. Molly Haskell, *From Reverence to Rape*, Baltimore, Penguin Books, 1974, p. 154.
23. Irigaray, 'Women's Exile', op. cit., p. 65.
24. Mulvey, 'Afterthoughts ... inspired by Duel in the Sun', *Framework* (Summer 1981), p. 13.

25. Joan Riviere, 'Womanliness as a Masquerade', *Psychoanalysis and Female Sexuality*, ed. Hendrik M. Ruitenbeek, New Haven, College and University Press, 1966, p. 213. My analysis of the concept of masquerade differs markedly from that of Luce Irigaray. See *Ce sexe qui n'en est pas un* (Paris: Les Editions de Minuit, 1977), pp. 131–2. It also diverges to a great extent from the very important analysis of masquerade presented by Claire Johnston in 'Femininity and the Masquerade: Anne of the Indies', *Jacques Tourneur* London, British Film Institute, 1975, pp. 36–44. I am indebted to her for the reference to Riviere's article.
26. Moustafa Safouan, 'Is the Oedipus Complex Universal?', *m/f*, nos. 5–6 (1981), pp. 84–5.
27. Montrelay, op.cit., p. 93.
28. Silvia Bovenschen, 'Is There a Feminine Aesthetic?' *New German Critique*, no. 10 (Winter 1977), p. 129.
29. Montrelay, op.cit., p. 93.
30. Linda Williams, 'When the Woman Looks . . .', in *Revision: Feminist Essays in Film Criticism*, ed. Mary Ann Doane, Pat Mellencamp and Linda Williams, Los Angeles, American Film Institute, 1984.
31. Johnson, op. cit., p. 40.
32. Freud, *Jokes and Their Relation to the Unconscious*, trans. James Strachey, New York, W.W. Norton & Company, Inc., 1960, p. 99.
33. Ibid, p. 98.
34. Weston J. Naef, *Counterparts: Form and Emotion in Photographs*, New York, E. P. Dutton and the Metropolitan Museum of Art, 1982, pp. 48–9.
35. Ibid.
36. Michel Foucault, *The History of Sexuality*, trans. Robert Hurley, New York: Pantheon Books, 1978.

12

'WOMEN'S GENRES: MELODRAMA, SOAP OPERA AND THEORY'

Annette Kuhn

I

Television soap opera and film melodrama, popular narrative forms aimed at female audiences, are currently attracting a good deal of critical and theoretical attention. Not surprisingly, most of the work on these 'gynocentric' genres is informed by various strands of feminist thought on visual representation. Less obviously, perhaps, such work has also prompted a series of questions which relate to representation and cultural production in a more wide-ranging and thoroughgoing manner than a specifically feminist interest might suggest. Not only are film melodrama (and more particularly its subtype the 'woman's picture') and soap opera directed at female audiences, they are also actually enjoyed by millions of women. What is it that sets these genres apart from representations which possess a less gender-specific mass appeal?

One of the defining generic features of the woman's picture as a textual system is its construction of narratives motivated by female desire and processes of spectator identification governed by female point-of-view. Soap opera constructs woman-centred narratives and identifications, too, but it differs textually from its cinematic counterpart in certain other respects: not only do soaps never end, but their beginnings are soon lost sight of. And whereas in the woman's picture the narrative process is characteristically governed by the enigma-retardation-resolution structure which marks the classic narrative, soap opera narratives propose

*From *Screen* 25:1, 1984, pp. 18–28.

competing and intertwining plot lines introduced as the serial progresses. Each plot ... develops at a different pace, thus preventing any clear resolution of conflict. The completion of one story generally leads into others, and ongoing plots often incorporate parts of semi-resolved conflicts.[1]

Recent work on soap opera and melodrama has drawn on existing theories, methods and perspectives in the study of film and television, including the structural analysis of narratives, textual semiotics and psychoanalysis, audience research, and the political economy of cultural institutions. At the same time, though, some of this work has exposed the limitations of existing approaches, and in consequence been forced if not actually to abandon them, at least to challenge their characteristic problematics. Indeed, it may be contended that the most significant developments in film and television theory in general are currently taking place precisely within such areas of feminist concern as critical work on soap opera and melodrama.

In examining some of this work, I shall begin by looking at three areas in which particularly pertinent questions are being directed at theories of representation and cultural production. These are, first, the problem of gendered spectatorship; second, questions concerning the universalism as against the historical specificity of conceptualizations of gendered spectatorship; and third, the relationship between film and television texts and their social, historical and institutional contexts. Each of these concerns articulates in particular ways with what seems to me the central issue here – the question of the audience, or audiences, for certain types of cinematic and televisual representation.

II

Film theory's appropriation to its own project of Freudian and post-Freudian psychoanalysis places the question of the relationship between text and spectator firmly on the agenda. Given the preoccupation of psychoanalysis with sexuality and gender, a move from conceptualizing the spectator as a homogeneous and androgynous effect of textual operations[2] to regarding her or him as a gendered subject constituted in representation seems in retrospect inevitable. At the same time, the interests of feminist film theory and film theory in general converge at this point in a shared concern with sexual difference. Psychoanalytic accounts of the formation of gendered subjectivity raise the question, if only indirectly, of representation and feminine subjectivity. This in turn permits the spectator to be considered as a gendered subject position, masculine or feminine: and theoretical work on soap opera and the woman's picture may take this as a starting point for its inquiry into spectator – text relations. Do these 'gynocentric' forms address, or construct, a female or a feminine spectator? If so, how?

On the question of film melodrama, Laura Mulvey, commenting on King Vidor's *Duel in the Sun*,[3] argues that when, as in this film, a woman is at the centre of the narrative, the question of female desire structures the hermeneutic: 'what does *she* want?' This, says Mulvey, does not guarantee the constitution of the spectator as feminine so much as it implies a contradictory, and in the final instance impossible, 'phantasy of masculinisation' for the female spectator. This is in line with the author's earlier suggestion that cinema spectatorship involves masculine identification for spectators of either gender.[4] If cinema does thus construct a masculine subject, there can be no unproblematic feminine subject position for any spectator. Pam Cook, on the other hand, writing about a group of melodramas produced during the 1940s at the Gainsborough Studios, evinces greater optimism about the possibility of a feminine subject of classic cinema. She does acknowledge, though, that in a patriarchal society female desire and female point-of-view are highly contradictory, even if they have the potential to subvert culturally dominant modes of spectator – text relation. The character-istic 'excess' of the woman's melodrama, for example, is explained by Cook in terms of the genre's tendency to '[pose] problems for itself which it can scarcely contain'.[5]

Writers on television soap opera tend to take views on gender and spectator-ship rather different from those advanced by film theorists. Tania Modleski, for example, argues with regard to soaps that their characteristic narrative patterns, their foregrounding of 'female' skills in dealing with personal and domestic crises, and the capacity of their programme formats and scheduling to key into the rhythms of women's work in the home, all address a female spectator. Furthermore, she goes so far as to argue that the textual processes of soaps are in some respects similar to those of certain 'feminine' texts which speak to a decentred subject, and so are 'not altogether at odds with ... feminist aesthetics'.[6] Modleski's view is that soaps not only address female spectators, but in so doing construct feminine subject positions which transcend patriarchal modes of subjectivity.

Different though their respective approaches and conclusions may be, however, Mulvey, Cook and Modleski are all interested in the problem of gendered spectatorship. The fact, too, that this common concern is informed by a shared interest in assessing the progressive or transformative potential of soaps and melodramas is significant in light of the broad appeal of both genres to the mass audiences of women at which they are aimed.

But what precisely does it mean to say that certain representations are aimed at a female audience? However well theorized they may be, existing concep-tualizations of gendered spectatorship are unable to deal with this question. This is because spectator and audience are distinct concepts which cannot – as they frequently are – be reduced to one another. Although I shall be considering some of its consequences more fully below, it is important to note a further problem for film and television theory, posed in this case by the distinction between spectator and audience. Critical work on the woman's picture and on soap opera has necessarily, and most productively, emphasized the question of gendered spectatorship. In doing this, film theory in particular has taken on board a conceptualization of the spectator derived from psychoanalytic accounts of the formation of human subjectivity.

Such accounts, however, have been widely criticized for their universalism. Beyond, perhaps, associating certain variants of the Oedipus complex with family forms characteristic of a patriarchal society and offering a theory of the construction of gender, psychoanalysis seems to offer little scope for theorizing subjectivity in its cultural or historical specificity. Although in relation to the specific issues of spectatorship and representation there may, as I shall argue, be a way around this apparent impasse, virtually all film and television theory – its feminist variants included – is marked by the dualism of universalism and specificity.

Nowhere is this more evident than in the gulf between textual analysis and contextual inquiry. Each is done according to different rules and procedures, distinct methods of investigation and theoretical perspectives. In bringing to the fore the question of spectator–text relations, theories deriving from psycho-analysis may claim – to the extent that the spectatorial apparatus is held to be coterminous with the cinematic or televisual institution – to address the relationship between text and context. But as soon as any attempt is made to combine textual analysis with analysis of the concrete social, historical and institutional conditions of production and reception of texts, it becomes clear that the context of the spectator/subject of psychoanalytic theory is rather different from the context of production and reception constructed by con-junctural analyses of cultural institutions.

The disparity between these two 'contexts' structures Pam Cook's article on the Gainsborough melodrama, which sets out to combine an analysis of the characteristic textual operations and modes of address of a genre with an examination of the historical conditions of a particular expression of it. Gainsborough melodrama, says Cook, emerges from a complex of determi-nants, including certain features of the British film industry of the 1940s, the nature of the female cinema audience in the post World War II period, and the textual characteristics of the woman's picture itself.[7] While Cook is correct in pointing to the various levels of determination at work in this instance, her lengthy preliminary discussion of spectator–text relations and the woman's picture rather outbalances her subsequent investigation of the social and industrial contexts of the Gainsborough melodrama. The fact, too, that analysis of the woman's picture in terms of its interpellation of a female/feminine spectator is simply placed alongside a conjunctural analysis tends to vitiate any attempt to reconcile the two approaches, and so to deal with the broader issue of universalism as against historical specificity. But although the initial problem remains, Cook's article constitutes an important intervention in the debate because, in tackling the text–context split head-on, it necessarily exposes a key weakness of current film theory.

In work on television soap opera as opposed to film melodrama, the dualism of text and context manifests itself rather differently, if only because – unlike film theory – theoretical work on television has tended to emphasize the determining character of the contextual level, particularly the structure and organization of television institutions. Since this has often been at the expense of attention to the operation of television texts, television theory may perhaps be regarded as innovative in the extent to which it attempts to deal specifically with texts as well as contexts. Some feminist critical work has in fact already begun to address the question of television as text, though always with characteristic emphasis on the issue of gendered spectatorship. This emphasis constitutes a common concern of work on both television soaps and the woman's picture, but a point of contact between text and context in either medium emerges only when the concept of social audience is considered in distinction from that of spectator.

III

Each term – spectator and social audience – presupposes a different set of relations to representations and to the contexts in which they are received. Looking at spectators and at audiences demands different methodologies and theoretical frameworks, distinct discourses which construct distinct subjectivities and social relations. The *spectator*, for example, is a subject constituted in signification, interpellated by the film or television text. This does not necessarily mean that the spectator is merely an effect of the text, however, because modes of subjectivity which also operate outside spectator–text relations in film or television are activated in the relationship between spectators and texts.

This model of the spectator/subject is useful in correcting more deterministic communication models which might, say, pose the spectator not as actively constructing meaning but simply as a receiver and decoder of preconstituted 'messages'. In emphasizing spectatorship as a set of psychic relations and focusing on the relationship between spectator and text, however, such a model does disregard the broader social implications of filmgoing or televiewing. It is the social act of going to the cinema, for instance, that makes the individual cinemagoer part of an audience. Viewing television may involve social relations rather different from filmgoing, but in its own ways television does depend on individual viewers being part of an audience, even if its members are never in one place at the same time. A group of people seated in a single auditorium looking at a film, or scattered across thousands of homes watching the same television programme, is a *social audience*. The concept of social audience, as against that of spectator, emphasizes the status of cinema and television as social and economic institutions.

Constructed by discursive practices both of cinema and television and of social science, the social audience is a group of people who buy tickets at the box office, or who switch on their television sets: people who can be surveyed, counted and categorized according to age, sex and socioeconomic status.[8] The cost of a cinema ticket or television licence fee, or a readiness to tolerate commercial breaks, earns audiences the right to look at films and television programmes, and so to be spectators. Social audiences become spectators in the moment they engage in the processes and pleasures of meaning-making attendant on watching a film or television programme. The anticipated pleasure of spectatorship is perhaps a necessary condition of existence of audiences. In taking part in the social act of consuming representations, a group of spectators becomes a social audience.

The consumer of representations as audience member and spectator is involved in a particular kind of psychic and social relationship: at this point, a conceptualization of the cinematic or televisual apparatus as a regime of pleasure intersects with sociological and economic understandings of film and television as institutions. Because each term describes a distinct set of relationships, though, it is important not to conflate social audience with spectators. At the same time, since each is necessary to the other, it is equally important to remain aware of the points of continuity between the two sets of relations.

These conceptualizations of spectator and social audience have particular implications when it comes to a consideration of popular 'gynocentric' forms such as soap opera and melodrama. Most obviously, perhaps, these centre on the issue of gender, which prompts again the question: what does 'aimed at a female audience' mean? What exactly is being signalled in this reference to a gendered audience? Are women to be understood as a subgroup of the social audience, distinguishable through discourses which construct *a priori* gender categories? Or does the reference to a female audience allude rather to gendered spectatorship, to sexual difference constructed in relations between spectators and texts? Most likely it condenses the two meanings; but an examination of the distinction between them may nevertheless be illuminating in relation to the broader theoretical issues of texts, contexts, social audiences and spectators.

The notion of a female social audience, certainly as it is constructed in the discursive practices through which it is investigated, presupposes a group of individuals already formed as female. For the sociologist interested in such matters as gender and lifestyles, certain people bring a pre-existent femaleness to their viewing or film and television. For the business executive interested in selling commodities, television programmes and films are marketed to individuals already constructed as female. Both, however, are interested in the same kind of woman. On one level, then, soap operas and women's melodramas address themselves to a social audience of women. But they may at the same time be regarded as speaking to a female, or a feminine, spectator. If soaps and melodramas inscribe femininity in their address, women – as well as being already formed *for* such representations – are in a sense also formed *by* them.

In making this point, however, I intend no reduction of femaleness to femininity: on the contrary, I would hold to a distinction between femaleness as social gender and femininity as subject position. For example, it is possible for a female spectator to be addressed, as it were, 'in the masculine', and the converse is presumably also true. Nevertheless, in a culturally pervasive operation of ideology, femininity is routinely identified with femaleness and masculinity with maleness. Thus, for example, an address 'in the feminine' may be regarded in ideological terms as privileging, if not necessitating, a socially constructed female gender identity.

The constitutive character of both the woman's picture and the soap opera has in fact been noted by a number of feminist commentators. Tania Modleski, for instance, suggests that the characteristic narrative structures and textual operations of soap operas both address the viewer as an 'ideal mother' – ever-understanding, ever-tolerant of the weaknesses and foibles of others – and also posit states of expectation and passivity as pleasurable: 'the narrative, by placing ever more complex obstacles between desire and fulfilment, makes anticipation of an end an end in itself'.[9] In our culture, tolerance and passivity are regarded as feminine attributes, and consequently as qualities proper in women but not in men.

Charlotte Brunsdon extends Modleski's line of argument to the extratextual level: in constructing its viewers as competent within the ideological and moral frameworks of marriage and family life, soap opera, she implies, addresses both a feminine spectator and female audience.[10] Pointing to the centrality of intuition and emotion in the construction of the woman's point-of-view, Pam Cook regards the construction of a feminine spectator as a highly problematic and contradictory process: so that in the film melodrama's construction of female point-of-view, the validity of femininity as a subject position is necessarily laid open to question.[11]

This divergence on the question of gendered spectatorship within feminist theory is significant. Does it perhaps indicate fundamental differences between film and television in the spectator–text relations privileged by each? Do soaps and melodramas really construct different relations of gendered spectatorship, with melodrama constructing contradictory identifications in ways that soap opera does not? Or do these different positions on spectatorship rather signal an unevenness of theoretical development – or, to put it less teleologically, reflect the different intellectual histories and epistemological groundings of film theory and television theory?

Any differences in the spectator–text relations proposed respectively by soap opera and by film melodrama must be contingent to some extent on more general disparities in address between television and cinema. Thus film spectatorship, it may be argued, involves the pleasures evoked by looking in a more pristine way than does watching television. Whereas in classic cinema the concentration and involvement proposed by structures of the look, identification and point-of-view tend to be paramount, television spectatorship is more likely to be characterized by distraction and diversion.[12] This would suggest that each medium constructs sexual difference through spectatorship in rather different ways: cinema through the look and spectacle, and television – perhaps less evidently – through a capacity to insert its flow, its characteristic modes of address, and the textual operations of different kinds of programmes into the rhythms and routines of domestic activities and sexual divisions of labour in the household at various times of day.

It would be a mistake, however, simply to equate current thinking on spectator – text relations in each medium. This is not only because theoretical work on spectatorship as it is defined here is newer and perhaps not so highly developed for television as it has been for cinema, but also because conceptualizations of spectatorship in film theory and in television theory emerge from quite distinct perspectives. When feminist writers on soap opera and on film melodrama discuss spectatorship, therefore, they are usually talking about different things. This has partly to do with the different intellectual histories and methodological groundings of theoretical work on film and on television. Whereas most television theory has until fairly recently existed under the sociological rubric of media studies, film theory has on the whole been based in the criticism-oriented tradition of literary studies. In consequence, while the one tends to privilege contexts over texts, the other usually privileges texts over contexts.

However, some recent critical work on soap opera, notably work produced within a cultural studies context, does attempt a *rapprochement* of text and context. Charlotte Brunsdon, writing about the British soap opera *Crossroads*, draws a distinction between subject positions proposed by texts and a 'social subject' who may or may not take up these positions.[13] In considering the interplay of 'social reader and social text'. Brunsdon attempts to come to terms with problems posed by the universalism of the psychoanalytic model of the spectator/subject as against the descriptiveness and limited analytical scope of studies of specific instances and conjunctures. In taking up the instance of soap opera, then, one of Brunsdon's broader objectives is to resolve the dualism of text and context.

'Successful' spectatorship of a soap like *Crossroads*, it is argued, demands a certain cultural capital: familiarity with the plots and characters of a particular serial as well as with soap opera as a genre. It also demands wider cultural competence, especially in the codes of conduct of personal and family life. For Brunsdon, then, the spectator addressed by soap opera is constructed within culture rather than by representation. This, however, would indicate that such a spectator, a 'social subject', might – rather than being a subject in process of gender positioning – belong after all to a social audience already divided by gender.

The 'social subject' of this cultural model produces meaning by decoding messages or communications, an activity which is always socially situated.[14] Thus although such a model may move some way towards reconciling text and context, the balance of Brunsdon's argument remains weighted in favour of context: spectator – text relations are apparently regarded virtually as an effect of sociocultural contexts. Is there a way in which spectator/subjects of film and television texts can be thought in a historically specific manner, or indeed a way for the social audience to be rescued from social/historical determinism?

Although none of the feminist criticism of soap opera and melodrama reviewed here has come up with any solution to these problems, it all attempts, in some degree and with greater or lesser success, to engage with them. Brunsdon's essay possibly comes closest to an answer, paradoxically because its very failure to resolve the dualism which ordains that spectators are constructed by texts while audiences have their place in contexts begins to hint at a way around the problem. Although the hybrid 'social subject' may turn out to be more a social audience member than a spectator, this concept does suggest that a move into theories of discourse could prove productive.

Both spectators and social audience may accordingly be regarded as discursive constructs. Representations, contexts, audiences and spectators would then be seen as a series of interconnected social discourses, certain discourses possessing greater constitutive authority at specific moments than others. Such a model permits relative autonomy for the operations of texts, readings and contexts, and also allows for contradictions, oppositional readings and varying degrees of discursive authority. Since the state of a discursive formation is not constant, it can be apprehended only by means of inquiry into specific instances or conjunctures. In attempting to deal with the text – context split and to address the relationship between spectators and social audiences, therefore, theories of representation may have to come to terms with discursive formations of the social, cultural and textual.

IV

One of the impulses generating feminist critical and theoretical work on soap opera and the woman's picture is a desire to examine genres which are popular, and popular in particular with women. The assumption is usually that such popularity has to do mainly with the social audience: television soaps attract large numbers of viewers, many of them women, and in its heyday the woman's picture also drew in a mass female audience. But when the nature of this appeal is sought in the texts themselves or in relations between spectators and texts, the argument becomes rather more complex. In what specific ways do soaps and melodramas address or construct female/feminine spectators?

To some extent, they offer the spectator a position of mastery: this is certainly true as regards the hermeneutic of the melodrama's classic narrative, though perhaps less obviously so in relation to the soap's infinite process of narrativity. At the same time, they also place the spectator in a masochistic position of either – in the case of the woman's picture – identifying with a female character's renunciation or, as in soap opera, forever anticipating an endlessly held-off resolution. Culturally speaking, this combination of mastery and masochism in the reading competence constructed by soaps and melodramas suggests an interplay of masculine and feminine subject positions. Culturally dominant codes inscribe the masculine, while the feminine bespeaks a 'return of the repressed' in the form of codes which may well transgress culturally dominant subject positions, though only at the expense of proposing a position of subjection for the spectator.

At the same time, it is sometimes argued on behalf of both soap opera and film melodrama that in a society whose representations of itself are governed by the masculine, these genres at least raise the possibility of female desire and female point-of-view. Pam Cook advances such a view in relation to the woman's picture, for example.[15] But how is the oppositional potential of this to be assessed? Tania Modleski suggests that soap opera is 'in the vanguard not just of TV art but of all popular narrative art'.[16] But such a statement begs the question: in what circumstances can popular narrative art itself be regarded as transgressive? Because texts do not operate in isolation from contexts, any answer to these questions must take into account the ways in which popular narratives are read, the conditions under which they are produced and consumed, and the ends to which they are appropriated. As most feminist writing on soap opera and the woman's melodrama implies, there is ample space in the articulation of these various instances for contradiction and for struggles over meaning.

The popularity of television soap opera and film melodrama with women raises the question of how it is that sizeable audiences of women relate to these representations and the institutional practices of which they form part. It provokes, too, a consideration of the continuity between women's interpellation as spectators and their status as a social audience. In turn, the distinction between social audience and spectator/subject, and attempts to explore the relationship between the two, are part of a broader theoretical endeavour: to deal in tandem with texts and contexts. The distinction between social audience and spectator must also inform debates and practices around cultural production, in which questions of context and reception are always paramount. For anyone interested in feminist cultural politics, such considerations will necessarily inform any assessment of the place and the political usefulness of popular genres aimed at, and consumed by, mass audiences of women.

NOTES

1. Muriel G. Cantor and Suzanne Pingree, *The Soap Opera*, Beverly Hills, Sage Publications, 1983, p. 22. Here 'soap opera' refers to daytime (US) or early evening (UK) serials, not prime-time serials like *Dallas* and *Dynasty*.
2. See Jean-Louis Baudry, 'Ideological Effects of the Basic Cinematographic Apparatus', *Film Quarterly*, 1974–5, vol. 28, no. 2, pp. 39–47; Christian Metz, 'The Imaginary Signifier', *Screen*, Summer 1975, vol. 16, no. 2, pp. 14–76.
3. Laura Mulvey, 'Afterthoughts on "Visual Pleasure and Narrative Cinema" ... Inspired by *Duel in the Sun*', *Framework*, 1981, nos. 15–17, pp. 12–15.
4. Laura Mulvey, 'Visual Pleasure and Narrative Cinema', originally published in *Screen*, Autumn 1975, vol. 16, no. 3, pp. 6–18.
5. Pam Cook, 'Melodrama and the Women's Picture', in Sue Aspinall and Robert Murphy (eds), *Gainsborough Melodrama*, London, British Film Institute, 1983, p. 17.
6. Tania Modleski, *Loving with a Vengeance: Mass Produced Fantasies for Women*, Hamden Connecticut, Shoe String Press, 1982, p. 105. See also Tania Modleski, 'The Search for Tomorrow in Today's Soap Operas', *Film Quarterly*, 1979, vol. 33, no. 1, pp. 12–21.
7. Cook, op. cit.
8. Methods and findings of social science research on the social audience for American daytime soap operas are discussed in Cantor and Pingree, op. cit., chapter 7.

9. Modleski, *Loving with a Vengeance*, op. cit., p. 88.
10. Charlotte Brunsdon, '*Crossroads*: Notes on Soap Opera', *Screen*, Winter 1981, vol. 22, no. 4, pp. 32–7.
11. Cook, op. cit., p. 19.
12. John Ellis, *Visible Fictions*, London, Routledge & Kegan Paul, 1982.
13. Brunsdon, op. cit., p. 32.
14. A similar model is also adopted by Dorothy Hobson in *Crossroads: The Drama of a Soap Opera*, London, Methuen, 1982.
15. Cook, op. cit.; E. Ann Kaplan takes a contrary position in 'Theories of Melodrama: a Feminist Perspective', *Women and Performance: a Journal of Feminist Theory*, 1983, vol. 1, no. 1, pp. 40–8.
16. Modleski, *Loving with a Vengeance*, op. cit., p. 87.

PART III
FURTHER READING

Bergstrom, Janet and Doane, Mary Ann 1989: The Female Spectator: Contexts and Directions. *Camera Obscura* 20–1 pp. 5–27.

Doane, Mary Ann 1991 (1988–9): Masquerade Reconsidered: Further Thoughts on the Female Spectator. In *Femmes Fatales: Feminism, Film Theory, Psychoanalysis*. New York and London: Routledge pp. 33–43.

Erens, Patricia (ed.) 1990: *Issues in Feminist Film Criticism*. Bloomington and Indianapolis: Indiana University Press.

Gamman, Lorraine and Marshment, Margaret (ed.) 1988: *The Female Gaze: Women as Viewers of Popular Culture*. London: The Women's Press.

Gledhill, Christine (ed.) 1987: *Home is Where the Heart is: Studies in Melodrama and the Woman's Film*. London: BFI.

Kaplan, E. Ann 1983: *Women and Film: Both Sides of the Camera*. New York and London: Methuen.

Kuhn, Annette 1982: *Women's Pictures: Feminism and Cinema*. London: Routledge & Kegan Paul.

Mayne, Judith 1990: *Woman at the Keyhole: Feminism and Women's Cinema*. Bloomington and Indianapolis: Indiana University Press.

Mayne, Judith 1993: *Cinema and Spectatorship*. London and New York: Routledge.

Mulvey, Laura 1989: *Visual and Other Pleasures*. Basingstoke and London: Macmillan.

Mulvey, Laura 1989: British Feminist Film Theory's Female Spectators: Presence and Absence. *Camera Obscura* 20/21, pp. 68–81.

Pribram, E. Deidre (ed.) 1988: *Female Spectators: Looking at Film and Television*. London and New York: Verso.

Riviere, Joan 1986 (1929): Womanliness as a Masquerade. In Burgin, V., Donald, J. and Kaplan, C. (eds), *Formations of Fantasy*. London and New York: Routledge, pp. 35–44.

Screen 1992: *The Sexual Subject: A* Screen *Reader in Sexuality*. London and New York: Routledge.

Stacey, Jackie 1994: *Star Gazing: Hollywood Cinema and Female Spectatorship*. London and New York: Routledge.

Thornham, Sue 1997: Female Spectators, Melodrama and the 'Woman's Film'. In *Passionate Detachments: An Introduction to Feminist Film Theory*. London: Arnold, pp. 45–66.

Walsh, Andrea S. 1984: *Women's Film and Female Experience 1940–1950*. New York and London: Praeger.

Williams, Linda 1984: When the Woman Looks. In Doane, M.A., Mellencamp, P., and Williams, L. (eds), *Re-Vision: Essays in Feminist Film Criticism*. Los Angeles: American Film Institute, pp. 83–99.

PART IV
TEXTUAL NEGOTIATIONS

INTRODUCTION

In her 1978 essay, 'Recent Developments in Feminist Criticism', Christine Gledhill expressed her sense of unease at the direction taken by 1970s feminist film theory. Like the participants in the 'Women and Film' discussion (Chapter 9), she was concerned at the distance between the theoretical work being produced by feminist film critics and the kind of knowledge that would be 'really useful' to a feminist politics. As a socialist-feminist, she felt the need to close the gap between 'current theories of culture' and 'political practice', and between the readings of films made by feminist film theorists and the ways in which these films are 'understood and used by women at large' (Gledhill 1978: 457; 461). It is a concern that was to lead her, as it did Annette Kuhn (Chapter 12), away from what she calls 'cine-psychoanalysis', and towards an engagement with the perspectives emerging in the 1970s within British cultural studies.

Under the directorship of Stuart Hall (1968–79), the Centre for Contemporary Cultural Studies (CCCS) at Birmingham University inaugurated an interdisciplinary study of popular culture that sought to combine textual analysis with a focus on historical and social context. What was needed, argued Hall, was a model of the text–viewer relationship that would account for the whole of the communicative process, not just for texts, or for 'effects' on audiences. In his 1973 paper, 'Encoding and Decoding in the Television Discourse', Hall describes this process as operating through three linked but distinctive 'moments'. The first is the moment of production (or 'encoding'), the second is that of the text, and the third is the moment of reception (or 'decoding'). Each is envisaged as the site of a struggle over meaning: the meanings given to an event or narrative ('encoded') by the producers; the meanings embodied in the text;

and the meanings read ('decoded') by the audience/spectator' (Hall 1980: 128). It is this model which, in her 1988 essay, 'Pleasurable Negotiations', Christine Gledhill appropriates for a feminist analysis.

'Meaning', she argues, 'is neither imposed, not passively imbibed, but arises out of a struggle or negotiation between competing frames of reference, motivation and experience. This can be analysed at three different levels: institutions, texts and audiences'. Gledhill's own focus is on the film text, and in particular on the way in which popular texts may become the site of 'a struggle between male and female voices over the meaning of the symbol "woman"' (1987: 37). If 'woman' is a sign, Gledhill argues, she is a sign whose meaning is not fixed, but competed over by the different social groups who have a stake in that struggle. And the traces of that struggle are evident in the text, in whose 'negotiations' we can distinguish both 'the patriarchal *symbol* of "woman"' and 'discourses which speak from and to the historical socio-cultural experience of "women"'. But if the text does not present a single position from which it must be understood, as 'cine-psychoanalysis' might suggest, it is still the case that as viewers we use the identifications it offers us in order to construct and confirm our own sense of identity. It is the task of the feminist critic to ask what range of positions the text makes available, a task to which the knowledge gained from studies of the audience can contribute. But such a task, argues Gledhill, is not neutral. The feminist critic is 'interested in some readings more than others': her own interpretation is also an intervention into the process of meaning-negotiation. Seeking to 'draw the text into a female and/or feminist orbit', the critic offers a reading that will then become subject, in its turn, to further 'negotiation'.

Despite her adoption of a cultural studies perspective, the focus of Christine Gledhill's work is still on the film text. As Jackie Stacey has observed, most cultural studies work on audiences has concentrated on television, and most feminist work on film focuses on the text. Writing in 1994, Stacey comments that if feminists looking at television have over-emphasised the audience, 'in feminist film criticism the exploration of women as cinema spectators has barely begun'. What is needed, argues Stacey, is 'an interactive model of text/audience/context to account for the complexity of the viewing process' – a model which should also incorporate a concept of the spectator as historically situated (1994: 47). Such a model requires a shift in research methodology to one that considers audiences as well as texts. In consequence, it must also address the political and ethical questions raised by the feminist researcher's role as interpreter (and judge?) of female audiences, their pleasures and their readings, questions that can be evaded by the textual critic, whose judgements remain more safely focused upon the text. The remaining three chapters in this section all work in some way towards the construction of such a model, seeking to bridge the gap between psychoanalytic theory and audience studies, between theories of unconscious identificatory processes and models of cultural negotiation.

Valerie Walkerdine's (1986) 'Video Replay: Families, Film and Fantasy' analyses the video viewing of *Rocky II* (1979) by a working-class family, the

Coles, combining this with a critique of Walkerdine's own role as academic 'spectator' of this process. Walkerdine opposes 'universalistic' models of cinema spectatorship, distinguishing between the textual position produced for the spectator by the film text and the actual spectator who is positioned in more complex ways. Her methodology brings together psychoanalytic theory and ethnography in an analysis of the relation between fantasy and lived social practices. For Mr Cole, she argues, *Rocky II* offers fantasies of 'omnipotence, heroism and salvation' which are the product of a very specific male working-class experience of oppression and powerlessness. As fantasies, these are not, however, separate from Mr Cole's everyday life. The fantasy of masculinity as 'fighting/being a fighter' structures Mr Cole's conscious self-identification and regulates his domestic relations, as well as reaching back into his unconscious as 'a defence against powerlessness, a defence against femininity'.

Walkerdine's analysis of Mr Cole's daughter Joanne ('Dodo') draws on her own childhood experiences. Mr Cole's infantilization of his daughter as 'Dodo' confirms his self-identification as a 'fighter' on her behalf, but it also creates a fantasy identification for Joanne, one which is, however, 'fractured', since she is seen by Mr Cole both as the fragile and feminine 'Dodo' and as a working-class 'fighter' like himself. Joanne, like Walkerdine before her, must somehow inhabit such a fractured identity. The 'fantasy-structure' of *Rocky II*, then, not only intersects with the specific subject positionings of the members of the Cole family in different ways; it also helps structure the power relations within the family. Walkerdine's final point is that the researcher/observer, too, is a viewer/ voyeur. She too occupies a fantasy space, one in which fictions of 'knowledge' and 'truth' mask complex desires and struggles.

Walkerdine's combination of ethnography with psychoanalytic theory marks an important break with existing divisions between 'textual spectators' and 'social audiences'. Its textual reading of *Rocky II* remains undeveloped, however, as does its account of exactly how fantasy, power relations and gendered subjectivity intersect within the family and its members. A final difficulty is that her foregrounding of the autobiographical may be a solution to the tendency of academic analyses to produce 'fictions' of knowledge that seek to obscure their own origins, but it has the uncomfortable effect of shifting the focus of research away from the spectator–film relation and on to the researcher herself.

Jackie Stacey's research, too, seeks to bring together what she sees as the antagonistic traditions of feminist film theory and cultural studies audience research. Her study of British female spectators' memories of Hollywood stars of the 1940s and 1950s, summarised in the chapter reproduced here, investigates how the processes of cinematic spectatorship 'produce and reform feminine identities', identities which she sees as always 'in process', continually being transformed. Like Walkerdine, she asks how spectators' fantasies and desires are formed differently within specific contexts and seeks to investigate the relationship between psychic and social formations.

The material for Stacey's ethnographic study comes from responses to an advertisement placed in two women's magazines inviting readers to write to her about memories of their favourite stars. Insisting both that ' "identity", be it gender, nationality or ethnicity, should be seen as partial, provisional and constantly "in process" ' and that 'identities are fixed by particular discourses, however unsuccessfully, temporarily or contradictorily' (1994: 226), Stacey argues from her research that the ideal images of Hollywood's female stars function as one such discourse. Her examination of her respondents' memories of such stars suggests the ways in which this relationship between stars and spectators involves the 'complex negotiation of self and other, image and ideal, and subject and object' (1994: 227).

Her analysis focuses centrally on a rethinking of the concept of identification, a concept more often theorised in terms of unconscious processes and studied via textual analysis. Like Walkerdine, Stacey considers both *'identificatory fantasies'* and *'identificatory practices'*. The former, she argues relate to cinematic processes of spectatorship, and involve fantasised negotiations of boundaries between self and ideal. The latter extend into the everyday lives of spectators and involve active use of the star image to transform the spectator's own sense of identity. The concept of identification is here expanded from its use within psychoanalytic theory to become a more active and diverse process of negotiation. As such, it does not operate simply to confirm or fix existing gendered identities, as psychoanalytic theory might suggest. It can also involve processes of transformation and the production of new, perhaps more contingent, partial and fragmented identities.

The final chapter in this section takes us from a focus on private identificatory fantasies and practices to the public discourses that shape the range of possible readings and interpretive strategies available to us at any historical moment. Here Janet Staiger applies what she calls 'historical reception studies' to the cultural event – or set of socially produced interpretations – that was the release of the 1991 film, *Silence of the Lambs* and the resultant 'outing' of its star, Jodie Foster.

Staiger's 'historical reception studies' draws on Hall's 'encoding/decoding' model, but broadens his original conceptualising of the reception process via its use of discourse rather than ideology as its organising principle. Staiger traces, then, the range of reading strategies drawn on by US reviewers that led to the figuring of Starling/Foster as lesbian both by critics and – though with very different inflections – by gay activists. Her analysis draws on contemporary critical and cultural theory – psychoanalysis, literary and film theory, for example – in order to understand not the text itself but the range of cultural meanings available for its reading.

Staiger's material, then, is not the film itelf but press reviews and articles. But her move 'beyond text-centred analyses' is also implicitly a theory of the text. Meaning, she writes, is not immanent in the text. It is constructed in the context of specific social formations and individual identities-in-process. Nor, because of the contradictory nature of discursive formations at any given historical moment, can any reading be unified, 'correct' or whole. Her focus is on the range of possible readings, their determinants – textual and extratextual – and what they suggest about contemporary cultural understandings.

Staiger's work, like that of Walkerdine and Stacey, raises particular theoretical and methodological issues. 'Interpreting interpretations', as she comments, 'is viciously circular'. It raises questions about the status of the interpreter's reading, about its theoretical and political basis, and about the material used. Both the public discourse of the review and the private discourse of directly elicited audience response are caught up in processes of (re-)construction, mediation, framing and re-framing. Whatever else they give us, they do not give us access to how the film works. Whilst all three writers are acutely aware of these issues, it remains a source of some unease for the feminist film theorist that, whether seen as source of identificatory fantasy/practice or as cultural event, film as text tends in these accounts to slip out of focus altogether.

NOTES

1. Hall's original concept envisaged audience readings as falling into three groups. The 'preferred' or 'dominant' reading adopts the ideological framework foregrounded by the text. The 'negotiated' reading adopts its broad outlines but negotiates on detail. The 'oppositional' reading adopts a critical stance towards the text's ideological framework. If, however, we view audience readings as framed instead by the range of discourses – or culturally available organisations of meaning – operating within a social formation at any particular moment, our model of audience readings becomes much more open and more complex. See Macdonell 1986.

REFERENCES

Gledhill, Christine 1978: Recent Developments in Feminist Criticism. *Quarterly Review of Film Studies* 3, 4, pp. 457–93.

Gledhill, Christine 1987: The Melodramatic Field: An Investigation. In Gledhill, *Home is Where the Heart is: Studies in Melodrama and the Woman's Film*. London: BFI, pp. 5–39.

Hall, Stuart 1980: Encoding/decoding. In Hall, S., Hobson, D., Lowe, A. and Willis, P. (eds), *Culture, Media, Language*. London: Hutchinson, 1980 pp. 128–138.

Macdonell, Diane 1986: *Theories of Discourse: An Introduction*. Oxford: Blackwell.

Stacey, Jackie 1994: *Star Gazing: Hollywood Cinema and Female Spectatorship*. London and New York: Routledge.

13

'PLEASURABLE NEGOTIATIONS'

Christine Gledhill

This essay takes as its starting-point the recent renewal of feminist interest in mainstream popular culture. Whereas the ideological analysis of the late 1970s and early 1980s, influenced by post-structuralism and cine-psychoanalysis, had rejected mainstream cinema for its production of patriarchal/bourgeois spectatorship and simultaneous repression of femininity, other approaches, developing in parallel, and sometimes in opposition to, psychoanalytic theories argued for socio-culturally differentiated modes of meaning production and reading.[1] Feminist analysis has focused in particular on forms directed at women. While feminist literary criticism recovers women's fiction – both Victorian and contemporary, written by women and/or for women – feminist work on film and television has particularly explored the woman's film, melodrama and soap opera.[2] A frequent aim of this enterprise, which relates commonly derided popular forms to the conditions of their consumption in the lives of socio-historically constituted audiences, is to elucidate women's cultural forms, and thereby to challenge the male canon of cultural worth. In this respect, feminist analysis of the woman's film and soap opera is beginning to counter more negative cine-psychoanalytic views of female spectatorship.

CINE-PSYCHOANALYSIS AND FEMINISM

The theoretical convergence of psychoanalysis and cinema has been problematic for feminism in that it has been theorised largely from the perspective of

* From Pribram, E. D. (ed.), *Female Spectators: Looking at Film and Television*. London and New York: Verso, 1988, pp. 64–77.

masculinity and its constructions. Notions of cinematic voyeurism and fetishism serve as norms for the analysis of classic narrative cinema, and early cine-psychoanalysis found it difficult to theorize the feminine as anything other than 'lack', 'absence', 'otherness'. Underpinning these concepts lay the homology uncovered between certain features of cinematic spectatorship and textual organization, and the Oedipal psycho-linguistic scenario theorized by Jacques Lacan in which the child simultaneously acquires identity, language and the Unconscious.[3] In this structure, the child's perception of sexual difference as the maternal figure's castration and the consequent repression of this perception are linked to the similarly hidden role of phonological and linguistic difference in the operation of language and production of meaning (it is the difference between 't' and 'd' that enables the formation of different words, and the difference between 'sheep' and 'mutton' that enables meaning to arise from such linguistic forms). This homology between the psychic and the linguistic, it is argued, enables the (male) child both to enter the symbolic order and to master language. It also, however, results in the repression of femininity. Thus the patriarchal subject is constructed as a unified, consistent, but illusory identity – a 'self' whose words appear to give it control of a world to which it is central. (In this respect, the identity of the patriarchal subject coalesces with the centrality of the 'individual' in bourgeois ideology.) Underlying these constructs there exists another reality – language and subjectivity as processes that produce each other, ever in flux, and based in linguistic and psychic 'difference'. Self, speech and meaning can never coincide with each other and fail to provide more than the illusion of mastery. For both bourgeois and patriarchal subjects, 'difference' – gender, sex, class, race, age, and so on – is alienated as 'otherness' and repressed. The repressed threatens to return, however, through the processes of the 'Unconscious'.

According to cine-psychoanalysis, classic narrative cinema reproduces such psycho-linguistic and ideological structures, offering the surface illusion of unity, plenitude and identity as compensation for the underlying realities of separation and difference.[4] The subject of mainstream narrative is the patri-archal, bourgeois individual: that unified, centred point from which the world is organized and given meaning. Narrative organization hierarchizes the different aesthetic and ideological discourses which intersect in the processes of the text, to produce a unifying, authoritative voice or viewpoint. This is the position – constructed outside the processes of contradiction, difference and meaning production – which the spectator must occupy in order to participate in the pleasures and meaning of the text.

Since in this argument narrative organization is patriarchal, the spectator constructed by the text is masculine. Pleasure is largely organized to flatter or console the patriarchal ego and its Unconscious. Simultaneous sublimation and repression of femininity is literally re-enacted in the way plot and camera place the female figure in situations of fetishistic idealization or voyeuristic punish-ment. This has led to the argument that female representations do not represent women at all, but are figures cut to the measure of the patriarchal Unconscious.

In particular the 'look' of the camera – mediated through the 'gaze' of a generally male hero – has been identified as male.[5] While these arguments have attracted feminists for their power to explain the alternate misogyny and idealization of cinema's female representations, they offer largely negative accounts of female spectatorship, suggesting colonized, alienated or masochistic positions of identification. Moreover, given the absorption of class struggle within patriarchal narrative structures – the textual spectator is a trans-class construct – this perspective has difficulty in dealing with the female image or spectator in terms of class difference.

While the theoretical gap between textual and social subject may seem unproblematic when considering male spectatorship – perhaps because the account of the male spectator fits our experience of the social subject – this distinction is crucial for feminist criticism, with its investment in cultural and political change for women in society. The psycho-linguistic location of the feminine in the repressed semiotic processes of signification leads to the advocacy of the 'feminine' avant-garde or the 'deconstructive' text as a means of countering the patriarchal mainstream. Such works, it is argued, counteract the power of the classic narrative text to reduce the play of semiotic and sexual difference to the 'fixed position' and 'identity' of the patriarchal subject. The avant-garde or deconstructive text foregrounds the means of its construction, refuses stable points of identification, puts 'the subject into process' and invites the spectator into a play with language, form and identity. The more politically tendentious work literally 'deconstructs' the text, taking it apart to expose the mechanisms of mainstream narrative.[6] However, such procedures do not, in my view, avoid the problems of positioning. While the political avant-garde audience deconstructs the pleasures and identities offered by the mainstream text, it participates in the comforting identity of critic or *cognoscente*, positioned in the sphere of 'the ideologically correct', and the 'radical' – a position which is defined by its difference from the ideological mystification attributed to the audiences of the mass media. This suggests that the political problem is not positioning as such, but which positions are put on offer, or audiences enter into.

Recent initiatives in feminist film theory – drawing on the work of feminist psychoanalysts and social psychologists such as Luce Irigaray, Julia Kristeva, Nancy Chodorow and Dorothy Dinnerstein – have made possible considerable revisions to the cine-psychoanalytic construction of the classic narrative text, faciliating attempts to take account of the 'female spectator'.[7] However, as Annette Kuhn points out, this work draws on theoretically divergent analytical approaches. 'Female spectatorship' elides conceptually distinct notions: the 'feminine spectator', constructed by the text, and the female audience, constructed by the socio-historical categories of gender, class, race, and so on.[8] The question now confronting feminist theory is how to conceive their relationship.

One approach to the problem of their elision is to question the identification of mainstream narrative structures with patriarchal/bourgeois ideology on which it is based. For while avant-garde practices may produce a spectator 'fixed' in the avant-garde, recent work suggests that the textual possibilities of resistant or deconstructive reading exist in the processes of the mainstream text. To pursue this avenue, however, we require a theory of texts which can also accommodate the historical existence of social audiences. For 'femininity' is not simply an abstract textual position; and what women's history tells us about femininity lived as a socio-culturally, as well as a psychically differentiated category, must have consequences for our understanding of the formation of feminine subjectivity, of the feminine textual spectator and the viewing/reading of female audiences. Work on women's cultural forms, female audiences and female spectatorship poses this problem in acute form.

CULTURE AS NEGOTIATION

Arguments which support the notion of a specific, socio-historically constructed female cultural space come from diverse intellectual contexts and traditions and do not yet form a coherent theory. A range of concepts have been drawn on, including sub-cultural reading, cultural competence, decoding position and so on. A notion frequently deployed in various contexts is that of 'negotiation'.[9] It is the purpose of this piece to suggest that this concept might take a central place in rethinking the relations between media products, ideologies and audiences – perhaps bridging the gap between textual and social subject. The value of this notion lies in its avoidance of an overly deterministic view of cultural production, whether economistic (the media product reflects dominant economic interests outside the text), or cine-psychoanalytic (the text constructs spectators through the psycho-linguistic mechanisms of the patriarchal Unconscious). For the term 'negotiation' implies the holding together of opposite sides in an ongoing process of give-and-take. As a model of meaning production, negotiation conceives cultural exchange as the intersection of processes of production and reception, in which overlapping but non-matching determinations operate. Meaning is neither imposed, nor passively imbibed, but arises out of a struggle or negotiation between competing frames of reference, motivation and experience. This can be analysed at three different levels: institutions, texts and audiences – although distinctions between levels are ones of emphasis, rather than of rigid separation.

A theory of 'negotiation' as a tool for analysing meaning production would draw on a number of tenets of neo-Marxism, semiotics and psychoanalysis, while at the same time challenging the textual determinism and formalism of these approaches in the ideological analyses of the 1970s. In place of 'dominant ideology' – with its suggestion either of conspiratorial imposition or of unconscious interpellation – the concept of 'hegemony', as developed by Antonio Gramsci, underpins the model of negotiation.[10] According to Gramsci, since ideological power in bourgeois society is as much a matter of persuasion as of force, it is never secured once and for all, but has continually to be re-established in a constant to and fro between contesting groups. 'Hegemony' describes the ever shifting, ever negotiating play of ideological, social and political forces through which power is maintained and contested. The culture industries of bourgeois democracy can be conceptualized in a similar way: ideologies are not simply imposed – although this possibility always remains an institutional option through mechanisms such as censorship – but are subject to continuous (re-)negotiation.

INSTITUTIONAL NEGOTIATIONS

The economics and ideologies of the 'free market' produce a contradictory situation which lays capitalist production open to the necessity of negotiation. Terry Lovell argues that the search for new markets requires new products, exchanged for a range of ever extending use-values.[11] But these values vary according to particular groups of users and contexts of use. Even consumer products such as cars or washing-machines, which might seem predictable and amenable to ideological control (through advertising, for instance), may have unforeseen social and cultural uses for specific social groups.[12] If this is true of consumer products, then the use values of media texts (which lie in a complex of pleasures and meanings operating at different levels – aesthetic, emotional, ideological, intellectual) are far less easily predicted and controlled. Thus the use-value to a particular group of a profitable (in the short-term) media product may be in contradiction with the ideologies which in the long term maintain capitalism. An obvious example of this is the publishing industry, for certain branches of which Marxist and feminist books make profitable commodities.

Negotiation at the point of production is not, however, simply a matter of potential contradiction between the needs of the media industries and user groups. Within media institutions, the professional and aesthetic practices of 'creative' personnel operate within different frameworks from, and often in conflict with, the economic or ideological purposes of companies and share-holders. Such conflict is, indeed, part of the ideology of creativity itself. Aesthetic practice includes, as well as formal and generic traditions, codes of professional and technical performance, of cultural value and, moreover, must satisfy the pressure towards contemporary renewal and innovation. These traditions, codes and pressures produce their own conflicts which media professionals must attempt to solve.

An example of the kind of negotiation provoked by the inherent contra-dictoriness of the media industries is offered in Julie D'Acci's chronicle of struggles over the American television series, *Cagney and Lacey*, between CBS network executives and their advertisers, its independent writing/producing team (two women friends, plus a husband) and sections of the American women's movement.[13] According to D'Acci, the series would not have originated without the public spread of ideas circulated by the women's movement – with which the producing trio identified and which could be called on in times of trouble to support the programme. What made the series saleable was not its incipient 'feminism', but the innovation of a female buddy pairing in the cop show – an idea inspired by Molly Haskell's critique of the 1960s–1970s male buddy movie for its displacement of good female roles.[14] The series, however, despite successful ratings and an Emmy award, had been under frequent threat of cancellation from CBS, in large part, D'Acci argues, because of the problematic definitions of 'woman' and female sexuality that it invokes, particularly in relation to the unmarried Christine Cagney, whose fierce independence and intense relation to another woman has led to three changes of actress in an effort to bring the series under control and reduce the charge of lesbianism – something such strategies have singularly failed to do.

TEXTUAL NEGOTIATIONS

The example of *Cagney and Lacey* suggests how the product itself becomes a site of textual negotiation. Contradictory pressures towards programming that is both recognizably familiar (that conforms to tradition, to formal or generic convention) and also innovative and realistic (offering a twist on, or modernizing, traditional genres) leads to complex technical, formal and ideological negotiations in mainstream media texts. For example, the decision by the makers of *Cagney and Lacey* to put a female buddy pair inside a cop series, as well as using gender reversal to breathe new life into an established genre, immediately raises aesthetic and ideological problems. Conflicting codes of recognition are demanded by the different generic motifs and stereotypes drawn into the series: the cop show, the buddy relationship, the woman's film, the independent heroine. Moreover, the female 'buddy' relationship can be 'realistically' constructed only by drawing on the sub-cultural codes of women's social intercourse and culture. Inside a soap opera, such codes are taken for granted. Inside a police series, however, they have a range of consequences for both genre and ideology. When female protagonists have to operate in a fictional world organized by male authority and criminality, gender conflict is inevitable. But the series could not evoke such gender conflict with any credibility if it did not acknowledge discourses about sexism already made public by the women's movement in America. Such discourses in their turn become an inevitable source of drama and ideological explanation. The plotting of *Cagney and Lacey* is itself made out of a negotiation, or series of negotiations, around definitions of gender roles and sexuality, definitions of heterosexual relations and female friendships, as well as around the nature of the law and policing.

Crucial to such a conception of the text are the semiotic notions of textual production, work and process. According to this perspective, meanings are not fixed entities to be deployed at the will of a communicator, but products of textual interactions shaped by a range of economic, aesthetic and ideological factors that often operate unconsciously, are unpredictable and difficult to control.

RECEPTION AS NEGOTIATION

To the institutional and aesthetic vagaries of production is added the frequent diminution of textual control at the third level of media analysis – reception. The viewing or reading situation affects the meanings and pleasures of a work by introducing into the cultural exchange a range of determinations, potentially resistant or contradictory, arising from the differential social and cultural constitution of readers or viewers – by class, gender, race, age, personal history, and so on. This is potentially the most radical moment of negotiation, because the most variable and unpredictable. Moreover we are not dealing with solitary viewers or readers. Ien Ang and Janice Radway, writing respectively on soap opera viewing and romance reading, discuss viewing and reading as a social practice, which differs between groups and historical periods and shapes the meanings which audiences derive from cultural products. This line of argument points beyond textual analysis, to the field of anthropological and ethnographic work with 'real' audiences.[15]

A frequent aim of this research is to rescue the female sub-cultural activity, resistance and pleasure that may be embedded in popular, mainstream culture. However, to start from the perspective of audiences and their putative pleasures is not without problems of its own. Such an approach is open to charges of relativism – in other words, there is no point to ideological analysis because meaning is so dependent on variable contexts. Or it may be accused of populism – a media product cannot be critiqued if audiences demonstrably enjoy it.[16] Counter-readings of popular texts often get caught up in arguments about whether particular films or television programmes are 'progressive' or 'subversive'. And concern with the pleasures or identifications of actual audiences seems to ignore the long-term task of overthrowing dominant structures, within which resistant or emergent voices struggle on unequal terms. In any case, it is often argued, capitalism cannot ignore the potential market represented by groups emerging into new public self-identity and its processes invariably turn alternative life-styles and identities into commodities, through which they are subtly modified and thereby recuperated for the status quo. Thus the media appropriate images and ideas circulating within the women's movement to supply a necessary aura of novelty and contemporaneity. In this process, bourgeois society adapts to new pressures, while at the same time bringing them under control.[17] To such criticisms, cine-psychoanalysis adds the argument that approaches from the perspective of the audience ignore the role of language and the Unconscious in the construction of subjectivity, assuming that external socio-economic or cultural determinations provide material for the class or gender consciousness of otherwise free-thinking subjects.

To characterize cultural exchange between text and reader as one of negotiation, however, does not necessitate a return to an economistic view of language and cultural form as transparent instruments of subjective expression. The concept of negotiation allows space to the play of unconscious processes in cultural forms, but refuses them an undue determination. For if ideologies operate on an unconscious level through the forms of language, the role of the 'other' in these processes is not passively suffered. The everyday working of argument and misunderstanding – in which contesting parties are positioned by, and struggle to resist, the unarticulated, 'unconscious' meanings running through their opponents' words, tones and gestures – demonstrates the extent to which 'otherness' may be negotiated. In this process, such constraints may become available to conscious understanding. A similar struggle can be posited of cultural exchange. Language and cultural forms are sites in which different subjectivities struggle to impose or challenge, to confirm, negotiate or displace, definitions and identities. In this respect, the figure of woman, the look of the camera, the gestures and signs of human interaction, are not given over once and for all to a particular ideology – unconscious or otherwise. They are cultural signs and therefore sites of struggle; struggle between male and female voices, between class voices, ethnic voices, and so on.

NEGOTIATION AND CULTURAL ANALYSIS

The value of 'negotiation', then, as an analytical concept is that it allows space to the subjectivities, identities and pleasures of audiences. While acknowledging the cine-psychoanalytic critique of the notion 'selfhood' – of 'fixed' and centred identity – the concept of negotiation stops short at the dissolution of identity suggested by avant-garde aesthetics. For if arguments about the non-identity of self and language, words and meaning, desire and its objects challenge bourgeois notions of the centrality and stability of the ego and the transparency of language, the political consequence is not to abandon the search for identity. As has been frequently noted, social out-groups seeking to identify themselves against dominant representations – the working class, women, blacks, gays – need clearly articulated, recognizable and self-respecting self-images. To adopt a political position is of necessity to assume for the moment a consistent and answerable identity. The object of attack should not be identity as such but its dominant construction as total, non-contradictory and unchanging. We need representations that take account of identities – representations that work with a degree of fluidity and contradiction – and we need to forge different identities – ones that help us to make productive use of the contradictions of our lives. This means entering socio-economic, cultural and linguistic struggle to define and establish them in the media, which function as centres for the production and circulation of identity.

However, knowledge of the instability of identity, its continual process of construction and reconstruction, warns the cultural critic not to look for final and achieved models of representation. Paradoxically, cine-psychoanalytic arguments about ideological effects, in their dependence on the centrality of language acquisition to the formation of subjectivity, make the text a moment of 'fixation' in the process of cultural exchange. Too frequently, cine-psycho-analytic analyses suggest that to read a mainstream text, to 'submit' to its pleasures, is to take a single position from which it can be read or enjoyed – that of the textual (patriarchal) subject, bound into ideological submission. However such analysis relies on a complete reading, on tracing the play of narrative processes through to narrative closure, which it is assumed conclusively ties up any ambiguity or enigmatic 'false' trails generated by the processes of the text.

Such textual analysis depends on total consumption of the cultural product and merges with the economistic critique of the spectator as passive consumer. Janice Radway, in her work on romance reading, has pointed to the 'culinary fallacy' in the notion of viewer as consumer – one who, meeting with the media product as a discrete object, swallows it whole, an already textually processed package of the same order as a television dinner. It seems highly improbable that cultural experiences are 'consumed' in quite this totalistic way. The notion of 'process' suggests flux, discontinuities, digressions, rather than fixed positions. It suggests that a range of positions of identification may exist within any text; and that, within the social situation of their viewing, audiences may shift subject positions as they interact with the text. Such processes – far from being confined to the 'high art' or political avant-garde work – are also a crucial source of cultural and formal regeneration, without which the culture industries would dry up.

The complete reading – from narrative disruption, to enigma development, to resolution – that arises from repeated viewings and close analysis is the product of the critical profession and does not replicate the 'raw' reading/viewing of audiences. The notion that the last word of the text is also the final memory of the audience – a notion frequently critiqued from Molly Haskell's account of classic romantic comedy, onwards – derives more from the exigencies of the critical essay than from the *experience* of films, which has no such neat boundaries. It is this haphazard, unsystematic viewing experience, and its aftermath that the cultural analyst must investigate if she/he wants to determine the political *effects* of textual ideologies. The text alone does not provide sufficient evidence for conclusions on such questions, but requires the researches of the anthropologist or ethnographer.

NEGOTIATION AND TEXTUAL CRITICISM

This returns me to a final question concerning the role of textual criticism in cultural analysis – a particularly pressing question in that I want to go on to consider the film *Coma* as an example of textual negotiation and do not have ethnographic skills. To limit the textual critic's authority in the analysis of *ideological effects* need not, however, lead to critical relativism, passivity, nor even unemployment – even if it does mean that textual analysis cannot alone determine the progressiveness or otherwise of a particular work. Semioticians argue that while the majority of cultural products are polysemic, they are not open to any and every interpretation. Aesthetic constraints intersect with the institutional in conscious or unconscious effort to contain or to open out the possibilities of negotiation. By studying the history and forms of aesthetic practices, codes and traditions as they operate within institutions, by studying narrative forms and genres, or the interpretative frameworks and viewing habits suggested by ethnographic research, the textual critic analyses the *conditions and possibilities of reading*.

Approached from this perspective, the cultural 'work' of the text concerns the generation of different readings; readings which challenge each other, provoke social negotiation of meanings, definitions and identities. Cultural history demonstrates that changes in context can render previous 'dominant' readings outmoded, enabling texts to be restructured in preference for alternative readings. For example, film criticism in the 1960s struggled to win 'commercial' Hollywood cinema for 'art', a project rejected by the ideological concerns of the 1970s as 'bourgeois humanism'. While some films disappeared from view (for instance, Fred Zinneman's social problem western, *High Noon*) others were saved by a re-evaluation and re-reading of their textual operations (John Ford's *Young Mr Lincoln*), and yet others were 'discovered' for the critical canon (for instance, Douglas Sirk's family melodrama, *Written on the Wind*).[18] In this respect criticism represents the professionalization of meaning production. The critic, attuned by training to the semiotic and social possibilities of texts, produces sophisticated, specialist readings. To the critical enterprise, ethnographic work contributes knowledge of the network of cultural relations and interactions in which texts are caught and which help shape their possibilities, suggesting what they are capable of generating for different social audiences. But the critical act is not finished with the 'reading' or 'evaluation' of a text. It generates new cycles of meaning production and negotiation – journalistic features, 'letters to the editor', classroom lectures, critical responses, changes in distribution or publication policy, more critical activity, and so on. In this way traditions are broken and remade. Thus critical activity itself participates in social negotiation of meaning, definition, identity. The circulation of the mainstream Hollywood film *Coma* into the orbit of feminist debates about cinema offers a good example of this interchange between general and specialized critical discourses.[19]

FEMINIST FILM ANALYSIS

A problem for feminist analysis is that it enters critical negotiation from a specific political position, often beginning with the aim of distinguishing 'progressive' from 'reactionary' texts. Yet, as we have seen, any attempt to fix meaning is illusory. Moreover, the feminist project seeks to open up definitions and identities, not to diminish them. While the attempt to define the ideological status of texts may stimulate debate, such judgements also threaten to foreclose prematurely on critical and textual negotiation. It is necessary, then, for feminist criticism to perform a dual operation. In the first instance, the critic uses textual and contextual analysis to determine the conditions and possibilities of gendered readings. The critic opens up the negotiations of the text in order to animate the contradictions in play. But the feminist critic is also interested in some readings more than others. She enters into the polemics of negotiation, exploiting textual contradiction to put into circulation readings that draw the text into a female and/or feminist orbit. For example, *Coma* (Michael Crichton, 1977) was conceived, publicized and discussed critically as a futuristic thriller exploiting public concern about organ transplants. But the film also makes the central investigative protagonist a woman doctor. This produces a series of textual negotiations which are both ideologically interesting to feminists and a considerable source of the film's generic pleasure. My analysis of the film is partisan to the extent that it focuses on these considerations at the expense of the issues of medical science.

CONDITIONS AND POSSIBILITIES OF TEXTUAL NEGOTIATION

A major issue for the analysis of textual negotiations is how 'textual' and 'social' subjects intersect in a cultural product; how the aesthetic and fictional practices engaged by a particular text meet and negotiate with extra-textual social practices; and, more specifically, how we can distinguish the patriarchal *symbol* of 'woman' from those discourses which speak from and to the historical socio-cultural experience of 'women'.

It is my argument that a considerable source of textual negotiation lies in the use by many mainstream film and television genres of both melodramatic and realist modes.[20] This dual constitution enables a text to work both on a symbolic, 'imaginary' level, internal to fictional production and on a 'realist' level, referring to the socio-historical world outside the text. Thus two aesthetic projects may co-exist in the same work. Popular culture draws on a melodramatic framework to provide archetypal and atavistic symbolic enactments; for the focus of melodrama is a moral order constructed out of the conflict of Manichaean, polar opposites – a struggle between good and evil, personified in the conflicts of villain, heroine and hero. At the same time such conflicts have power only on the premiss of a recognizable, socially constructed world; the pressure towards realism and contemporaneity means that a popular text must also conform to ever shifting criteria of relevance and credibility.

If, however, melodramatic conflicts still have imaginative resonance in twentieth-century culture, melodrama as a category is rejected for its association with a discarded Victorianism – for its simplistically polarized personifications of good and evil and 'feminized' sentimentalism. In order, therefore, to find credible articulations of such conflict, which will re-solicit the recognition of continually shifting audiences, current melodramatic forms draw on those contemporary discourses which apportion responsibility, guilt and innocence in 'modern' terms – psychoanalysis, for example, marriage guidance, medical ethics, politics, even feminism. The modern popular drama, then, exists as a negotiation between the terms of melodrama's Manichaean moral frameworks and conflicts and those contemporary discourses which will ground the drama in a recognizable verisimilitude. These conditions of aesthetic existence ensure the continuing renewal of popular forms, the generation of renewed use values that will bring audiences back to the screen.

Gender representation is at the heart of such cultural negotiation. For during a period of active feminism, of social legislation for greater sexual equality and corresponding shifts in gender roles, gender and sexual definitions themselves become the focus of intense cultural negotiation. Central to such negotiation is the figure of woman, which has long served as a powerful and ambivalent patriarchal symbol, heavily over-determined as expression of the male psyche. But while film theory suggests how narrative, visual and melodramatic pleasures are organized round this symbol, feminist cultural history also shows that the figure of woman cannot be fixed in her function as patriarchal value. The 'image of woman' has also been a site of gendered discourse, drawn from the specific socio-cultural experiences of women and shared by women, which negotiates a space within, and sometimes resists, patriarchal domination. At the same time new definitions of gender and sexuality circulated by the women's movement contest the value and meaning of the female image, struggling for different, female recognitions and identifications. When popular cultural forms, operating within a melodramatic framework, attempt to engage contemporary discourses about women or draw on women's cultural forms in order to renew their gender verisimilitude and solicit the recognition of a female audience, the negotiation between 'woman' as patriarchal symbol and woman as generator of women's discourse is intensified. While melodrama orchestrates gender conflicts on a highly symbolic level to produce the clash of identities that will adumbrate its moral universe, the codes of women's discourse work in a more direct and articulate register to produce realist and gendered recognitions [. . .]

NOTES

1. For example, cultural studies in England, and reader-response theory in the United States have explored the cultural processes and textural procedures that make differential readings possible.
2. For examples of feminist analysis of women's fiction, see: Nina Baym, *Woman's Fiction: A Guide to Novels by and About Women in America, 1920–1970*, Ithaca: Cornell University Press, 1978; Janice A. Radway, *Reading the Romance: Women, Patriarchy, and Popular Literature*, London: Verso, 1987; Jane Tompkins, *Sensational Designs: The Cultural Work of American Fiction, 1790–1860s*, Oxford: Oxford University Press, 1985. For feminist work on the woman's film, melodrama and soap opera, see: Tania Modleski, *Loving with a Vengeance*, Hamden, Connecticut: The Shoe String Press, 1982; Charlotte Brunsdon, 'Crossroads: Notes on Soap Opera', in E. Ann Kaplan (ed.), *Regarding Television: Critical Approaches – An Anthology*, Los Angeles: American Film Institute, 1983; Dorothy Hobson, *Crossroads: The Drama of a Soap Opera*, London: Methuen, 1982; Ien Ang, *Watching Dallas*, London: Methuen, 1985; Maria LaPlace, 'Producing and Consuming the Woman's Film: Discursive Struggle in *Now, Voyager*', and Linda Williams, ' "Something Else Besides a Mother": *Stella Dallas* and the Maternal Melodrama', both in Christine Gledhill (ed.), *Home Is Where the Heart Is*, London: British Film Institute, 1987.
3. For an account of Lacanian psychoanalysis, see Steve Burniston, Frank Mort and Christine Weedon, 'Psychoanalysis and the Cultural Acquisition of Sexuality and Subjectivity', in Women's Studies Group, Centre for Contemporary Cultural Studies, University of Birmingham (ed.), *Women Take Issue*, London: Hutchinson, 1978.
4. The psychoanalytic underpinnings of classic narrative cinema were first signalled in a special issue of *Screen*, vol. 14 no. 1/2 (Spring/Summer 1973), dealing with semiotics and cinema, and were developed by Colin MacCabe in 'The Politics of Separation', and by Stephen Heath in 'Lessons from Brecht', both in *Screen*, vol. 15,

no. 2 (Summer 1974). *Screen*, vol. 16, no. 2, translated Christian Metz's 'The Imaginary Signifier' in a special issue on psychoanalysis and the cinema.

5. Claire Johnston's 'Women's Cinema as Counter-Cinema'. *Screen* Pamphlet, no. 2, September 1972, is an early and influential exposition of this view. Laura Mulvey's 'Visual Pleasure and Narrative Cinema' in *Screen*, vol. 16, no. 3 (Autumn 1975), provided an influential development of feminist cine-psychoanalysis. Annette Kuhn's book *Women's Picture: Feminism and Cinema*, London: Routledge and Kegan Paul, 1982 offers succinct and critical introduction to this work, and Ann Kaplan's *Women and Film: Both Sides of the Camera*, New York: Methuen, 1983, a distinctive development of it, dealing in particular with the notion of the 'male gaze' in classic narrative cinema. See also my 'Recent Developments in Feminist Film Criticism' in Mary Ann Doane, Patricia Mellencamp and Linda Williams (eds), *Re-Vision: Essays in Feminist Film Criticism*, Frederick, Maryland: University Publications of America, in association with the American Film Institute, 1984, for an account of feminist engagement with psychoanalysis.

6. See Annette Kuhn, *Women's Pictures*.

7. For example, Tania Modleski, 'Never To Be Thirty-Six Years Old: *Rebecca* as Female Oedipal Drama', *Wide Angle*, vol. 5, no. 1 (1982), and Linda Williams, ' "Something Else Besides a Mother": *Stella Dallas* and the Maternal Melodrama', and Tania Modleski, 'Time and Desire in the Woman's Film', in Gledhill 1987.

8. Annette Kuhn, 'Women's Genres: Melodrama, Soap Opera and Theory', *Screen*, vol. 25, no. 1 (1984), reprinted in Gledhill.

9. For example, Stuart Hall, 'Encoding/Decoding', in Hall *et al.* (eds), *Culture, Media, Language*, London: Hutchinson, 1980, David Morley, *The Nationwide Audience*, London: British Film Institute Television Monograph II, 1980, Richard Dyer, *Stars*, London: British Film Institute, 1980.

10. See Antonio Gramsci, *Selections from the Prison Notebooks*, Quintin Hoare and Geoffrey Nowell-Smith (ed. and trans.), London: Lawrence and Wishart, 1971. For discussion and application of the notion of hegemony to cultural products, see Terry Lovell, 'Ideology and Coronation Street', in Richard Dyer *et al.*, *Coronation Street*, London: British Film Institute Television Monograph 13, 1981, and Geoff Hurd, 'Notes on Hegemony, the War and Cinema', in *National Fictions: World War Two in British Films and Television*, London: British Film Institute, 1985.

11. See Terry Lovell, *Pictures of Reality: Aesthetics, Politics and Pleasure*, London: British Film Institute, 1980, pp. 56–63. She defines the 'use-value' of a commodity as 'the ability of the commodity to satisfy some human want', which, according to Marx, 'may spring from the stomach or from the fancy'. 'The use-value of a commodity is realised only when it is consumed, or used' (p. 57).

12. See Maria LaPlace, 'Producing and Consuming the Woman's Film: Discursive Struggle in *Now, Voyager*', in Gledhill 1987, for a discussion of the contradictions of consumerism for women.

13. Julie D'Acci, 'The Case of *Cagney and Lacey*', in Helen Baehr and Gillian Dyer (eds), *Boxed In: Women and Television*, London: Pandora, 1987.

14. Molly Haskell, *From Reverence to Rape: The Treatment of Women in the Movies*, Harmondsworth: Penguin, 1979.

15. Ien Ang, *Watching Dallas*, London: Methuen, 1985, and Janice Radway, *Reading the Romance: Women, Patriarchy and Popular Literature*, London: Verso, 1987.

16. See, for example, Judith Williamson, 'The Problems of Being Popular', *New Socialist*, September 1986.

17. For examples of fully developed textual analysis of the 'recuperative' strategies of mainstream cinema, see Peter Steven (ed.), *Jump Cut: Hollywood, Politics and Counter-Cinema*, New York, Praeger, 1985.

18. For a translation of the seminal analysis of *Young Mr Lincoln* by the editors of *Cahiers du Cinéma*, see *Screen*, vol. 13, no. 3 (Autumn 1972), reprinted in Bill Nichols (ed.) *Movies and Methods*, Berkeley: University of California Press, 1976.

For work on Douglas Sirk, see Jon Halliday (ed.), *Sirk on Sirk*, London: Secker and Warburg/British Film Institute, 1971, a special issue of *Screen*, vol. 12, no. 2 (Summer 1971), and Laura Mulvey and Jon Haliday (eds), *Douglas Sirk*, Edinburgh: Edinburgh Film Festival, 1972.

19. See, for example, Elizabeth Cowie's account of press coverage of *Coma* in 'The Popular Film as a Progressive Text – a discussion of *Coma* Part 1', *m/f*, no. 3, 1979. Part 2 of this article appeared in *m/f*, no. 4, 1980. *Coma* was discussed by Christine Geraghty under the heading, 'Three Women's Films', in *Movie*, nos. 27/28, Winter/Spring 1980–81, an article which is reprinted in Charlotte Brunsdon (ed.), *Films for Women*, London: British Film Institute, 1986, as is also an extract from Part 1 of Elizabeth Cowie's piece. The film frequently appears in film study courses dealing with feminism and cinema.

20. See 'The Melodramatic Field: An Investigation', in Gledhill 1987.

14

'VIDEO REPLAY: FAMILIES, FILMS AND FANTASY'

Valerie Walkerdine

I am seated in the living room of a council house in the centre of a large English city. I am there to make an audio-recording as part of a study of 6-year-old girls and their education. While I am there, the family watches a film, *Rocky II*, on the video. I sit, in my armchair, watching them watching television. How to make sense of this situation?

Much has been written about the activity of watching films in terms of scopophilia. But what of that other activity, film theory, or, more specifically, what about this activity of research, of trying so hard to understand what people see in films? Might we not call this the most perverse voyeurism?[1] Traditionally, of course, observation – like all research methods in the human and social sciences – has been understood as, at worst, minimally intrusive on the dynamics and interaction unfolding before the eyes of the observer, who is herself outside the dynamic. My argument is that such observation, like all scientific activity, constitutes a voyeurism in its will to truth, which invests the observer with 'the knowledge', indeed the logos. The observer then should be seen as the third term, the law which claims to impose a reading on the interaction. This is offered as an explanation to which the observed have no access and yet which is crucial in the very apparatuses which form the basis of their regulation. In addition, the observer becomes the silent Other who is present in, while apparently absent from, the text. Clearly, I cannot escape the contradictions and effects of my own need here to produce a reading, an analysis, an account of what happened. But in

* From Burgin, V. et al. (eds), *Formations of Fantasy*. London: Routledge, 1986, pp. 167–99.

order to insert myself explicitly into the text, I shall attempt to speak also of my own identification with the film I watched with this family.

My concern is therefore not just with the voyeurism of the film spectator, but also with the voyeurism of the theorist – in whose desire for knowledge is inscribed a will to truth of which the latent content is a terror of the other who is watched.

From this perspective, I shall explore, in a preliminary way, the relationship of families to television and video and, more particularly, the effectivity of the films they watch upon the constitution of family dynamics. Within film theory concepts from psychoanalysis do not seem to have been used to examine how specific films have been read in practice, nor how they produce their specific effects. Identification, for example, is often discussed in terms of the effectivity of representation as distorted perception – the viewer is accorded no status which pre-exists the film. Psychoanalysis is used, in the end, to explore the relations within a film rather than to explain the engagement with the film by viewers already inserted in a multiplicity of sites for identification.

The family I shall be discussing did not watch *Rocky II* as ideal, acultural viewers, for example, but in relation to complex and already constituted dynamics. And these dynamics cannot simply be reduced to differences of class, gender and ethnicity – although the question of how these enter into the divided relations of domestic practices is, nevertheless, central.

Such differences themselves exist within a regime of practices, in which 'fantasy' and 'reality' already operate in a complex and indiscernible dynamic.[2] In trying to understand the domestic and family practices in which adults and children are inscribed, therefore, I examine the play of discourses and the relations of signification which already exist. And I approach the viewing of the film in the same way, as a dynamic intersection of viewer and viewed, a chain of signification in which a new sign is produced – and thus a point of production or creation in its own right.

In discussing families watching films, I try to show how aspects of the filmic representations are incorporated into the domestic practices of the family. This explains the themes and emphases in my argument. First, there is the question of how to understand the act of *watching*. I shall describe the watching of families as a surveillant voyeurism, a 'will to tell the truth' about families which contains a set of desperate desires – for power, for control, for vicarious joining-in – as well as a desperate fear of the other being observed. Secondly, I want to challenge the 'intellectualization of pleasures' which seems to be the aim of much analysis of mass film and television. In opposition to the implicit contrast between the masses narcotized by the mass fantasies produced by the consciousness industry and the intellectual unbefuddled by the opium of ideology, it seems to me that we should look at the desire for forms of mastery that are present in our own subjectification as cultural analysts before rushing to 'save' 'the masses' from the pleasures of imaginary wish-fulfilment. Thirdly, therefore, I stress the materiality of power and oppression. Politics, in other words, are central to the analysis.

ROCKY II

The Coles are a working-class family. They live on a council estate and have three children – Joanne, aged 6, Robert, 9, and James, 13 – together with a large Alsatian dog, named Freeway.[3] I am seated in their living room. The video of *Rocky II* is being watched, sporadically, by the whole family. I sit there, almost paralysed by the continued replay of round 15 of the final boxing sequence, in which Mr Cole is taking such delight. Paralysed by the violence of the most vicious kind – bodies beaten almost to death. How can they? What do they see in it? The voyeuristic words echo inside my head, the typical response of shame and disgust which condemns the working class for overt violence and sexism (many studies show, for example, how much more sex-role stereotyping there is amongst working-class families). In comparison with a bourgeois liberalism it seems shameful, disgusting (key aspects of voyeurism) and quite inexplicable except by reference to a model of pathology.

I do not remember if I saw all of the film then. All I recall now is the gut-churning horror of the constant replay. Much later, when beginning to do the work for an analysis, I hired the video of *Rocky II* and watched it in the privacy of my office, where no one could see. And at that moment I recognized something that took me far beyond the pseudo-sophistication of condemning its macho sexism, its stereotyped portrayals. The film brought me up against such memories of pain and struggle and class that it made me cry. I cried with grief for what was lost and for the terrifying desire to be somewhere and someone else: the struggle to 'make it'. No longer did I stand outside the pleasures of engagement with the film. I too wanted Rocky to win. Indeed, I *was* Rocky – struggling, fighting, crying to get out. I am not saying that there is one message or reading here for all to pick up. On the contrary the film engages me as a viewer at the level of fantasy because I can insert myself into, position myself with, the desires and pain woven into its images. Someone else might have identified with Rocky's passive and waiting wife. But Rocky's struggle to become bourgeois is what reminded me of the pain of my own.[4] The positions set up within the film then create certain possibilities, but it seems to be the convergence of fantasies and dream which is a significant in terms of engaging with a film.

One aspect of the popularity of Hollywood films like the *Rocky* series is that they *are* escapist fantasies: the imaginary fulfilment of the working-class dream for bourgeois order. And they reveal an escape route, one which is all the more enticing given the realistic mode of its presentation, despite the very impossibility of its realism.[5] Such are popular films then, not because violence or sex-role stereotyping is part of the pathology of working-class life, but because escape is what we are set up to want, whatever way we can get it. For the majority of women and men, the escape-route open to me, that of the mind, of being clever, is closed. It is the body which presents itself either as the appropriate vehicle for bourgeois wardship (all those women starlets, beauty queens and 'kept' women) or for the conquering champion who has beaten the opponents into submission.

What is important for me about watching a film like this is the engagement, the linking, of the fantasy space of the film and viewer. Watching *Rocky II*, to be effective, necessitates an already existent constitution of pains, of losses and desires for fulfilment and escape, inhabiting already a set of fantasy spaces inscribing us in the 'everyday life' of practices which produce us all. This does not imply a concept of a unitary subject, whose location in a 'social totality' determines the reading of a film, but rather a fragmented subjectivity in which signifying practices produce manifest and latent contents for the inscription of fantasy. Such wishes cannot be understood outside signifying activity – which is itself also discursive and involves aspects of power and regulation.

The magic convergence, therefore, is an act of signification, the fusion of signifier and signified to produce a new sign, a new place, desire leaping across the terminals, completing the circuit, producing the current. These multiple sites of my formation, these dynamic relations, are the diversity of practices in which power and desire inscribe me. The reader is *not* simply in the text, not then the spectator in the film, motivated simply by a pathological scopophilia. The *position* produced for the reader or spectator is not identical with an actual reader constituted in multiple sites and positions. Perhaps the 'desire to look' belongs with the film theorist and social or behavioural scientist who disavow their own engagement and subsume their own fantasies into a move into the symbolic, the desire for the mastery of explanation. Just as there is no 'reader' (simply and exclusively) 'in the text' nor is there a preformed subject whose experience is reflected, biased or distorted in the film. If fantasies of escape are what we are set up for, then any amount of cinematic fantasy posing as realism about the drudgery of our lives will not convince us to abandon our enticing fantasies.

There is, in this watching, a moment of *creation* – if it is effective and successful as a cultural product for the mass market whose desires it helps to form. There is certainly an aesthetic or a pleasure, and yet each of these terms is more redolent of an up-market art movie in which there are taken only to be acceptable, not nasty, pleasures. An aesthetic is cold. What I am talking about is red hot. It is what makes the youths in cinema audiences cheer and scream for Rocky to win the match – including many black youths, even though the Mr Big of boxing, whom he defeats, is black. It is what makes Mr Cole want to have the fight on continuous and instant replay forever, to live and triumph in that moment. And it is what makes me throb with pain [. . .]

Fighting enters into the Coles' domestic practices as a relation in a way which is totally consonant with its presentation in *Rocky II*. That relation was crystallized in the watching of the film and the repetition of the final round. In terms of 'forwards' movements therefore, I am placing the relations of signification within history, and within an experience of gendered and class-specific lived oppression. Fighting is a key term in a discourse of powerlessness, of a constant struggle not to sink, to get rights, not to be pushed out. It is quite unlike the pathological object of a liberal anti-sexist discourse which would understand fighting as 'simply' macho violence and would substitute covert regulation and reasoning in language as less sexist.

It is in this way that I am aiming to demonstrate the *fixing* of fighting in that lived historicity – the *point de capiton*. I am stressing too that 'fight/ing/er' as a relation is quite specific in its meaning and therefore *not* co-terminous with what fighting would mean in, for example, a professional middle-class household where both the regulation of conflict and the relation to oppression are quite different. This is an argument *against* a universalism of meaning, reading and interpretation. However, having examined the manifest content in which the relations of signification are historically fixed, this is not all there is. If we are to explore the latent content, it is necessary to ask what is suppressed/repressed/ forgotten beneath the term? The working-class male body is a site of struggle and of anxiety, as well as pleasure. Mr Cole is a very small man. Fighting is a way of gaining power, of celebrating or turning into a celebration that which is constituent of oppression. Power in its manifest content covers over a terror of powerlessness, an anxiety beneath the pleasure.

Mr Cole is afraid of being 'soft', of a femininity lurking beneath the surface. This is referred to while the family watch the musical film *Annie* on video. It is seen as a 'women's film', and its fantasies, its dancing and singing, are constantly held up for ridicule. It is as though Mr Cole cannot bear to be seen (by me?) as liking such a film, as having passive, romantic fantasies. In this analysis, masculinity as fighting is a defence, a defence against powerlessness, a defence against femininity. The backwards movement can be articulated in relation to several points. The fear of being watched or monitored (counterpointed by my voyeurism), the expectation of female servicing (when his wife is at home), the *struggle* to fight against a fear: all these suggest that fighting represents a triumph over, repression of, defence against, the terror of powerlessness. This powerlessness, as in *Rocky II*, is presented as the humiliation of cowardice – of the man who cannot work, fight, protect women, and who is therefore feminized. Latent beneath Mr Cole's conscious self-identification as a fighter may lurk the fear of a small man whose greatest fear is his cowardice and femininity. It is this which has to be displaced by projection on to, and investment in, others (his wife, Joanne) who can be the objects of his protection and for whom he fights.

In psychoanalytic terms, such a reading keys into the necessity for – but also the fraudulence of – the phallus as a sign of power. Whether one finds in this an Oedipal struggle or an omnipotent, pre-Oedipal one, might be a point of dispute. However, my aim is not to suggest that the historical 'fighting' is really about a psychic relation. Far from it. It is to demonstrate the centrality of sexuality and power in the lived historicity of current struggles and the interminable intertwining of present and past, of material conditions and psychic relations. What is being fought for and fought against by Mr Cole can therefore be understood as having a manifest and latent content. But, since Mr Cole's (childhood) anxieties were and are produced in specific historical conditions, it is quite impossible and indeed dangerous to separate the one from the other.

PSYCHICAL REALITY

In suggesting that the practices in which Mr Cole is inscribed locate him as a 'fighter', I have argued for a reading of the manifest and latent content of the term. In understanding the relation between the manifest content of *Rocky II* and that of the Coles' domestic practices, it is necessary to examine the chains of signification produced which link the two. This is particularly possible with a video-recording, since it is watched partly as a backdrop to other practices rather than in a darkened cinema.

Identifications, like those of Rocky and Mr Cole as fighters, may be fictions inscribed in fantasy, set and worked out in the film itself, but they are also lived out in the practices in which Mr Cole is inserted. There is no 'real' of these practices which stands outside fantasy, no split between fantasy as a psychic space and a reality which can be known. If such fictional identities become 'real' in practices, they must have a psychical reality which has a positive effectivity in the lived materiality of the practices themselves. Such fictional identities must be created in the plays of power and desire. They are also therefore created in relational dynamics in which others can project fantasies on to, and invest them in, subjects within the family and other relations. I want to point up the psychical reality of such projections by dwelling for a moment upon Mr Cole's nickname for his daughter, Joanne: Dodo. Although I have suggested that this may well be derived from a childish mispronounciation 'Jo-Jo', it has other associations, which Mr Cole makes, of the Dodo as an extinct bird.

It is not uncommon for men to give baby names such as Dodo to women and girls in their wardship. Deborah Cherry and Griselda Pollock, for example, have analysed Rossetti's use of 'Guggums' for his model and mistress, Elizabeth Siddall.[6] They make reference to Lacan's statement that 'woman does not exist' except as a symptom and myth of a male fantasy. Like his later statement that the 'phallus is a fraud', Lacan sets up there the possibility that subjectivity is created not in a fixed and certain gender-identity, but in shifting and uncertain relations. The desire of the Other, the fears and fantasies inscribed in and projected on to that Other, help to fix what 'woman' and 'man' are taken to be, not the essentiality of their nature. In addition, actual men and women strive and struggle to be 'man' and 'woman' within specific regimes of representation [...]

The important point is that such fantasies have a psychical reality which has positive and material effects when its significations are inscribed in actual practices. When Mr Cole calls his daughter 'Dodo', for example, that suggests not only his desire to infantilize his daughter, but also his identification of himself as a 'fighter' for her and on her behalf. He becomes her Other – the big man, the protector. This is then inscribed in the semiotics of their relating and their positioning within practices. But Joanne is not only infantilized as Dodo. She is also positioned, in contradiction as a 'fighter' like her father – Dodo and yet a 'tomboy'. This reveals the complexity of his identification with, and investment in, her as he makes her simultaneously his feminine ward to be protected and later 'married off' and his masculinized working-class fighter, like her brothers. Joanne's fractured subjectivity is therefore lived not without some pain produced by this splitting.

RECOGNITION AND LATENT CONTENT

I argued at the beginning of this article that psychoanalytically oriented film theory, despite its many strengths, still elides certain problems about subjectivity when it implies that subject-positions are produced *within* the discourses of filmic representations. To some extent that should be read as a self-criticism too. Like many other people, I have drawn on the work of Althusser, Lacan and Foucault to understand the relation between 'positioning in discourse', 'modes of signification' and the 'semiotics of the psyche'.[7] Although the centrality of plays of signification to the formation of subjectivity has been emphasized within such modes of analysis, very little empirical work has been done on how the process actually works in the regulative practices of daily life. As a result of concentrating on the dynamics within regimes of representation, we risk ending up with a sense of the determined and passive subject we had hoped to avoid. Hence the question I have tackled here: how do we reassert the importance of the creation of subjectivity as active, even if the subject is caught at an intersection of discourses and practices?

The subject is positioned or produced in multiple sites. These are not all-embracing, but may work with or against each other. The person watching a film, for example, will always be already inscribed in practices which have multiple significations. That is why the film cannot in and of itself produce a reading which 'fixes' the subject. Rather the viewing constitutes a point of dynamic intersection, the production of a new sign articulated through the plays of significance of the film and those which already articulate the subject. This sort of approach should make it possible to deal with the issue of specific readings, and the location of readers/viewers, without collapsing into essentialism. Thus Claire Johnston has argued for:

> a move away from a notion of the text as an autonomous object of study and towards the more complex question of subjectivity seen in historical/ social terms. Feminist film practice can no longer be seen simply in terms of the effectivity of a system of representation, but rather as a production of and by subjects already in social practices, which always involve hetero-geneous and often contradictory positions in ideologies.[8]

As I say, though, the problem has been that, however clearly this agenda has been set, there has been little empirical work to back it up so far. My account of how the Coles (and I) watched *Rocky II* is an attempt to show the effectivity of filmic representations within the lived relations of domestic practices – signifying and discursive practices which are historically constituted and regulated.[9]

This means attempting to examine the relations between domestic practices (and other practices and discourses) in a number of ways. We need to understand how these 'lived relations' are formed through régimes of meanings which position the participants and which 'lock into' relations of signification in the media. But more than this, we need to go beyond the present use of psycho-analysis. That is, by using psychoanalysis to understand relations *within* a film and then using voyeurism to understand the viewer, we are left in a sterile situation which assumes that all viewers 'take on' the psycho-dynamic of the film as far as it relates to the Oedipal conflict. As Laura Mulvey and others have pointed out, this leaves women as viewers in a difficult position. As ethno-graphic studies such as those of Janice Radway have shown, it also imposes universalistic meanings on particularistic viewing situations.[10] Radway and others, however, are almost forced back on to an 'effects' model because they end up having to understand readers and viewers as pre-located and pre-determined. Cathy Urwin has pointed out that children's use of figures from the popular media in their therapy is not necessarily Oedipal.[11] Using a Kleinian framework she finds pre-Oedipal struggles. Importantly she suggests that the use made by the children of these figures, although it relates in some ways to the dynamic in the film or television programme, particularly relates to their own struggles in therapy. Hence a young boy can use the figure of Superman, not in relation to an Oedipal resolution, but as a carrier for his fantasies of omnipotent power. This suggests that different readers will 'read' films, not in terms of a pre-existing set of relations of significantion or through a pathology of scopophilia, but by what those relations *mean to them*.

Although we have to understand the dynamics within which the viewer is already inscribed in order to engage with viewing, I do not wish to resort to an essentialistic reading, nor to a notion of a preformed subject. It is important not to reduce each viewer to some 'stage' in the analytic move from infancy to maturity. Rather the viewers are themselves created in dynamics which are understood through, and inscribed in, historically specific practices and relations of power and oppression. The fantasies, anxieties and psychical states cannot be understood outside that history.

This, as I have stressed throughout this article, applies as much to the position of the researcher as to the families or viewers being observed. I have already considered my own relation to *Rocky II* and to fathers' infantilization of girl children. But what of my position as researcher? As I suggested in the introduction, this itself constitutes part of the dynamic I was studying. It has to be understood not as a problem of 'intrusiveness', but in terms of the power/ knowledge couplet.

As observer, I became a 'Surveillant Other' not only watching but also producing a knowledge that feeds into the discursive practices regulating families. The 'social scientist' is the producer of a 'truth' which claims to 'know' those whom it describes. Together, observer and observed constitute a couple in the play of power and desire. We therefore need to examine the response of the observed to their experience of surveillance. Equally important, however, is the theorist's 'desire to know', for this contains both a fantasy of power and also a fear of the observed. (Scientific objectivity might therefore be seen as the suppression or disavowal of this desire.)

Humanistic forms of social science often attempt to escape this inevitable power dynamic by reducing 'power-differentials' or by 'putting subjects at ease'. Despite these patronizing attempts to get 'beyond power', I would argue that most therapeutically and psychoanalytically oriented work on families and films or television clearly remains normative and regulative.[12]

However disguised, the observer's account is a *regulative* reading which pathologizes the participants' actions. The knowledge it produces will inevitably differ from the meanings ascribed to them by the participants – meanings they produce as they live out the practices in which they are formed. But the struggle between them is not simply about the 'values' attached to meanings. Nor is it about validating people's interpretations. It is a struggle about power with a clear material effectivity. One might therefore ask how far it is possible for the observer to 'speak for' the observed.

The families I was studying in my research (which, as I have noted, concerned the education of 6-year-old girls rather than film or television watching) clearly indicated on many occasions that they experienced me as surveillant Other. Their responses to my presence cannot be understood without taking this into consideration. Equally I was struck by the fantasies, anxieties and pain triggered in me by being perceived as a middle-class academic confronting a working-class family. Although I invested considerable desire into wanting to 'be one of them' at the same time as 'being different', no amount of humanistic seeking for the 'beyond ideology' would get them to see in me a working-class girl 'like them'. Rather than disavow that dynamic, therefore, it became necessary to work *with* it and to acknowledge the clear effectivity of their reading of me as middle class in the data I collected.

But I also wanted to examine my multiple positioning as both middle-class academic *and* working-class child, to use my own fantasies in exploring how the participants perceived me and how they understood their experience. In this work I developed the term *recognition* as a reworking of Althusser's concept of 'mis-recognition'. Rather than engage with its negative connotations for the study of ideological (i.e. always-already distorting) interpellation, I wanted to use the idea of recognition *positively* in my work on domestic practices. Recognition is what places the subject in the historical moment. It is achieved through the circulation of the signifier as a relation in present discursive practices. Like Lacan's *point de capiton*, recognition acts as a nodal point (involving also forgetting and the repression of what went before): it provides the post-structure. In my own research, therefore, I wanted to use my own fantasied positions within those practices as a way of engaging with their unconscious and conscious relations of desire and the plays of anxiety and meaning. Often when interviewing the participants I felt that I 'knew what they meant', that I recognized how the practices were regulated or that I understood what it was like to be a participant.[13] Using this 'recognition' to explore the positivity of how domestic relations are lived seems to me an important step beyond assertions that academics should side with the oppressed, that film-makers should see themselves as workers or that teachers should side with pupils. Such rhetoric may represent *our* wish-fulfilling denial of power and responsibility – a way of disavowing our position instead of accounting for it.

To take a rather mischievous example, Paul Willis's *Learning to Labour* could be interpreted from this perspective as the story of an 'earole' who wants to become a 'lad', a male academic vicariously becoming one of the boys. What is missing from such work is any account of the ethnographer's own position in the web of power/knowledge/desire. Another problem with much ethnographic work (my own included) has been the way it takes discourse at face value. In working with a transcript, for example, of what can we take it as evidence? Ethnographic interviews with adolescent working-class girls are often used to justify theories of girls' resistance, as is their anti-school behaviour and taking on of feminity (through using make-up or subverting uniform). Yet could these discourses and actions not equally well hide pain and anxiety in relation to academic failure? The problem of ethnographic work is how to take adequate account of the psychical reality of both observer and observed.

This means disrupting the commonsense split between 'fantasy' and 'reality'. Fantasy is invested in domestic relations just as much as it is in films – that is the point I have been making in drawing out the intersection between the fantasy-structure of *Rocky II* and the domestic dynamics of the Cole family. The fiction, the fantasy is created in this interaction, not only in the projection and introjection between the voyeuristic observer and the observed.[14] This emphasis on the inscription of fantasies within family practices raises the question of the power relations within those practices and their regulation. Power, however, as Cathy Urwin has demonstrated[15] is inextricably intertwined with desire. If positions created within the regulation of domestic practices also generate fantasy and desire, it becomes necessary to dig beneath the surface of the discourse – its manifest content – to find the latent content behind it.

Here, for example, I have attempted to analyse the constitution of subjectivity within a variety of cultural practices, of which watching videos is one. I have tried to avoid either essentializing social differences between viewers or reducing the relations of fantasy and desire inscribed within a film to any one reading without engaging with the family relations and domestic practices into which the video is inserted. Instead, I have asked how people make sense of what they watch and how this sense is incorporated into an existing fantasy-structure.

The basis for this approach is to be found in Freud's analysis of dreaming, where he explores the relationship between dreams as fantasy-scenarios and the inscription of those fantasies in everyday life. He takes their manifest content, as consciously described by the patient, and then focuses on the dream-work – the chains of associations, the changing patterns of condensation and displacement – to discover their latent content. Just as Freud drew on associations made by the patient and also on issues which had previously surfaced in the analysis, I have taken certain key signifiers which feature both in the film and in the domestic practices and examined how associations, either of equation or opposition, are made by the participants at various points in the dialogue.

Although this mode of analysis remains to be developed, I would like to stress two kinds of movement within these relations of signification. One, which I call the forwards movement, anchors and fixes the signifier within current practices, producing the regulative effectivity of the term as it operates as a relation within a régime of representation and truth. The other is a backwards movement which traces the associations of the signifier into the unconscious. This may relate not only to the history of the subject, but also to the forgotten relations inside the practice itself. (Some working-class domestic practices, for example, may have developed in relation to defences against poverty, and yet they may persist as cultural practices even when there is no threat of poverty.) By focusing on the relation between these two movements, it is possible to identify latent content without implying (as happens in certain forms of psychoanalysis) that there must be a psychical Originary Moment which is not also social-historical. Equally my approach acknowledges the effectivity of the manifest content: manifest/latent is not the same as phenomenal/real. It therefore engages with the positivity of recognition as it is lived. The signifiers generate their meanings from the living out of historically specific relations, not from the internal rules of a Saussurian sign system. Meanings inscribed within power/knowledge relations provide a basis for surveillant and regulative practices; other meanings are produced in opposition to them from people's lived historicity. Meaning thus becomes a site of oppression, contestation and political struggle. The subject therefore cannot be positioned in a single textual location which can be put under erasure to reveal the infinity of traces. As Derrida remarks, this activity contains a fiction of mastery over the process of uncovering, the deconstructing of the truth beyond the telling of the truth.

The examination of latent content would involve an infinite historical regression, were it not for the forwards movement which anchors the subject in history. We might make our own history, but in conditions which are not of our choosing – that is, in relations of domination and subordination/subjectification. Derrida accuses Foucault of forgetting that the subject is to be put under erasure. But if we are to produce a history of reading of *the present* and a political practice that is adequate to it, then we need to understand how surveillance functions, how power works, where the buck stops. We need to examine how existing discursive régimes function 'in truth' and have a positive effectivity in positioning the subject. The quasi-Foucauldian approach to how the truth operates is an attempt to produce the forwards movement of which I have spoken.

FANTASY AND INTELLECTUALIZATION

How finally are we to come to terms with the voyeuristic social scientist? The 'space' of observation, I would argue, like that of watching videos, is a fantasy space in which certain fictions are produced. One effect of these fictions is to constitute a knowledge, a truth that is incorporated into the regulation of families. At the same time, the 'claim to truth' designates the social scientist as an expert in the bourgeois order which produces this intellectuality. But it also, I have suggested, hides the fear that motivates it. The masses must be known because they represent a threat to the moral and political order; the theorist/ voyeur expresses shame and disgust at the 'animal passions' which have to be monitored and regulated – and which she cannot enjoy. This logic of intellectualization is evident in many studies of audiences. I therefore want to consider how the fantasies and fictions embodied in academic accounts as well as in films are inscribed in the daily lives of ordinary people.

Modern apparatuses of social regulation, along with other social and cultural practices, produce knowledges which claim to 'identify' individuals. These knowledges create the possibility of multiple practices, multiple positions. To be a 'clever child' or a 'good mother', for example, only makes sense in the terms given by pedagogic, welfare, medical, legal and other discourses and practices. These observe, sanction and correct how we act; they attempt to define who and what we are. They are, however, criss-crossed by other discourses and practices – including those of popular entertainment, for example. This multiplicity means that the practices which position us may often be mutually contradictory. They are also sites of contestation and struggle. We never quite fit the 'positions' provided for us in these regulatory practices. That failure is, in Freudian psycho-analysis, both the point of pain and the point of struggle. It shows repeatedly that the imposition of fictional identities – or socialization – does not work.[16]

What I am proposing here is a model of how subjectification is produced: how we struggle to become subjects and how we resist provided subjectivities in relation to the regulative power of modern social apparatuses. This model rejects the old image of the masses trapped in false consciousness, waiting to be led out of ideology by radical intellectuals. Rather, I would argue, these two categories form a couple defined and produced in relation to each other. The modern bourgeois order depends upon a professional intellectual élite which 'knows' and regulates the proletariat.[17] One side effect of the creation of this 'new middle class' has been that some of its radical members, having themselves achieved social mobility through the route of higher education, claim that it is *only* through rationality and intellectualization that the masses can see through the workings of ideology and so escape its snares.

The audience for popular entertainment, for example, is often presented as sick (voyeuristic, scopophilic) or as trapped within a given subjectivity (whether defined by the social categories of class, race and gender or by a universalized Oedipal scenario). What is disavowed in such approaches is the complex relation of 'intellectuals' to 'the masses': 'our' project of analysing 'them' is itself one of the regulative practices which produce *our* subjectivity as well as theirs. We are each Other's Other – but not on equal terms. Our fantasy investment often seems to consist in believing that we can 'make them see' or that we can see or speak *for* them. If we do assume that, then we continue to dismiss fantasy and the Imaginary as snares and delusions. We fail to acknowledge how the insistent demand to see through ideology colludes in the process of intellectualizing bodily and other pleasures.

It was in opposition to that approach that I tried to make sense of Mr Cole's self-identification as a fighter. I argued that fighting relates not only to masculinity, but also to lived oppression, to the experience of powerlessness and the fear of it. The implication is that we should stop being obsessed by the illusory tropes of an oppressive ideology, and that we should start to look at fantasy spaces as places for hope and for escape from oppression as well.

Asked why they read romantic fiction, the women Janice Radway spoke to said that it helped them to escape from the drudgery of servicing their families – and thus to cope with it. They read at quiet moments (in bed, in the bath) when they could recall the tattered dreams of their youth and long for someone to love them as they wanted to be loved. Their reading was therefore double-edged: not only a way of coming to terms with their daily lives, but also an act of resistance and hope. It is this question of the hope and pleasure that women invest in romantic fiction, which Radway brings out very clearly, that I want to dwell on. But I depart from Radway's analysis, because she remains caught up with the idea that these readers might move 'beyond' such romantic notions; she also rejects psychoanalytic explanations for failing to engage with the specificity of readers' lives.[18] That seems to underestimate both the material *and* the psychical reality of these women's servitude and the pain of their longing for something else.

The danger with such approaches to the study of the audience, however radical in intent, is that their insistence on the transcendence of ideology through the intellectualization of pleasure(s) can itself become part of a broader regulatory project of intellectualization. This seems to be implicit, for example, in the description of a course for women about women and/in the cinema.[19] When the students were encouraged to deconstruct the codes of representation in various types of film, some found it difficult because it meant giving up, or supplanting, the pleasure they had previously felt in watching movies. Similarly, in many media studies courses in schools, children are asked to analyse popular television programmes. What concerns me is how these women, children, whoever, are being asked to deal with their previous enjoyment of such things – a pleasure shared with family, friends and their general social and cultural environment. It seems that they are being left little room for any response other than feeling stupid, or despising those who are still enjoying these 'perverse' pleasures.

What this typically academic emphasis on rationality and intellectualization can overlook are the specific conditions of the formation of pleasures for particular groups at a given historical moment. Rather than seeing the pleasures of 'the masses' as perverse, perhaps we should acknowledge that it is the bourgeois 'will to truth' that is perverse in its desire for knowledge, certainty and mastery. This is the proper context in which to understand the *desire* to know the masses, the voyeurism of the (social) scientist. The crusade to save the masses from the ideology that dupes them can obscure the real social significance of their pleasures and, at the same time, blind us to the perversity of radical intellectual pleasures. The alternative is not a populist defence of Hollywood, but a reassessment of what is involved in watching films. This becomes part of the experience of oppression, pain and desire. Watching a Hollywood movie is not simply an escape from drudgery into dreaming: it is a place of desperate dreaming, of hope for transformation.

Popular pleasures produced in/under oppression can be contrasted with the more cerebral pleasures of discrimination or deconstruction. These ultimately derive from the scientific project of intellectualization, the Cogito, which culminates in the scientific management of populations, the power/knowledge of the modern social order. The intellectualization of pleasures, in other words, is linked not just to the desire to know but also to the project of controlling nature. This has had as its other and opposite a fear of the powers of the unknown, the animal, the unlawful, the insane, the masses, women, blacks. These 'others' became objects to be known and thus civilized and regulated. There exists among the bourgeoisie a terror of the pleasures of the flesh, of the body, of the animal passions seen to be burning darkly in sexuality and also in violent uprisings. No surprise then that the regulation of children's consumption of the modern media focuses so obsessively on sex and violence.

In the end then the 'problem' of popular pleasures – the Coles' enjoyment of *Rocky II* – turns out to lie not (only) with 'the masses' but (also) with the fears and desires of the bourgeois intellectual. The desire to know and to master conceals the terror of a lack of control, a paranoia which is the opposite of omnipotent fantasy, a megalomania. These I have called perversions to point up the way in which they project their own terror of the masses on to the masses themselves. It is this projection that motivates the desire to rationalize the pleasures of the body, to transform them into pleasures of the mind. This body/mind dualism valorizes mental labour as genius or creativity and denigrates the servicing and manual work which make them possible – the labour of the masses and their terrifying physicality. It is in this context of the mental/manual division that the physicality of *Rocky*, expressed so clearly in its violence, should be placed.

I have tried to establish the difference between the 'cold' aesthetic of high culture, with its cerebral and intellectualized appreciation, and the bodily and sensuous pleasures of 'low' cultures.[20] What is most important is to understand the different conditions in which these pleasures – and their associated pains and hopes – are produced. In the oppressive conditions of the bourgeois order 'animal passions' are regulated, the 'rising of the masses' is feared, the individual is defined in terms of brain or brawn, the only way out offered is through cleverness, guile, making it, working, trying. And so embourgeoisement is the only dream left in all those desires for, and dreams of, difference . . .

NOTES

This analysis would not have been possible without the work and insights of Helen Lucey and Diana Watson of the Girls and Mathematics Unit, University of London

Institute of Education. Many of the arguments are developed in my 'On the regulation of speaking and silence', in C. Steedman, C. Urwin and V. Walkerdine (eds), *Language, Gender and Childhood*, London, Routledge & Kegan Paul, 1985; V. Walkerdine *Surveillance, Subjectivity and Struggle*, Minneapolis, University of Minnesota Press, 1986; and *The Mastery of Reason*, London, Routledge & Kegan Paul, 1988; V. Walkerdine and H. Lucey, *Final Report of Grant No.C/00/23/033/1 to the Economic and Social Research Council*, 1985; and V. Walkderine and H. Lucey, *Democracy in the Kitchen: Regulating Mothers and Socialising Daughters*, London, Virago, 1989. I would also like to thank Philip Corrigan, Dick Hebdige and David Morley for helpful comments and criticism.

1. Foucault has documented this in relation to a 'will to truth' in which the production of a knowledge has real effects in the surveillance and regulation of the Other. I add the dimension of *voyeurism* to this perverse will to truth because it allows us to explore the fears and fantasies present in this watching, classifying surveillance – the desire to *know* the Other and therefore to have power over, to control, to explain, to regulate it. This claim to certainty and truth becomes not normal, but profoundly perverse. It is linked both with disgust and with shame: shame at watching – desire to see how 'the other half lives' – and the vicarious excitement in that which is forbidden to the bourgeois researcher and in which s/he profoundly desires to engage but must only monitor, watch, describe and moralistically criticize and prevent. (Cf. S. Freud, *Standard Edition of the Complete Psychological Works*, ed. James Strachey, London, Hogarth. Press, 1955, vol. VII, pp.156–7.)

2. In that sense I shall argue that the 'truths' which create the modern form of sociality are fictions and therefore themselves invented in fantasy. 'The real' therefore becomes a problematic category which I shall deal with only by reference to 'veridicality', on the one hand, and cultural forms and practices, on the other. That is, both scientific and cultural practices produce régimes of meaning, truth, representation in which there are particular relations of signification. What is important in respect of these is the production of a *sign* – i.e. how we enter as 'a relation' and how in actual social practices and cultural forms we become 'positioned'. The concept of positioning relies upon the importance attached to signifier/signified relations. In addition, we can utilize the concept of fantasy to understand our insertion within other 'dramas'. In this respect then the mode of analysis is similar, and also potentially allows an examination of fantasies inscribed in *both* the imaginary and the symbolic.

3. Freeway is the name of an extremely small dog in the television series *Hart to Hart* Using it as the Alsatian's name is therefore something of a joke.

4. That pain of becoming bourgeois through work: a route opened to working-class women, perhaps for the first time, in the post-war educational expansion. See my 'Dreams from an ordinary childhood', in L. Heron (ed.), *Truth, Dare or Promise*, London, Virago, 1985.

5. The dramatic butchery of the fights in the *Rocky* films would be impossible under the existing laws of amateur and professional boxing. Kathryn Kalinak makes a similar point about the impossibility of the escape route though dance presented in *Flashdance*; the heroine is simply much too old to take up a classical ballet career. See 'Flashdance: the Dead End Kind', in *Jump Cut*, no. 29 (1984), pp. 3–4.

6. D. Cherry and G. Pollock, 'Women as sign: the representation of Elizabeth Siddall in Pre-Raphaelite literature', *Art History*, vol. 7, no. 2 (1984). This analysis owes much to the work of Diane Watson: *Woman as Sign in Educational Discourse*, MSc Dissertation, University of London, 1984.

7. See J. Henriques, W. Hollway, C. Urwin, C. Venn and V. Walkerdine, *Changing the Subject: Psychology, Social Regulation and Subjectivity*, London, Methuen, 1984.

8. C. Johnston, *Edinburgh Television Papers, 1979*. For elaboration on this issue, see D. Morley, 'Texts, readers, subjects', in S. Hall, D. Hobson, A. Lowe and P. Willis (eds), *Culture, Media, Language*, London, Hutchinson, 1980.

9. For further discussions of families watching television, see D. Morley, *Family Television*, London, Comedia, 1986, and A. Gray, 'Behind Closed Doors: Video Recorders in the Home', in Helen Baehr and Gillian Dyer (eds), *Boxed In: Women and Television*, London, Pandora Press, 1987.

10. L. Mulvey, 'Visual pleasure and narrative cinema', in *Screen*, vol. 16, no. 3 (1975), J. Radway, 'Women read the romance: the interaction of text and context', *Feminist Studies*, vol. 9, no. 1 (1983).

11. C. Urwin, (1985), 'Wonder People', BPS Developmental Psychology Conference, Belfast.

12. For examples of current work on family dynamics and television which use various therapeutic models to identify normal and pathological viewing, see Goodman 'Television's role in family interaction', *Journal of Family Issues*, vol. 14, no. 2 (1983), pp. 405–24.

13. It is here that a struggle must be located. This takes us away from the implied determinism and fixity of 'interpellation' to the possibility of a struggle over meaning.

14. Rather than analysing fantasy and reality as dichotomous, I approach *positions* and *meanings* as fictional spaces in which fantasy is lived out. The actual operations of fantasy are complex: they are inscribed not only in the lived relations of the family, I am suggesting, but also in the relations between observer and observed, in transference and counter-transference. Such relations are characterized by power.

15. C. Urwin, 'Power relations and the emergence of language', in Henriques, Urwin, Venn and Walkerdine, op. cit.

16. J. Rose, 'Femininity and its discontents', *Feminist Review*, no. 14 (1983), p. 9.

17. For a discussion of intellectuals, see P. Schlesinger, 'In search of the intellectuals: some comments on recent theory', *Media, Culture and Society*, no. 4 (1982).

18. Radway's rejection seems to rest on an equation between psychoanalysis and a purely formalist account of how texts 'position' subjects. Although there have been occasional attempts at just such a synthesis, at a theoretical level the equation is misleading. It seems to me that psychoanalysis might open up a way of engaging with the reality of women's fantasies, pleasures and desires as they read the novels – see, for example, Cora Kaplan, '*The Thorn Birds*: Fiction, Fantasy, Femininity', in Victor Burgin, James Donald and Cora Kaplan (eds), *Formations of Fantasy* London Routledge 1986, pp. 142–66.

19. S. Clayton, 'Notes on teaching film', *Feminist Review*, no. 14 (1983).

20. P. Bourdieu, *Distinction: A Social Critique of the Judgement of Taste*, London, Routledge & Kegan Paul, 1984, ch. 1.

15

'FEMININE FASCINATIONS: FORMS OF IDENTIFICATION IN STAR-AUDIENCE RELATIONS'

Jackie Stacey

[...] The term 'identification' has been central to many debates within psycho-analytic theory and film studies. Within psychoanalytic theory, 'identification' has been seen as the key mechanism for the production of identities. Freud analysed the unconscious mechanisms through which the self is constituted in relation to external objects. In her paper 'Identification and the Star: A Refusal of Difference', Anne Friedberg quotes Freud on identification:

> First, identification is the original form of emotional tie with an object; secondly, in a regressive way it becomes a substitute for a libidinal object-tie, as it were by means of introjection of the object into the ego; and thirdly, it may arise with any new perception of a common quality shared with some other person who is not an object of sexual instinct. The more important this common quality is, the more successful may this partial identification become, and it may thus represent the beginning of a new tie.[1]

The role of vision in identification has always been part of the Freudian formulation (the emphasis on the moment of the sight of sexual difference, for example) but the 'specular role of identification' has taken centre stage in Lacan's theories of the mirror phase, through which subjects are 'constituted through a specular misrecognition of an *other*'.[2]

These models of identification employed within psychoanalysis to explore the developments of unconscious identities have been seen by some film theorists,

---

* From Gledhill, C. (ed.), *Stardom: Industry of Desire*. London: Routledge, 1991, pp. 141–63.

such as Christian Metz,[3] as analogous to the cinematic experience of spectatorship. As Friedberg outlines:

> Primary identification as Metz describes it (as distinct from Freud's 'original and emotional tie') means a spectator who identifies with both camera and projector, and like the child positioned in front of the mirror, constructs an imaginary notion of wholeness, of a unified body ... Secondary identification is with an actor, character or star ... any body becomes an opportunity for an identificatory investment, a possible suit for the substitution/misrecognition of self.[4]

Psychoanalytic film theorists have thus developed a complex analysis of cinematic identification, based on an analogy between the construction of individual identities in infancy in relation to others, and the process of watching a film on a screen. Whilst this may be an appealing analogy, especially given the centrality of the specular in later psychoanalytic accounts of the development of identity, the question remains as to the validity of such a straightforward transposition: how similar are these processes, and what is being left out of the account of spectatorship by focusing so exclusively on its psychic dimensions? Such a framework offers limited purchase on understanding cinematic identification, with no evidence other than a conceptual analogy of the processes occurring in individual psyches.

In film studies more generally, the term 'identification' has been widely used to suggest a broader set of processes. Drawing on literary analysis, identification has often been used rather loosely to mean sympathising or engaging with a character. It has also been used in relation to the idea of 'point of view', watching and following the film from a character's point of view. This involves not only *visual* point of view, constructed by type of shot, editing sequences and so on, but also *narrative* point of view, produced through the sharing of knowledge, sympathy or moral values with the protagonist. Identification has thus been used as a kind of common-sense term within film and literary studies, referring to a very diverse set of processes, and has yet to be adequately theorised in a manner which provides a satisfactory alternative to the more reductive psychoanalytic models.

Interestingly, feminist writing on the subject of identification in relation to gender identities has developed in two opposing directions. On the one hand, the psychoanalytically informed film criticism following Laura Mulvey's original attack on the visual pleasure of narrative cinema is still marked by a suspicion of any kind of feminine role model, heroine or image of identification. Mulvey's films (such as *Amy!*, 1980), as well as her influential theoretical work, have advocated a rejection of the conventions of popular representations, not simply for the images of femininity constructed, but also for the processes of identification offered to the cinema spectator. 'Identification' itself has been seen as a cultural process complicit with the reproduction of dominant culture by reinforcing patriarchal forms of identity. Anne Freidberg sums up what feminists have seen as the problematic functions of identification thus:

> Identification can only be made through recognition, and all recognition is itself an implicit confirmation of an existing form. The institutional sanction of stars as ego ideals also operates to establish normative figures. Identification enforces a collapse of the subject onto the normative demand for sameness, which, under patriarchy, is always male.[5]

On the other hand, some feminist cultural theorists have attempted to rescue the process of identification from such criticism, and have instead drawn attention to the empowerment through certain forms of identification within the consumption of popular culture. Valerie Walkerdine, for example, offers an analysis of the way the different members of a working-class family read *Rocky II*, which demonstrates the shifting significance of the metaphor of fighting in Rocky's character.[6] Gender differences produce different and conflicting identifications in Walkerdine and the family members; nevertheless identification is reclaimed in Walkerdine's analysis as potentially producing rebellious feelings and a desire to fight the dominant system, as well as being a necessary aspect of cultural consumption.

These two perspectives, then, represent opposite positions on processes of identification in the visual media: the first criticises identification of any kind for reproducing sameness, fixity and the confirmation of existing identities, whilst the second reclaims it as potentially empowering and expressive of resistance. They coincide, however, in taking psychoanalytic accounts of identification as central to their understanding of spectatorship.

Whilst there are detailed psychoanalytic accounts of the psychic processes of identification,[7] however, there has been less investigation of the broader cultural and social dimensions of identification in the cinema. Therefore instead of applying psychoanalytic theory to a film text to investigate identification in the cinema, I shall take the audiences' representations of this process and its meanings as my starting point. This is not to argue that audiences are the source of 'the true meanings' of films or of stars; clearly audiences' recollections are themselves a highly mediated set of cultural representations ... Instead, the purpose of this investigation is to look at the production of the meaning of stars in the terms of how audiences construct them.

Particularly striking in the letters I received was the diversity of processes represented which could loosely be termed identification. To the extent that identification involves various processes which negotiate the boundaries between self and other,[8] these processes take on a particular significance in the context of popular cinema where women in the audience are offered idealised images of femininity in many different forms. Some of these quite clearly relate back to the psychic processes described by psychoanalysis, and others move into the domain of cultural consumption more generally.

There is a problem finding a term to refer to the women in the audience whose letters are used in this analysis. The term 'female spectator', used so widely within feminist film theory, has been a confusing one; it has been used to refer both to the textual positions constructed by the film, and, often implicitly, to the female members of the cinema audience.[9] At best it is acknowledged that the two processes may, to some extent, be separate, but generally an implicit textual determinism defines assumptions about spectatorship.[10] In addition, the singularity of the reference of the term spectator implies a unified viewing experience, and its usage carries with it a very passive model of how audiences watch films.

I am using 'spectator' here in a rather different way to refer to members of the cinema audience. However, there is a further problem using the term to discuss practices which take place beyond the cinema, since spectator, in this broader sense, refers to a person still in the cinema. This is itself symptomatic of the limited interest in what spectatorship might mean outside or beyond the cinema experience. Spectatorship, when considered as an aspect of cultural consumption, should no longer be seen simply as an extension of a film text replicating infantile misrecognition, nor as an isolated viewing process, but rather as part of a more general cultural construction of identities.

The analysis of the letters which follows is divided into two sections. The first addresses processes of identification which involve fantasies about the relationship between the identity of the star and the identity of the spectator. On the whole these forms of identification relate to the cinematic context. The second section examines forms of identification which involve practice as well as fantasy, in that spectators actually transform some aspect of their identity as a result of their relationship to their favourite star. These practices extend beyond the cinema itself and thus spectatorship is considered in relation to the construction of feminine identities more generally.

CINEMATIC IDENTIFICATORY FANTASIES

Devotion and Worship

> I wanted to write and tell you of my devotion to my favourite star Doris Day. I thought she was fantastic, and joined her fan club, collected all the photos and info I could. I saw *Calamity Jane* 45 times in a fortnight and still watch all her films avidly. My sisters all thought I was mad going silly on a woman, but I just thought she was wonderful, they were mad about Elvis, but my devotion was to Doris Day. (V. M.)

Some letters do not even mention the self, but simply offer evidence of devotion to a female star. However, this is unusual; most letters I received framed their comments on stars in relation to their own identities. In this first group, many of the letters speak of the pleasure produced by some kind of difference from the star, the distance produced by this difference providing a source of fascination. Stars are frequently written about as out of reach, and belonging to a different world or plane of existence:

> Film stars ... seemed very special people, glamorous, handsome and way above us ordinary mortals. (J. T.)

> I'll never forget the first time I saw her, it was in *My Gal Sal* in 1942, and her name was Rita Hayworth. I couldn't take my eyes off her, she was the most perfect woman I had ever seen. The old cliché 'screen goddess' was used about many stars, but those are truly the only words that define that divine creature . . . I was stunned and amazed that any human being could be that lovely. (V. H.)

> Stars were fabulous creatures to be worshipped from afar, every film of one's favourite gobbled up as soon as it came out. (P. K.)

These statements represent the star as something different and unattainable. Religious signifiers here indicate the special status and meaning of the stars, as well as suggesting the intensity of the devotion felt by the spectator. They also reinforce the 'otherness' of the stars who are not considered part of the mortal world of the spectator. The last example, however, does introduce the star into the mortal world by a metaphor of ingestion reminiscent of the act of communion. Worship of stars as goddesses involves a denial of self found in some forms of religious devotion. The spectator is only present in these quotes as a worshipper, or through their adoration of the star. There is no reference to the identity of the spectator or suggestion of closing the gap between star and fan by becoming more like a star; these are simply declarations of appreciation from afar. The boundaries between self and ideal are quite fixed and stable in these examples, and the emphasis is very strongly on the ideal rather than the spectator. Even in the last statement, where the self is implicit in that the star is to be gobbled up, the star none the less remains the subject of the sentence.

The Desire to Become

In other examples, the relationship between star and audience is also articulated through the recognition of an immutable difference between star and spectator: 'Bette Davis was the epitome of what we would like to be, but knew we never could!' (N. T.). Yet here the desire to move across that difference and become more like the star is expressed, even if this is accompanied by the impossibility of its fulfilment.[11] The distance between the spectator and her ideal seems to produce a kind of longing which offers fantasies of transformed identities.

These desires to become more like the stars occur on several levels. Many of them are predictably articulated in relation to appearance:

> I finally kept with Joan Crawford – every typist's dream of how they'd like to look. (M. R.).

> And of course her [Betty Grable's] clothes – how could a young girl not want to look like that? (S. W.)

> Although I wished to look like a different star each week depending what film I saw, I think my favourite was Rita Hayworth, I always imagined, if I

could look like her I could toss my red hair into the wind ... and meet the man of my dreams ... (R. A.)

Clearly, stars serve a normative function to the extent that they are often read as role models, contributing to the construction of the ideals of feminine attractiveness circulating in culture at any one time. The age difference between the star and the younger fans is central here: stars provide ideals of femity for adolescent women in the audience, preoccupied with attaining adult femininity. Part of this kind of identification involves recognising desirable qualities in the ideal and wanting to move towards it:

Doris Day ... seemed to epitomise the kind of person who, with luck, I as a child could aspire to be. (B. C.)

I loved to watch Deanna Durbin. I used to put myself in her place. She lived in a typical girl's dream. (J. G.)

These examples demonstrate not simply the desire to overcome the gap between spectator and star, but a fantasy of possible movement between the two identities, from the spectator to the star.

Pleasure in Feminine Power

However, the difference between the female star and the female spectator is a source of fascination not only with ideals of physical beauty, but also with the stars' personalities and behaviour, which are often admired or envied by spectators. These identifications demonstrate the contradictory pleasures offered by Hollywood stars, on the one hand reproducing normative models of feminine glamour, whilst on the other hand offering women fantasies of resistance. For example, some female stars represented images of power and confidence. These were frequent favourites because they offered spectators fantasies of power outside their own experience.

We liked stars who were most different to ourselves and Katharine Hepburn, with her self-assured romps through any situation was one of them. We were youngsters at the time, and were anything but self confident, and totally lacking in sophistication, so, naturally, Bette Davis took the other pedestal. She who could be a real 'bitch', without turning a hair, and quelled her leading men with a raised eyebrow and sneer at the corners of her mouth ... (N. T.)

Bette Davis ... was great, I loved how she walked across the room in her films, she seemed to have a lot of confidence and she had a look of her own, as I think a lot of female stars had at that time ... (E. M.)

Powerful female stars often play characters in punishing patriarchal narratives, where the woman is either killed off, or married, or both, but these spectators do not seem to select this aspect of their films to write about. Instead, the qualities of confidence and power are remembered as offering pleasure to female spectators in something they lack and desire.

Identification and Escapism

This movement from spectator to star is part of the pleasure of escapism articulated in many of the letters. Instead of the difference between the spectator and the star being recognised and maintained, the difference provides the possibility for the spectator to leave her world temporarily and become part of the star's world.[12]

> It made no difference to me if the film was ushered in by a spangled globe, the Liberty Lady or that roaring lion, I was no longer in my seat but right up there fleeing for my life from chasing gangsters, skimming effortlessly over silver ice, or singing high and sweet like a lark. (D. H.)

> I was only a girl, but I could be transported from the austerity and gloom of that time to that other world on the silver screen. (J. T.)

> Joan Crawford – could evoke such pathos, and suffer such martyrdom . . . making you live each part. (M. B.)

In these examples, the movement from self to other is more fluid than in the previous categories, and this fluidity provides the well-known pleasure of the cinema: 'losing oneself' in the film. Here, in contrast to the distinction between self and ideal maintained in the processes of spectatorship discussed above, the spectator's identity merges with the star in the film, or the character she is portraying.

In this first section I have discussed processes of spectatorship which involve negotiating the difference between the star and the spectator in various ways: beginning with the denial of self, in favour of praising the screen goddesses, and moving on to the desire to become like the star, but realising the impossibility of such desires, and ending with the pleasure in overcoming the difference and merging with the ideal on the screen.

EXTRA-CINEMATIC IDENTIFICATORY PRACTICES

Now I want to move on to discuss representations which concern what I shall call 'identificatory practices' of spectatorship. These nearly all relate to forms of identification which take place outside the cinematic context. These practices also involve the audience engaging in some kind of practice of transformation of the self to become more like the star they admire, or to involve others in the recognition of their similarity with the star.

Pretending

> . . . there was a massive open-cast coal site just at the tip of our estate – there were 9 of us girls – and we would go to the site after school, and play on the mounds of soil removed from the site. The mounds were known to us as

'Beverley Hills' and we all had lots of fun there. Each of us had our own spot where the soil was made into a round – and that was our mansion. We played there for hours – visiting one mansion after another and each being our own favourite film star ... (M. W.)

I really loved the pictures, they were my life, I used to pretend I was related to Betty Grable because my name was Betty, and I used to get quite upset when the other children didn't believe me. (B. C.)

Pretending to be particular film stars involves an imaginary practice, but one where the spectator involved knows that it is a game. This is rather different from the processes of escapism in the cinema discussed above whereby the spectator feels completely absorbed in the star's world and which thus involves a temporary collapsing of the self into the star identity. The first example given above is also different in that it involves a physical as well as an imaginary transformation. Furthermore pretending does not simply involve the privatised imagination of the individual spectator, as in the process of escapism, but also involves the participation of other spectators in the collective fantasy games. This kind of representation of the relationship between star and fan is based more on similarity than difference, since the fan takes on the identity of the star in a temporary game of make-believe, and the difference between them is made invisible, despite the recognition of the whole process as one of pretending.

Resembling

Bette Davis – her eyes were fabulous and the way she walked arrogantly ... I have dark eyes, in those days I had very large dark eyebrows ... and my Dad used to say ... 'Don't you roll those Bette Davis eyes at me young lady ...' ... Now Doris Day, that's a different thing – we share the same birthday ... (P. O.)

There are numerous points of recognition of similarities between the spectator and the star. These are not based on pretending to be something one is not, but rather selecting something which establishes a link between the star and the self based on a pre-existing part of the spectator's identity which bears a resemblance to the star. This does not necessarily involve any kind of transformation, but rather a highlighting of star qualities in the individual spectator. The significance of particular features, such as 'Bette Davis eyes', seems to exceed physical likeness, to suggest a certain kind of femininity, in this case a rebellious one which represented a challenge to the father's authority.

Imitating

Unlike the above process of recognising a resemblance to a star, many spectators wrote about practices which involved transforming themselves to be more like the star. This is different from the fantasy of becoming the star whilst viewing a film, or even expressing the desire to become more like the star generally, since it involves an actual imitation of a star or of her particular characteristics in a particular film. In other words this identificatory practice involves a form of pretending or play-acting, and yet it is also different from pretending, since pretending is represented as a process involving the whole star persona, whereas imitation is used here to indicate a partial taking-on of part of a star's identity.

Several letters gave examples of imitating singing and dancing of favourite stars after the film performance:

> We used to go home and do concerts based on the songs and dances we had seen in the films, and one of my friends had an auntie who was a mine of information on the words of songs from films ... (B. F.)

> The films we saw made us sing and sometimes act our way home on the bus ... (J. T.)

> My favourite female star was Betty Grable. The songs she sang in the film, I would try to remember, I would sing and dance all the way home ... (P. G.)

The imitation of stars was not limited to singing and dancing, but was clearly a pleasure in terms of replicating gestures, speech and star personalities: 'I had my favourites of course ... One week I would tigerishly pace about like Joan Crawford, another week I tried speaking in the staccato tones of Bette Davis and puffing a cigarette at the same time' (D. H.).

Copying

Although imitation and copying are very closely linked as practices, I want to use them here differently to distinguish between audiences *imitating* behaviour and activities, and copying appearances. As the attempted replication of appearance, then, *copying* relates back to the desire to look like stars discussed above. However it is not simply expressed as an unfulfillable desire or pleasurable fantasy, as in the earlier examples, it is also a practice which transforms the spectators' physical appearance.

Copying is the most common form of identificatory practice outside the cinema. Perhaps this is not surprising given the centrality of physical appearance to femininity in general in this culture, and to female Hollywood stars in particular. The 'visual pleasure' offered by the glamour and sexual appeal of Hollywood stars has been thoroughly criticised by feminists elsewhere[13]. Here I am interested in how women audiences related to these ideals of femininity as presented by Hollywood stars on the screen, and particularly in how identification extends beyond individualised fantasies into practices aimed at the transformation of identity.

> I was a very keen fan of Bette Davis and can remember seeing her in *Dark Victory* ... That film had such an impact on me. I can remember coming

home and looking in the mirror fanatically trying to comb my hair so that I could look like her. I idolised her . . . thought she was a wonderful actress. (V. C.)

This process involves an intersection of self and other, subject and object. The impact of the film on the spectator was to produce a desire to resemble physically the ideal. In front of a reflection of herself, the spectator attempts to close the gap between her image and her ideal image, by trying to produce a new image, more like her ideal. In this instance, her hair is the focus of this desired transformation. Indeed hairstyle is one of the most frequently recurring aspects of the star's appearance which the spectators try to copy:

My friends and I would try and copy the hair styles of the stars, sometimes we got it right, and other times we just gave up, as we hadn't the looks of the stars or the money to dress the way they did. (E. M.)

Now Doris Day . . . I was told many times around that I looked like her, so I had my hair cut in a D.A. style. Jane Wyman was a favourite at one stage and I had hair cut like hers, it was called a tulip . . . Now Marilyn Monroe was younger and by this time I had changed my image, my hair was almost white blonde and longer and I copied her hairstyle, as people said I looked like her. (P. O.)

These forms of copying involve some kind of self-transformation to produce an appearance more similar to Hollywood stars. Some spectators clearly have a stronger feeling of their success than others; the first example includes a sense of defeat whilst the last seems to be able to achieve several desired likenesses, especially bearing in mind this respondent is the one who had 'Bette Davis eyes'. The difference then between the star and the spectator is transformable into similarity through the typical work of femininity: the production of oneself simultaneously as subject and object in accordance with cultural ideals of femininity.

Copying and Consumption

Copying the hairstyles of famous film stars can be seen as a form of cultural production and consumption. It involves the production of a new self-image through the pleasure taken in a star image. In this last section I want to consider an extension of the identificatory practice of copying where it intersects with the consumption of cultural products in addition to the star image. The construction of women as cinema spectators overlaps here with their construction as consumers.

To some extent copying the hairstyles of the stars overlaps with this. However I have separated hairstyles from other aspects of this process, since changing hairstyles does not necessarily involve the actual purchasing of other products to transform the identity of the spectator, although it may do. The purchasing of items such as clothing and cosmetics in relation to particular stars brings into particularly sharp focus the relationship between the cinema industries and other forms of capitalist industry. Stars are consumable feminine images which female spectators then reproduce through other forms of consumption.

> ... and I bought clothes like hers [Doris Day] ... dresses, soft wool, no sleeves, but short jackets, boxy type little hats, half hats we used to call them and low heeled court shoes to match your outfit, kitten heels they were called ... as people said I looked like her [Marilyn Monroe] I even bought a suit after seeing her in *Niagara*. (P. O.)

> It was fun trying to copy one's favourite stars with their clothes, hats and even make-up, especially the eyebrows. Hats were very much in vogue at that time and shops used to sell models similar to the styles the stars were wearing. I was very much into hats myself and tried in my way (on a low budget) to copy some of them. Naturally I bought a Deanna Durbin model hat and a Rita Hayworth one. (V. C.)

> I'd like to name Deanna Durbin as one of my favourite stars. Her beautiful singing voice, natural personality and sparkling eyes made her films so enjoyable, and one always knew she would wear boleros; in one film she wore six different ones. I still like wearing boleros – so you can tell what a lasting effect the clothes we saw on the screen made on us. (J. D. Member of the Deanna Durbin Society)

Stars are thus identified with particular commodities which are part of the reproduction of feminine identities. The female spectators in these examples produce particular images of femininity which remind them of their favourite stars. In so doing they produce a new feminine identity, one which combines an aspect of the star with their own appearance. This is different from imitation, which is more of a temporary reproduction of a particular kind of behaviour which resembles the star. It transforms the spectators' previous appearance, and in doing so offers the spectator the pleasure of close association with her ideal.

> As teenagers and young girls we did not have the vast variety of clothing and choices of make-up that is available today, so hairstyles and make-up were studied with great interest and copied ... I seem to remember buying a small booklet by Max Factor with pictures of the stars, M.G.M. mostly, with all the details of their make-up and how to apply it ... (E. H.)

> Their make-up was faultless and their fashion of the forties platform shoes, half hats with rows of curls showing at the back under the hat ... We used to call the shoes 'Carmen Miranda' shoes ... I felt like a film star using Lux Toilet soap, advertised as the stars' soap. (V. B.)

Through the use of cosmetic products, then, as well as through the purchasing and use of clothing, spectators take on a part of the star's identity and make it part of their own. The self and the ideal combine to produce another feminine identity, closer to the ideal. This is the direct opposite of the process of identification I began with in the first section, in which the spectator's own identity remained relatively marginal to the description of the pleasure taken in female Hollywood stars. In this final process, the star becomes more marginal and is only relevant in so far as the star identity relates to the spectator's own identity. As has been noted by other commentators, these latter practices demonstrate the importance of understanding Hollywood stars and their audiences in relation to other cultural industries of the 1940s and 1950s.[14]

CONCLUDING COMMENTS

Having outlined some of the different forms of identification in audience–star relationships represented in these letters, it is now important to reconsider some of the earlier models of identification and spectatorship in the light of this research. First, the diversity of processes of identification, including forms of desire, evident in these letters is striking. The idea of a singular process of identification, so often assumed in psychoanalytic film theory, seems unsatisfactory in the light of the range of processes discussed above. In addition, the use of the term 'female spectatorship' to refer to a single positioning by a film text seems equally inappropriate in the light of the diversity of readings of stars by different women in the cinema audiences in the 1940s and 1950s.

As well as categorising the many different kinds of identification in the relationships between audiences and stars, I have also drawn attention to the broad distinction between two different forms of identification: identificatory fantasies and identificatory practices. This is not to suggest that the practices do not also involve fantasies, nor that fantasies cannot also be considered as practices. But rather, it is important to extend our understanding of cinematic identification, previously analysed solely at the level of fantasy, to include the practices documented by these spectators, in order to understand the different forms of overlap between stars' and audiences' identities.

Another significant distinction is that between cinematic identification, which refers to the viewing experience, and extra-cinematic identification, referring to the use of stars' identities in a different cultural time and space. So far, film studies has, not surprisingly, been concerned with the former. However, the importance of these extra-cinematic forms of identification to the women who wrote to me came across very forcefully in their letters. Not only was this one of the most written-about aspects of the relationship between stars and audiences, but the pleasure and force of feeling with which they recalled the details of the significance of stars in this context was also striking.

All the above forms of identification relate to a final distinction which I have used to frame the sequence of the quotations: identification based on difference and identification based on similarity. The early categories of identification concern processes where the differences between the star and the spectator produce the sources of pleasure and fascination. The representations of these processes tended to emphasise the presence of the star and de-emphasise the identity of the spectator. The later categories concern processes where the similarity, or at least the possibility of closing the gap produced by the differences between stars and spectators, is the source of pleasure expressed. In these examples the reproduction of the spectators' identities tended to be the focus of the commentary. Thus identifications do not merely involve processes of recognition based on similarity, but also involve the productive recognition of differences between femininities.

Indeed the processes of identification articulated most strongly in terms of difference seem to be those relating more directly to the cinematic context where the image of the star is still present on the screen. The processes, and practices, which involve reproducing similarity seem to be those extra-cinematic identifications which take place more in the spectator's more familiar domestic context, where the star's identity is selectively reworked and incorporated into the spectator's new identity. Even in these cases, identification does not simply involve the passive reproduction of existing femininities, but rather an active engagement and production of changing identities.

The assumption behind much of the psychoanalytic work discussed earlier is that identification fixes identities: 'identification can only be made through recognition, and all recognition is itself an implicit confirmation of existing form'.[15] Many of the examples I have discussed contradict this assumption and demonstrate not only the diversity of existing forms, but also that recognition involves the production of desired identities, rather than simply the confirmation of existing ones. Many forms of identification involve processes of transformation and the production of new identities, combining the spectator's existing identity with her desired identity and her reading of the star's identity.

This research also challenges the assumption that identification is necessarily problematic because it offers the spectator the illusory pleasure of unified subjectivity. The identifications represented in these letters speak as much about partial recognitions and fragmented replications as they do about the misrecognition of a unified subjectivity in an ego ideal on the screen. Thus, cultural consumption does not necessarily fix identities, destroy differences and confirm sameness. If we take audiences as a starting point for understanding the consumption of stars, the active and productive elements of the star-audience relationships begin to emerge.

In challenging previous models of passive female spectatorship, and demonstrating the diversity and complexity of identifications between stars and women in the audience, however, I am not suggesting feminists look at cultural consumption uncritically. Taking audiences as a starting point can present problems for a feminist analysis: how can we remain critical of the dominant meanings of gender produced by Hollywood, whilst at the same time taking seriously the pleasures female spectators articulate about their favourite stars? Perhaps this problem is itself a reason for the reluctance by feminists to analyse female audiences and their relationship to dominant idealised feminine images, such as Hollywood stars.

In asking women to write to me about the appeal of Hollywood stars, it was inevitable I would receive an enthusiastic response. The discrepancy between the passion with which women spectators wrote about their Hollywood favourites and feminist criticisms of the patriarchal constructions of femininity in Hollywood produces a familiar dilemma for feminists working in many areas of cultural analysis. Simply to use what women wrote to me to illustrate the subordinating operations of patriarchal capitalism seems to me to be overwhelmingly patronising, as well as rather pessimistic. But simply to embrace the enthusiastic spirit of the pleasures they describe would be equally problematic, and would reproduce an uncritical populism which leaves behind crucial feminist insights. It therefore remains a challenge to feminists analysing Hollywood cinema to produce critical accounts of dominant cultural representations whilst at the same time developing theories of female cultural consumption as an active and productive process.

NOTES

1. S. Freud, *Group Psychology and the Analysis of the Ego*, 1921, chapter 7, quoted in Anne Friedberg, 'Identification and the Star: a refusal of difference', in Christine Gledhill, ed., *Star Signs* (London, BFI Publishing, 1982).
2. Ibid., 49.
3. Christian Metz, 'Le Signifiant imaginaire', *Communications*, 23 (1975); trans. Celia Britton, Anwyl Williams, Ben Brewster, Alfred Guzetti, *Psychoanalysis and Cinema: The Imaginary Signifier* (London, Macmillan, 1983).
4. Anne Friedberg, 'Identification and the Star', p. 50.
5. Ibid., 53.
6. Valerie Walkerdine, 'Video replay: families, films and fantasies', in Victor Burgin, James Donald and Cora Kaplan, eds, *Formations of Fantasy* (London, Methuen, 1986).
7. For example, see Jacqueline Rose, *Sexuality in the Field of Vision* (London, Verso, 1986), Mary Anne Doane, *The Desire to Desire: The Woman's Film of the 1940s* (Bloomington and Indianapolis, Indiana University Press, 1987), and Teresa De Lauretis, *Alice Doesn't: Feminism, Semiotics, Cinema* (London, Macmillan, 1984).
8. For a typology of audience–star relations, see Andrew Tudor, *Image and Influence: Studies in the Sociology of Film* (London, Allen & Unwin, 1974), 80.
9. See Tania Modleski, 'Introduction: Hitchcock, feminism and the patriarchal unconscious', in *The Women Who Knew Too Much: Hitchcock and Feminist Theory* (London, Methuen, 1988).
10. This problem is addressed by Annette Kuhn, 'Women's genres', in *Screen*, 25, 1 (1984), 18–28.
11. For a discussion of the representation of desire between women produced by their differences, see Jackie Stacey, 'Desperately seeking difference', in *Screen*, 28, 1 (1987), 48–61.
12. For a discussion of the pleasurable feelings escapism offers to the cinema audience, see Richard Dyer, 'Entertainment and utopia', *Movie*, 24 (Spring 1977), 2–13.
13. See Laura Mulvey, *Visual and other Pleasures* (London, Macmillan, 1989), and E. Ann Kaplan, *Women and Film: Both Sides of the Camera* (London, Methuen, 1983).
14. See Angela Partington, 'Melodrama's gendered audience' in Sarah Franklin, Celia Lury and Jackie Stacey, (eds), *Off Centre: Feminism and Cultural Studies* (London, HarperCollins, 1991) pp. 49–68.
15. Friedberg, 'Identification and the Star', 53.

16

'TABOOS AND TOTEMS: CULTURAL MEANINGS OF *THE SILENCE OF THE LAMBS'*

Janet Staiger

By the fifth week of the release of *Silence of the Lambs* (1991), the debates over the film had solidified into a set of propositions: 1) that whether or not Jonathan Demme had intended to create a homophobic film, the character of the serial murderer had attributes associated with stereotypes of gay men; 2) that in a time of paranoia over AIDS and increased violence directed toward gays in the United States, even suggesting connections between homosexuals and serial murderers was irresponsible; but 3) that the character of Clarice Starling played by Jodie Foster was a positive image of a woman working in a patriarchal society and, thus, empowering for women viewers. The diversion in views produced a consequent division: two non-dominant groups, some gay men and some feminists (both straight and lesbian), found themselves at odds over evaluating the film.

The controversy further escalated when several activists 'outed' Jodie Foster. 'Outing' is the recent practice by some people to declare publically that certain individuals are homosexual or bisexual[1] even though those people have not chosen to make their sexual preferences known. The argument for doing this is that it is hypocritical for famous people to remain private about such preferences if they participate in public activities which perpetuate homophobia. Rather they should help promote gay rights.

Foster's outing produced in the most vitriolic counter-analysis the claim that Foster was being outed because she was a strong woman and that she was being

* From Collins, J., Radner, H., and Collins, A. P. (eds), *Film Theory Goes to the Movies*. London: Routledge, 1993, pp. 142–54.

'offer[ed] up [by gay activists] as a sacrifice in the furtherance of gay visibility.'[2] 'You don't have to look far,' the woman argued,

> to find a reason why a culture with screen idols such as Marilyn Monroe and Judy Garland would object so vociferously to an actress like Jodie Foster. Like their straight brothers, the gay men who condemn Jodie Foster and *Lambs* are out to destroy a woman who doesn't put male interests first and doesn't conform to their idea of what a woman should be. Under the guise of promoting gay consciousness, they're falling back on the same reliable weapon that men have used for centuries against women who claim a little too much for themselves—they're calling her a dyke.

Although other women were not so strong in their condemnation of Foster's outing, all thirteen of those women whose views of the movie, *Silence of the Lambs*, I had available to me expressed praise for the film. These included at least two lesbians, one of whom criticized Larry Kramer of ACT UP for his 'patronizing' attitude toward Foster, trying to treat her as a 'disobedient daughter.'[3]

Whether Foster is or is not a lesbian or bisexual 'in real life' is not the point of this essay. Whether the character she plays in *Silence of the Lambs* is or is not a lesbian is also not at issue here. What I shall be pursuing instead is the ultimate *stitching* together of gay and woman that became the 'climax' of the discussion. I shall argue that this possibility, while not inevitable, is grounded in its reception context and process. What I shall be doing here is what I call historical reception studies. This research attempts to illuminate the cultural meanings of texts in specific times and social circumstances to specific viewers, and it attempts to contribute to discussions about the spectorial effects of films by moving beyond text-centered analyses.

Because I wish to give you an application of this rather than an extended theoretical argument, I will simply lay out several hypotheses informing my research:

1) Immanent meaning in a text is denied.

2) 'Free readers' do not exist either.

3) Instead, contexts of social formations and constructed identities of the self in relation to historical conditions explain the interpretation strategies and affective responses of readers. Thus, receptions need to be related to specific historical conditions as *events*.

4) Furthermore, because the historical context's discursive formation is contradictory and heterogeneous, *no* reading is unified.

5) The best means currently available for analyzing cultural meanings exist in poststructuralist and ideological textual analyses. These methods, of necessity, draw upon multiple theoretical frameworks

and perspectives such as deconstructionism, psychoanalysis, cognitive psychology, linguistics, anthropology, cultural studies Marxism, and feminist, ethnic and minority, lesbian and gay studies. They do so with a clear understanding that the connections and differences among the frameworks and perspectives must be theorized.

Consequently, historical reception studies work combines contemporary critical and cultural studies to understand why distinct interpretive and affective experiences circulate historically in specific social formations. In a case study, the following steps might occur:

1) An object of analysis is determined. This object is an *event*, not a text: that is, it is a set of interpretations or affective experiences produced by individuals from an encounter with a text or set of texts within a social situation. It is not an analysis of the text except in so far as to consider what textually might be facilitating the reading.

2) Traces of that event are located. Here I shall be using primarily traces in the form of printed prose and images, but when available, oral accounts would be very good sites of additional evidence. The print and images include about twenty reviews, news articles, letters to papers, advertisements, illustrations, and publicity which circulated in the major mass media.

3) The traces are analyzed textually and culturally. That is, as new historians elucidate causal processes to explain conjunctions called 'events' and then characterize the social significance of these events in relation to specific groups of people, so too does this research. Furthermore, the analyses avoid categorizing receptions into preferred, negotiated, or resistant readings. Rather the processes of interpretation are described since more richness in explanation can be achieved than by reducing readings to three specific generalizations.

4) Finally, the range of readings is considered not only by what seems possible at that moment but also by what the readings did not consider. That is, structuring absences are as important as well.

My project will be to work toward explicating the event of the 'sacrificial' outing of Jodie Foster. I shall argue that, although this event might be explained simply through contemporary US stereotypes of lesbians—i.e., a strong woman must be a lesbian—or even because of informal oral communication circulated by gays and lesbians about Foster's sexual preferences, the possibility of making such an inference was facilitated by the critical response *Silence of the Lambs* received. Furthermore, Foster's outing is symptomatic of current cultural taboos and totems. Thus, calling Foster a lesbian is more overdetermined linguistically, psychoanalytically, and culturally than it might appear.

In this initial study of the event, three specific reading strategies occur.[4] These are: 1) the construction of binary oppositions with deployments of high and low, good and bad attributions; 2) the use of metaphor and analogy; and 3), most pertinent to the event, the hybridization or grafting of incompatible terms together. This practice is activated from the prior two strategies and even finds its motivation from one of the dominant metaphors in the discourse.

TABOOS

Perhaps because many writers have gone to film school or because thinking in oppositions so colors our everyday lives, reviewers of *Silence of the Lambs* often structured their plot analyses around a central binary opposition. The most obvious opposition was one between Hannibal 'The Cannibal' Lecter and Jame 'Buffalo Bill' Gumb. One reviewer notices that Lecter is upper class and witty while Gumb is a 'working-class lout.'[5] The reviewer even emphasizes how this sets up an audience to sympathize with the 'good' Lecter and to find disgusting the 'bad' Gumb. He critically summarizes, 'Lecter: rich, wise, clever, helpful, and funny. Gumb: working-class, stupid, dense, and dull. Lecter: straight. Gumb: gay. Lecter: abstract evil; Gumb: evil incarnate.' David Denby characterizes the Lecter/Gumb opposition as between 'an unimaginable vicious genius; the other merely rabid and weird.'[6] Another reviewer writes that the film has 'two villains who represent quite different incarnations of evil. Buffalo Bill a grotesque enigma, has absolutely no redeeming virtues. But Lecter is strangely sympathetic, a symbol of muzzled rage.'[7]

Important to this evaluation is that Lecter's victims are bureaucrats and authority figures, such as the census taker whose liver he ate with a nice Chianti. Meanwhile, Gumb goes after young, overweight women. Additionally, of course, Gumb is played as effeminate—something remarked upon by several reviewers who also acknowledged the gay community's concern about the film.

Binary oppositions are commonly deployed in ways such that the two terms in the opposition are not equal. Peter Stallybrass and Allon White in *The Politics and Poetics of Transgression* argue that cultural oppositions often duplicate themselves in various discursive realms.[8] That is, hierarchies reproduce themselves across various symbolic systems such as psychic forms, the human body, geographical spaces, and social orders. To justify these figurations, one symbolic system will refer to the other to warrant its ordering. An obvious example would be the equation commonly made between the head as exalted and the lower anatomy as base; the physical body is written over by a metaphysical discourse.[9]

This hierarchization of binary oppositions functions analogically to legitimate Lecter's cannibalism. Thus, the class attributions, choice of victims, and socialized behavior patterns are read not merely as oppositions but ones with values attached which reinforced each other. Viewers routinely enjoyed Lecter, particularly as played by Anthony Hopkins. *Variety*'s reviewer symptomatically jokes: the 'juiciest part is Hopkins.'[10] Lecter, of course, offers an interesting problem since he breaks a taboo which would so normally be described as the horror for a film.

Can we explain the spectators' acceptance of this transgression beyond the functioning of the textual array of values attached to the binary oppositions? Freud writes in *Totem and Taboo* that taboos are occasionally breached only to reassert the boundaries authenticating them. One instance of such a breach is the ritual eating of something considered taboo. Such a thing might even be the plant or animal which the tribe considers to be its totem. Totems stand as symbols for the group.

But according to Freud, they are also causal explanations. The totem is the tribe's origin, the 'father' of the tribe. Thus, Freud links the ritual eating of totems to the Oedipal story and argues that what has been established as out-of-bounds (e.g., killing one's father) is in the ritual the symbolic consumption of the totem's character. A current example of such a ritual act, Freud writes, is the Christian communion. Drinking wine and eating bread is devouring one's own kind. Lecter, of course, foregoes the more oblique symbolism: he actually eats members of the tribe but for the same purpose.[11] Lecter's ingestation of his own kind, authorized as the incorporation of the bodies of authority figures and legitimated through socially originated hierarchies of binary oppositions, provides both textual and contextual determinations for spectators to accept, and even find pleasure in, his destruction of boundaries.

Consequently, and as part of the weirdly disconcerting pleasure of the event, the reviewers make all sorts of jokes about accepting the broken taboo as if they too wish to participate in the ritual. These jokes occur in the form of puns, doubly validating as they are by puns being a lawful disruption of traditional meanings. For example, Denby writes: 'The horrors of the scene are brought off with, well, taste.'[12] Another reviewer notes, 'Buffalo Bill is famous for killing women, skinning them and leaving the cocoon of an exotic moth in their mouths. Lecter made his name by eating the flesh of his victims raw. All of that may sound a little hard to swallow.'[13] One columnist gives Demme a 'C– in Mise-en-Scène 101 for the way he fleshes out (so to speak) the villainous Jame Gumb on screen.'[14] Notice that all of these wisecracks are made apologically, because they do, indeed, open fissures in social categorizing. Headlines are particularly susceptible to word play, and the discursive motif continues there. Examples include: 'Overcooked Lambs,' 'Skin Deep: Jonathan Demme's Chatter of the Hams,' and 'Gluttons for Punishment.'[15]

Thus, a very powerful and significant binary opposition between Lecter and Gumb is constructed and circulated by viewers of the film. A second structuring binary opposition is proposed by Denby and J. Hoberman who point out that Clarice Starling has several fathers with which to contend.[16] Hoberman expands the comparison: Crawford, the FBI agent, is her daytime dad who is rational; Lecter, her nighttime father, is a 'charismatic suitor.'[17] This reading of the film as an incest story is transformed in other reviews. As one writer suggests, *Silence of the Lambs* can be seen as about Starling who is 'changing, trying to formulate an identity.'[18] Interpreting the film as an Oedipal passage for Starling is reinforced *visually* by iconographic materials published with the reviews. Most illustrations were supplied by Orion in its publicity kit. These feature Lecter standing behind Starling with Crawford behind both of them. Some illustrations cut out Crawford; others left him in. All three people face forward so that Crawford and Lecter seem to be peering over Starling's shoulder.

Reading *Silence of the Lambs* as an initiation/Oedipal story fits in an eerie way a discussion of the slasher genre by Carol Clover. She argues that in this genre women are victimized by psychopathic killers. However, she continues that it would be an error to assume that slasher pictures are simply cases of misogyny. For one thing, we ought not imagine that gender characteristics determine viewer identification.[19] This is particularly important with cinematic representation in which the physical body is often so powerful as an immediate signifier of gender. Furthermore, viewer identification does not necessarily remain stably located to a single character throughout a film. For instance, Clover believes that in slasher movies identification seems to alter during the course of the picture from sympathizing with the killer to identifying with the woman-hero. Clover also argues that the (apparently male) monster is usually characterized as bisexual while the woman-hero is not so simply a 'woman.' She is often 'unfeminine,' even tracking the killer into 'his underground labyrinth.'[20]

The ultimate confrontation in the slasher film, Clover believes, is between a 'shared femininity' and a 'shared masculinity' in which the monster is castrated. Thus, the woman-hero is able to appropriate, refering to Linda Williams's work, 'all those phallic symbols" of the killer's. Moreover, and important here, the woman-hero is 'a congenial double for the adolescent male' who is now negotiating sexual identity. The woman-hero is a safe identificatory substitute for a male, with the repressed plot about male-to-male relations. The woman-hero is thus a 'homoerotic stand-in.'

Psychoanalytical discourse is widespread, and Hoberman, among others, is familiar with it. Thus, the historical discourse of psychoanalysis may be abetting his reading the film as an Oedipal crisis for Starling, one that ends 'happily.' Starling is permitted to join the FBI; Lecter rewards her with unfettered independence from threats by him. Furthermore, and most significantly, Starling kills Gumb, symbol of aberrant sexual behavior, thus overtly denying homoeroticism while permitting it to exist in the apparently heterosexual Crawford-Starling pair.

Thus, one way some reviewers seem to have read the film is Starling-as-Masquerading-Woman who accedes into patriarchy. However, another way exists to understand parts of the interpretive reception of *Silence of the Lambs*. To explore that I need to draw out further the second interpretive strategy: the functions of metaphor and analogy.

TOTEMS

We can assume that some reviewers of the movie read the original novel which is thus part of the potential context for interpreting the film. The novel employs a rather hackneyed device: the various characters are linked to animals, with a theme of natural preying.[21] At the first meeting between Crawford and Starling, Crawford describes Lecter's behavior: 'It's the kind of curiosity that makes a snake look in a bird's nest' (6). Starling, of course, is thus forewarned. Later, added to Lecter's attributes is the classic connection of the snake being the devil: 'Dr Lecter's eyes are maroon and they reflect the light in pinpoints of red' (16); his tongue flickers in and out of his face (144). Thus, the metaphor builds a set of parallelisms: body attributes equal snake equals devil; therefore, evil.

The animal motif as metaphor and category for social cognition, perhaps set up by having read the novel, perhaps from Starling's name itself—or from the title of the film—perhaps from habit, permeates reception discourse about *Silence of the Lambs*. Lecter is a 'cobra'[22] who lives in a 'snake pit of an asylum.'[23] He makes 'hissing, vile, intimate remarks to women.'[24]

The initiation theme crisscrosses with this motif. Starling is described as 'molelike' for her penetration of the killers' habitats. She descends into the 'dungeon-like bowels' of the prison;[25] she raids the 'basement of death.'[26] Stuart Klawans points out that Starling must overcome all sorts of obstacles: the initial course in the opening shots, a 'labyrinth of offices,' 'a mazelike dungeon.'[27]

But Starling is not always, or usually, the one doing the preying. 'Lecter plays cat and mouse with Clarice.'[28] For viewers, Starling can become the totem animal with whom she identifies: *she* is the 'lamb in wolves' territory.'[29] Also crossing is the devil association. Starling 'must defend herself at all times, lest [Lecter] eat her soul.'[30]

Social discourses are never uniform nor logical even as they try to map hierarchies across semantic categories. In the reception of *Silence of the Lambs*, Lecter's meaning is mobile; some times on the top, other times on the bottom. This inversion is most obvious when he is positioned not to counsel but to threaten Starling. The photographs of the series of father figures with Starling could be read another way. Some men reviewers took Starling to be a woman-victim. Could readers perceive Starling as a woman in danger?

In a discussion of the representation of the naked female body, Margaret R. Miles points out that by the 15th century, a common visual motif is the positioning of a woman in a frontal pose with the figure of Adam, her lover, standing behind her.[31] Or, Adam is transformed into the Figure of Death and the woman dances with him. Or in even more threatening and troubling images, Death copulates with the woman in sadomasochistic brutalism. These images are reminiscent of representations of vampirism, a later connection of animals, eating, sexuality, and death. Miles argues that their significance is the patriarchal connection of woman with sin, sex, and death. But she also notes that 'Julia Kristeva has stated that [while] "significance is inherent in the human body," ... little more can be said about *what* is signified until one examines the meanings of bodies in their particular religious and social contexts.'[32]

Hauntingly, then, another theme in the critical reception of the film is the ambiguous threat of Lecter to Starling as woman-victim. When they discussed it, many reviewers did take the threat to be sexual in some way. Added to this was the suggestion of pandering by Crawford who sends Starling to Lecter hoping, as Vincent Canby puts it, 'to arouse his interest.'[33] This reading, however, does not mean that Starling is necessarily being read psychically as female, with the sexuality as heterosexual—in fact it would be repressed polymorphous sexuality—but it does open the space for such a reception. This opens for discussion another feature in the array of interpretations.

MINOTAURS AND MOTHS

Women who discussed the film in the public discourse that I surveyed liked *Silence of the Lambs* and seemed especially to sympathize with Starling. Julie Salamon describes Starling as 'an attractive woman of unexceptional size doing what used to be thought of as a man's job . . . She is a rare heroine, a woman who goes about her work the way men do in movies, without seeming less a woman.'[34] Amy Taubin praises the movie as a 'feminist film' which 'suggests that [sexuality and sexual role] fantasies can be exumed and examined, and that their meanings can be shifted.' Taubin goes on to invert traditional mythology: after describing Starling's discussions with Lecter as 'the meeting of Oedipus and the Sphinx,' she claims that the pleasure of the film is 'the two-hour spectacle of a woman solving the perverse riddles of patriarchy—all by herself.'[35]

Again, Starling is being placed in the narrative position traditionally given to a male. However, in Taubin's scenario, Lecter is not the patriarchal father. Rather, Lecter must fit in the slot of the Sphinx, the monstrous hybrid with the upper torso of a woman and the lower torso an amalgamation of animal body parts. Although symptomatically its gender is unknown, the Sphinx has traditionally been associated with the 'maternal.' Interestingly, however, no other reviewer surveyed suggested that Lecter had any feminine traits, perhaps because by contrast he seemed masculine compared with Gumb.[36]

Another monstrous hybrid is also mentioned in the reviews. Hoberman retitles the movie 'Nancy Drew Meets the Minotaur.' The Minotaur is a double inversion of the Sphinx, for its lower body is that of a human male while its head is that of a bull.[37] Thus, the human body halves that define the two beasts are reversed as well as the genders. Furthermore, the Minotaur is absolutely knowable as male since the lower portion of its body is entirely visible—the area legitimated by medical discourse as that which defines and describes sexual difference.[38] This Minotaur association is reinforced through the labyrinth metaphors mentioned earlier.

The third reading strategy is hybridization, the grafting together of irreconcilables. The associations with these particular mythical beasts are some evidence of this. Note, in particular, that what is grotesque is not the blurring of boundaries or even their transgression, which is the case for Lecter's cannibalism in which he ingests another and takes on its attributes. Rather what is disturbing is the all-too-apparent, the *see-able*, combination of disparate semantical categories: human/animal. Again, Hoberman's discourse is particularly insightful. About Gumb, he writes, '[Buffalo Bill] is a jarring billboard of discordant signs—a figure stitched together like the Frankenstein monster.'[39]

Hoberman's vocabulary, then, gives us the thread to another pattern of interpretation motivated by the text and mobilized by the historical context. Gumb received his nickname because he skins his victims and sews those skins together to make himself an outfit. Literally stripping the women of their outer raiment, Gumb tries to fashion himself into the woman he desires to be. All of the reviewers decide he is the ultimate monster.

Working from Kristeva's thoughts about the abject, Barbara Creed has recently argued that the horror to be confronted in some films is not just the phallic mother but, finally, the archaic mother of the imaginary, pre-Oedipal experience.[40] The monstrous horror is not the castrated female but the maternal authority which threatens the 'obliteration of the self.'

Many of the reviewers observe that Gumb's behavior is readable as effeminate, leading to the inference, despite lines of dialogue, that he is homosexual. As the reviewer for the Los Angeles *Reader* puts it, Gumb has a 'swishy stage-homosexual posturing.'[41] This association seems to be emphasized and commented upon by a sketch accompanying a *Village Voice* article in which Gumb holds a needle and thread while Starling has a pencil and paper. Again, Starling is face forward in the foreground with the threat behind her, looking toward her. No matter her gender, Gumb's is by cultural categories feminized.

Also reinforcing this threat of the engulfing maternal monster is Gumb's totem: the death's-head moth, so named because the markings on its back resemble those of a skull. It is this animal which he wishes to imitate in its transformation into beauty; it is this totem which he shoves down his victims' throats. Klawans observes that Jack the Ripper is considered to be the first serial killer, whom Klawans notes arrives when women start living on their own in the city.[42] Furthermore, to make his self apparent, to construct his own identity, the serial killer will repeat his signature at each crime scene. By 'pattern, [the killer] writes in code with his victims' bodies.'[43] The film, then, meticulously follows common lore about such behavior. The death's-head moth functions symbolically to write 'Gumb' on the bodies of women. According to the movie plot, Gumb did this as well to forecast his forthcoming transformation and new link to the identity 'woman.' Holding the moth in their mouths, the women's interiors are now exteriorized—their skins gone but their bodies the cocoon for a new beauty.

This association of moth, maternity, and monster is strongly prepared for extratextually, so the fact that viewers responded to it is not surprising. For *Silence of the Lambs*, the moth was a major motif in the advertising campaign through the posters of it covering Starling's mouth.[44] But the ad's image does not have the moth *in* Starling's throat. It would not be visible. It covers her mouth, hiding an orifice. In this film, and in symptomatic displacement, inversions have existed all over the interpretational landscape. Outsides become insides both in Lecter's cannibalism and Gumb's scripting his forthcoming transformation.

Furthermore, the moth is *stitched* across her mouth. Starling is figured and readable as a hybrid monster as well. If she is easily thought of as an individual in search of her identity, she, like Gumb, can be associated with the moth. She is interpretable as part of his clan. But this stitching is across the mouth, leaving Starling, like that of so many victims, silenced.

Recall that readers have also equated Starling with the lambs she tried to save from slaughter. After death, lambs have two functions: they can be eaten; their hides can be worn. In both cases, the sacrifice is incorporated by the killer—internally via swallowing and externally via masquerading as an other. In both cases, difference and identity are threatened. Klawans writes, why is the audience being worked over in *Silence of the Lambs*? 'The best answer . . . and it's a good one—is that the protagonist is a woman. She might even be a lesbian.' Other *male* writers also publicly regarded this a distinct possibility prior to the outing of Foster.[45] Thus, although Starling *is* a woman, she may not be a *'normal'* woman. We thus have a complete quadrant of gender and sexual preferences available in the film: Lecter: heterosexual male; female victims: (heterosexual) females; Gumb: homosexual male; Starling: homosexual female. Reading Starling as a lesbian, however, is not a direct result of textual evidence but an inference from the interpretive strategies and the discursive context of the film.

Mary Douglas writes in *Purity and Danger* that social pollution comes from threats to the political and cultural unity of a group.[46] Social pollution anxieties can be rewritten over the human body in a concern for its orifices since body openings 'are connected symbolically to social preoccupations about exits and entrances.'[47] In my analysis of this public discourse, the most apparent danger was from incorporating or transgressing traditional oppositions. Douglas believes that one way to cancel such a social pollution is a confessional rite.

As the release date for *Silence of the Lambs* neared, Orion and the producers used the Hollywood strategy of attracting attention to it by giving several benefit shows. One party was for the AIDS Project in Los Angeles. In the United States in 1991, this gesture of concern cannot be disassociated with the public assumption that AIDS is primarily a disease of gay men and lower-class drug-users. Gay activists immediately read the event as a pollution rite: 'They [are attempting] to launder the film by using . . . an organization whose clients are mostly gay to offset criticism.'[48] To gay activists, the act of trying to imply concern for homosexuals was thus an inverted confession of the homophobia of the film.

This event occurred extratextually and prior to the film's opening. Thus, its existence determined the reception of the film for many viewers. When the film went on to do good box office, the intensity of the threat increased. For gay activists, an external threat—wide reinforcement of the notion that effeminate men are psychopathic serial killers—was not only being ignored by massive numbers of audience members but likely being, again, incorporated into public mythologies. Thus, some gay activists chose to blur the line which is so often crossed: the difference between fiction and real social life.

Notice that gay activists did not try to argue that *Starling* was a lesbian. Like Orion, they made the argument that the movie had some (obscure) value to social life. Like Orion, they made the argument extratextually: *Jodie Foster* was a lesbian. In a time in which homo- or bisexuality is threatened as a personal identity—threatened not just by social stereotyping but by real physical threats from homophobic violence—'sacrificing' Foster seems logical. That is, pointing out the hypocrisy of the filmmakers by arguing that Foster had not yet come to terms with her own identity and sexual preferences was necessary if society was ever to come to terms with its notions of 'monsters.'

As I have indicated, Foster might well have come under attack simply because of stereotypes of the strong woman as a lesbian as well as informal oral communication about her, but motifs in the advertising and film, combined with reading strategies by its viewers, reinforced the credibility of the accusation by those who chose to out her. Starling's gender is ambiguous. She is easily read as a 'son' in a patriarchal identity crisis; she is easily read as 'unfeminine,' tracking archaic mothers in their lairs; she is easily read as a hybrid—a moth-person. And within a structural square of oppositions and inversions, her position is the most 'other': not heterosexual, not male. She could be the lamb sacrificed in punishment for the film's expressed homophobia and repressed polymorphous sexuality.

Of course, other people pointed out that those choosing to out her were in an odd way accepting the notion that being called a lesbian would be humiliating. And that, in any case, Foster was being denegrated or patronized just as women so often are in our culture. As I mentioned earlier, women—both straight and lesbian—uniformly defended her and the movie as a positive, powerful representation of a female.

In closing I wish to underline what I have been doing theoretically. This study is an attempt to indicate how contemporary theoretical frameworks can be useful in determining the cultural meanings (with the plural emphasized) of a specific text. What I have not done is to try to unify the text or the readings by asserting that one reading or set of oppositions or displacements is more viable than another. I have tried to provide the *range* of readings and to give an initial account of what might explain that range.

Additionally, my *primary* evidence for the cultural meanings of the events was not derived from a textual reading of the film. It came from public discourse. From that discourse, mediated though it is, I determined what textual, extratextual, and social determinants might account for the readings in my sample. I did not, although I might have, discuss significant absences in the discourse, a critical one being 'blood,' which is obviously significant considering how AIDS is transmitted.

Determining the cultural meaning of a text is full of assumptions and pitfalls. Interpreting interpretations is viciously circular. Additionally, the discourse I used is public and therefore already suspect. It is by no means representative of its culture—although I would be willing to argue that it has some relation to it as well as an effect on it. Given these (and other) problems, however, I still believe that research of this sort is helpful in a project of trying to understanding how individuals interpret the world and how they use discourse to shape, or reshape, that world. While I have made no decision about the political gesture of outing, I do believe I need to work toward understanding what acts of resistance such as that one mean in my social formation.

What this investigation has reaffirmed for me, then, is that at this time homosexuality, bisexuality, or ambiguous sexual preference is threatening to a wide range of readers. Gumb's death as an 'unnatural' person is met with a sigh of relief. 'Sick' though the movie's ending may be, Lecter's continued career as a cannibal of authority figures is met with a shaky laugh of pleasure. Maybe this is because Lecter's act of murder is one that dominant culture takes to be a normal ritual of incorporation: father to son, not the hybridizing of monsters such as men who sew rather than model themselves after appropriately masculine authority figures.

NOTES

I would like to thank Eithne Johnson for preparing such an interesting Ph.D. reading list, Beth Wichterich for helping me understand parts of the events, and audiences at the 1991 Nordiskt Filmsymposium (Lund, Sweden), the Women's Research Seminars at the University of Texas at Austin, and the University of Wisconsin-Madison for giving me very valuable responses to drafts of this essay.

1. In this paper I will usually not refer to bisexuality as a sexual preference. However, bisexuality should be considered an implied option throughout.
2. Leslie Larson, 'Foster Freeze,' [Letter to] *Village Voice* (April 2, 1991) from *Silence of the Lambs* clipping file, Academy of Motion Picture Arts and Sciences Margaret Herrick Library—hereafter SLfile]. Background, descriptions, and debates preceding this can be found in David J. Fox, 'Gays Decry Benefit Screening of "Lambs,"' *Los Angeles Times* (February 4, 1991) [n.p. SLfile]; Michael Musto, 'La Dolce Musto,' *Village Voice* (February 12, 1991) [n.p. SLfile]; Amy Taubin, 'Demme's Monde,' *Village Voice* (February 19, 1991), pp. 64, 76–77; Lisa Kennedy, ed., 'Writers on the *Lamb*,' *Village Voice* (March 5, 1991), pp. 49, 56; Michelangelo Signorile, '*Lamb* Chops,' [Letter to] *Village Voice*, (March 12, 1991) [n.p. SLfile]; [Letters to] *Village Voice* (March 19, 1991) [n.p. SLfile]; Elaine Dutka, '"Silence" Fuels a Loud and Angry Debate,' *Los Angeles Times* (March 20, 1991) [n.p. SLfile]; and Michael Bronski, 'Reel Politic,' *Z Magazine* 4:5 (May, 1991), pp. 80–84.
3. Julie Salamon, 'Weirdo Killer Shrink Meets the G-Girl,' *Wall Street Journal* (February 14, 1991); Amy Taubin, 'Demme's Monde'; Lisa Kennedy, 'Writers'; Martha Gever (in Kennedy, ed., 'Writers'); C. Carr (in Kennedy, ed. 'Writers'); Sheila Benson, 'Why Do Critics Love These Repellent Movies?,' *Los Angeles Times Calendar* (March 17, 1991); Andrea Kusten, Letters, *Village Voice* (March 19, 1991); Anna Hamilton Phelan, Tammy Bruce, and Phyllis Frank quoted in Elaine Dutka, '"Silence" Fuels a Loud and Angry Debate'; Leslie Larson, 'Foster Freeze'; B. Ruby Rich, quoted in Bronski, 'Reel Politic'; Maria Magenit, quoted in Bronski, 'Reel Politic.'
4. If I were explaining something else about the reception of *Silence of the Lambs*, other features and practices in the discourse might be pertinent.
5. Henry Sheehan, 'Overcooked Lambs,' *Los Angeles Reader* (February 15, 1991), pp. 29–30. These footnotes contain only the sources which I quote from; other reviews were part of my sample.
6. David Denby, 'Something Wilder,' *New York* 24:7 (February 18, 1991), pp. 60–61.
7. Brian D. Johnson, 'The Evil That Men Do,' *Maclean's* (February 18, 1991), pp. 51–52.
8. Peter Stallybrass and Allon White, *The Politics and Poetics of Transgression* (London: Methuen, 1986).

9. 'A recurrent pattern emerges: the "top" attempts to reject and eliminate the "bottom" for reasons of prestige and status, only to discover, not only that it is in some way frequently dependent upon that low-Other . . . but also that the top *includes* the low symbolically, as a primary eroticized constituent of its own fantasy life. The result is a mobile, conflictual fusion of power, fear and desire in the construction of subjectivity: a psychological dependence upon precisely those Others which are being rigorously opposed and excluded at the social level. It is for this reason that what is *socially* peripheral is so frequently *symbolically* central (like long hair in the 1960s)' (Stallybrass and White, *Politics and Poetics*, p. 5).

10. 'Cart,' 'The Silence of the Lambs,' *Variety* (February 11, 1991), p. 109.

11. Sigmund Freud, *Totem and Taboo: Resemblances Between the Psychic Lives of Savages and Neurotics* [1918], trans. A.A. Brill (New York: Vintage Books, 1946). 'The cannibalism of primitive races derives its more sublime motivation in a similar manner. By absorbing parts of the body of a person through the act of eating we also come to possess the properties which belonged to that person' (p. 107).

12. Denby, 'Something Wilder.'

13. Johnson, 'The Evil.'

14. Stephen Harvey, in Kennedy, ed., 'Writers,' p. 49.

15. Henry Sheehan, 'Overcooked Lambs,' p. 29; John Powers, 'Skin Deep: Jonathan Demme's Chatter of the Hams,' *L.A. Weekly* (February 15–21, 1991), p. 27; Stanley Kauffmann, 'Gluttons for Punishment,' *New Republic* (February 18, 1991), p. 48.

16. J. Hoberman, 'Skin Flick,' *Village Voice* (February 19, 1991), p. 61.

17. As Hoberman notices, in the original novel, Starling's relation with her mother is a dominant theme. In the film, her mother's death and its meaning to Starling are repressed, with the film concentrating on Starling's need to deal with her father's death.

18. Terrence Rafferty, 'Moth and Flame,' *New Yorker* (February 25, 1991), pp. 87–88.

19. Carol J. Clover, 'Her Body, Himself: Gender in the Slasher Film,' *Representations* 20 (Fall, 1987), pp. 187–228.

20. Starling was widely perceived by the viewers to be unfeminine. She was variously referred to in her role as an FBI recruit. Although Orion's publicity materials described her as 'gutsy,' repeating verbatim studio handout sheets is taboo among reviewers; equally unsettling might have been the unconscious connection between that adjective and Lecter's idiosyncratic diet. Here, however, Starling is variously relabeled to be 'tenacious,' 'sturdy,' 'tough,' 'resourceful,' 'persistent,' 'ambitious,' 'driven.' The *Silence of the Lambs* publicity materials, Orion Pictures [SLfile].

21. Thomas Harris, *The Silence of the Lambs* (New York: St Martin's, 1988).

22. Rafferty, 'Moth and Flame.'

23. Peter Travers, 'Snapshots from Hell: The Silence of the Lambs,' *Rolling Stone* (March 7, 1991), pp. 87–88.

24. Denby, 'Something Wilder.'

25. Chuck Smith, 'Hollywood Horror,' *Vanguard* (April 19, 1991) [n.p. SLfile].

26. Hoberman, 'Skin Flick.'

27. Stuart Klawans, 'Films,' *The Nation* (February 25, 1991), pp. 246–247.

28. Powers, 'Skin Deep.'

29. Smith, 'Hollywood Horror.'

30. Richard A. Blake, 'Visions of Evil,' *America* 64:10 (March 16, 1991), p. 292. *Commonweal*'s reviewer implies the film is about Faust and Mephisto. The *Rolling Stone* headline says the film has 'snapshots from hell.'

31. Margaret R. Miles, *Carnal Knowing: Female Nakedness and Religious Meaning in the Christian West* (New York: Vintage Books, 1989).

32. Miles, *Carnal Knowing*, pp. 12 and xi.

33. Vincent Canby, 'Methods of Madness in "Silence of the Lambs,"' *New York Times* (February 14, 1991), p. C17.

34. Salamon, 'Wierdo Killer.'

35. Amy Taubin, in Kennedy, ed., 'Writers.'
36. Reviewers did at times discuss him not only as monstrous but as alien or an extraterrestrial.
37. In *Alice Doesn't: Feminism, Semiotics, Cinema* (Bloomington: Indiana University Press, 1984), Teresa de Lauretis's analysis of narrativity and gender uses the Oedipal myth with its stories of meeting the Sphinx and the Minotaur tale as part of her argument about patriarchy's construction of desire. This odd coincidence is not particularly troublesome to explain since the equation is widely known through feminist discourse, and Taubin and Hoberman both are familiar with that discourse. We do not need to assume anything more than common social and discursive networks provoked this conjunction of terms.
38. Arnold I. Davidson, 'Sex and the Emergence of Sexuality,' *Critical Inquiry* 14:1 (Autumn, 1987), pp. 16–48, writes that it was through psychiatry that a split was made between anatomical sex and psychological sex. Medicalization takes over, investigating for visual evidence of gender both externally and internally.
39. Hoberman, 'Skin Flick.'
40. Barbara Creed, 'Horror and the Monstrous-Feminine: An Imaginary Abjection,' *Screen* 27:1 (January-February, 1986), pp. 44–70.
41. Sheehan, 'Overcooked Lambs.'
42. And as psychoanalysis as a discourse begins its dissemination.
43. Klawans, 'Films.'
44. It was derived from the novel but appears even during publicity generated while the film was in production. Its potency is obvious from the fact that the ad campaign recently won an award for the best movie poster of the year. Eithne Johnson informs me that the posters used Dali's 'punning' picture of women to create the skull. Furthermore, moths and butterflies have a long-standing association with the vagina. No reviewer, however, made note of either.
45. Klawans, 'Films'; Smith, 'Hollywood Horror.'
46. Mary Douglas, *Purity and Danger: An Analysis of the Concepts of Pollution and Taboo* (New York: Praeger, 1966), p. 122.
47. Douglas, *Purity*, p. 126.
48. Richard Jennings quoted in Fox, 'Gays Decry Benefit Screening of "Lambs."'

PART IV
FURTHER READING

Ang, Ien 1985: *Watching Dallas: Soap Opera and the Melodramatic Imagination*. London: Methuen.

Ang, Ien and Hermes, Joke 1991: Gender and/in Media Consumption. In Curran, J. and Gurevitch, M. (ed.), *Mass Media and Society*. London: Edward Arnold, pp. 307–28.

Brown, Mary Ellen (ed.) 1990: *Television and Women's Culture*. London: Sage.

Byars, Jackie 1991: *All that Hollywood Allows: Re-Reading Gender in 1950s Melodrama*. London: Routledge.

Franklin, Sarah, Lury, Celia and Stacey, Jackie 1991: Feminism and Cultural Studies: Pasts, Presents, Futures. In Franklin, S., Lury, C. and Stacey, J. (eds), *Off Centre: Feminism and Cultural Studies*. London and New York: HarperCollins, pp. 1–19.

Gledhill, Christine 1978: 'Klute': A Contemporary Film Noir and Feminist Criticism. In E. A. Kaplan (ed.), *Women in Film Noir*. London: BFI.

Gledhill, Christine (ed.) 1987: *Home is Where the Heart is: Studies in Melodrama and the Woman's Film*. London: BFI.

Hall, Stuart 1980: Encoding/decoding. In Hall, S., Hobson, D., Lowe, A. and Willis, P. (eds), *Culture, Media, Language*. London: Hutchinson, 1980, pp. 128–38.

Hall, Stuart 1992: Cultural Studies and its Theoretical Legacies. In Grossberg, L., Nelson, C. and Treichler, P. (eds), *Cultural Studies*. New York and London: Routledge, pp. 277–94.

LaPlace, Maria 1987: Producing and Consuming the Woman's Film: Discursive Struggle in *Now, Voyager*. In Gledhill, C. (ed.) *Home is Where the Heart is: Studies in Melodrama and the Woman's Film*. London: BFI, pp. 138–66.

Partington, Angela 1991: Melodrama's Gendered Audience. In Franklin, S., Lury, C. and Stacey, J. (eds), *Off Centre: Feminism and Cultural Studies*. London and New York: HarperCollins, pp. 49–68.

Radway, Janice 1987: *Reading the Romance*. London: Verso.

Seiter, Ellen, Borchers, Hans, Kreutzner, Gabriele and Warth, Eva-Maria 1989:

Remote Control: Television, Audiences and Cultural Power. London and New York: Routledge.

Stacey, Jackie 1992 (1987): Desperately Seeking Difference. In *The Sexual Subject: A Screen Reader in Sexuality*. London and New York: Routledge, pp. 244–57.

Stacey, Jackie 1994: *Star Gazing: Hollywood Cinema and Female Spectatorship*. London and New York: Routledge.

Thornham, Sue 1997: Negotiating the Text: Spectator Positions and Audience Readings. In *Passionate Detachments: An Introduction to Feminist Film Theory*. London: Arnold, pp. 67–91.

PART V
FANTASY, HORROR AND THE BODY

INTRODUCTION

In Mary Ann Doane's work on the 'woman's film' (Chapter 6) she drew on Freud's account of masochistic fantasy, 'A Child is Being Beaten' (1919), to argue that it is precisely this kind of fantasy – of passivity, objectification, overidentification – which the 'woman's film' constructs for its female spectator. Increasingly in the 1980s, however, Freud's work on fantasy was re-interpreted very differently, so that it became the theoretical underpinning not for cinema's power to 'fix' its spectators within the structures of sexual difference, but for the reverse: the shifting and multiple positions that cinema offers to its fantasising spectator.

The key essay in this move was the (1964) essay, 'Fantasy and the Origins of Sexuality' by Jean Laplanche and Jean-Bertrand Pontalis. The essence of fantasy, argue Laplanche and Pontalis, is not 'the object of desire, but its setting' (1986: 26). Fantasy is the staging of desire, its *mise-en-scène*. Thus we are always present in our fantasies, but our place is not fixed. Our identification is shifting, unconfined by boundaries of biological sex, cultural gender or sexual preference. The structure of fantasy, they add, is formed from three (unconscious) 'original' fantasies. Fantasies of 'the primal scene' picture 'the origin of the individual; fantasies of seduction, [picture] the origin and upsurge of sexuality; and fantasies of castration, [picture] the origin of the difference between the sexes' (1986: 19). 'Secondary' fantasies – unconscious or conscious, dream, daydream or cinematic fiction – rework these original fantasies, using the 'kaleidoscopic material' of the present to construct their narratives. Any simple opposition between 'fantasy' and 'reality' thus disappears: fantasies draw on social reality as well as the unconscious in their reworking of the 'kaleidoscopic material' of our social existence.

The possible implications for feminist film theory of the work of Laplanche and Pontalis were explored in Elizabeth Cowie's (1984) essay, 'Fantasia'. Fantasy, argues Cowie, has presented a problem for feminist theory because it has seemed, in popular genres like romance fiction or the 'woman's film', to tie women into masochistic identifications which are the more powerful because they are unconscious. It has been assumed that women's point of identification in such structures must be with the passive and suffering fictional heroine, whilst the 'male gaze' is voyeuristic and sadistic. On the contrary, however, cinematic fantasies do not, Cowie argues, fix the spectator in a specific gendered position. Instead, they 'join with the "original" fantasies in visualising the subject in the scene, and in presenting a varying of subject position so that the subject takes up more than one position and thus is not fixed' (1984: 80). Cinematic conventions – of realism, of narrative, of genre – provide the means through which the private structuring of desire can be represented in public forms.

The three essays in this section all draw on this re-thinking of Freud's work on fantasy, though the conclusions they draw are not always as optimistic as Cowie's. Carol J. Clover's investigation of the contemporary slasher film challenges existing assumptions that 'screen males represent the Male and screen females the Female [and] that this identification along gender lines authorises impulses towards sexual violence in males and encourages impulses towards victimisation in females'. How, she asks, can such theories explain the appeal to a largely male audience of a film genre that features a female victim-hero?

Clearly, argues Clover, viewers are performing cross-gender identifications in these films. But, she adds, neither the (ostensibly male) killer/monster nor the (ostensibly female) victim/hero is quite what s/he seems. The killer, often transvestite, transsexual or otherwise gender-impaired, is a feminised male, and the hero – the active and 'unfeminine' Final Girl – a masculinised female. The Final Girl, she argues, makes a 'congenial double' for the adolescent male: masculine enough to perform the Oedipal journey as his surrogate, but with a female body on which may be enacted – at a safe distance – the masochistic fantasies of the male spectator; the 'Final Girl is (apparently) female not despite the maleness of the audience but because of it'.

Clover is drawing here not only on the re-reading by Laplanche and Pontalis of Freud's work on masochistic fantasy, but also on its further development in the work of Kaja Silverman (see Chapter 8). Silverman, as we have seen, argues that mainstream cinema persistently displaces on to the figure of woman the sense of 'lack' that the male subject himself feels. With this displacement, she argues, comes a projection on to the female character/spectator of a masochism that properly belongs to the male spectator. As Clover notes, for Silverman 'it is always the victim – the figure who occupies the passive position – who is really the focus of attention, and whose subjugation the subject (whether male or female) experiences as a pleasurable repetition of his/her own history' (1980: 5). The ambiguous and oscillating gender identity of the slasher film's Final Girl allows its male spectator, too, to oscillate between 'feminine' and 'masculine' viewing positions. The emergence of the female victim-hero in the slasher movie, then, speaks much more of male anxieties and desires, argues Clover, than it does of the impact of feminism. Nevertheless, she concludes, the emergence of this ambiguous figure does give evidence of some shift in the terms of gender representation, if only for the male viewer.

Barbara Creed also draws on Freud's work on fantasy to explain the horror film. Like the primal fantasies, she argues, horror narratives – and Creed's example here is the sci-fi horror film, *Alien* – are particularly concerned with origins. However, the horror film represents its 'primal fantasies' in terms of the abject. Creed's concept of 'the abject' is drawn from the work of Julia Kristeva, whose *Powers of Horror* (1982), Creed argues, 'provides us with a preliminary hypothesis' for an analysis of the representation of woman as monstrous in the horror film. The abject, defined by Kristeva as that which does not 'respect borders, positions, rules', that which 'disturbs identity, system, order', is linked by her to the pre-linguistic maternal realm. For the child to leave this realm, she argues, it must first delimit its own 'clean and proper' body, separating its bounded, unified self from 'the improper, the unclean and the disorderly' (Grosz 1989: 71). Yet, argues Kristeva, what is excluded 'can never be fully obliterated but hovers at the borders of our existence, threatening the apparently settled unity of the subject with disruption and possible dissolution' (Grosz 1989: 71). It is this confrontation that the horror film repeatedly enacts, argues Creed: in its images of mutilation, bodily wastes and putrefying flesh, in its preoccupation with the transgression of borders, but above all in its construction of the maternal as abject – the 'monstrous-feminine'.

The maternal figure as monster has various guises, she writes, dominant amongst which is the figure of 'the archaic mother'. This figure, 'the generative mother', the 'mother as the origin of all life', is monstrous not because of her perceived 'lack', or because, like the imagined mother of Freud's pre-Oedipal infant, she 'possesses' the phallus. Instead, her monstrousness arises from her perceived self-sufficiency. As parthenogenic mother, she offers 'a notion of the feminine which does not depend for its definition on a concept of the masculine'. In the patriarchal world of the horror film, this 'horrifying image' has two manifestations. One is the image of the 'gestating, all-devouring womb'; the other is the threat of obliteration, of re-incorporation, which she poses. It is this threat, argues Creed, that produces a spectator-positioning unique to the horror film: those moments when the spectator is forced to look away. At these points, argues Creed, cinema's identificatory structures threaten to draw the spectator into identification with a screen image of the disintegration and collapse of identity. The spectator withdraws his gaze to preserve his sense of self.

The horror narrative ends with the restoration of boundaries, and it is in this light, argues Creed, that we should view the much-discussed ending of *Alien*, with its 're-feminising' of the film's hero, Ripley/Sigourney Weaver. The function of the horror film for a patriarchal culture, she argues, is to stage and re-stage confrontation with, and repudiation of, the monstrous-feminine. Like

Clover, then, she argues that the fantasy structures of the horror film, with their shifting subject positions and blurring of gender boundaries, reveal a great deal about male fears and desires – including the perverse desire for the collapse of boundaries – but tell us nothing about female desire.

The relation between 'gender, genre, fantasy and structures of perversion' is also explored in the final chapter in this section, Linda Williams' (1991) study of 'body genres', 'Film Bodies: Gender, Genre and Excess'. The 'body genres' that Williams discusses are pornography, horror and melodrama, genres marked respectively by 'gratuitous sex, gratuitous violence and terror, [and] gratuitous emotion'. All have in common a quality of excess that marks them as 'low genres', an excess which is 'written across the body'. All measure their success by the extent to which the spectator, too, is caught up in the sensations of the body on the screen; there is, writes Williams, 'a sense of over-involvement in sensation and emotion'. Williams' analysis, then, brings together the work of theorists like Mary Ann Doane[1] on the 'woman's film' (see Chapter 6) and that of Barbara Creed and Carol J. Clover on the horror film. In all three genres, she writes, it is the bodies of women that have 'functioned traditionally as the primary *embodiments* of pleasure, fear, and pain'. All, too, are genres 'in which fantasy predominates', fantasy that is marked not only by an oscillation of identificatory subject positions but by an oscillation which is, as in Freud's 'A Child is Being Beaten', between the poles of sadism and masochism, powerlessness and power.

Even the predominantly masochistic woman's film, argues Williams, exhibits this oscillation. Thus, despite the apparently gendered address of these 'body genres', Williams argues that the viewing positions constructed are not as gender-linked and as gender-fixed as has been supposed. These are 'genres of gender fantasy' which explore basic problems related to sexual identity. As such, each can be seen to correspond with one of the three 'original fantasies' described by Laplanche and Pontalis: pornography with the fantasy of primal seduction, horror with the castration fantasy, and melodrama with the fantasy of the primal scene. But whilst each constantly (and repetitively) reworks its 'original fantasy' of sexual identity, each is also historically specific, recasting its story and its pattern of identifications in response to cultural shifts. As forms of 'cultural problem-solving', they can offer only 'solutions' that remain bound within the terms of the problem (more, different or better sex as the solution to the problem of sex, more violence related to sexual difference as the answer to the problem of violence related to sexual difference, more loss as the answer to the pathos of loss). Nevertheless, the problems that they address are constantly recast in response to the changing nature of gendered power relations.

Williams' use of fantasy theory, then, relates it back to perversion (though with the understanding that, in terms of sexuality, 'we are all perverts') and to the body – specifically, to the spectacle of the 'sexually saturated' female body. Like Clover and Creed, she argues that the popularity of contemporary 'body genres' can be linked to current uncertainties about gender identities. But her concern is with the female spectator as well as with her male counterpart. Even in the most masochistic of melodramas, she argues, 'identification is neither fixed nor entirely passive'. The 'new fluidity and oscillation' in the 'body genres', then, offer pleasures to the female as well as the male spectator.

NOTES

1. See also Williams' own essay on the maternal melodrama, ' "Something Else besides a Mother": *Stella Dallas* and the Maternal Melodrama', in Christine Gledhill (ed.) (1987), *Home is Where the Heart Is*.

REFERENCES

Cowie, Elizabeth 1984: Fantasia. *m/f* no. 9, pp. 71–104.

Freud, Sigmund 1979 (1919): 'A Child is Being Beaten'. In Freud, S., *On Psychopathology*. Pelican Freud Library Vol. 10. London: Penguin, pp. 159–93.

Gledhill, Christine (ed.) 1987: *Home is Where the Heart is: Studies in Melodrama and the Woman's Film*. London: BFI.

Grosz, Elizabeth 1989: *Sexual Subversions*. Sydney: Allen & Unwin.

Kristeva, Julia 1982: *Powers of Horror: An Essay on Abjection*. New York: Columbia University Press.

Laplanche, Jean and Pontalis, Jean-Bertrand 1986 (1964): Fantasy and the Origins of Sexuality. In Burgin, V., Donald, J. and Kaplan, C., *Formations of Fantasy*. London and New York: Routledge, pp. 5–34.

Silverman, Kaja 1980: Masochism and Subjectivity. *Framework* 12, pp. 2–9.

Williams, Linda 1987 (1984): 'Something Else Besides a Mother': *Stella Dallas* and the Maternal Melodrama. In Gledhill, C. (ed.) *Home is Where the Heart is: Studies in Melodrama and the Woman's Film*. London: BFI, pp. 299–325.

17

'HER BODY, HIMSELF:
GENDER IN THE SLASHER FILM'

Carol J. Clover

[...] On the face of it, the relation between the sexes in slasher films could hardly be clearer. The killer is with few exceptions recognizably human and distinctly male; his fury is unmistakably sexual in both roots and expression; his victims are mostly women, often sexually freed and always young and beautiful. Just how essential this victim is to horror is suggested by her historical durability. If the killer has over time been variously figured as shark, fog, gorilla, birds, and slime, the victim is eternally and prototypically the damsel. Cinema hardly invented the pattern. It has simply given visual expression to the abiding proposition that, in Poe's famous formulation, the death of a beautiful woman is the 'most poetical topic in the world'.[1] As slasher director Dario Argento puts it, 'I like women, especially beautiful ones. If they have a good face and figure, I would much prefer to watch them being murdered than an ugly girl or a man.'[2] Brian De Palma elaborates: 'Women in peril work better in the suspense genre. It all goes back to the *Perils of Pauline* ... If you have a haunted house and you have a woman walking around with a candelabrum, you fear more for her than you would for a husky man.'[3] Or Hitchcock, during the filming of *The Birds*: 'I always believe in following the advice of the playwright Sardou. He said "Torture the women!" The trouble today is that we don't torture women enough.'[4] What the directors do not say, but show, is that 'Pauline' is at her very most effective in a state of undress, borne down upon by a blatantly phallic murderer, even gurgling orgasmically as she dies. The case could be made that

* From Donald, J. (ed.), *Fantasy and the Cinema* London: BFI, 1989, pp. 91–133.

the slasher films available at a given neighborhood video rental outlet recor
mend themselves to censorship under the Dworkin-MacKinnon guidelines ...
least as readily as the hard-core films the next section over, at which that
legislation is aimed; for if some victims are men, the argument goes, most are
women, and the women are brutalised in ways that come too close to real life for
comfort. But what this line of reasoning does not take into account is the figure
of the (Final Girl) Because slashers lie for all practical purposes beyond the
purview of legitimate criticism, and to the extent that they have been reviewed at
all have been reviewed on an individual basis, (the phenomenon of the female
victim-hero has scarcely been acknowledged.)

It is, of course, 'on the face of it' that most of the public discussion of film takes
place – from the Dworkin-MacKinnon legislation to Siskel's and Ebert's reviews
to our own talks with friends on leaving the movie house Underlying that
discussion is the assumption that the sexes are what they seem; that screen males
represent the Male and screen females the Female; that this identification along
gender lines authorises impulses towards sexual violence in males and encourages impulses towards victimisation in females.) In part because of the massive
authority cinema by nature accords the image, even academic film criticism has
been slow – slower than literary criticism – to get beyond appearances. Film may
not appropriate the mind's eye, but it certainly encroaches on it; the gender
characteristics of a screen figure are a visible and audible given for the duration of
the film. To the extent that the possibility of cross-gender identification has been
entertained, it has been in the direction female-with-male. Thus some critics have
wondered whether the female viewer, faced with the screen image of a
masochistic/narcissistic female, might not rather elect to 'betray her sex and
identify with the masculine point of view'.[5] The reverse question – whether men
might not also, on occasion, elect to betray their sex and identify with screen
females – has scarcely been asked, presumably on the assumption that men's
interests are well served by the traditional patterns of cinematic representation.
Then too there is the matter of the 'male gaze'. As E. Ann Kaplan sums it up:
'Within the film text itself, men gaze at women, who become objects of the gaze;
the spectator, in turn, is made to identify with this male gaze, and to objectify the
women on the screen; and the camera's original "gaze" comes into play in the
very act of filming.'[6] But if it is so that all of us, male and female alike, are by these
processes 'made to' identify with men and 'against' women, how are we then to
explain the appeal to a largely male audience of a film genre that features a female
victim-hero? The slasher film brings us squarely up against a fundamental
question of film analysis: where does the literal end and the figurative begin; how
do the two levels interact and what is the significance of the particular
interaction; and to which, in arriving at a political judgment (as we are inclined
to do in the case of low horror and pornography), do we assign priority?

A figurative or functional analysis of the slasher begins with the processes of
point of view and identification. The male viewer seeking a male character, even

a vicious one, with whom to identify in a sustained way has little to hang on to in the standard example. On the good side, the only viable candidates are the schoolmates or friends of the girls. They are for the most part marginal, undeveloped characters; more to the point, they tend to die early in the film. If the traditional horror film gave the male spectator a last-minute hero with whom to identify, thereby 'indulging his vanity as protector of the helpless female',[7] the slasher eliminates or attenuates that role beyond any such function; indeed, would-be rescuers are not infrequently blown away for their efforts, leaving the girl to fight her own fight. Policemen, fathers, and sheriffs appear only long enough to demonstrate risible incomprehension and incompetence. On the bad side, there is the killer. The killer is often unseen, or barely glimpsed, during the first part of the film, and what we do see, when we finally get a good look, hardly invites immediate or conscious empathy. He is commonly masked, fat, deformed, or dressed as a woman. Or 'he' *is* a woman: woe to the viewer of *Friday the Thirteenth I* who identifies with the male killer only to discover, in the film's final sequences, that he was not a man at all but a middle-aged woman. In either case, the killer is himself eventually killed or otherwise evacuated from the narrative. No male character of any stature lives to tell the tale.

(The one character of stature who does live to tell the tale is of course female.) The Final Girl is introduced at the beginning and is the only character to be developed in any psychological detail.)We understand immediately from the attention paid it that here is the main story line. She is intelligent, watchful, level-headed; the first character to sense something amiss and the only one to deduce from the accumulating evidence the patterns and extent of the threat; the only one, in other words, whose perspective approaches our own privileged under-standing of the situation. We register her horror as she stumbles on the corpses of her friends; her paralysis in the face of death duplicates those moments of the universal nightmare experience on which horror frankly trades. When she downs the killer, we are triumphant. She is by any measure the slasher film's hero. This is not to say that our attachment to her is exclusive and unremitting, only that it adds up, and that in the closing sequence it is very close to absolute.

An analysis of the camerawork bears this out. Much is made of the use of the I-camera to represent the killer's point of view. In these passages – they are usually few and brief, but powerful – we see through his eyes and (on the sound track) hear his breathing and heartbeat. His and our vision is partly obscured by bushes or windowblinds in the foreground. By such means we are forced, the argument goes, to identify with the killer. In fact, however, the relation between camera point of view and the processes of viewer identification are poorly understood; the fact that Steven Spielberg can stage an attack in *Jaws* from the shark's point of view (underwater, rushing upward towards the swimmer's flailing legs) or Hitchcock an attack in *The Birds* from the birds-eye perspective (from the sky, as they gather to swoop down on the streets of Bodega Bay) would seem to suggest either that the viewer's identificatory powers are unbelievably elastic or that point-of-view shots can sometimes be pro forma.[8] But let us for the moment accept the equation point of view = identification. We are linked, in this way, with the killer in the early part of the film, usually before we have seen him directly and before we have come to know the Final Girl in any detail. Our closeness to him wanes as our closeness to the Final Girl waxes – a shift underwritten by story line as well as camera position. By the end, point of view is hers: we are in the closet with her, watching with her eyes the knife blade stab through the door; in the room with her as the killer breaks through the window and grabs at her; in the car with her as the killer stabs through the convertible top, and so on. With her, we become if not the killer of the killer then the agent of his expulsion from the narrative vision. (If, during the film's course, we shifted our sympathies back and forth, and dealt them out to other characters along the way, we belong in the end to the Final Girl; there is no alternative.) When Stretch eviscerates Chop Top at the end of *Texas Chainsaw II*, she is literally the only character left alive, on either side.

Audience response ratifies this design. Observers unanimously stress the readiness of the 'live' audience to switch sympathies in midstream, siding now with the killer and now, and finally, with the Final Girl. As Schoell, whose book on shocker films wrestles with its own monster, 'the feminists', puts it:

> Social critics make much of the fact that male audience members cheer on the misogynous misfits in these movies as they rape, plunder, and murder their screaming, writhing female victims. Since these same critics walk out of the moviehouse in disgust long before the movie is over, they don't realize that these same men cheer on (with renewed enthusiasm, in fact) the heroines, who are often as strong, sexy, and independent as the [earlier] victims, as they blow away the killer with a shotgun or get him between the eyes with a machete. All of these men are said to be identifying with the maniac, but they enjoy *his* death throes the most of all, and applaud the heroine with admiration.[9]

What film-makers seem to know better than film critics is that gender is less a wall than a permeable membrane.[10]

No one who has read 'Red Riding Hood' to a small boy or participated in a viewing of, say, *Deliverance* (an all-male story that women find as gripping as men) or, more recently, *Alien* and *Aliens*, with whose space-age female Rambo, herself a Final Girl, male viewers seem to engage with ease, can doubt the phenomenon of cross-gender identification.[11] This fluidity of engaged perspective is in keeping with the universal claims of the psychoanalytic model: the threat function and the victim function coexist in the same unconscious, regardless of anatomical sex. (But why, if viewers can identify across gender lines and if the root experience of horror is sex blind, are the screen sexes not interchangeable? Why not more and better female killers, and why (in light of the maleness of the majority audience) not Pauls as well as Paulines? (The fact that horror film so stubbornly genders the killer male and the principal victim female would seem to suggest that representation itself is at issue – that the sensation of bodily fright derives not exclusively from repressed content, as Freud insisted, but also from the bodily manifestations of that content.

Nor is the gender of the principals as straightforward as it first seems. The killer's phallic purpose, as he thrust his drill or knife into the trembling bodies of young women, is unmistakable. At the same time, however, his masculinity is severely qualified: he ranges from the virginal or sexually inert to the transvestite or transsexual, is spiritually divided ('the mother half of his mind') or even equipped with vulva and vagina. Although the killer of *God Told Me To* is represented and taken as a male in the film text, he is revealed, by the doctor who delivered him, to have been sexually ambiguous from birth: 'I truly could not tell whether that child was male or female; it was as if the sexual gender had not been determined ... as if it were being developed.'[12] In this respect, slasher killers have much in common with the monsters of classic horror – monsters who, in Linda Williams's formulation, represent not just 'an eruption of the normally repressed animal sexual energy of the civilised male' but also the 'power and potency of a *non-phallic* sexuality'. To the extent that the monster is constructed as feminine, the horror film thus expresses female desire only to show how monstrous it is.[13] The intention is manifest in *Aliens*, in which the Final Girl, Ripley, is pitted in the climactic scene against the most terrifying 'alien' of all: an egg-laying Mother.

Nor can we help noticing the 'intrauterine' quality of the Terrible Place, dark and often damp, in which the killer lives or lurks and whence he stages his most terrifying attacks. 'It often happens,' Freud wrote,

> that neurotic men declare that they feel there is something uncanny about the female genital organs. This *unheimlich* place, however, is an entrance to the former *Heim* [home] of all human beings, to the place where each one of us lived once upon a time and in the beginning ... In this case too then, the *unheimlich* is what once was *heimisch*, familiar; the prefix *'un'* ['un –'] is the token of repression.[14]

It is the exceptional film that does not mark as significant the moment that the killer leaps out of the dark recesses of a corridor or cavern at the trespassing victim, usually the Final Girl. Long after the other particulars have faded, the viewer will remember the images of Amy assaulted from the dark halls of a morgue (*He Knows You're Alone*), Sally or Stretch facing dismemberment in the ghastly dining room or underground labyrinth of the slaughterhouse family (*Texas Chainsaw I-II*), or Melanie trapped in the attic as the savage birds close in (*The Birds*). In such scenes of convergence the Other is at its bisexual mightiest, the victim at her tiniest, and the component of sadomasochism at its most blatant.

The gender of the Final Girl is likewise compromised from the outset by her masculine interests, her inevitable sexual reluctance (penetration, it seems, constructs the female), her apartness from other girls, sometimes her name. At the level of the cinematic apparatus, her unfemininity is signalled clearly by her exercise of the 'active investigating gaze' normally reserved for males and hideously punished in females when they assume it themselves; tentatively at first and then aggressively, the Final Girl looks *for* the killer, even tracking him to his forest hut or his underground labyrinth, and then *at* him, therewith bringing him, often for the first time, into our vision as well.[15] When, in the final scene, she stops screaming, looks at the killer, and reaches for the knife (sledge hammer, scalpel, gun, machete, hanger, knitting needle, chainsaw), she addresses the killer on his own terms. To the critics' objection that *Halloween* in effect punished female sexuality, director John Carpenter responded:

> They [the critics] completely missed the boat there, I think. Because if you turn it around, the one girl who is the most sexually uptight just keeps stabbing this guy with a long knife. She's the most sexually frustrated. She's the one that killed him. Not because she's a virgin, but because all that repressed energy starts coming out. She uses all those phallic symbols on the guy … She and the killer have a certain link: sexual repression.[16]

For all its perversity, Carpenter's remark does underscore the sense of affinity, even recognition, that attends the final encounter. But the 'certain link' that puts killer and Final Girl on terms, at least briefly, is more than 'sexual repression'. It is also a shared masculinity, materialised in 'all those phallic symbols' – and it is also a shared femininity, materialised in what comes next (and what Carpenter, perhaps significantly, fails to mention): the castration, literal or symbolic, of the killer at her hands. His eyes may be put out, his hand severed, his body impaled or shot, his belly gashed, or his genitals sliced away or bitten off. The Final Girl has not just manned herself; she specifically unmans an oppressor whose masculinity was in question to begin with. By the time the drama has played itself out, darkness yields to light (often as day breaks) and the close quarters of the barn (closet, elevator, attic, basement) give way to the open expanse of the yard (field, road, lakescape, cliff). With the Final Girl's appropriation of 'all those phallic symbols' comes the quelling, the dispelling, of the 'uterine' threat as well. Consider again the paradigmatic ending of *Texas Chainsaw II*. From the underground labyrinth, murky and bloody, in which she faced saw, knife, and hammer, Stretch escapes through a culvert into the open air. She clambers up the jutting rock and with a chainsaw takes her stand. When her last assailant comes at her, she slashes open his lower abdomen – the sexual symbolism is all too clear – and flings him off the cliff. Again, the final scene shows her in extremely long shot, standing on the pinnacle, drenched in sunlight, buzzing chainsaw held overhead.

The tale would indeed seem to be one of sex and parents. The patently erotic threat is easily seen as the materialised projection of the dreamer's (viewer's) own incestuous fears and desires. It is this disabling cathexis to one's parents that must be killed and rekilled in the service of sexual autonomy. When the Final Girl stands at last in the light of day with the knife in her hand, she has delivered herself into the adult world. Carpenter's equation of the Final Girl with the killer has more than a grain of truth. The killers of *Psycho*, *The Eyes of Laura Mars*, *Friday the Thirteenth II–VI*, and *Cruising*, among others, are explicitly figured as sons in the psychosexual grip of their mothers (or fathers, in the case of *Cruising*). The difference is between past and present and between failure and success. The Final Girl enacts in the present, and successfully, the parenticidal struggle that the killer himself enacted unsuccessfully in his own past – a past that constitutes the film's backstory. She is what the killer once was; he is what she could become should she fail in her battle for sexual selfhood. 'You got a choice, boy,' says the tyrannical father of Leatherface in *Texas Chainsaw II*, 'sex or the saw; you never know about sex, but the saw – the saw is the family.'

But the tale is no less one of maleness. If the early experience of the Oedipal drama can be – is perhaps ideally – enacted in female form, the achievement of full adulthood requires the assumption and, apparently, brutal employment of the phallus. The helpless child is gendered feminine; the autonomous adult or subject is gendered masculine; the passage from childhood to adulthood entails a shift from feminine to masculine. It is the male killer's tragedy that his incipient femininity is not reversed but completed (castration) and the Final Girl's victory that her incipient masculinity is not thwarted but realised (phallicisation). When De Palma says that female frailty is a predicate of the suspense genre, he proposes, in effect, that the lack of the phallus, for Lacan the privileged signifier of the symbolic order of culture, is itself simply horrifying, at least in the mind of the male observer. Where pornography (the argument goes) resolves that lack through a process of fetishisation that allows a breast or leg or whole body to stand in for the missing member, the slasher film resolves it either through eliminating the woman (earlier victims) or reconstituting her as masculine (Final Girl). The moment at which the Final Girl is effectively phallicised is the moment that the plot halts and horror ceases. Day breaks, and the community returns to its normal order.

Casting psychoanalytic verities in female form has a venerable cinematic history. Ingmar Bergman has made a career of it, and Woody Allen shows signs of following his lead. One immediate and practical advantage, by now presumably unconscious on the part of the makers as well as viewers, has to do with a preestablished cinematic 'language' for capturing the moves and moods of the female body and face. The cinematic gaze, we are told, is male, and just as that gaze 'knows' how to fetishise the female form in pornography (in a way that it does not 'know' how to fetishise the male form),[17] so it 'knows', in horror, how to track a woman ascending a staircase in a scary house and how to study her face from an angle above as she first hears the killer's footfall. A set of conventions we now take for granted simply 'sees' males and females differently.

To this cinematic habit may be added the broader range of emotional expression traditionally allowed women. Angry displays of force may belong to the male, but crying, cowering, screaming, fainting, trembling, begging for mercy belong to the female. (Abject terror, in short, is gendered feminine, and the more concerned a given film with that condition – and it is the essence of modern horror – the more likely the femaleness of the victim. It is no accident that male victims in slasher films are killed swiftly or offscreen, and that prolonged struggles, in which the victim has time to contemplate her imminent destruction, inevitably figure female.)Only when one encounters the rare expression of abject terror on the part of a male (as in *I Spit on Your Grave*) does one apprehend the full extent of the cinematic double standard in such matters.[18]

It is also the case that gender displacement can provide a kind of identificatory buffer, an emotional remove, that permits the majority audience to explore taboo subjects in the relative safety of vicariousness. Just as Bergman came to realise that he could explore castration anxiety more freely via depictions of hurt female bodies (witness the genital mutilation of Karin in *Cries and Whispers*), so the makers of slasher films seem to know that sadomasochistic incest fantasies sit more easily with the male viewer when the visible player is female. It is one thing for that viewer to hear the psychiatrist intone at the end of *Psycho* that Norman as a boy (in the backstory) was abnormally attached to his mother; it would be quite another to see that attachment dramatised in the present, to experience in nightmare form the elaboration of Norman's (the viewer's own) fears and desires. If the former is playable in male form, the latter, it seems, is not.

(The Final Girl is, on reflection, a congenial double for the adolescent male. She is feminine enough to act out in a gratifying way, a way unapproved for adult males, the terrors and masochistic pleasures of the underlying fantasy, but not so feminine as to disturb the structures of male competence and sexuality.) Her sexual inactivity, in this reading, becomes all but inevitable; the male viewer may be willing to enter into the vicarious experience of defending himself from the possibility of symbolic penetration on the part of the killer, but real vaginal penetration on the diegetic level is evidently more femaleness than he can bear. The question then arises whether the Final Girls of slasher films – Stretch, Stevie, Marti, Will, Terry, Laurie, and Ripley – are not boyish for the same reason that the female 'victims' in Victorian flagellation literature – 'Georgy', 'Willy' – are boyish: because they are transformed males. The transformation, Steven Marcus writes, 'is itself both a defense against and a disavowal of the fantasy it is simultaneously expressing – namely, that a *boy* is being beaten – that is, loved – by another man'.[19] What is represented as male-on-female violence, in short, is figuratively speaking male-on-male sex. For Marcus, the literary picture of flagellation, in which *girls* are beaten, is utterly belied by the descriptions (in *My Secret Life*) of real-life episodes in which the persons being beaten are not girls at all but 'gentlemen' dressed in women's clothes ('He had a woman's dress on tucked up to his waist, showing his naked rump and thighs. . . . On his head was a woman's cap tied carefully round his face to hide whiskers') and whipped by prostitutes. Reality, Marcus writes, 'puts the literature of flagellation out of the running . . . by showing how that literature is a completely distorted and idealised version of what actually happens'.[20] (Applied to the slasher film, this logic reads the femaleness of the Final Girl (at least up to the point of her transformation) and indeed of the women victims in general as only apparent, the artifact of heterosexual deflection. It may be through the female body that the body of the audience is sensationalised, but the sensation is an entirely male affair.)

At least one director, Hitchcock, explicitly located thrill in the equation victim = audience. So we judge from his marginal jottings in the shooting instructions for the shower scene in *Psycho*: 'The slashing. An impression of a knife slashing, as if tearing at the very screen, ripping the film.'[21] Not just the body of Marion is to be ruptured, but also the body on the other side of the film and screen: our witnessing body. As Marion is to Norman, the audience of *Psycho* is to Hitchcock; as the audiences of horror film in general are to the directors of those films, female is to male. Hitchcock's 'torture the women' then means, simply, torture the audience. De Palma's remarks about female frailty likewise contemplate a male-on-'female' relationship between director and viewer. Cinefantastic horror, in short, succeeds in the production of sensation to more or less the degree that it succeeds in incorporating its spectators as 'feminine' and then violating that body – which recoils, shudders, cries out collectively – in ways otherwise imaginable, for males, only in nightmare. The equation is nowhere more plainly put than in David Cronenberg's *Videodrome*. Here the threat is a mind-destroying video signal and the victims television viewers. Despite the (male) hero's efforts to defend his mental (and physical) integrity, a deep, vagina-like gash appears on his lower abdomen. Says the media conspirator as he thrusts a videocassette into the victim's gaping wound, 'You must open yourself completely to this.'

[If the slasher film is 'on the face of it' a genre with at least a strong female presence, it is in these figurative readings a thoroughly strong male exercise, one that finally has very little to do with femaleness and very much to do with phallocentrism.) Figuratively seen, the Final Girl is a male surrogate in things oedipal, a homoerotic stand-in, the audience incorporate; to the extent she 'means' girl at all, it is only for purposes of signifying phallic lack, and even that meaning is nullified in the final scenes. Our initial question – how to square a female victim-hero with a largely male audience – is not so much answered as it is obviated in these readings. The Final Girl is (apparently) female not despite the maleness of the audience, but precisely because of it. The discourse is wholly masculine, and females figure in it only insofar as they 'read' some aspect of male experience. [To applaud the Final Girl as a feminist development, as some reviews of *Aliens* have done with Ripley, is, in light of her figurative meaning, a particularly grotesque expression of wishful thinking.][22] She is simply an agreed-upon fiction, and the male viewer's use of her as a vehicle for his own sadomasochistic fantasies an act of perhaps timeless dishonesty.

[...] If we define the Final Girl as nothing more than a figurative male, what do we then make of the context of the spectacular gender play in which she is emphatically situated? In his essay on the uncanny, Freud rejected out of hand Jentsch's theory that the experience of horror proceeds from intellectual uncertainty (curiosity?) – feelings of confusion, induced by an author or a coincidence, about who, what, and where one is.[23] One wonders, however, whether Freud would have been quite so dismissive if, instead of the mixed materials he used as evidence, he were presented with a coherent story corpus – forty slashers, say – in which the themes of incest and separation were relentlessly played out by a female character, and further in which gender identity was repeatedly thematised as an issue in and of itself. For although the factors we have considered thus far – the conventions of the male gaze, the feminine constitution of abject terror, the value for the male viewer of emotional distance from the taboos in question, the special horror that may inhere, for the male audience, in phallic lack, the homoerotic deflection – go a long way in explaining why it is we have Pauline rather than Paul as our victim-hero, they do not finally account for our strong sense that gender is simply being played with, and that part of the thrill lies precisely in the resulting 'intellectual uncertainty' of sexual identity.

The 'play of pronoun function' that underlies and defines the cinefantastic is nowhere more richly manifested than in the slasher; if the genre has an aesthetic base, it is exactly that of a visual identity game. Consider, for example, the by now standard habit of letting us view the action in the first person long before revealing who or what the first person *is*. In the opening sequence of *Halloween I*, 'we' are belatedly revealed to ourselves, after committing a murder in the cinematic first person, as a six-year-old boy. The surprise is often within gender, but it is also, in a striking number of cases, across gender. Again, *Friday the Thirteenth I*, in which 'we' stalk and kill a number of teenagers over the course of an hour of screen time without even knowing who 'we' are; we are invited, by conventional expectation and by glimpses of 'our' own bodily parts – a heavily booted foot, a roughly gloved hand – to suppose that 'we' are male, but 'we' are revealed, at film's end, as a woman. If this is the most dramatic case of pulling out the gender rug, it is by no means the only one. In *Dressed to Kill*, we are led to believe, again by means of glimpses, that 'we' are female – only to discover, in the denouement, that 'we' are a male in drag. In *Psycho*, the dame we glimpse holding the knife with a 'visible virility quite obscene in an old lady' is later revealed, after additional gender teasing, to be Norman in his mother's clothes.[24] *Psycho II* plays much the same game. *Cruising* (in which, not accidentally, transvestites play a prominent role) adjusts the terms along heterosexual/homosexual lines. The tease here is whether the originally straight detective assigned to the string of murders in a gay community does or does not succumb to his assumed homosexual identity; the camerawork leaves us increasingly uncertain as to his (our) sexual inclinations, not to speak of his (our) complicity in the crimes. Even at film's end we are not sure who 'we' were during several of the first-person sequences.[25]

The gender-identity game, in short, is too patterned and too pervasive in the slasher film to be dismissed as supervenient. It would seem instead to be an integral element of the particular brand of bodily sensation in which the genre trades. Nor is it exclusive to horror. It is directly thematised in comic terms in the recent 'gender benders' *Tootsie* (in which a man passes himself off as a woman) and *All of Me* (in which a woman is literally introjected into a man and affects his speech, movement, and thought). It is also directly thematised, in the form of bisexual and androgynous figures and relations, in such cult films as *Pink Flamingos* and *The Rocky Horror Picture Show* [...]

It may be just this theatricalisation of gender that makes possible the willingness of the male viewer to submit himself to a brand of spectator experience that Hitchcock designated as 'feminine' in 1960 and that has become only more so since then. In classic horror, the 'feminization' of the audience is intermittent and ceases early. Our relationship with Marion's body in *Psycho* halts abruptly at the moment of its greatest intensity (slashing, ripping, tearing). The considerable remainder of the film distributes our bruised sympathies among several lesser figures, male and female, in such a way and at such length as to ameliorate the Marion experience and leave us, in the end, more or less recuperated in our (presumed) masculinity. (Like Marion, the Final Girl is the designated victim, the incorporation of the audience, the slashing, ripping, and tearing of whose body will cause us to flinch and scream out in our seat. But unlike Marion, she does not die.) If *Psycho*, like other classic horror films, solves the femininity problem by obliterating the female and replacing her with representatives of the masculine order (mostly but not inevitably males), the modern slasher solves it by regendering the woman. We are, as an audience, in the end 'masculinized' by and through the very figure by and through whom we were earlier 'feminized'. The same body does for both, and that body is female.

The last point is the crucial one: the same *female* body does for both. The Final Girl 1) undergoes agonising trials, and 2) virtually or actually destroys the antagonist and saves herself. By the lights of folk tradition, she is not a heroine, for whom phase 1 consists in being saved by someone else, but a hero, who rises to the occasion and defeats the adversary with his own wit and hands. Part 1 of the story sits well on the female; it is the heart of heroine stories in general (Red Riding Hood, Pauline), and in some figurative sense, in ways we have elaborated in some detail, it is gendered feminine even when played by a male. Odysseus's position, trapped in the cave of the Cyclops, is after all not so different from Pauline's position tied to the tracks or Sally's trapped in the dining room of the slaughterhouse family. (The decisive moment, as far as the fixing of gender is concerned, lies in what happens next: those who save themselves are male, and those who are saved by others are female. No matter how 'feminine' his experience in phase 1, the traditional hero, if he rises against his adversary and saves himself in phase 2, will be male.)

What is remarkable about the slasher film is that it comes close to reversing the priorities. Presumably for the various functional or figurative reasons we have considered in this essay, phase 1 wants a female: on that point all slashers from *Psycho* on are agreed. Abject fear is still gendered feminine, and the taboo anxieties in which slashers trade are still explored more easily via Pauline than Paul. The slippage comes in phase 2. As if in mute deference to a cultural imperative, slasher films from the 1970s bring in a last-minute male, even when he is rendered supernumerary by the Final Girl's sturdy defense. By 1980, however, the male rescuer is either dismissably marginal or dispensed with altogether; not a few films have him rush to the rescue only to be hacked to bits, leaving the Final Girl to save herself after all. (At the moment that the Final Girl becomes her own saviour, she becomes a hero, and the moment that she becomes a hero is the moment that the male viewer gives up the last pretense of male identification. Abject terror may still be gendered feminine, but the willingness of one immensely popular current genre to re-represent the hero as an anatomical female would seem to suggest that at least one of the traditional marks of heroism, triumphant self-rescue, is no longer strictly gendered masculine.)

So too the cinematic apparatus. The classic split between 'spectacle and narrative', which 'supposes the man's role as the active one of forwarding the story, making things happen', is at least unsettled in the slasher film.[26] When the Final Girl (in films like *Hell Night*, *Texas Chainsaw II*, and even *Splatter University*) assumes the 'active investigating gaze', she exactly reverses the look, making a spectacle of the killer and a spectator of herself. Again, it is through the killer's eyes (I-camera) that we saw the Final Girl at the beginning of the film, and through the Final Girl's eyes that we see the killer, often for the first time with any clarity, towards the end. The gaze becomes, at least for a while, female. More to the point, the female exercise of scopic control results not in her annihilation, in the manner of classic cinema, but in her triumph; indeed, her triumph *depends* on her assumption of the gaze. It is no surprise, in light of these developments, that the Final Girl should show signs of boyishness. Her symbolic phallicisation, in the last scenes, may or may not proceed at root from the horror of lack on the part of audience and maker. But it certainly proceeds from the need to bring her in line with the epic laws of Western narrative tradition – the very unanimity of which bears witness to the historical importance, in popular culture, of the literal representation of heroism in male form – and it proceeds no less from the need to render the reallocated gaze intelligible to an audience conditioned by the dominant cinematic apparatus.

It is worth noting that the higher genres of horror have for the most part resisted such developments. The idea of a female who outsmarts, much less outfights – or outgazes – her assailant is unthinkable in the films of De Palma and Hitchcock. Although the slasher film's victims may be sexual teases, they are not in addition simple-minded, scheming, physically incompetent, and morally deficient in the manner of these film-makers' female victims. And however revolting their special effects and sexualised their violence, few slasher murders approach the level of voluptuous sadism that attends the destruction of women in De Palma's films. For reasons on which we can only speculate, femininity is more conventionally elaborated and inexorably punished, and in an emphatically masculine environment, in the higher forms – the forms that *are* written up, and not by Joe Bob Briggs.

That the slasher film speaks deeply and obsessively to male anxieties and desires seems clear – if nothing else from the maleness of the majority audience. And yet these are texts in which the categories masculine and feminine, traditionally embodied in male and female, are collapsed into one and the same character – a character who is anatomically female and one whose point of view the spectator is unambiguously invited, by the usual set of literary-structural and cinematic conventions, to share. The willingness and even eagerness (so we judge from these films' enormous popularity) of the male viewer to throw in his emotional lot, if only temporarily, with not only a woman but a woman in fear and pain, at least in the first instance, would seem to suggest that he has a vicarious stake in that fear and pain. If it is also the case that the act of horror spectatorship is itself registered as a 'feminine' experience – that the shock effects induce bodily sensations in the viewer answering the fear and pain of the screen victim – the charge of masochism is underlined. This is not to say that the male viewer does not also have a stake in the sadistic side; narrative structure, cinematic procedures, and audience response all indicate that he shifts back and forth with ease. It is only to suggest that in the Final Girl sequence his emphathy with what the films define as the female posture is fully engaged, and further, because this sequence is inevitably the central one in any given film, that the viewing experience hinges on the emotional assumption of the feminine posture. Kaja Silverman takes it a step further: 'I will hazard the generalisation that it is always the victim – the figure who occupies the passive position – who is really the focus of attention, and whose subjugation the subject (whether male or female) experiences as a pleasurable repetition from his/her own story', she writes. 'Indeed, I would go so far as to say that the fascination of the sadistic point of view is merely that it provides the best vantage point from which to watch the masochistic story unfold.'[27]

The slasher is hardly the first genre in the literary and visual arts to invite identification with the female; one cannot help wondering more generally whether the historical maintenance of images of women in fear and pain does not have more to do with male vicarism than is commonly acknowledged. What distinguishes the slasher, however, is the absence or untenability of alternative perspectives and hence the exposed quality of the invitation. As a survey of the tradition shows, this has not always been the case. The stages of the Final Girl's evolution – her piecemeal absorption of functions previously represented in males – can be located in the years following 1978. The fact that the typical patrons of these films are the sons of marriages contracted in the 1960s or even early seventies leads us to speculate that the dire claims of that era – that the women's movement, the entry of women into the workplace, and the rise of divorce and woman-headed families would yield massive gender confusion in the next generation – were not entirely wrong. We may prefer, in the eighties, to speak of the cult of androgyny, but the point is roughly the same. The fact that we have in the killer a feminine male and in the main character a masculine female – parent and Everyteen, respectively – would seem, especially in the latter case, to suggest a loosening of the categories, or at least of the equation sex = gender. It is not that these films show us gender and sex in free variation; it is that they fix on the irregular combinations, of which the combination masculine female repeatedly prevails over the combination feminine male. The fact that masculine males (boyfriends, fathers, would-be rescuers) are regularly dismissed through ridicule or death or both would seem to suggest that it is not masculinity per se that is being privileged, but masculinity in conjunction with a female body – indeed, as the term victim-hero contemplates, masculinity in conjunction with femininity. For if 'masculine' describes the Final Girl some of the time, and in some of her more theatrical moments, it does not do justice to the sense of her character as a whole. She alternates between registers from the outset; before her final struggle she endures the deepest throes of 'femininity'; and even during that final struggle she is now weak and now strong, now flees the killer and now charges him, now stabs and is stabbed, now cries out in fear and now shouts in anger. She is a physical female and a characterological androgyne: like her name, not masculine but either/or, both, ambiguous.[28]

Robin Wood speaks of the sense that horror, for him the by-product of cultural crisis and disintegration, is 'currently the most important of all American [film] genres and perhaps the most progressive, even in its overt nihilism'.[29] Likewise Vale and Juno say of the 'incredibly strange films', mostly low-budget horror, that their volume surveys: 'They often present unpopular – even radical – views addressing the social, political, racial, or sexual inequities, hypocrisy in religion or government.'[30] And Tania Modleski rests her case against the standard critique of mass culture (stemming from the Frankfurt School) squarely on the evidence of the slasher, which does *not* propose a spurious harmony; does *not* promote the 'specious good' (but indeed often exposes and attacks it); does *not* ply the mechanisms of identification, narrative continuity, and closure to provide the sort of narrative pleasure constitutive of the dominant ideology.[31] One is deeply reluctant to make progressive claims for a body of cinema as spectacularly nasty towards women as the slasher film is, but the fact is that the slasher does, in its own perverse way and for better or worse, constitute a visible adjustment in the terms of gender representation. That it is an adjustment largely on the male side, appearing at the furthest possible remove from the quarters of theory and showing signs of trickling upwards, is of no small interest.

NOTES

I owe a special debt of gratitude to James Cunniff and Lynn Hunt for criticism and encouragement. Particular thanks to James (not Lynn) for sitting with me through not a few of these movies.

1. 'The Philosophy of Composition', in *Great Short Works of Edgar Allan Poe*, ed. G. R. Thompson (New York, 1970), p. 55.
2. As quoted in William Schoell, *Stay Out of the Shower* (New York, 1985), p. 56.
3. As quoted in Schoell, p. 41.
4. Donald Spoto, *Dark Side of Genius: The Life of Alfred Hitchcock* (New York, 1983), p. 483.
5. Silvia Bovenschen, 'Is There a Feminine Aesthetic?' *New German Critique* 10, 1977,

p. 114. See also Mary Ann Doane, 'Misrecognition and Identity', *Cine-Tracts* 11, 1980, pp. 25–32.

6. Ann Kaplan, *Women and Film: Both Sides of the Camera* (London and New York, Methuen, 1983), p. 15. The discussion of the gendered 'gaze' is lively and extensive. See above all Laura Mulvey, 'Visual Pleasure and Narrative Cinema', *Screen* vol. 16 no. 3, Autumn 1975, pp. 6–18; also Christine Gledhill, 'Recent Developments in Feminist Criticism', *Quarterly Review of Film Studies* (1978); reprinted in Mast and Cohen, *Film Theory and Criticism*, pp. 817–45.

7. Robin Wood, 'Beauty Bests the Beast', *American Film* 8, 1983, p. 64.

8. The locus classicus in this connection is the view-from-the-coffin shot in Carl Dreyer's *Vampyr*, in which the I-camera sees through the eyes of a dead man. See Mark Nash, '*Vampyr* and the Fantastic', *Screen*, vol. 17 no. 3, Autumn 1976, esp. pp. 32–3. The 1987 remake of *The Little Shop of Horrors* (itself originally a low-budget horror film, made the same year as *Psycho* in two days) lets us see the dentist from the proximate point of view of the patient's tonsils.

9. Two points in this paragraph deserve emending. One is the suggestion that rape is common in these films; it is in fact virtually absent, by definition. The other is the characterization of the Final Girl as 'sexy'. She may be attractive (through typically less so than her friends), but she is with few exceptions sexually inactive. For a detailed analysis of point-of-view manipulation, together with a psychoanalytic interpretation of the dynamic, see Steve Neale, '*Halloween*: Suspense, Aggression, and the Look'. *Framework* 14 (1981).

10. Wood is struck by the willingness of the teenaged audience to identify 'against' itself, with the forces of the enemy of youth. 'Watching it [*Texas Chainsaw Massacre I*] recently with a large, half-stoned youth audience, who cheered and applauded every one of Leatherface's outrages against their representatives on the screen, was a terrifying experience'. 'Return of the Repressed', *Film Comment* 14, 1978, p. 32.

11. 'I really appreciate the way audiences respond', Gail Anne Hurd, producer of *Aliens*, is reported to have said, 'They buy it. We don't get people, even rednecks, leaving the theater saying, "That was stupid. No woman would do that." You don't have to be a liberal ERA supporter to root for Ripley'; as reported in the *San Francisco Examiner Datebook*, 10 August 1986, p. 19. *Time*, 28 July 1986, p. 56, suggests that Ripley's maternal impulses (she squares off against the worst aliens of all in her quest to save a little girl) give the audience 'a much stronger rooting interest in Ripley, and that gives the picture resonances unusual in a popcorn epic'.

12. Further, 'When she [the mother] referred to the infant as a male, I just went along with it. Wonder how that child turned out – male, female, or something else entirely?' The birth is understood to be parthenogenetic, and the bisexual child, literally equipped with both sets of genitals, is figured as the reborn Christ.

13. Linda Williams, 'When the Woman Looks', in *Re-Vision: Essays in Feminist Film Criticism*, eds Mary Ann Doane, Patricia Mellencamp, and Linda Williams, American Film Institute Monograph Series (Los Angeles: The American Film Institute/Frederick, Maryland, University Publishers of America, 1984), p. 90. Williams's emphasis on the phallic leads her to dismiss slasher killers as a 'non-specific male killing force' and hence a degeneration in the tradition. 'In these films the recognition and affinity between women and monster of classic horror film gives way to pure identity; she *is* the monster, her mutilated body is the only visible horror' (p. 96). This analysis does not do justice to the obvious bisexuality of slasher killers, nor does it take into account the new strength of the female victim. The slasher film may not, in balance, be more subversive than traditional horror, but it is certainly not less so.

14. S. Freud, 'The "Uncanny"' in *The Standard Edition of the Complete Psychological Works of Sigmund Freud* ed. and transl. James Strachey, 24 Vols (London: Hogarth

Press, 1953–66), vol 17, p. 245. See also Neale, '*Halloween*', esp. pp. 28–9.

15. 'The woman's exercise of an active investigating gaze can only be simultaneous with her own victimization. The place of her specularization is transformed into the locus of a process of seeing designed to unveil an aggression against itself': Mary Ann Doane, 'The "Woman's Film" ', in *Re-Vision*, p. 72.

16. John Carpenter interviewed by Todd McCarthy, 'Trick and Treat', *Film Comment* 16, 1980 pp. 23–4.

17. This is not so in traditional film, nor in heterosexual pornography, in any case. Gay male pornography, however, films some male bodies in much the same way that heterosexual pornography films female bodies.

18. Compare the visual treatment of the (male) rape in *Deliverance* with the (female) rapes in Hitchcock's, *Frenzy*, or Wes Craven's *Last House on the Left* or Ingmar Bergman's *The Virgin Spring*. The latter films study the victims' faces at length and in closeup during the act: the first looks at the act intermittently and in long shot, focusing less on the actual victim than on the victim's friend who must look on.

19. Steven Marcus, *The Other Victorians: A Study of Sexuality and Pornography in Mid-Nineteenth-Century England* (New York: 1964), pp. 260–61. Marcus distinguishes two phases in the development of flagellation literature: one in which the figure being beaten is a boy, and the second, in which the figure is a girl. The very shift indicates, at some level, the irrelevance of apparent sex. 'The sexual identity of the figure being beaten is remarkably labile. Sometimes he is represented as a boy, sometimes as a girl, sometimes as a combination of the two – a boy dressed as a girl, or the reverse.' The girls often have sexually ambiguous names, as well. The beater is a female, but in Marcus's reading a phallic one – muscular, possessed of body hair – representing the father.

20. Marcus, pp. 125–7.

21. Further: 'Suspense is like a woman. The more left to the imagination, the more the excitement ... The perfect "woman of mystery" is one who is blonde, subtle, and Nordic ... Movie titles, like women, should be easy to remember without being familiar, intriguing but never obvious, warm yet refreshing, suggest action, not impassiveness, and finally give a clue without revealing the plot. Although I do not profess to be an authority on women, I fear that the perfect title, like the perfect woman, is difficult to find'; as quoted by Spoto, *Dark Side of Genius*, p. 431.

22. This would seem to be the point of the final sequence of Brian De Palma's *Blow-Out*, in which we see the boyfriend of the victim-hero stab the killer to death but later hear the television announce that the woman herself vanquished the killer. The frame plot of the film has to do with the making of a slasher film ('Co-Ed Frenzy'), and it seems clear that De Palma means his ending to stand as a comment on the Final Girl formula of the genre. De Palma's (and indirectly Hitchcock's) insistence that only men can kill men, or protect women from men, deserves a separate essay.

23. Freud, 'The "Uncanny"', esp. pp. 219–21 and pp. 226–7.

24. Raymond Durgnat, *Films and Feelings* (Cambridge, Mass., 1967), p. 216.

25. Not a few critics have argued that the ambiguity is the unintentional result of bad film-making.

26. Mulvey, 'Visual Pleasure and Narrative Cinema', p. 12.

27. Kaja Silverman, 'Masochism and Subjectivity', *Framework* 12, 1979, 5. Needless to say, this is not the explanation for the girl-hero offered by the industry. *Time* magazine on *Aliens*: 'As Director Cameron says, the endless "remulching" of the masculine hero by the "male-dominated industry" is, if nothing else, commercially shortsighted. "They choose to ignore that 50% of the audience is female. And I've been told that it has been proved demographically that 80% of the time it's women who decide which film to see" '; 28 July 1986. It is of course not Cameron who established the female hero of the series but Ridley Scott (in *Alien*), and it is fair to assume, from his careful manipulation of the formula, that Scott got her from the slasher film, where she has flourished for some time with audiences that are heavily

male. Cameron's analysis is thus both self-serving and beside the point.

28. If this analysis is correct, we may expect horror films of the future to feature Final Boys as well as Final Girls. Two recent figures may be incipient examples: Jesse, the pretty boy in *A Nightmare on Elm Street II*, and Ashley, the character who dies last in *The Evil Dead* (1983). Neither quite plays the role, but their names, and in the case of Jesse the characterization, seem to play on the tradition.

29. For the opposite view (based on classic horror in both literary and cinematic manifestations), see Franco Moretti, 'The Dialectic of Fear', *New Left Review* 136, 1982, pp. 67–85.

30. *Incredibly Strange Films*, eds V. Vale and Andrea Juno, *Re/Search* 10, San Francisco, 1986, p. 5.

31. Tania Modleski, 'The Terror of Pleasure: The Contemporary Horror Film and Post-modern Theory', in *Studies in Entertainment: Critical Approaches to Mass Culture*, ed. Tania Modleski (Bloomington, Ind., 1986), pp. 155–66. (Like Modleski, I stress that my comments are based on many slashers, not all of them.) This important essay (and volume) appeared too late for me to take it into full account in the text.

18

'HORROR AND THE MONSTROUS-FEMININE: AN IMAGINARY ABJECTION'

Barbara Creed

I

Mother's not herself today. – Norman Bates, *Psycho*

All human societies have a conception of the monstrous-feminine, of what it is about woman that is shocking, terrifying, horrific, abject. 'Probably no male human being is spared the terrifying shock of threatened castration at the sight of the female genitals,' Freud wrote in his paper, 'Fetishism' in 1927.[1] Joseph Campbell, in his book, *Primitive Mythology*, noted that:

> ...there is a motif occurring in certain primitive mythologies, as well as in modern surrealist painting and neurotic dream, which is known to folklore as 'the toothed vagina' – the vagina that castrates. And a counterpart, the other way, is the so-called 'phallic mother,' a motif perfectly illustrated in the long fingers and nose of the witch.[2]

Classical mythology also was populated with gendered monsters, many of which were female. The Medusa, with her 'evil eye', head of writhing serpents and lolling tongue, was queen of the pantheon of female monsters; men unfortunate enough to look at her were turned immediately to stone.

It is not by accident that Freud linked the sight of the Medusa to the equally horrifying sight of the mother's genitals, for the concept of the monstrous-feminine, as constructed within/by a patriarchal and phallocentric ideology, is

* From *Screen* 27:1, 1986, pp. 44–70.

related intimately to the problem of sexual difference and castration. In 1922 he argued that the 'Medusa's head takes the place of a representation of the female genitals';[3] if we accept Freud's interpretation, we can see that the Perseus myth is mediated by a narrative about the *difference* of female sexuality as a difference which is grounded in monstrousness and which invokes castration anxiety in the male spectator. 'The sight of the Medusa's head makes the spectator stiff with terror, turns him to stone.'[4] The irony of this was not lost on Freud, who pointed out that becoming stiff also means having an erection. 'Thus in the original situation it offers consolation to the spectator: he is still in possession of a penis, and the stiffening reassures him of the fact.'[5] One wonders if the experience of horror – of viewing the horror film – causes similar alterations in the body of the male spectator. And what of other phrases that apply to both male and female viewers – phrases such as: 'It scared the shit out of me'; 'It made me feel sick'; 'It gave me the creeps'? What is the relationship between physical states, bodily wastes (even if metaphoric ones) and the horrific – in particular, the monstrous-feminine?

II

Julia Kristeva's *Powers of Horror*[6] provides us with a preliminary hypothesis for an analysis of these questions. Although this study is concerned with literature, it nevertheless suggests a way of situating the monstrous-feminine in the horror film in relation to the maternal figure and what Kristeva terms 'abjection', that which does not 'respect borders, positions, rules' ... that which 'disturbs identity, system, order' (p. 4). In general terms, Kristeva is attempting to explore the different ways in which abjection, as a source of horror, works within patriarchal societies, as a means of separating the human from the non-human and the fully constituted subject from the partially formed subject. Ritual becomes a means by which societies both renew their initial contact with the abject element and then exclude that element [...]

A full examination of this theory is outside the scope of this article; I propose to draw mainly on Kristeva's discussion of abjection in its construction in the human subject in relation to her notions of (a) the 'border' and (b) the mother-child relationship. At crucial points, I shall also refer to her writing on the abject in relation to religious discourses. This area cannot be ignored, for what becomes apparent in reading her work is that definitions of the monstrous as constructed in the modern horror text are grounded in ancient religious and historical notions of abjection – particularly in relation to the following religious 'abominations': sexual immorality and perversion; corporeal alteration, decay and death; human sacrifice; murder; the corpse; bodily wastes; the feminine body and incest.

The place of the abject is 'the place where meaning collapses' (p. 2), the place where 'I' am not. The abject threatens life; it must be 'radically excluded' (p. 2) from the place of the living subject, propelled away from the body and deposited on the other side of an imaginary border which separates the self from that which threatens the self. Kristeva quotes Bataille: 'Abjection (. . .) is merely the inability to assume with sufficient strength the imperative act of excluding abject things (and that act establishes the foundations of collective existence)' (p. 56). Although the subject must exclude the abject, it must, nevertheless, be tolerated, for that which threatens to destroy life also helps to define life. Further, the activity of exclusion is necessary to guarantee that the subject take up his/her proper place in relation to the symbolic [. . .]

To the extent that abjection works on the socio-cultural arena, the horror film would appear to be, in at least three ways, an illustration of the work of abjection. Firstly, the horror film abounds in images of abjection, foremost of which is the corpse, whole and mutilated, followed by an array of bodily wastes such as blood, vomit, saliva, sweat, tears and putrifying flesh. In terms of Kristeva's notion of the border, when we say such-and-such a horror film 'made me sick' or 'scared the shit out of me'[7] we are actually foregrounding that specific horror film as a 'work of abjection' or 'abjection at work' – in both a literal and metaphoric sense. Viewing the horror film signifies a desire not only for perverse pleasure (confronting sickening, horrific images, being filled with terror/desire for the undifferentiated) but also a desire, having taken pleasure in perversity, to throw up, throw out, eject the abject (from the safety of the spectator's seat).

Secondly, there is, of course, a sense in which the concept of a border is central to the construction of the monstrous in the horror film; that which crosses or threatens to cross the 'border' is abject. Although the specific nature of the border changes from film to film, the function of the monstrous remains the same – to bring about an encounter between the symbolic order and that which theatens its stability. In some horror films the monstrous is produced at the border between human and inhuman, man and beast (*Dr Jekyll and Mr Hyde*, *Creature from the Black Lagoon*, *King Kong*); in others the border is between the normal and the supernatural, good and evil (*Carrie*, *The Exorcist*, *The Omen*, *Rosemary's Baby*); or the monstrous is produced at the border which separates those who take up their proper gender roles from those who do not (*Psycho*, *Dressed to Kill*, *Reflection of Fear*); or the border is between normal and abnormal sexual desire (*Cruising*, *The Hunger*, *Cat People*).

In relation to the construction of the abject within religious discourses, it is interesting to note that various sub-genres of the horror film seem to correspond to religious categories of abjection. For instance, blood as a religious abomination becomes a form of abjection in the 'splatter' movie (*Texas Chainsaw Massacre*); cannibalism, another religious abomination, is central to the 'meat' movie (*Night of the Living Dead*, *The Hills Have Eyes*); the corpse as abomination becomes the abject of ghoul and zombie movies (*The Evil Dead*; *Zombie Flesheaters*); blood as a taboo object within religion is central to the vampire film (*The Hunger*) as well as the horror film in general (*Bloodsucking Freaks*); human sacrifice as a religious abomination is constructed as the abject of virtually all horror films; and bodily disfigurement as a religious abomination is also central to the slash movie, particularly those in which woman is slashed, the mark a sign of her 'difference', her impurity (*Dressed to Kill, Psycho*).

III

The third way in which the horror film illustrates the work of abjection refers to the construction of the maternal figure as abject. Kristeva argues that all individuals experience abjection at the time of their earliest attempts to break away from the mother. She sees the mother-child relation as one marked by conflict: the child struggles to break free but the mother is reluctant to release it. Because of the 'instability of the symbolic function' in relation to this most crucial area – 'the prohibition placed on the maternal body (as a defence against autoeroticism and incest taboo)' (p. 14) – Kristeva argues that the maternal body becomes a site of conflicting desires. 'Here, drives hold sway and constitute a strange space that I shall name, after Plato (*Timeus*, 48–53), a *chora*, a receptacle' (p. 14). The position of the child is rendered even more unstable because, while the mother retains a close hold over the child, it can serve to authenticate her existence – an existence which needs validation because of her problematic relation to the symbolic realm.

> It is a violent, clumsy breaking away, with the constant risk of falling back under the sway of a power as securing as it is stifling. The difficulty the mother has in acknowledging (or being acknowledged by) the symbolic realm – in other words, the problem she has with the phallus that her father or husband stands for – is not such as to help the future subject leave the natural mansion. (p. 13)

In the child's attempts to break away, the mother becomes an abject; thus, in this context, where the child struggles to become a separate subject, abjection becomes 'a precondition of narcissism' (p. 13). Once again we can see abjection at work in the horror text where the child struggles to break away from the mother, representative of the archaic maternal figure, in a context in which the father is invariably absent (*Psycho, Carrie, The Birds*). In these films, the maternal figure is constructed as the monstrous-feminine. By refusing to relinquish her hold on her child, she prevents it from taking up its proper place in relation to the Symbolic. Partly consumed by the desire to remain locked in a blissful relationship with the mother and partly terrified of separation, the child finds it easy to succumb to the comforting pleasure of the dyadic relationship. Kristeva argues that a whole area of religion has assumed the function of tackling this danger:

> This is precisely where we encounter the rituals of defilement and their derivatives, which, based on the feeling of abjection and all converging on the maternal, attempt to symbolize the other threat to the subject: that of being swamped by the dual relationship, thereby risking the loss not of a part (castration) but of the totality of his living being. The function of these

religious rituals is to ward off the subject's fear of his very own identity sinking irretrievably into the mother. (p. 64)

How, then, are prohibitions against contact with the mother enacted and enforced? In answering this question, Kristeva links the universal practices of rituals of defilement to the mother. She argues that within the practices of all rituals of defilement, polluting objects fall into two categories: excremental, which threatens identity from the outside, and menstrual, which threatens from within.

> Excrement and its equivalents (decay, infection, disease, corpse, etc.) stand for the danger to identity that comes from without: the ego threatened by the non-ego, society threatened by its outside, life by death. Menstrual blood, on the contrary, stands for the danger issuing from within identity (social or sexual); it threatens the relationship between the sexes within a social aggregate and, through internalisation, the identity of each sex in the face of sexual difference. (p.71)

Both categories of polluting objects relate to the mother; the relation of menstrual blood is self-evident, the association of excremental objects with the maternal figure is brought about because of the mother's role in sphincteral training. Here, Kristeva argues that the subject's first contact with 'authority' is with the maternal authority when the child learns, through interaction with the mother, about its body: the shape of the body, the clean and unclean, the proper and improper areas of the body. Kristeva refers to this process as a 'primal mapping of the body' which she calls 'semiotic'. She distinguishes between maternal 'authority' and 'paternal laws': 'Maternal authority is the trustee of that mapping of the self's clean and proper body; it is distinguished from paternal laws within which, with the phallic phase and acquisition of language, the destiny of man will take shape'. (p. 72).

In her discussion of rituals of defilement in relation to the Indian caste system, Kristeva draws a distinction between the maternal authority and paternal law. She argues that the period of the 'mapping of the self's clean and proper body' is characterised by the exercise of 'authority without guilt', a time when there is a 'fusion between mother and nature'. However, the symbolic ushers in a 'totally different universe of socially signifying performances where embarrassment, shame, guilt, desire etc. come into play – the order of the phallus'. In the Indian context, these two worlds exist harmoniously side by side because of the working of defilement rites. Here, Kristeva is referring to the practice of public defecation in India. She quotes V. S. Naipaul who says that no one ever mentions 'in speech or in books, those squatting figures, because, quite simply, no one sees them'. Kristeva argues that this split between the world of the mother (a universe without shame) and the world of the father (a universe of shame), would in other social contexts produce psychosis; in India it finds a 'perfect socialization':

> This may be because the setting up of the rite of defilement takes on the function of the hyphen, the virgule, allowing the two universes of *filth* and *prohibition* to brush lightly against each other without necessarily being identified as such, as *object* and as *law*. (p. 74)

Images of blood, vomit, pus, shit, etc, are central to our culturally/socially constructed notions of the horrific. They signify a split between two orders: the maternal authority and the law of the father. On the one hand, these images of bodily wastes threaten a subject that is already constituted, in relation to the symbolic, as 'whole and proper'. Consequently, they fill the subject – both the protagonist in the text and the spectator in the cinema – with disgust and loathing. On the other hand, they also point back to a time when a 'fusion between mother and nature' existed; when bodily wastes, while set apart from the body, were not seen as objects of embarrassment and shame. Their presence in the horror film may invoke a response of disgust from the audience situated as it is within the symbolic but at a more archaic level the representation of bodily wastes may invoke pleasure in breaking the taboo on filth – sometimes described as a pleasure in perversity – and a pleasure in returning to that time when the mother-child relationship was marked by an untrammelled pleasure in 'playing' with the body and its wastes.

The modern horror film often 'plays' with its audience, saturating it with scenes of blood and gore, deliberately pointing to the fragility of the symbolic order in the domain of the body which never ceases to signal the repressed world of the mother. This is particularly evident in *The Exorcist*, where the world of the symbolic, represented by the priest-as-father, and the world of the pre-symbolic, represented by woman aligned with the devil, clashes head-on in scenes where the foulness of woman is signified by her putrid, filthy body covered in blood, urine, excrement and bile. Significantly, a pubescent girl about to menstruate played the woman who is possessed – in one scene blood from her wounded genitals mingles with menstrual blood to provide one of the film's key images of horror. In *Carrie*, the film's most monstrous act occurs when the couple are drenched in pig's blood which symbolises menstrual blood – women are referred to in the film as 'pigs', women 'bleed like pigs', and the pig's blood runs down Carrie's body at a moment of intense pleasure, just as her own menstrual blood runs down her legs during a similar pleasurable moment when she enjoys her body in the shower. Here, women's blood and pig's blood flow together, signifying horror, shame and humiliation. In this film, however, the mother speaks for the symbolic, identifying with an order which has defined women's sexuality as the source of all evil and menstruation as the sign of sin.

The horror film's obsession with blood, particularly the bleeding body of woman, where her body is transformed into the 'gaping wound', suggests that castration anxiety is a central concern of the horror film – particularly the slasher sub-genre. Woman's body is slashed and mutilated, not only to signify her own castrated state, but also the possibility of castration for the male. In the guise of a 'madman' he enacts on her body the one act he most fears for himself, transforming her entire body into a bleeding wound.

Kristeva's semiotic posits a pre-verbal dimension of language which relates to sounds and tone and to direct expression of the drives and physical contact with the maternal figure; 'it is dependent upon meaning, but in a way that is not that of *linguistic* signs nor of the *symbolic* order they found' (p. 72). With the subject's entry into the symbolic, which separates the child from the mother, the maternal figure and the authority she signifies are repressed. Kristeva argues that it is the function of defilement rites, particularly those relating to menstrual and excremental objects, to point to the 'boundary' between the maternal semiotic authority and the paternal symbolic law.

> Through language and within highly hierarchical religious institutions, man hallucinates partial 'objects' – witnesses to an archaic differentiation of the body on its way toward ego identity, which is also sexual identity. The *defilement* from which ritual protects us is neither sign nor matter. Within the rite that extracts it from repression and depraved desire, defilement is the translinguistic spoor of the most archaic boundaries of the self's clean and proper body. In that sense, if it is a jettisoned object, it is so from the mother . . . By means of the symbolic institution of ritual, that is to say, by means of a system of ritual exclusions, the partial-object consequently becomes *scription* – an inscription of limits, an emphasis placed not on the (paternal) Law but on (maternal) Authority through the very signifying order. (p. 73)

Kristeva argues that, historically, it has been the function of religion to purify the abject but with the disintegration of these 'historical forms' of religion, the work of purification now rests solely with 'that catharsis par excellence called art' (p. 17).

> In a world in which the Other has collapsed, the aesthetic task – a descent into the foundations of the symbolic construct – amounts to retracing the fragile limits of the speaking being, closest to its dawn, to the bottomless 'primacy' constituted by primal repression. Through that experience, which is nevertheless managed by the Other, 'subject' and 'object' push each other away, confront each other, collapse, and start again – inseparable, contaminated, condemned, at the boundary of what is assimilable, thinkable: abject. (p. 18)

This, I would argue, is also the central ideological project of the popular horror film – purification of the abject through a 'descent into the foundations of the symbolic construct'. In this way, the horror film brings about a confrontation with the abject (the corpse, bodily wastes, the monstrous-feminine) in order, finally, to eject the abject and re-draw the boundaries between the human and non-human. As a form of modern defilement rite, the horror film works to separate out the symbolic order from all that threatens its stability, particularly the mother and all that her universe signifies. In Kristeva's terms, this means separating out the maternal authority from paternal law [...]

IV

The science-fiction horror film *Alien* is a complex representation of the monstrous-feminine in terms of the maternal figure as perceived within a patriarchal ideology. She is there in the text's scenarios of the primal scene, of birth and death; she is there in her many guises as the treacherous mother, the oral sadistic mother, the mother as primordial abyss; and she is there in the film's images of blood, of the all-devouring vagina, the toothed vagina, the vagina as Pandora's box; and finally she is there in the chameleon figure of the alien, the monster as fetish-object of and for the mother. But it is the archaic mother, the reproductive/generative mother, who haunts the *mise-en-scène* of the film's first section, with its emphasis on different representations of the primal scene.

According to Freud, every child either watches its parents in the act of sexual intercourse or has phantasies about that act – phantasies which relate to the problem of origins. Freud left open the question of the cause of the phantasy but suggested that it may initially be aroused by 'an observation of the sexual intercourse of animals'.[8] In his study of 'the Wolf Man', Freud argued that the child did not initially observe his parents in the act of sexual intercourse but that he witnessed the copulation of animals whose behaviour he then displaced onto his parents. In situations where the child actually witnesses sexual intercourse between its parents, Freud argued that all children arrive at the same conclusion: 'They adopt what may be called a *sadistic view of coition*'.[9] If the child perceives the primal scene as a monstrous act – whether in reality or phantasy – it may phantasise animals or mythical creatures as taking part in the scenario. Possibly the many mythological stories in which humans copulate with animals and other creatures (Europa and Zeus, Leda and the Swan) are reworkings of the primal scene narrative. The Sphinx, with her lion's body and woman's face, is an interesting figure in this context. Freud suggested that the Riddle of the Sphinx was probably a distorted version of the great riddle that faces all children – Where do babies come from? An extreme form of the primal phantasy is that of 'observing parental intercourse while one is still an unborn baby in the womb'.[10]

One of the major concerns of the sci-fi horror film (*Alien, The Thing, Invasion of the Body Snatchers, Altered States*) is the reworking of the primal scene in relation to the representation of other forms of copulation and procreation. *Alien* presents various representations of the primal scene. Behind each of these lurks the figure of the archaic mother, that is, the image of the mother in her generative function – the mother as the origin of all life. This archaic figure is somewhat different from the mother of the semiotic chora, posed by Kristeva, in that the latter is the pre-Oedipal mother who exists in relation to the family and the symbolic order. The concept of the parthenogenic, archaic mother adds another dimension to the maternal figure and presents us with a new way of understanding how patriarchal ideology works to deny the 'difference' of woman in her cinematic representation.

The first birth scene occurs in *Alien* at the beginning, where the camera/spectator explores the inner space of the mother-ship whose life support system is a computer aptly named – 'Mother'. This exploratory sequence of the inner body of the 'Mother' culminates with a long tracking shot down one of the corridors which leads to a womb-like chamber where the crew of seven are woken up from their protracted sleep by Mother's voice monitoring a call for help from a nearby planet. The seven astronauts emerge slowly from their sleep pods in what amounts to a re-birthing scene which is marked by a fresh, antiseptic atmosphere. In outer space, birth is a well controlled, clean, painless affair. There is no blood, trauma or terror. This scene could be interpreted as a primal fantasy in which the human subject is born fully developed – even copulation is redundant.

The second representation of the primal scene takes place when three of the crew enter the body of the unknown space-ship through a 'vaginal' opening: the ship is shaped like a horseshoe, its curved sides like two long legs spread apart at the entrance. They travel along a corridor which seems to be made of a combination of inorganic and organic material – as if the inner space of this ship were alive. Compared to the atmosphere of the *Nostromo*, however, this ship is dark, dank and mysterious. A ghostly light glimmers and the sounds of their movements echo throughout the caverns. In the first chamber, the three explorers find a huge alien life form which appears to have been dead for a long time. Its bones are bent outward as if it exploded from the inside. One of the trio, Kane, is lowered down a shaft into the gigantic womb-like chamber in which rows of eggs are hatching. Kane approaches one of the eggs; as he touches it with his gloved hand it opens out, revealing a mass of pulsating flesh. Suddenly, the monstrous thing inside leaps up and attaches itself to Kane's helmet, its tail penetrating Kane's mouth in order to fertilise itself inside his stomach. Despite the warnings of Ripley, Kane is taken back on board the Nostromo where the alien rapidly completes its gestation processes inside Kane.

This representation of the primal scene recalls Freud's reference to an extreme primal scene fantasy where the subject imagines travelling back inside the womb to watch her/his parents having sexual intercouse, perhaps to watch her/himself being conceived. Here, three astronauts explore the gigantic, cavernous, malevolent womb of the mother. Two members of the group watch the enactment of the primal scene in which Kane is violated in an act of phallic penetration – by the father or phallic mother? Kane himself is guilty of the strongest transgression; he actually peers into the egg/womb in order to investigate its mysteries. In so doing, he becomes a 'part' of the primal scene, taking up the place of the mother, the one who is penetrated, the one who bears the offspring of the union. The primal scene is represented as violent, monstrous (the union is between human and alien), and is mediated by the question of incestuous desire. All re-stagings of the primal scene raise the question of incest, as the beloved parent (usually the mother) is with a rival. The first birth scene, where the astronauts emerge from their sleep pods, could be viewed as a representation of incestuous desire *par excellence*: the father is completely absent; here, the mother is sole parent and sole life-support.

From this forbidden union, the monstrous creature is born. But man, not woman, is the 'mother' and Kane dies in agony as the alien gnaws its way through his stomach. The birth of the alien from Kane's stomach plays on what Freud described as a common misunderstanding that many children have about birth, that is, that the mother is somehow impregnated through the mouth – she may eat a special food – and the baby grows in her stomach from which it is also born. Here, we have a third version of the primal scene.

A further version of the primal scene – almost a convention[11] of the science fiction film – occurs when smaller crafts or bodies are ejected from the mother-ship into outer space; although sometimes the ejected body remains attached to the mother-ship by a long life-line or umbilical chord. This scene is presented in two separate ways: one when Kane's body, wrapped in a white shroud, is ejected from the mother-ship; and the second, when the small space capsule, in which Ripley is trying to escape from the alien, is expelled from the underbelly of the mother-ship. In the former, the 'mother's' body has become hostile; it contains the alien whose one purpose is to kill and devour all of Mother's children. In the latter birth scene the living infant is ejected from the malevolent body of the 'mother' to avoid destruction; in this scenario, the 'mother's' body explodes at the moment of giving birth.

Although the 'mother' as a figure does not appear in these sequences – nor indeed in the entire film – her presence forms a vast backdrop for the enactment of all the events. She is there in the images of birth, the representations of the primal scene, the womb-like imagery, the long winding tunnels leading to inner chambers, the rows of hatching eggs, the body of the mother-ship, the voice of the life-support system and the birth of the alien. She is the generative mother, the pre-phallic mother, the being who exists prior to knowledge of the phallus.

V

[...] Clearly, it is difficult to separate out completely the figure of the archaic mother, as defined above, from other aspects of the maternal figure – the maternal authority of Kristeva's semiotic, the mother of Lacan's imaginary, the phallic woman, the castrated woman. While the different figures signify quite separate things about the monstrous-feminine, as constructed in the horror film, each one is also only part of the whole – a different aspect of the maternal figure. At times the horrific nature of the monstrous-feminine is totally dependent on the merging together of all aspects of the maternal figure into one – the horrifying image of woman as archaic mother, phallic woman and castrated body represented as a single figure within the horror film. However, the archaic mother is clearly present in two distinct ways in the horror film.

(i) The archaic mother – constructed as a negative force – is represented in her phantasmagoric aspects in many horror texts, particularly the sci-fi horror film. We see her as the gaping, cannibalistic bird's mouth in *The Giant Claw*; the terrifying spider of *The Incredible Shrinking Man*; the toothed vagina/womb of *Jaws*; and the fleshy, pulsating, womb of *The Thing* and the *Poltergeist*. What is common to all of these images of horror is the voracious maw, the mysterious black hole which signifies female genitalia as a monstrous sign which threatens to give birth to equally horrific offspring as well as threatening to incorporate everything in its path. This is the generative archaic mother, constructed within patriarchal ideology as the primeval 'black hole'. This, of course, is also the hole which is opened up by the absence of the penis; the horrifying sight of the mother's genitals – proof that castration can occur.

However, in the texts cited above, the emphasis is not on castration; rather it is the gestating, all-devouring womb of the archaic mother which generates the horror. Nor are these images of the womb constructed in relation to the penis of the father. Unlike the female genitalia, the womb cannot be constructed as a 'lack' in relation to the penis. The womb is not the site of castration anxiety. Rather, the womb signifies 'fullness' or 'emptiness' but always it is its *own point of reference*. This is why we need to posit a more archaic dimension to the mother. For the concept of the archaic mother allows for a notion of the feminine which does not depend for its definition on a concept of the masculine. The term 'archaic mother' signifies woman as sexual difference. In contrast the maternal figure of the pre-Oedipal is always represented in relation to the penis – the phallic mother who later becomes the castrated mother. Significantly, there is an attempt in *Alien* to appropriate the procreative function of the mother, to represent a man giving birth, to deny the mother as signifier of sexual difference – but here birth can exist only as the other face of death.

(ii) The archaic mother is present in all horror films as the blackness of extinction – death. The desires and fears invoked by the image of the archaic mother, as a force that threatens to re-incorporate what it once gave birth to, are always there in the horror text – all pervasive, all encompassing – because of the constant presence of death. The desire to return to the original oneness of things, to return to the mother/womb, is primarily a desire for non-differentiation. If, as Georges Bataille[12] argues, life signifies discontinuity and separateness, and death signifies continuity and non-differentiation, then the desire for and attraction of death suggests also a desire to return to the state of original oneness with the mother. As this desire to merge occurs after differentiation, that is after the subject has developed as separate, autonomous self, then it is experienced as a form of psychic death. In this sense, the confrontation with death as represented in the horror film, gives rise to a terror of self-disintegration, of losing one's self or ego – often represented cinematically by a screen which becomes black, signifying the obliteration of self, the self of the protagonist in the film and the spectator in the cinema. This has important consequences for the positioning of the spectator in the cinema.

One of the most interesting structures operating in the screen-spectator relationship relates to the sight/site of the monstrous within the horror text. In contrast to the conventional viewing structures working within other variants of the classic text, the horror film does not constantly work to suture the spectator into the viewing processes. Instead, an unusual phenomenon arises whereby the suturing processes are momentarily undone while the horrific image on the screen challenges the viewer to run the risk of continuing to look. Here, I refer to those moments in the horror film when the spectator, unable to stand the images of horror unfolding before his/her eyes, is forced to look away, to not-look, to look anywhere but at the screen. Strategies of identification are temporarily broken, as the spectator is constructed in the place of horror, the place where the sight/site can no longer be endured, the place where pleasure in looking is transformed into pain and the spectator is punished for his/her voyeuristic desires. Perhaps, this should be referred to as a *fifth* look operating alongside the other 'looks' which have been theorised in relation to the screen-spectator relationship.[13]

Confronted by the sight of the monstrous, the viewing subject is put into crisis – boundaries, designed to keep the abject at bay, threaten to disintegrate, collapse. According to Lacan, the self is constituted in a process which he called the 'mirror phase', in which the child perceives its own body as a unified whole in an image it receives from outside itself. Thus, the concept of identity is a structure which depends on identification with another. Identity is an imaginary construct, formed in a state of alienation, grounded in mis-recognition. Because the self is constructed on an illusion, Lacan argues that it is always in danger of regressing:

> Here we see the ego, in its essential resistance to the elusive process of Becoming, to the variations of Desire. This illusion of unity, in which a human being is always looking forward to self-mastery, entails a constant danger of sliding back again into the chaos from which he started; it hangs over the abyss of a dizzy Assent in which one can perhaps see the very essence of Anxiety.[14]

The horror film puts the viewing subject's sense of a unified self into crisis, specifically in those moments when the image on the screen becomes too threatening or horrific to watch, when the abject threatens to draw the viewing subject to the place 'where meaning collapses', the place of death. By not-looking, the spectator is able momentarily to withdraw identification from the image on the screen in order to reconstruct the boundary between self and screen and reconstitute the 'self' which is threatened with disintegration. This process of reconstitution of the self is reaffirmed by the conventional ending of the horror narrative in which the monster is usually 'named' and destroyed.[15]

Fear of losing oneself and one's boundaries is made more acute in a society which values boundaries over continuity and separateness over sameness. Given that death is represented in the horror film as a threat to the self's boundaries, symbolised by the threat of the monster, death images are most likely to cause the spectator to look away, to not-look. Because the archaic mother is closely associated with death in its negative aspects, her presence is marked negatively within the project of the horror film. Both signify a monstrous obliteration of the self and both are linked to the demonic. Again, Kristeva presents a negative image of the maternal figure in her relationship to death:

> What is the demoniacal – an inescapable, repulsive, and yet nurtured abomination? The fantasy of an archaic force, on the near side of separation, unconscious, tempting us to the point of losing our differences, our speech, our life; to the point of aphasia, decay, opprobrium, and death? (p. 107)

[...] The other face of the monstrous-feminine in *Alien* is the phallic mother. Freud argued that the male child could either accept the threat of castration, thus ending the Oedipus complex, or disavow it. The latter response requires the (male) child to mitigate his horror at the sight of the mother's genitals – proof that castration can occur – with a fetish object which substitutes for her missing penis. For him, she is still the phallic mother, the penis-woman. In 'Medusa's Head' Freud argued that the head with its hair of writhing snakes represented the terrifying genitals of the mother, but that this head also functioned as a fetish object.

> The hair upon the Medusa's head is frequently represented in works of art in the form of snakes, and these once again are derived from the castration complex. It is a remarkable fact that, however frightening they may be in themselves, they nevertheless serve actually as a mitigation of horror, for they replace the penis, the absence of which is the cause of horror.[16]

Freud noted that a display of the female genitals makes a woman 'unapproachable and repels all sexual desires'. He refers to the section in Rabelais which relates 'how the Devil took flight when the woman showed him her vulva'.[17] Perseus' solution is to look only at a reflection, a mirror-image of her genitals. As with patriarchal ideology, his shield reflects an 'altered' representation, a vision robbed of its threatening aspects. The full difference of the mother is denied; she is constructed as other, displayed before the gaze of the conquering male hero, then destroyed.[18] The price paid is the destruction of sexual heterogeneity and repression of the maternal signifier. The fetishisation of the mother's genitals could occur in those texts where the maternal figure is represented in her phantasmagoric aspects as the gaping, voracious vagina/womb. Do aspects of these images work to mitigate the horror by offering a substitute for the penis? [...]

In *Alien*, the monstrous creature is constructed as the phallus of the negative mother. The image of the archaic mother – threatening because it signifies woman as difference rather than constructed as opposition – is, once again, collapsed into the figure of the pre-Oedipal mother. By re-locating the figure of woman within an Oedipal scenario, her image can be recuperated and controlled. The womb, even if represented negatively, is a greater threat than the mother's phallus. As phallic mother, woman is again represented as monstrous. What is horrific is her desire to cling to her offspring in order to continue to 'have the phallus'. Her monstrous desire is concretised in the figure of the alien; the creature whose deadly mission is represented as the same as that of the archaic mother – to reincorporate and destroy all life.

If we consider *Alien* in the light of a theory of female fetishism, then the chameleon nature of the alien begins to make sense. Its changing appearance represents a form of doubling or multiplication of the phallus, pointing to the mother's desire to stave off her castration. The alien is the mother's phallus, a fact which is made perfectly clear in the birth scene where the infant alien rises from Kane's stomach and holds itself erect, glaring angrily around the room, before screeching off into the depths of the ship. But the alien is more than a phallus; it is also coded as a toothed vagina, the monstrous-feminine as the cannibalistic mother. A large part of the ideological project of *Alien* is the representation of the maternal fetish object as an 'alien' or foreign shape. This is why the body of the heroine becomes so important at the end of the film.

Much has been written about the final scene, in which Ripley/Sigourney Weaver undresses before the camera, on the grounds that its voyeurism undermines her role as successful heroine. A great deal has also been written about the cat. Why does she rescue the cat and thereby risk her life, and the lives of Parker and Lambert, when she has previously been so careful about quarantine regulations? Again, satisfactory answers to these questions are provided by a phallocentric concept of female fetishism. Compared to the horrific sight of the alien as fetish object of the monstrous feminine, Ripley's body is pleasurable and reassuring to look at. She signifies the 'acceptable' form and shape of woman. In a sense the monstrousness of woman, represented by Mother as betrayer (the computer/life support system), and Mother as the uncontrollable, generative, cannibalistic mother (the alien), is controlled through the display of woman as reassuring and pleasurable sign. The image of the cat functions in the same way; it signifies an acceptable, and in this context, a reassuring, fetish object for the 'normal' woman.[19] Thus, Ripley holds the cat to her, stroking it as if it were her 'baby', her 'little one'. Finally, Ripley enters her sleep pod, assuming a virginal repose. The nightmare is over and we are returned to the opening sequence of the film where birth was a pristine affair. The final sequence works, not only to dispose of the alien, but also to repress the nightmare image of the monstrous-feminine, constructed as a sign of abjection, within the text's patriarchal discourses.

Kristeva's theory of abjection, if viewed as description rather than prescription, provides a productive hypothesis for an analysis of the monstrous-feminine in the horror film.[20] If we posit a more archaic dimension to the mother, we can see how this figure, as well as Kristeva's maternal authority of the semiotic, are both constructed as figures of abjection within the signifying practices of the horror film. We can see its ideological project as an attempt to shore up the

264

symbolic order by constructing the feminine as an imaginary 'other' which must be repressed and controlled in order to secure and protect the social order. Thus, the horror film stages and re-stages a constant repudiation of the maternal figure.

But the feminine is not *per se* a monstrous sign; rather, it is constructed as such within a patriarchal discourse which reveals a great deal about male desires and fears but tells us nothing about feminine desire in relation to the horrific. When Norman Bates remarked to Marion Crane in *Psycho* that: 'Mother is not herself today', he was dead right. Mother wasn't herself. She was someone else. Her son – Norman.

NOTES

1. Sigmund Freud, 'Fetishism', *On Sexuality*, Harmondsworth, Penguin, Pelican Freud Library, vol. 7, 1981, p. 354.
2. Joseph Campbell, *The Masks of God: Primitive Mythology*, New York, Penguin, 1969, p. 73.
3. Sigmund Freud, 'Medusa's Head', in James Strachey (ed., *The Standard Edition of the Complete Psychological Works of Sigmund Freud*, vol. 18, London, Hogarth Press, 1964, pp. 273–4.
4. Ibid, p. 273.
5. Ibid.
6. Julia Kristeva, *Powers of Horror: An Essay on Abjection*, New York, Columbia University Press, 1982. All page citations will be included in the text.
7. For a discussion of the way in which the modern horror film works upon its audience see Philip Brophy, 'Horrality', in *Screen*, 27, 1.
8. Sigmund Freud, 'From the History of an Infantile Neurosis', *Case Histories II*, Harmondsworth, Penguin, Harmondsworth, Pelican Freud Library, vol. 9, 1981, p. 294.
9. Sigmund Freud, 'On the Sexual Theories of Children', *On Sexuality*, Harmondsworth, Penguin, Pelican Freud Library, vol. 7, 1981, p. 198.
10. Sigmund Freud, 'The Paths to the Formation of Symptoms', *Introductory Lectures on Psychoanalysis*, Harmondsworth, Penguin, Pelican Freud Library, vol. 1, 1981, p. 417.
11. Daniel Dervin argues that this structure does deserve the status of a convention. For a detailed discussion of the primal scene phantasy in various film genres, see his 'Primal Conditions and Conventions: The Genres of Comedy and Science Fiction', *Film/Psychology Review*, Winter-Spring 1980, pp. 115–47.
12. Georges Bataille, *Death and Sensuality: A Study of Eroticism and the Taboo*, New York, Walker and Company, 1962, p. 200.
13. For a discussion of cinema and the structures of the 'look' see Paul Willemen, 'Letter To John', *Screen* Summer, 1980, vol. 21 no. 2, pp. 53–66.
14. Jacques Lacan, 'Some Reflections on the Ego', *The International Journal of Psychoanalysis*, vol. 24, 1953, p. 15.
15. For a discussion of the relationship between the female spectator, structures of looking and the horror film see Linda Williams, 'When The Woman Looks', in Mary Anne Doane, Patricia Mellencamp and Linda Williams (eds), *Re-Vision*, American Film Institute Monograph Series, vol. 3, University Publications of America, 1984.
16. Sigmund Freud, 'Medusa's Head', p. 105.
17. Ibid, p. 106.
18. For a fascinating discussion of the place of woman as monster in the Oedipal narrative see Teresa de Lauretis, *Alice Doesn't: Feminism, Semiotics, Cinema*, Indiana University Press, 1984, chapter 5.

19. The double bird images of Hitchcock's *The Birds* function in the same way: the love birds signify an 'acceptable' fetish, the death birds a fetish of the monstrous woman.
20. For an analysis of the horror film as a 'return of the repressed' see Robin Wood's articles: 'Return of the Repressed', *Film Comment*, July-August, 1978; and 'Neglected Nightmares', *Film Comment*, March-April, 1980.

19

'FILM BODIES: GENDER, GENRE AND EXCESS'

Linda Williams

When my seven-year-old son and I go to the movies we often select from among categories of films that promise to be sensational, to give our bodies an actual physical jolt. He calls these movies 'gross.' My son and I agree that the fun of 'gross' movies is in their display of sensations that are on the edge of respectable. Where we disagree – and where we as a culture often disagree, along lines of gender, age, or sexual orientation – is in which movies are over the edge, too 'gross.' To my son the good 'gross' movies are those with scary monsters like Freddy Krueger (of the *Nightmare on Elm Street* series) who rip apart teenagers, especially teenage girls. These movies both fascinate and scare him; he is actually more interested in talking about than seeing them.

A second category, one that I like and my son doesn't, are sad movies that make you cry. These are gross in their focus on unseemly emotions that may remind him too acutely of his own powerlessness as a child. A third category, of both intense interest and disgust to my son (he makes the puke sign when speaking of it), he can only describe euphemistically as 'the "K" word.' K is for kissing. To a seven-year-old boy it is kissing precisely which is obscene.

There is no accounting for taste, especially in the realm of the 'gross.' As a culture we most often invoke the term to designate excesses we wish to exclude; to say, for example, which of the Robert Mapplethorpe photos we draw the line at, but not to say what form and structure and function operate within the representations deemed excessive. Because so much attention goes to determin-

* *Film Quarterly* Vol. 44, No. 4, 1991, pp. 2–13.

ing where to draw the line, discussions of the gross are often a highly confused hodgepodge of different categories of excess. For example, pornography is today more often deemed excessive for its violence than for its sex, while horror films are excessive in their displacement of sex onto violence. In contrast, melodramas are deemed excessive for their gender- and sex-linked pathos, for their naked displays of emotion; Ann Douglas once referred to the genre of romance fiction as 'soft-core emotional porn for women' (Douglas, 1980).

Alone or in combination, heavy doses of sex, violence, and emotion are dismissed by one faction or another as having no logic or reason for existence beyond their power to excite. Gratuitous sex, gratuitous violence and terror, gratuitous emotion are frequent epithets hurled at the phenomenon of the 'sensational' in pornography, horror, and melodrama. This essay explores the notion that there may be some value in thinking about the form, function, and system of seemingly gratuitous excesses in these three genres. For if, as it seems, sex, violence, and emotion are fundamental elements of the sensational effects of these three types of films, the designation 'gratuitous' is itself gratuitous. My hope, therefore, is that by thinking comparatively about all three 'gross' and sensational film body genres we might be able to get beyond the mere fact of sensation to explore its system and structure as well as its effect on the bodies of spectators.

BODY GENRES

The repetitive formulas and spectacles of film genres are often defined by their differences from the classical realist style of narrative cinema. These classical films have been characterized as efficient action-centered, goal-oriented linear narratives driven by the desire of a single protagonist, involving one or two lines of action, and leading to definitive closure. In their influential study of the Classical Hollywood Cinema, Bordwell, Thompson, and Staiger call this the Classical Hollywood style (1985).

As Rick Altman has noted in a recent article (1989), both genre study and the study of the somewhat more nebulous category of melodrama has long been hampered by assumptions about the classical nature of the dominant narrative to which melodrama and some individual genres have been opposed. Altman argues that Bordwell, Thompson, and Staiger, who locate the Classical Hollywood Style in the linear, progressive form of the Hollywood narrative, cannot accommodate 'melodramatic' attributes like spectacle, episodic presentation, or dependence on coincidence except as limited exceptions or 'play' within the dominant linear causality of the classical (Altman, 1989, 346).

Altman writes: 'Unmotivated events, rhythmic montage, highlighted parallelism, overlong spectacles – these are the excesses in the classical narrative system that alert us to the existence of a competing logic, a second voice.' (345–6) Altman, whose own work on the movie musical has necessarily relied upon analyses of seemingly 'excessive' spectacles and parallel constructions, thus makes a strong case for the need to recognize the possibility that excess may itself be organized as a system (347). Yet analyses of systems of excess have been much slower to emerge in the genres whose non-linear spectacles have centered more directly upon the gross display of the human body. Pornography and horror films are two such systems of excess. Pornography is the lowest in cultural esteem, gross-out horror is next to lowest.

Melodrama, however, refers to a much broader category of films and a much larger system of excess. It would not be unreasonable, in fact, to consider all three of these genres under the extended rubric of melodrama, considered as a filmic mode of stylistic and/or emotional excess that stands in contrast to more 'dominant' modes of realistic, goal-oriented narrative. In this extended sense melodrama can encompass a broad range of films marked by 'lapses' in realism, by 'excesses' of spectacle and displays of primal, even infantile emotions, and by narratives that seem circular and repetitive. Much of the interest of melodrama to film scholars over the last fifteen years originates in the sense that the form exceeds the normative system of much narrative cinema. I shall limit my focus here, however, to a more narrow sense of melodrama, leaving the broader category of the sensational to encompass the three genres I wish to consider. Thus, partly for purposes of contrast with pornography, the melodrama I will consider here will consist of the form that has most interested feminist critics – that of 'the woman's film' or 'weepie.' These are films addressed to women in their traditional status under patriarchy – as wives, mothers, abandoned lovers, or in their traditional status as bodily hysteria or excess, as in the frequent case of the woman 'afflicted' with a deadly or debilitating disease.[1]

What are the pertinent features of bodily excess shared by these three 'gross' genres? First, there is the spectacle of a body caught in the grip of intense sensation or emotion. Carol Clover, speaking primarily of horror films and pornography, has called films which privilege the sensational 'body' genres (Clover, 1987, 189). I am expanding Clover's notion of low body genres to include the sensation of overwhelming pathos in the 'weepie.' The body spectacle is featured most sensationally in pornography's portrayal of orgasm, in horror's portrayal of violence and terror, and in melodrama's portrayal of weeping. I propose that an investigation of the visual and narrative pleasures found in the portrayal of these three types of excess could be important to a new direction in genre criticism that would take as its point of departure – rather than as an unexamined assumption – questions of gender construction, and gender address in relation to basic sexual fantasies.

Another pertinent feature shared by these body genres is the focus on what could probably best be called a form of ecstasy. While the classical meaning of the original Greek word is insanity and bewilderment, more contemporary meanings suggest components of direct or indirect sexual excitement and rapture, a rapture which informs even the pathos of melodrama.

Visually, each of these ecstatic excesses could be said to share a quality of uncontrollable convulsion or spasm – of the body 'beside itself' with sexual pleasure, fear and terror, or overpowering sadness. Aurally, excess is marked by

269

recourse not to the coded articulations of language but to inarticulate cries of pleasure in porn, screams of fear in horror, sobs of anguish in melodrama.

Looking at, and listening to, these bodily ecstasies, we can also notice something else that these genres seem to share: though quite differently gendered with respect to their targeted audiences, with pornography aimed, presumably, at active men and melodramatic weepies aimed, presumably, at passive women, and with contemporary gross-out horror aimed at adolescents careening wildly between the two masculine and feminine poles, in each of these genres the bodies of women figured on the screen have functioned traditionally as the primary *embodiments* of pleasure, fear, and pain.

In other words, even when the pleasure of viewing has traditionally been constructed for masculine spectators, as is the case in most traditional hetero-sexual pornography, it is the female body in the grips of an out-of-control ecstasy that has offered the most sensational sight. So the bodies of women have tended to function, ever since the eighteenth-century origins of these genres in the Marquis de Sade, Gothic fiction, and the novels of Richardson, as both the *moved* and the *moving*. It is thus through what Foucault has called the sexual saturation of the female body that audiences of all sorts have received some of their most powerful sensations (Foucault, 1978, 104).

There are, of course, other film genres which both portray and affect the sensational body – e.g., thrillers, musicals, comedies. I suggest, however, that the film genres that have had especially low cultural status – which have seemed to exist as excesses to the system of even the popular genres – are not simply those which sensationally display bodies on the screen and register effects in the bodies of spectators. Rather, what may especially mark these body genres as low is the perception that the body of the spectator is caught up in an almost involuntary mimicry of the emotion or sensation of the body on the screen along with the fact that the body displayed is female. Physical clown comedy is another 'body' genre concerned with all manner of gross activities and body functions – eating shoes, slipping on banana peels. Nonetheless, it has not been deemed gratuitously excessive, probably because the reaction of the audience does not mimic the sensations experienced by the central clown. Indeed, it is almost a rule that the audience's physical reaction of laughter does not coincide with the often dead-pan reactions of the clown.

In the body genres I am isolating here, however, it seems to be the case that the success of these genres is often measured by the degree to which the audience sensation mimics what is seen on the screen. Whether this mimicry is exact, e.g., whether the spectator at the porn film actually orgasms, whether the spectator at the horror film actual shudders in fear, whether the spectator of the melodrama actually dissolves in tears, the success of these genres seems a self-evident matter of measuring bodily response. Examples of such measurement can be readily observed: in the 'peter meter' capsule reviews in *Hustler* magazine, which measure the power of a porn film in degrees of erection of little cartoon penises; in horror films which measure success in terms of screams, fainting, and heart attacks in the audience (horror producer William Castle specialized in this kind of thing with such films as *The Tingler*, 1959); and in the longstanding tradition of women's films measuring their success in terms of one-, two-, or three-handkerchief movies.

What seems to bracket these particular genres from others is an apparent lack of proper esthetic distance, a sense of over-involvement in sensation and emotion. We feel manipulated by these texts – an impression that the very colloquialisms of 'tear jerker' and 'fear jerker' express – and to which we could add pornography's even cruder sense as texts to which some people might be inclined to 'jerk off.' The rhetoric of violence of the jerk suggests the extent to which viewers feel too directly, too viscerally manipulated by the text in specifically gendered ways. Mary Ann Doane, for example, writing about the most genteel of these jerkers – the maternal melodrama – equates the violence of this emotion to a kind of 'textual rape' of the targeted female viewer, who is 'feminized through pathos' (Doane, 1987, 95).

Feminist critics of pornography often evoke similar figures of sexual/textual violence when describing the operation of this genre. Robin Morgan's slogan 'pornography is the theory, and rape is the practice' is well known (Morgan, 1980, 139). Implicit in this slogan is the notion that women are the objectified victims of pornographic representations, that the image of the sexually ecstatic woman so important to the genre is a celebration of female victimization and a prelude to female victimization in real life.

Less well known, but related, is the observation of the critic of horror films, James Twitchell, who notices that the Latin *horrere* means to bristle. He describes the way the nape hair stands on end during moments of shivering excitement. The aptly named Twitchell thus describes a kind of erection of the hair founded in the conflict between reactions of 'fight and flight' (Twitchell, 1985, 10). While male victims in horror films may shudder and scream as well, it has long been a dictum of the genre that women make the best victims. 'Torture the women!' was the famous advice given by Alfred Hitchcock.[2]

In the classic horror film the terror of the female victim shares the spectacle along with the monster. Fay Wray and the mechanized monster that made her scream in *King Kong* is a familiar example of the classic form. Janet Leigh in the shower in *Psycho* is a familiar example of a transition to a more sexually explicit form of the tortured and terrorized woman. And her daughter, Jamie Lee Curtis in *Halloween*, can serve as the more contemporary version of the terrorized woman victim. In both of these later films the spectacle of the monster seems to take second billing to the increasingly numerous victims slashed by the sexually disturbed but entirely human monsters.

In the woman's film a well-known classic is the long-suffering mother of the two early versions of *Stella Dallas* who sacrifices herself for her daughter's upward mobility. Contemporary film goers could recently see Bette Midler going through the same sacrifice and loss in the film *Stella*. Debra Winger in *Terms of Endearment* is another familiar example of this maternal pathos.

With the above genre stereotypes in mind we should now ask about the status of bodily excess in each of these genres. Is it simply the unseemly, 'gratuitous' presence of the sexually ecstatic woman, the tortured woman, the weeping woman – and the accompanying presence of the sexual fluids, the blood and the tears that flow from her body and which are presumably mimicked by spectators – that mark the excess of each type of film? How shall we think of these bodily displays in relation to one another, as a system of excess in the popular film? And finally, how excessive are they really?

The psychoanalytic system of analysis that has been so influential in film study in general and in feminist film theory and criticism has been remarkably ambivalent about the status of excess in its major tools of analysis. The categories of fetishism, voyeurism, sadism, and masochism frequently invoked to describe the pleasures of film spectatorship are by definition perversions. Perversions are usually defined as sexual excesses, specifically as excesses which are deflected away from 'proper' end goals onto substitute goals or objects – fetishes instead of genitals, looking instead of touching, etc. – which seem excessive or gratuitous. Yet the perverse pleasures of film viewing are hardly gratuitous. They have been considered so basic that they have often been presented as norms. What is a film, after all, without voyeurism? Yet, at the same time, feminist critics have asked, what is the position of women within this pleasure geared to a presumably sadistic 'male gaze'? (Mulvey, 1975) To what extent is she its victim? Are the orgasmic woman of pornography and the tortured woman of horror merely in the service of the sadistic male gaze? And is the weeping woman of melodrama appealing to the abnormal perversions of masochism in female viewers?

These questions point to the ambiguity of the terms of perversion used to describe the normal pleasures of film viewing. Without attempting to go into any of the complexities of this discussion here – a discussion which must ultimately relate to the status of the term perversion in theories of sexuality themselves – let me simply suggest the value of not invoking the perversions as terms of condemnation. As even the most cursory reading of Freud shows, sexuality is by definition perverse. The 'aims' and 'objects' of sexual desire are often obscure and inherently substitutive. Unless we are willing to see reproduction as the common goal of the sexual drive, we have to admit, as Jonathan Dollimore has put it, that we are all perverts. Dollimore's goal of retrieving the 'concept of perversion as a category of cultural analysis' – as a structure intrinsic to all sexuality rather than extrinsic to it – is crucial to any attempt to understand cultural forms – such as our three body genres – in which fantasy predominates.[3]

STRUCTURES OF PERVERSION IN THE 'FEMALE BODY GENRES'

Each of the three body genres I have isolated hinges on the spectacle of a 'sexually saturated' female body, and each offers what many feminist critics would agree to be spectacles of feminine victimization. But this victimization is very different in each type of film and cannot be accounted for simply by pointing to the sadistic power and pleasure of masculine subject positions punishing or dominating feminine objects.

Many feminists have pointed to the victimization of the woman performers of pornography who must actually do the acts depicted in the film, as well as to the victimization of characters within the films (Dworkin, 1979; MacKinnon, 1987). Pornography, in this view, is fundamentally sadistic. In women's weepies, on the other hand, feminists have pointed to the spectacles of intense suffering and loss as masochistic.

In horror films, while feminists have often pointed to the women victims who suffer simulated torture and mutilation as victims of sadism (Williams, 1983), more recent feminist work has suggested that the horror film may present an interesting, and perhaps instructive, case of oscillation between masochistic and sadistic poles. This more recent argument, advanced by Carol J. Clover, has suggested that pleasure, for a masculine-identified viewer, oscillates between identifying with the initial passive powerlessness of the abject and terrorized girl-victim of horror and her later, active empowerment (Clover, 1987).

This argument holds that when the girl-victim of a film like *Halloween* finally grabs the phallic knife, or axe, or chain saw to turn the tables on the monster-killer, that viewer identification shifts from an 'abject terror gendered feminine' to an active power with bisexual components. A gender-confused monster is foiled, often symbolically castrated by an 'androgynous' 'final girl' (Clover, 1987, 206–9). In slasher films, identification with victimization is a roller-coaster ride of sadomasochistic thrills.

We could thus initially schematize the perverse pleasures of these genres in the following way: pornography's appeal to its presumed male viewers would be characterized as sadistic, horror films' appeal to the emerging sexual identities of its (frequently adolescent) spectators would be sadomasochistic and women's films' appeal to presumed female viewers would be masochistic.

The masochistic component of viewing pleasure for women has been the most problematic term of perversion for feminist critics. It is interesting, for example, that most of our important studies of masochism – whether by Deleuze (1971), Silverman (1980; 1988) or Studlar (1985) – have all focused on the exoticism of masculine masochism rather than the familiarity of female masochism. Masochistic pleasure for women has paradoxically seemed either too normal – too much the normal yet intolerable condition of women – or too perverse to be taken seriously as pleasure.

There is thus a real need to be clearer than we have been about what is in masochism for women – how power and pleasure operate in fantasies of domination which appeal to women. There is an equal need to be clearer than we have about what is in sadism for men. Here the initial opposition between these two most gendered genres – women's weepies and male heterosexual pornography – needs to be complicated. I have argued elsewhere, for example, that pornography has too simplistically been allied with a purely sadistic fantasy structure. Indeed, those troubling films and videos which deploy instruments of torture on the bodies of women have been allied so completely with masculine viewing pleasures that we have not paid enough attention to their appeal to women except to condemn such appeal as false consciousness (Williams, 1989, 184–228).

One important complication of the initial schema I have outlined would thus be to take a lesson from Clover's more bisexual model of viewer identification in horror film and stress the sadomasochistic component of each of these body genres through their various appropriations of melodramatic fantasies that are, in fact, basic to each. All of these genres could, for example, be said to offer highly melodramatic enactments of sexually charged, if not sexually explicit, relations. The sub-genre of sadomasochistic pornography, with its suspension of pleasure over the course of prolonged sessions of dramatic suffering, offers a particularly intense, almost parodic, enactment of the classic melodramatic scenario of the passive and innocent female victim suffering at the hands of a leering villain. We can also see in horror films of tortured women a similar melodramatization of the innocent victim. An important difference, of course, lies in the component of the victim's overt sexual pleasure in the scenario of domination.

But even in the most extreme displays of feminine masochistic suffering, there is always a component of either power or pleasure for the woman victim. In slasher horror films we have seen how identification seems to oscillate between powerlessness and power. In sadomasochistic pornography and in melodramatic woman's weepies, feminine subject positions appear to be constructed which achieve a modicum of power and pleasure within the given limits of patriarchal constraints on women. It is worth noting as well that *non*-sadomasochistic pornography has historically been one of the few types of popular film that has not punished women for actively pursuing their sexual pleasure.

In the subgenre of sadomasochistic pornography, however, the female masochist in the scenario must be devious in her pursuit of pleasure. She plays the part of passive sufferer in order to obtain pleasure. Under a patriarchal double standard that has rigorously separated the sexually passive 'good' girl from the sexually active 'bad' girl, masochistic role-playing offers a way out of this dichotomy by combining the good girl with the bad: the passive 'good girl' can prove to her witnesses (the super-ego who is her torturer) that she does not will the pleasure that she receives. Yet the sexually active 'bad' girl enjoys this pleasure and has knowingly arranged to endure the pain that earns it. The cultural law which decides that some girls are good and others are bad is not defeated but within its terms pleasure has been negotiated and 'paid for' with a pain that conditions it. The 'bad' girl is punished, but in return she receives pleasure.[4]

In contrast, the sadomasochistic teen horror films kill off the sexually active 'bad' girls, allowing only the non-sexual 'good' girls to survive. But these good girls become, as if in compensation, remarkably active, to the point of

An anatomy of film bodies

Genre:	Pornography	Horror	Melodrama
Bodily excess	sex	violence	emotion
Ecstasy: – shown by	ecstatic sex orgasm ejaculation	ecstatic violence shudder blood	ecstatic woe sob tears
Presumed audience:	men (active)	adolescent boys (active/passive)	girls, women (passive)
Perversion:	sadism	sadomasochism	masochism
Originary fantasy:	seduction	castration	origin
Temporality of fantasy:	on time!	too early!	too late!
Genre cycles: 'classic'	stag films (20s–40s) *The Casting Couch*	'classic' horror: *Dracula* *Frankenstein* *Dr Jekyll/Mr Hyde* *King Kong*	'classic' women's films: maternal melodrama: *Stella Dallas* *Mildred Pierce* romance: *Back Street* *Letter from an Unknown Woman*
contemporary	feature-length hard core porn: *Deep Throat*, etc. *The Punishment of Anne* Femme Productions Bi-sexual Tri-sexual	post-*Psycho*: *Texas Chainsaw Massacre* *Halloween* *Dressed to Kill* *Videodrome*	male and female 'weepies' *Steel Magnolias* *Stella* *Dad*

appropriating phallic power to themselves. It is as if this phallic power is granted so long as it is rigorously separated from phallic or any other sort of pleasure. For these pleasures spell sure death in this genre.

In the melodramatic woman's film we might think to encounter a purer form of masochism on the part of female viewers. Yet even here the female viewer does not seem to be invited to identify wholly with the sacrificing good woman, but rather with a variety of different subject positions, including those which empathically look on at her own suffering. While I would not argue that there is a very strong sadistic component to these films, I do argue that there is a strong mixture of passivity and activity, and a bisexual oscillation between the poles of each, in even this genre.

For example, the woman viewer of a maternal melodrama such as *Terms of Endearment* or *Steel Magnolias* does not simply identify with the suffering and dying heroines of each. She may equally identify with the powerful matriarchs, the surviving mothers who preside over the deaths of their daughters, experiencing the exhilaration and triumph of survival. The point is simply that identification is neither fixed nor entirely passive.

While there are certainly masculine and feminine, active and passive, poles to the left and right of the chart on which we might position these three genres (see above), the subject positions that appear to be constructed by each of the genres are not as gender-linked and as gender-fixed as has often been supposed. This is especially true today as hard-core pornography is gaining appeal with women viewers. Perhaps the most recent proof in this genre of the breakdown of rigid dichotomies of masculine and feminine, active and passive is the creation of an alternative, oscillating category of address to viewers. Although heterosexual hard core once addressed itself exclusively to heterosexual men, it has now begun to address itself to heterosexual couples and women as well; and in addition to homosexual hard core, which has addressed itself to gay and (to a lesser extent) lesbian viewers, there is now a new category of video called bisexual. In these videos men do it with women, women do it with women, men do it with men and then all do it with one another, in the process breaking down a fundamental taboo against male-to-male sex.[5]

A related interpenetration of once more separate categories of masculine and feminine is what has come to be known in some quarters as the 'male weepie.' These are mainstream melodramas engaged in the activation of the previously repressed emotions of men and in breaking the taboos against male-to-male hugs and embraces. The father-son embrace that concludes *Ordinary People* (1980) is exemplary. More recently, paternal weepies have begun to compete with the maternal – as in the conventional *Dad* (1989) or the less conventional, wild paternal displays of *Twin Peaks*.

The point is certainly not to admire the 'sexual freedom' of this new fluidity and oscillation – the new femininity of men who hug and the new masculinity of women who leer – as if it represented any ultimate defeat of phallic power. Rather, the more useful lesson might be to see what this new fluidity and oscillation permits in the construction of feminine viewing pleasures once thought not to exist at all. (It is instructive, for example, that in the new bisexual pornography women characters are shown verbally articulating their visual pleasure as they watch men perform sex with men.)

The deployment of sex, violence, and emotion would thus seem to have very precise functions in these body genres. Like all popular genres, they address persistent problems in our culture, in our sexualities, in our very identities. The deployment of sex, violence, and emotion is thus in no way gratuitous and in no way strictly limited to each of these genres; it is instead a cultural form of problem solving. As I have argued in *Hard Core*, pornographic films now tend to present sex as a problem, to which the performance of more, different, or better sex is posed as the solution (Williams, 1989). In horror a violence related to sexual difference is the problem, more violence related to sexual difference is also the solution. In women's films the pathos of loss is the problem, repetitions and variations of this loss are the generic solution.

STRUCTURES OF FANTASY

All of these problems are linked to gender identity and might be usefully explored as genres of gender fantasy. It is appropriate to ask, then, not only about the structures of perversion, but also about the structures of fantasy in each of these genres. In doing so, we need to be clear about the nature of fantasy itself. For fantasies are not, as is sometimes thought, wish-fulfilling linear narratives of mastery and control leading to closure and the attainment of desire. They are marked, rather, by the prolongation of desire, and by the lack of fixed position with respect to the objects and events fantasized.

In their classic essay 'Fantasy and the Origins of Sexuality,' Jean Laplanche and J. B. Pontalis (1968) argue that fantasy is not so much a narrative that enacts the quest for an object of desire as it is a setting for desire, a place where conscious and unconscious, self and other, part and whole meet. Fantasy is the place where 'desubjectified' subjectivities oscillate between self and other occupying no fixed place in the scenario (16).

In the three body genres discussed here, this fantasy component has probably been better understood in horror film, a genre often understood as belonging to the 'fantastic.' However, it has been less well understood in pornography and women's film melodrama. Because these genres display fewer fantastic special effects and because they rely on certain conventions of realism – the activation of social problems in melodrama, the representation of real sexual acts in pornography – they seem less obviously fantastic. Yet the usual criticisms that these forms are improbable, that they lack psychological complexity and narrative closure, and that they are repetitious, become moot as evaluation if such features are intrinsic to their engagement with fantasy.

There is a link, in other words, between the appeal of these forms and their ability to address, if never *really* to 'solve,' basic problems related to sexual identity. Here, I would like to forge a connection between Laplanche and Pontalis's structural understanding of fantasies as myths of origins which try to cover the discrepancy between two moments in time and the distinctive temporal structure of these particular genres. Laplanche and Pontalis argue that fantasies which are myths of origins address the insoluble problem of the discrepancy between an irrecoverable original experience presumed to have actually taken place – as in the case, for example, of the historical primal scene – and the uncertainty of its hallucinatory revival. The discrepancy exists, in other words, between the actual existence of the lost object and the sign which evokes both this existence and its absence.

Laplanche and Pontalis maintain that the most basic fantasies are located at the juncture of an irrecoverable real event that took place somewhere in the past and a totally imaginary event that never took place. The 'event' whose temporal and spatial existence can never be fixed is thus ultimately, according to

Laplanche and Pontalis, that of 'the origin of the subject' – an origin which psychoanalysts tell us cannot be separated from the discovery of sexual difference (11).

It is this contradictory temporal structure of being situated somewhere between the 'too early' and the 'too late' of the knowledge of difference that generates desire that is most characteristic of fantasy. Freud introduced the concept of 'original fantasy' to explain the mythic function of fantasies which seem to offer repetitions of and 'solutions' to major enigmas confronting the child (Freud, 1915). These enigmas are located in three areas: the enigma of the origin of sexual desire, an enigma that is 'solved,' so to speak, by the fantasy of seduction; the enigma of sexual difference, 'solved' by the fantasy of castration; and finally the enigma of the origin of self, 'solved' by the fantasy of family romance or return to origins (Laplanche and Pontalis, 1968, 11).

Each of the three body genres I have been describing could be seen to correspond in important ways to one of these original fantasies: pornography, for example, is the genre that has seemed to endlessly repeat the fantasies of primal seduction, of meeting the other, seducing or being seduced by the other in an ideal 'pornotopia' where, as Steven Marcus has noted, it is always bedtime (Marcus, 1964/74, 269). Horror is the genre that seems to endlessly repeat the trauma of castration as if to 'explain,' by repetitious mastery, the originary problem of sexual difference. And melodramatic weepie is the genre that seems to endlessly repeat our melancholic sense of the loss of origins – impossibly hoping to return to an earlier state which is perhaps most fundamentally represented by the body of the mother.

Of course each of these genres has a history and does not simply 'endlessly repeat.' The fantasies activated by these genres are repetitious, but not fixed and eternal. If traced back to origins each could probably be shown to have emerged with the formation of the bourgeois subject and the intensifying importance to this subject of specified sexualities. But the importance of repetition in each genre should not blind us to the very different temporal structure of repetition in each fantasy. It could be, in fact, that these different temporal structures constitute the different utopian component of problem-solving in each form. Thus the typical (non-sadomasochistic) pornographic fantasies of seduction operate to 'solve' the problem of the origin of desire. Attempting to answer the insoluble question of whether desire is imposed from without through the seduction of the parent or whether it originates within the self, pornography answers this question by typically positing a fantasy of desire coming from within the subject *and* from without. Non-sadomasochistic pornography attempts to posit the utopian fantasy of perfect temporal coincidence: a subject and object (or seducer and seduced) who meet one another 'on time!' and 'now!' in shared moments of mutual pleasure that it is the special challenge of the genre to portray.

In contrast to pornography, the fantasy of recent teen horror corresponds to a temporal structure which raises the anxiety of not being ready, the problem, in effect, of 'too early!' Some of the most violent and terrifying moments of the horror film genre occur in moments when the female victim meets the psycho-killer-monster unexpectedly, before she is ready. The female victims who are not ready for the attack die. This surprise encounter, too early, often takes place at a moment of sexual anticipation when the female victim thinks she is about to meet her boyfriend or lover. The monster's violent attack on the female victims vividly enacts a symbolic castration which often functions as a kind of punishment for an ill-timed exhibition of sexual desire. These victims are taken by surprise in the violent attacks which are then deeply felt by spectators (especially the adolescent male spectators drawn to the slasher subgenre) as linked to the knowledge of sexual difference. Again the key to the fantasy is timing – the way the knowledge of sexual difference too suddenly overtakes both characters and viewers, offering a knowledge for which we are never prepared.

Finally, in contrast to pornography's meeting 'on time!' and horror's unexpected meeting 'too early!,' we can identify melodrama's pathos of the 'too late!' In these fantasies the quest to return to and discover the origin of the self is manifest in the form of the child's fantasy of possessing ideal parents in the Freudian family romance, in the parental fantasy of possessing the child in maternal or paternal melodrama, and even in the lovers' fantasy of possessing one another in romantic weepies. In these fantasies the quest for connection is always tinged with the melancholy of loss. Origins are already lost, the encounters always take place too late, on death beds or over coffins. (Neale, 1988).

Italian critic Franco Moretti has argued, for example, that literature that makes us cry operates via a special manipulation of temporality: what triggers our crying is not just the sadness or suffering of the character in the story but a very precise moment when characters in the story catch up with and realize what the audience already knows. We cry, Moretti argues, not just because the characters do, but at the precise moment when desire is finally recognized as futile. The release of tension produces tears – which become a kind of homage to a happiness that is kissed goodbye. Pathos is thus a surrender to reality but it is a surrender that pays homage to the ideal that tried to wage war on it (Moretti, 1983, 179). Moretti thus stresses a subversive, utopian component in what has often been considered a form of passive powerlessness. The fantasy of the meeting with the other that is always too late can thus be seen as based upon the utopian desire that it not be too late to remerge with the other who was once part of the self.

Obviously there is a great deal of work to be done to understand the form and function of these three body genres in relation to one another and in relation to the fundamental appeal as 'original fantasies.' Obviously also the most difficult work of understanding this relation between gender, genre, fantasy, and structures of perversion will come in the attempt to relate original fantasies to historical context and specific generic history. However, there is one thing that already seems clear: these 'gross' body genres which may seem so violent and inimical to women cannot be dismissed as evidence of a monolithic and unchanging misogyny, as either pure sadism for male viewers or masochism for females. Their very existence and popularity hinges upon rapid changes taking place in relations between the 'sexes' and by rapidly changing notions of gender – of what it means to be a man or a woman. To dismiss them as bad excess whether of explicit sex, violence, or emotion, or as bad perversions, whether of masochism or sadism, is not to address their function as cultural problem-solving. Genres thrive, after all, on the persistence of the problems they address; but genres thrive also in their ability to recast the nature of these problems.

Finally, as I hope this most recent example of the melodrama of tears suggests, we may be wrong in our assumption that the bodies of spectators simply reproduce the sensations exhibited by bodies on the screen. Even those masochistic pleasures asssociated with the powerlessness of the 'too late!' are not absolutely abject. Even tear jerkers do not operate to force a simple mimicry of the sensation exhibited on the screen. Powerful as the sensations of the jerk might be, we may only be beginning to understand how they are deployed in generic and gendered cultural forms.

Notes

I owe thanks to Rhona Berenstein, Leo Braudy, Ernest Callenbach, Paul Fitzgerald, Jane Gaines, Mandy Harris, Brian Henderson, Marsha Kinder, Eric Rentschler, and Pauline Yu for generous advice on drafts of this essay.

1. For an excellent summary of many of the issues involved with both film melodrama and the 'women's film,' see Christine Gledhill's introduction to the anthology *Home is Where the Heart Is: Studies in Melodrama and the Woman's Film* (Gledhill, 1987). For a more general inquiry into the theatrical origins of melodrama, see Peter Brooks's (1976) *The Melodramatic Imagination*. And for an extended theoretical inquiry and analysis of a body of melodramatic women's films, see Mary Ann Doane (1987), *The Desire to Desire*.
2. Carol J. Clover (1987) discusses the meanings of this famous quote in her essay, 'Her Body/Himself: Gender in the Slasher Film.'
3. Dollimore (1990, 13). Dollimore's project, along with Teresa de Lauretis's more detailed examination of the term perversion in Freudian psychoanalysis is central to any more detailed attempts to understand the perverse pleasures of these gross body genres.
4. I discuss these issues at length in a chapter on sadomasochistic pornography in my book *Hard Core* (1989).
5. Titles of these relatively new (post 1986) hard-core videos include: *Bisexual Fantasies; Bi-Mistake; Karen's Bi-Line; Bi-Dacious; Bi-Night; Bi and Beyond: The Ultimate Fantasy; Bi and Beyond II; Bi and Beyond III: Hermaphrodites.*

Works Cited

Altman, Rick, 1989. 'Dickens, Griffith, and Film Theory Today.' *South Atlantic Quarterly* 88:321–59.
Bordwell, David, Janet Staiger and Kristin Thompson. 1985. *The Classical Hollywood Cinema: Film Style and Mode of Production to 1960*. New York: Columbia University Press.
Brooks, Peter. 1976. *The Melodramatic Imagination*. New Haven: Yale University Press.

Clover, Carol J. 1987. 'Her Body, Himself: Gender in the Slasher Film.' *Representations* 20 (Fall): 187–228.

De Lauretis, Teresa. 1994. *The Practice of Love: Lesbian Sexuality and Perverse Desire.* Bloomington: Indiana University Press.

Deleuze, Gilles. 1971. *Masochism: An Interpretation of Coldness and Cruelty.* Translated by Jean McNeil. New York: Braziller.

Doane, Mary Ann. 1987. *The Desire to Desire: The Woman's Film of the 1940's.* Bloomington: Indiana University Press.

Doane, Mary Ann, Patricia Mellencamp, and Linda Williams, eds. 1983. *Re-Vision: Essays in Feminist Film Criticism.* American Film Institute Monograph Series, vol. 3. Frederick, MD: University Publications of America.

Dollimore, Jonathan. 1990. 'The Cultural Politics of Perversion: Augustine, Shakespeare, Freud, Foucault.' *Genders* 8.

Douglas, Ann. 1980. 'Soft-Porn Culture.' *The New Republic*, 30 August 1980.

Dworkin, Andrea. 1979. *Pornography: Men Possessing Women.* New York: Perigee Books.

Foucault, Michel. 1978. *The History of Sexuality* Vol. 1: *An Introduction.* Translated by Robert Hurley. New York: Pantheon Books.

Freud, Sigmund. 1915. 'Instincts and their Vicissitudes.' Vol. 14 of the *Standard Edition of The Complete Psychological Works of Sigmund Freud.* London: Hogarth. 14.

Gledhill, Christina. 1987. *Home is Where the Heart Is: Studies in Melodrama and the Woman's Film.* London: BFI.

Laplanche, Jean, J. B. Pontalis. 1968. 'Fantasy and the Origins of Sexuality.' *The International Journal of Psycho-Analysis.* 49: 1–18.

MacKinnon. 1987. *Feminism Unmodified: Discourses on Life and Law.* Cambridge, MA: Harvard University Press.

Marcus, Steven, 1964/74. *The Other Victorians: A Study of Sexuality and Pornography in Mid-Nineteenth Century England.* New York: New American Library.

Morgan, Robin, 1980, 'Theory and Practice: Pornography and Rape.' In *Take Back the Night: Women on Pornography*, edited by Laura Lederer. New York: Morrow.

Moretti, Franco. 1983. 'Kindergarten.' In *Signs Taken for Wonders*. London: Verso.

Mulvey, Laura. 1975. 'Visual Pleasure and Narrative Cinema.' *Screen* 16, no. 3: 6–18.

Neale, Steve. 1986. 'Melodrama and Tears.' *Screen* 27 (Nov.–Dec.): 6–22.

Silverman, Kaja. 1980. 'Masochism and Subjectivity.' *Framework* 12: 2–9.

Silverman, Kaja. 1988. 'Masochism and Male Subjectivity.' *Camera Obscura* 17: 31–66.

Studlar, Gaylyn. 1985. *In the Realm of Pleasure: Von Sternberg, Dietrich and the Masochistic Aesthetic.* Urbana: University of Illinois Press.

Twitchell, James, 1985. *Dreadful Pleasures: An Anatomy of Modern Horror.* New York: Oxford.

Williams, Linda. 1983. 'When the Woman Looks.' In *Re Vision: Essays in Feminist Film Criticism.* See Doane (1983).

William, Linda 1989. *Hard Core: Power, Pleasure and the 'Frenzy of the Visible.'* Berkeley: University of California Press.

PART V
FURTHER READING

Adams, Parveen 1988: Per Os(cillation). *Camera Obscura* 17, pp. 6–29.

Burgin, Victor, Donald, James and Kaplan, Cora (eds) 1989: *Formations of Fantasy*. London and New York: Routledge.

Clover, Carol J. 1992: *Men, Women and Chainsaws: Gender in the Modern Horror Film*. London: BFI.

Cook, Pam and Dodd, Philip (eds) 1993: *Women and Film: A Sight and Sound Reader*. London: Scarlett Press.

Cowie, Elizabeth 1984: Fantasia. *m/f* no. 9, pp.71–104.

Creed, Barbara 1987: From Here to Modernity – Feminism and Postmodernism. *Screen* 28, 2, pp. 47–67.

Creed, Barbara 1988: A Journey Through *Blue Velvet, New Formations* Vol. 6, pp.97–117.

Creed, Barbara 1993: *The Monstrous Feminine: Film, Feminism, Psychoanalysis*. London: Routledge.

Creed, Barbara 1993: Dark Desires: Male Masochism in the Horror Film. In Cohan, S. and Hark, I. R., *Screening the Male: Exploring Masculinities in Hollywood Cinema*. London and New York: Routledge, pp. 118–33.

De Lauretis, Teresa 1995: On the Subject of Fantasy. In Pietropaolo, L. and Testaferri, A. (eds), *Feminisms in the Cinema*. Bloomington and Indianapolis: Indiana University Press, pp. 63–85.

Donald, James (ed.) 1989: *Fantasy and the Cinema*. London: BFI, pp. 136–45.

Grosz, Elizabeth 1989: *Sexual Subversions*. Sydney: Allen & Unwin.

Kaplan, E. Ann (ed.) 1990: *Psychoanalysis and Cinema*. London: Routledge.

Kristeva, Julia 1982: *Powers of Horror: An Essay on Abjection*. New York: Columbia University Press.

Kuhn, Annette (ed.) 1990: *Alien Zone: Cultural Theory and Contemporary Science Fiction Cinema*. London: Verso.

Laplanche, Jean and Pontalis, Jean-Bertrand 1986 (1964): Fantasy and the Origins of Sexuality. In Burgin, V., Donald, J. and Kaplan, C., *Formations of Fantasy*.

London and New York: Routledge, pp.5–34.

Penley, Constance 1989: *The Future of an Illusion: Film, Feminism and Psychoanalysis*. London: Routledge.

Penley, Constance 1992: Feminism, Psychoanalysis, and the Study of Popular Culture. In Grossberg, L., Nelson, C. and Treichler, P. (ed.), *Cultural Studies*. New York and London: Routledge, pp. 479–500.

Silverman, Kaja 1980: Masochism and Subjectivity. *Framework* 12, pp. 2–9.

Silverman, Kaja 1988: *The Acoustic Mirror: The Female Voice in Psychoanalysis and Cinema*. Bloomington and Indianapolis: Indiana University Press.

Silverman, Kaja 1988: Masochism and Male Subjectivity. *Camera Obscura* 17, pp. 31–67.

Stacey, Jackie 1994: *Star Gazing: Hollywood Cinema and Female Spectatorship*. London and New York: Routledge.

Studlar, Gaylyn 1985 (1984): Masochism and the Perverse Pleasures of the Cinema. In Nichols, B. (ed.), *Movies and Methods* Vol. II. London: University of California Press, pp. 602–21.

Tasker, Yvonne 1993: *Spectacular Bodies: Gender, Genre and the Action Cinema*. London and New York: Routledge.

Thornham, Sue 1997: Fantasy, Horror and the Body. In *Passionate Detachments: An Introduction to Feminist Film Theory*. London: Arnold, pp. 92–116.

Williams, Linda 1984: When the Woman Looks. In Doane, M.A., Mellencamp, P., and Williams, L. (eds), *Re-Vision: Essays in Film Criticism*. Los Angeles: American Film Institute, pp. 83–99.

Williams, Linda 1990: *Hard Core*. London: Pandora.

PART VI
RE-THINKING DIFFERENCES

INTRODUCTION

The essays in the preceding two sections can be seen in their different ways as responses to the limitations of psychoanalytic theory as it had been employed within feminist film theory of the 1970s and early 1980s. Those in this final section explore its limitations when confronted by two groups of female spectators whose cinematic pleasures and identifications seem unassimilable to the theoretical structures of a psychoanalytically-based feminist film theory: black women and lesbian women.[1] As Jane Gaines writes in the opening essay, the opposition male/female, so central to feminist theory, 'is a powerful, but sometimes blinding construct'. It can blind the theorist, for example, to the inability of a structure based on theories of a 'male gaze' and masculine spectatorial pleasure to theorise a lesbian viewing position. It can blind her, too, to the elision of the specificity of black women's positioning that goes on when Freud's metaphor of woman as 'the dark continent'[2] is used to describe woman's positioning as 'other' within patriarchy.[3] As Lola Young puts it:

> There has been white feminist overinvestment in the gender component of the 'dark continent', which has resulted in the virtual elimination of the racial and colonial implications. Thus this most racialized of sexual metaphors has become synonymous with the concerns of white women. (Young 1996: 177)

It is this issue that Jane Gaines discusses. Like Christine Gledhill (Chapter 13), she criticises the inability of a psychoanalytically-based feminist film criticism to deal with issues of history, experience, and political practice, and she draws for support on the work of Stuart Hall within cultural studies. But, focusing on the experience of black American women, her charge is not just that the broad categories of 'cine-psychoanalysis' cannot deal with the specificities of their history; it is that the theoretical framework offered by psychoanalysis is inadequate as a conceptual tool.

As Gaines points out, African-American feminist criticism has grounded its critique on the claims of a distinctive black – specifically black American – experience.[4] It has been race, rather than gender, which has formed its structuring principle, so that white women, rather than sharing a common oppression, may be seen as themselves oppressors, and black men can be seen to share a common history of oppression under slavery. Moreover, femininity within American culture has been defined as white femininity, so that the body of the black woman may function not as the objectified image of 'woman' of white feminist theory, but as the site of resistance to invisibility.

Gaines explores these issues in relation to *Mahogany*, a 1975 star vehicle for Diana Ross. The film, she points out, can be analysed using a psychoanalytically-grounded feminist film criticism: it exemplifies issues of male voyeurism/ sadism and female objectification. But to perform such an analysis is to miss the lack of power afforded the black male gaze in the film, a powerlessness whose explanation lies not in psychoanalytic theory but in the cultural history of African-American men, for whom the sexual gaze, if directed at a white woman, could carry the penalty of literal castration or death. It is to miss, too, the very different significance of the central character's thoroughly conventional decision to abandon career for love, in a context where that decision is also a decision to abandon white 'acceptance' for black community solidarity. The crucial importance of these issues for an understanding of the film, argues Gaines, suggests that we must not only 'rethink film theory along more materialist lines' but also reconsider our understanding of cinematic language, for which the opposition black/white may be as important a structuring principle as the opposition male/female.

bell hooks also criticises feminist film theory for its reliance on a psychoanalytic perspective that places sexual difference as 'the primary and/or exclusive signifier of difference' and thus allows the white woman to believe she is speaking for all women. Positioning herself within a cultural studies framework, hooks argues that 'the field of representation' must be seen as 'a place of struggle' (1992: 3) in which both text and audience are engaged. Her critique thus echoes that of other feminist theorists within a cultural studies tradition (see Part IV), but its central focus is on the black woman as image and spectator. If, argues hooks, processes of identification depend on the imaginary closing of the gap between self and other, then the gap between black female spectator and idealised *white* image of femininity is one that can be imaginatively closed only through 'the masochistic look of victimization'. The black female spectator, however, more often resists that process, she argues, placing herself outside the structures of cinematic visual pleasure proposed by Laura Mulvey or Mary Ann Doane (see Part II), and developing instead a critical or oppositional gaze.

For hooks, as for Gaines, the power of the gaze is materially as well as psychoanalytically constructed. If the politics of slavery denied the slave the right to look, then a 'critical' or oppositional gaze has long been a strategy of resistance and an assertion of agency in the face of domination. For black men, in the darkened space of the cinema, this might mean the possibility of a fantasised phallocentric power denied them in a racist society. Black female spectators, however, refusing to identify with 'the phallocentric gaze of desire and possession', can create a critical space where Mulvey's opposition of 'woman as image, man as bearer of the look' can be deconstructed and negative images of black women reclaimed. Whilst it is the product of a specific black history, however, such a critical gaze is not its inevitable result. It has to be actively asserted in the face of 'dominant ways of knowing and looking'. Finally, hooks affirms the importance of an emerging black feminist film-making in opening up new ways of thinking about black female subjectivity and creating new spaces for the assertion of a critical black female spectatorship.

Tania Modleski's 'Cinema and the Dark Continent' returns us, as its title suggests, to an engagement both with psychoanalytic theory and with the relationship between representations of racial and sexual difference within mainstream cinema. Modleski points out that both Frantz Fanon and Homi Bhabha[5] have brought a psychoanalytic perspective to bear on the processes of colonial stereotyping. Just as feminist theorists like Luce Irigaray[6] have argued that Freud's (and Western culture's) representation of woman as 'castrated' male is a fetishised image that simultaneously recognises sexual difference and disavows it (the woman is only an 'inferior man'), so Bhabha has argued that colonial stereotypes exhibit a similar ambivalence, simultaneously acknowledging and disavowing racial difference (the black man as like/unlike the white). Both forms of fetishised body, too, exhibit a 'splitting' in their stereotypical representations: into childlike innocence/savage bestiality and into virgin/whore.

Neither Fanon nor Bhabha consider the ways in which race and gender might intersect in these representations, however. Indeed both, as Modleski suggests, whilst constructing their psychoanalytic accounts of the construction of racial difference on the model of Freud's account of the construction of sexual difference, elide the question of sexual difference altogether. How then, she asks, can we avoid a theoretical privileging of either racial or sexual difference but instead seek to understand how the two interrelate in popular culture. Her answer focuses on representations in popular film, first of the relationship between black men and white women, and second of black women.

Her analysis of the 1989 film, *Gorillas in the Mist*, sees it as 'an updated, middlebrow version of the King Kong tale', in which, in Bhabha's words, black skin 'splits' into images of a perverse and bestial 'coupling' between white woman and gorilla on the one hand, and those of the benign, 'maternal' gaze of the black male servant/guide on the other. Black men, then, are 'either self-sacrificing servants or threatening monsters'; the white woman is both 'noble savior of innocent creatures' and witch/monster. Both are products of the fears and fantasies of the white male, whose surrogate in the film is the figure of the photographer-lover for whom the pairing white woman/gorilla acts as both voyeuristic object and vicarious fulfilment of desire.

If white women in film have served as signifiers of male desire, continues Modleski, then black women, when present at all, have served quite different functions. Most frequently they serve as an embodiment either of female sexuality (black female body as sexualized body) or of the maternal (black female body as procreative body). Elsewhere, as 'unfeminine' women, they seem to be coded as in the history of slavery – as not really women at all. Dressed in sexy evening wear, as for example Whoopi Goldberg is in a number of films cited by Modleski, they may seem to be in drag. Modleski concludes with an exhortation to white feminist theorists to recognise their own participation in racist structures within cinema – as both filmmakers and spectators – and within theory. She ends, however, on an optimistic note: the hegemony of white heterosexual masculinity can be overcome.

If black women can be rendered invisible within the terms of a white feminist film theory that accords primacy to sexual difference, then lesbian desire can seem unthinkable within its terms.[7] Judith Butler's theorising of sexual identity argues that it should be seen not as the fixed binary opposition of male/female but as performance. She argues that the very category of gender is what she terms a 'regulatory fiction' (1990: 339), a myth which functions to enforce compulsory heterosexuality (everyone is gendered either male or female and opposites complement/attract). For Butler, gender is instead 'a kind of impersonation and approximation … but … *a kind of imitation for which there is no original*' (1991: 21). The appearance of 'naturalness' that accompanies heterosexual gender identity is simply the effect of a repeated imitative performance. What is being imitated, however, is only a fantasised ideal. There is no essence of heterosexual masculinity or femininity that precedes our performance of these roles; we construct the ideal of that essence through our performances.

For Butler, then, the conscious performance of gender, as for example in drag, may subvert assumed gender norms because it draws attention to the non-identity of gender and sexuality and implies that all gendering is 'a kind of impersonation and approximation' (1991: 21). The 1991 film, *Paris is Burning*, deals with just such performance, but since its male drag performers are all African-American or Latino, it also raises issues of racial difference. In a review of the film to which Butler refers, bell hooks criticises it for its failure to interrogate whiteness. Within the world of the black-gay-drag-ball culture voyeuristically depicted by the film, she writes, 'the idea of womanness and femininity is totally personified by whiteness': it is to this ideal of white femininity that its drag artists aspire. The film, she writes, never questions its own standpoint, that of its white lesbian director, passing itself off instead as a 'neutral' ethnographic account (1992: 147, 151).

hooks' criticism finds an echo in that of Tania Modleski in Chapter 22. As we have seen, for Modleski, too, drag may not be the subversive masquerade that

Butler suggests, particularly when it involves black 'performance' of white femininity. Butler's analysis of *Paris is Burning* seeks to answer these criticisms. Drag, she writes, is not in itself subversive; it may function to deflect anxieties about homosexuality. Nevertheless, as conscious performance, it is a site of ambivalence, and to the extent that it de-naturalises gender and heterosexuality it may also be subversive. *Paris is Burning* exhibits just such an ambivalence, she suggests. Its drag pageantry both appropriates and subverts 'racist, misogynist, and homophobic norms of oppression'. Insofar as its performers seek to inhabit the privileged identity of white femininity, it operates within dominant norms. Insofar as they *perform* this identity, and that of the feminized black masculinity which straight culture accords to gay black men, they create a performative excess. Such excess, whilst it cannot offer liberation from hegemonic constraints, can at least open them up to question. In a similar manner, insofar as the film itself offers its gaze as neutral, it 'allows the performance to become an exotic fetish'. Insofar as it draws attention, however, to the 'ambivalence of embodying – and failing to embody – that which one sees', it opens up for its spectators a critical distance from which may be viewed our own 'performance' of (racialised) gender identity.

NOTES

1. For a black lesbian perspective, see also The Combahee River Collective, 'A Black Feminist Statement, in Beverly Guy-Sheftall (ed.) (1995), *Words of Fire: An Anthology of African-American Thought.*
2. 'We know less about about the sexual life of little girls than of boys. But we need not feel ashamed of this distinction; after all, the sexual life of adult women is a "dark continent" for psychology'. (Freud 1953: 212).
3. The equation, 'woman = black', has been made within feminist film criticism since the 1970s. See, for example, Siew Hwa Beh's 1971 review of *The Woman's Film*, which celebrates its 'raising of consciousness about women's real position in life', a position which can be characterised as: 'The parallel: "women as niggers," the private property of one man to another, from father to husband' (Beh 1976: 202).
4. Barbara Smith, for example, begins her 1977 manifesto for a black feminist literary criticism, 'Towards a Black Feminist Criticism', with 'I do not know where to begin ... This invisibility, which goes beyond anything that either Black men or white women experience and tell about in their writing, is one reason it is so difficult for me to know where to start' (1986: 168). She goes on to argue that there is an identifiable literary and historical tradition of black women's writing to be uncovered, since 'thematically, stylistically, aesthetically, and conceptually Black women writers manifest common approaches to the act of creating literature as a direct result of the specific political, social, and economic experience they have been obliged to share' (1986: 174). It is the task of the black feminist critic, she writes, to recover this tradition with its common language and cultural experience, and, writing out of her own identity within such a tradition, to make explicit the ideas and political implications expressed within its writings.
5. See particularly Fanon (1952), *Black Skin, White Masks* and Bhabha (1983), 'The Other Question – the Stereotype and Colonial Discourse'.
6. See Irigaray (1985).
7. Elizabeth Grosz, for example, argues that current feminist theory is simply inadequate as a framework within which to theorise lesbian sexuality: 'In the terms we have most readily available, it seems impossible to think lesbian desire' (1995: 179).

REFERENCES

Beh, Siew Hwa 1976 (1971): *The Woman's Film*. In Nichols, B. (ed.), *Movies and Methods*. Berkeley, Los Angeles and London: University of California Press, pp. 201–4.

Bhabha, Homi K. 1983: The Other Question – the Stereotype and Colonial Discourse. In *Screen*, 24, 6, pp. 18–36.

Butler, Judith 1990: Gender Trouble, Feminist Theory, and Psychoanalytic Discourse. In Nicholson, L. J. (ed.), *Feminism/Postmodernism*. New York and London: Routledge, pp. 324–40.

Butler, Judith 1991: Imitation and Gender Insubordination. In Fuss, D. (ed.), *Inside/Out: Lesbian Theories, Gay Theories*. New York and London: Routledge, pp. 13–31.

Combahee River Collective 1995 (1977): A Black Feminist Statement. In Guy-Sheftall, B. (ed.), *Words of Fire: An Anthology of African-American Feminist Thought*. New York: The New Press.

Fanon, Frantz 1986 (1952): *Black Skin, White Masks*. London: Pluto.

Freud, Sigmund 1953 (1925–6): The Question of Lay Analysis: Conversations with an Impartial Person. In Strachey, J. (ed.), *The Standard Edition of the Complete Psychological Works of Sigmund Freud* Vol. 20. London: Hogarth.

Grosz, Elizabeth 1995: *Space, Time, and Perversion*. New York and London: Routledge.

hooks, bell 1992: *Black Looks: Race and Representation*. London: Turnaround.

Irigaray, Luce 1985: *Speculum of the Other Woman*, trans. Gillian C. Gill. Ithaca: Cornell University Press.

Smith, Barbara 1986 (1977): Toward a Black Feminist Criticism. In Showalter, E. (ed.), *The New Feminist Criticism: Essays on Women, Literature, and Theory*. London: Virago, pp. 168–85.

Young, Lola 1996: *Fear of the Dark: 'Race', Gender and Sexuality in the Cinema*. London and New York: Routledge.

20

'WHITE PRIVILEGE AND LOOKING RELATIONS: RACE AND GENDER IN FEMINIST FILM THEORY'

Jane Gaines

[...] In the US, lesbian feminists raised the first objections to the way in which film theory explained the operation of the classic realist text in terms of tensions between masculinity and femininity. The understanding of spectatorial pleasure in classical cinema as inherently male drew an especially sharp response from critics who argued that this theory cancelled the lesbian spectator whose viewing pleasure could never be construed as anything like male voyeurism. Positing a lesbian spectator would significantly change the trajectory of the gaze. It might even lead us to see how the eroticised star body might be not just the object, but what I would term the visual objective of another female gaze within the film's diegesis – a gaze with which the viewer might identify; following this argument, Marilyn Monroe and Jane Russell in *Gentlemen Prefer Blondes* are 'only for each other's eyes'.[1] Two influential studies building on the lesbian reading of *Gentlemen Prefer Blondes* suggested that the lesbian reception of *Personal Best* held a key to challenging the account of cinema as producing patriarchal subject positions – since lesbian viewers, at least, were subverting dominant meanings and confounding textual structures.[2]

Consistently, lesbians have charged that cultural theory posed in psychoanalytic terms is unable to conceive of desire or explain pleasure without reference to the binary oppositions male/female. This is the function of what Monique Wittig calls the heterosexual assumption, or the 'straight mind', that unacknowledged structure not only built into Lacanian psychoanalysis, but

* From *Screen* 29:4, 1988, pp. 12–27.

underlying the basic divisions of Western culture; organising all knowledge, yet escaping any close examination.[3] Male/female is a powerful, but sometimes blinding construct. And it is difficult to see that the paradigm which we embraced so quickly in our first lessons in feminism may have been standing in the way of our further education.

The male/female opposition, seemingly so fundamental to feminism, may actually lock us into modes of analysis which will continually misinterpret the position of many women. Thus it is that women of colour, like lesbians, an afterthought in feminist analysis, remain unassimilated by this problematic. Feminist anthologies consistently include articles on black female and lesbian perspectives as illustration of the liberality and inclusiveness of feminism; however, the very concept of 'different perspectives', while validating distinctness and maintaining woman as common denominator, still places the categories of race and sexual preference in theoretical limbo. Our political etiquette is correct, but our theory is not so perfect.

In Marxist feminist analysis, the factors of race and sexual preference have remained loose ends; as categories of oppression they fit somewhat awkwardly into a model based on class relations in capitalist society. Although some gay historians see a relationship between the rise of capitalism and the creation of the social homosexual, only with a very generous notion of sexual hierarchies – such as the one Gayle Rubin has suggested – can sexual oppression (as distinct from gender oppression) be located within a framework based on class.[4] Race has folded into Marxist models more neatly than sexual preference, but the orthodox formulation which understands racial conflict as class struggle, is still unsatisfactory to Marxist feminists who want to know exactly how gender intersects with race. The oppression of *women* of colour remains incompletely grasped by the classical Marxist paradigm.

Just as the Marxist model based on class has obscured the function of gender, the feminist model based on the male/female division under patriarchy has obscured the function of race. The dominant feminist paradigm actually encourages us not to think in terms of any oppression other than male dominance and female subordination. Thus it is that feminists and lesbians, says Barbara Smith, seem '... blinded to the implications of any womanhood that is not white womanhood ...'[5] For purposes of analysis, black feminists agree that class is as significant as race; however, if these feminists hesitate to emphasise gender as a factor, it is in deference to the way black women describe their experience, for it is clear that Afro-American women have historically formulated identity and political allegiance in terms of race rather than gender or class.[6] Feminism, however, seems not to have heard the statements of women of colour who say that they experience oppression first in relation to race rather than gender, and that for them exploitation can be personified by a white female.[7] Even more difficult for feminist theory to digest is black female identification with the black male. On this point, black feminists diverge from white feminists, in repeatedly reminding us that they do not necessarily see the black male as patriarchal antagonist, but feel instead that their racial oppression is 'shared' with men.[8] In the most comprehensive analysis of all, black lesbian feminists have described race, class and gender oppression as an 'interlocking' synthesis in the lives of black women.[9]

The point here is not to rank the structures of oppression in a way that implies the need for black women to choose between solidarity with men or solidarity with women, between race or gender as the basis for a political strategy. At issue is the question of the fundamental antagonism which has been so relevant for Marxist feminist theory. Where we have foregrounded one antagonism in our analysis, we have misunderstood another, and this is most dramatically illustrated in applying the notion of patriarchy. Feminists have not been absolutely certain what they mean by patriarchy: alternately it has referred to either father-right or domination of women; but what is consistent about the use of the concept is the rigidity of the structure it describes.[10] Patriarchy is incompatible with Marxism where it is used trans-historically without qualification, and where it becomes the source from which all other oppressions are tributary, as in the radical feminist theory of patriarchal order, which sees oppression in all forms and through all ages as derived from the male/female division.[11] This deterministic model, which Sheila Rowbotham says functions like a 'feminist base-superstructure', has the disadvantage of leaving us with no sense of movement, or no idea of how women have acted to change their condition, especially in comparison with the fluidity of the Marxist conception of class.[12]

The radical feminist notion of absolute patriarchy has also one-sidedly portrayed the oppression of women through an analogy with slavery, and since this theory has identified woman as man's savage or repressed Other it competes with theories of racial difference which understand the black as the 'unassimilable Other.'[13] Finally, the notion of patriarchy is most obtuse when it disregards the position white women occupy over black men as well as black women.[14] In order to rectify this tendency in feminism, black feminists refer to 'racial patriarchy', which is based on an analysis of the white patriarch/master in US history, and his dominance over the black male as well as the black female.[15]

I

I want now to reconsider the connotations of sexual looking, with reference to a film in which racial difference structures a hierarchy of access to the female image. In *Mahogany*, her follow-up to *Lady Sings The Blues*, Diana Ross plays an aspiring fashion designer who dreams of pulling herself up and out of her Chicago South Side neighbourhood by means of a high-powered career. During the day, Tracy Chambers is assistant to the modelling supervisor for a large department store. At night she attends design school, where the instructor reprimands her for sketching a cocktail dress instead of completing the assignment, the first suggestion of the exotic irrelevance of her fantasy career. She loses her job, but the famous fashion photographer Sean McEvoy (Anthony

Perkins) discovers her as a model and whisks her off to Rome. There, Tracy finally realises her ambition to become a designer, when a wealthy Italian admirer gives her a business of her own. After the grand show unveiling her first collection of clothes, she returns to Chicago and is reunited with community organiser Brian Walker (Billy Dee Williams), whose political career is a counterpoint to Tracy's modelling career.

With its long fashion photography montage sequences temporarily interrupting the narrative, *Mahogany* invites a reading based on the alternation between narrative and woman-as-spectacle as theorised by Laura Mulvey in 'Visual Pleasure and Narrative Cinema'. To the allure of pure spectacle these sequences add the fascination of masquerade and transformation. Effected with wigs and make-up colours, the transformations are a play on and against 'darkness'; Diana Ross is a high-tech Egyptian queen, a pale mediaeval princess, a turbaned Asiatic, a body-painted blue nymph. As her body colour is powdered over or washed out in bright light, and as her long-haired wigs blow around her face, she becomes suddenly 'white'.

Contemporary motion pictures never seem to exhaust the narrative possibilities associated with the camera-as-deadly-weapon metaphor; *Mahogany* adds to this the sadomasochistic connotations of high fashion photography with reference to the mid-seventies work of Guy Bourdin and Helmut Newton, linked to the tradition of 'attraction by shock'.[16] The montage sequences chronicling Tracy's career, from perfume ads to high fashion magazine covers, equate the photographic act with humiliation and violation. Camera zoom and freeze-frame effects translate directly into aggression, as in the sequence in which Sean pushes Tracy into a fountain and her dripping image solidifies into an Italian Revlon advertisement. Finally, the motif of stopping-the-action-as-aggression is equated with the supreme violation: attempted murder. Pressing his favourite model to her expressive limits, Sean drives her off an expressway ramp. Since this brutality escalates after the scene in which he fails with Tracy in bed, the film represents her punishment as a direct consequence of his impotence.

With its classic castration threat scenario, its connection between voyeurism and sadism, and its reference to fetishisation – as seen in Sean's photographic shrine to the models he has abused – *Mahogany* is the perfect complement to a psychoanalytic analysis of classical Hollywood's visual pleasure. The film further provides material for such an analysis by producing its own 'proof' that there is only an incremental difference between voyeurism (fashion photography) and sadism (murder). The black and white photographic blow-ups of Tracy salvaged from the death car seem undeniable evidence of the fine line between looking and killing, or, held at another angle, between advertising imagery and pornography.

This, then, is to suggest the kind of evidence in the film which would support an analysis of it as patriarchal discourse, in its use of the female image as fetish to assuage castration anxiety, and through its rich offering of views to please the male spectator. There's even an inescapable suggestion of voyeurism as pathology, since the gaze is that of the actor whose star persona is fatally haunted by the protagonist of *Psycho*. To explain the ideological function of the film in terms of the construction of male pleasure, however, is to 'aid and abet' the film's other ideological project. In following the line of analysis I have outlined, one is apt to step into an ideological signifying trap set up by the chain of meanings that lead away from seeing the film in terms of racial conflict. Because there are so many connotative paths – photographer exploits model, madman assaults woman, voyeur attempts murder – we may not immediately see white man as aggressor against black woman. Other strategies encourage the viewer to forget or not notice racial issues. For instance, the narrative removes Tracy from racially polarised Chicago to Rome, where the brown Afro-American woman with Caucasian features is added to the collection of a photographer who names his subjects after prized objects or their qualities. Losing her black community identity, Tracy becomes Mahogany, acquiring the darkness, richness and value the name connotes; that is, her blackness becomes commodified.

Mahogany functions ideologically for black viewers in the traditional Marxist sense, that is, in the way the film obscures the class nature of social antagonisms. This has certain implications for working-class black viewers, who would gain most from seeing the relationship between race, gender and class oppression. Further, *Mahogany* has the same trouble with representing black femaleness that the wider culture has had historically; a black female is either all woman and tinted black, or mostly black and scarcely woman. These two expectations correspond with the two worlds and two struggles which structure the film: the struggle over the sexual objectification of Tracy's body in the face of commercial exploitation, and the struggle of the black community in the face of class exploitation. But the film identifies this antagonism as the hostility between fashion and politics, embodied respectively by Tracy and Brian, and it is through them that it organises conflict and, eventually, reconciliation. Intensifying this conflict between characters, the film contrasts 'politics' and 'fashion' in one daring homage to the aesthetic of 'attraction by shock'; Sean arranges his models symmetrically on the back stairwell of a run-down Chicago apartment building and uses the confused tenants and street people as props. Flamboyant excess, the residue of capital, is juxtaposed with a kind of dumbfounded poverty. For a moment, the scene figures the synthesis of gender, class and race, but the political glimpse is fleeting. Forced together as a consequence of the avant-garde's socially irresponsible quest for a new outrage, the political antagonisms are suspended – temporarily immobilised as the subjects pose.

The connection between gender, class and race oppression is also denied as the ghetto photography session's analogy between commercial exploitation and race/class exploitation merely registers on the screen as visual incongruity. Visual discrepancy, which, as I have argued, is used for aesthetic effect, also makes it difficult to grasp the confluence of race, class and gender oppression in the image of Tracy Chambers. The character's class background magically becomes decor in the film – it neither radicalises her nor drags her down; instead it sets her off. Diana Ross is alternately weighed down by the glamour iconography of commercial modelling or stripped to a black body. But the *haute couture* iconography ultimately dominates the film. Since race is decorative and class does not reveal itself to the eye, Tracy can only be seen as exploited in terms of her role as a model.

If the film plays down race, it does not do so just to accommodate white audiences. In worshipping the success of the black cult star and combining this with Diana Ross's own dream-come-true – a chance to design all of the costumes in her own film – *Mahogany* hawks the philosophy of black enterprise and social aspiration. Here it does not matter where you come from, what you should be asking yourself, in the words of the theme song, is 'Where are you going, do you know?' Race, then, should be seen as any other obstacle – to be transcended through diligent work and dedication to a goal. Supporting the film's self-help philosophy is the related story of Diana Ross's 'discovery' as a skinny teenager singing in a Baptist Church in Detroit. With *Mahogany*, Motown president and founder Berry Gordy (who fired Tony Richardson and took over the film's direction) helps Diana Ross to make something of herself again, just as he helped so many aspiring recording artists, by coaching them in money management and social decorum in his talent school.[17]

The phenomenon of Motown Industries is less a comment on the popularity of the self-help philosophy than a verification of the discrepancy between the opportunity formula and the social existence of black Americans. Ironically, black capitalism's one big success thrives on the impossibility of black enterprise: soul entertainment as compensation and release sells because capitalism cannot deliver well-being to all.[18] Black music and performance, despite the homogenisation of the original forms, represents a utopian aspiration for black Americans, as well as for white suburbanites. Simon Frith describes the need supplied by rock fantasy:

> Black music had a radical, rebellious edge: it carried a sense of possibility denied in the labor market; it suggested a comradeship, a sensuality, a grace and joy and energy lacking in work ... the power of rock fantasy rests, precisely on utopianism.[19]

Given that popular culture can accommodate the possibility of both containment and resistance in what Stuart Hall calls its 'double movement', I want to turn to the ways *Mahogany* can be seen to move in the other direction.[20]

Racial conflict looms or recedes in this film rather like the perceptual trick in which, depending on the angle of view, one swirling pattern or the other pops out at the viewer. Some perceptual ambiguity, for instance, is built into the confrontation between black and white, as in the scene in which Sean lures Brian into a struggle over an unloaded weapon. The outcome, in which Sean, characterised as a harmless eccentric, manipulates Brian into pulling the trigger, could be read as confirming the racist conception that blacks who possess street reflexes are murderous aggressors. *Ebony* magazine, the black equivalent of *Life* magazine in the US, however, features a promotional still of the scene (representing Brian holding a gun over Sean), with a caption describing how Brian is tricked but still wins the fight.[21] Just as viewers choose the winners of such ambiguous conflicts, they may also choose to inhabit 'looking' structures. The studies of lesbian readership already cited show that subcultural groups can interpret popular forms to their advantage, even without invitation from the text. Certainly more work needs to be done with the positioning of the audience around the category of race, considering, for instance, the social prohibitions against the black man's sexual glance, the interracial intermingling of male 'looks', and other visual taboos related to sanctions against interracial sexuality, but these are beyond the scope of this article.

One of the original tenets of contemporary feminist film theory – that the (male) spectator possesses the female indirectly through the eyes of the male protagonist (his screen surrogate) – is problematised here by the less privileged black male gaze. Racial hierarchies of access to the female image also relate to other scenarios which are unknown by psychoanalytic categories. Considering the racial categories which psychoanalysis does not recognise, then, we see that the white male photographer monopolises the classic patriarchal look controlling the view of the female body, and that the black male protagonist's look is either repudiated or frustrated. The sumptuous image of Diana Ross is made available to the spectator via the white male character (Sean) but *not* through the look of the black male character (Brian). In the sequence in which Tracy and Brian first meet outside her apartment building, his 'look' is renounced. In each of the three shots of Tracy from Brian's point of view, she turns from him, walking out of his sight and away from the sound of his voice as he shouts at her through a megaphone. The relationship between the male and female protagonists is negotiated around Brian's bullhorn, emblem of his charismatic black leadership, through which he tries to reach both the black woman and his constituents. Both visual and audio control is thus denied the black male, and the failure of his voice is consistently associated with Tracy's publicity image in the white world. The discovery by Brian's aides of the Mahogany advertisement for Revlon in *Newsweek* coincides with the report that the Gallup polls show the black candidate trailing in the election. Later, the film cuts from the *Harper's Bazaar* cover featuring Mahogany to Brian's limping campaign where the sound of his voice magnified through a microphone is intermittently drowned out by a passing train as he makes his futile pitch to white factory workers. The manifest goal of the film, the reconciliation of the black heterosexual couple, is thwarted by the commercial appropriation of her image, but, in addition, its highly-mediated form threatens the black political struggle.

II

For black feminists, history seems to be the key to understanding black female sexuality. 'The construction of the sexual self of the Afro-American woman,' says Rennie Simson, 'has its roots in the days of slavery.'[22] Looking at this construction over time reveals a pattern of patriarchal phases and female sexual adjustments that has no equivalent in the history of white women in the US. In the first phase, characterised by the dominance of the white master during the period of slavery, black men and women were equal by default. To have allowed the black male any power over the black woman would have threatened the power balance of the slave system. Thus, as Angela Davis explains social control in the slave community, 'The man slave could not be the unquestioned superior within the "family" or community, for there was no such thing as the "family" provided among the Slaves.'[23] The legacy of this phase has involved both the rejection of the pedestal the white female has occupied, as well as the heritage of retaliation against white male abuse. If the strategy for racial survival was resistance during the first phase, it was accommodation during the next. During Reconstruction, the black family, modelled after the white bourgeois household, was constituted defensively in an effort to preserve the race.[24] Black women yielded to their men in deference to a tradition that promised respectability and safety. Re-evaluating this history, black feminists point out that, during Reconstruction, the black male, following the example of the white patriarch, 'learned' to dominate. Poet Audre Lorde, for instance, sees sexism in black communities as not original to them, but as a plague that has struck.[25] One of the most telling manifestations of the difference between the operation of patriarchy in the lives of black as opposed to white women is the way this is worked out *at the level of language* in the formal conventions organising the short stories and novels of Afro-American women. Particularly in the work of early writers such as Harriet E. Wilson, Frances E. W. Harper, and Pauline Hopkins, the black father is completely missing and, as Hazel Carby says, 'The absent space in fiction by black women confirms this denial of patriarchal power to black men'.[26] The position consistently taken by black feminists, that patriarchy was originally foreign to the Afro-American community and was introduced into it historically, then, represents a significant break with feminist theories which see patriarchal power invested equally in all men throughout history, and patriarchal form as colour blind.

Black history also adds another dimension to the concept of 'rape', which has emerged as the favoured metaphor for defining women's jeopardy in the second wave of feminism, replacing 'prostitution', which articulated women's fears in the nineteenth century.[27] The charge of rape, conjuring up a historical connection with lynching, is inextricably connected in North American history with the myth of the black man as archetypal rapist. We can never again use the concept of 'rape' quite so abstractly in its generic or metaphorical sense, after we have considered the way 'white' or 'black' has historically modified, or shall we say 'inflamed', the act and the term. During slavery, white male abuse of black women was a symbolic blow to black manhood, understood as rape only within the black community. With the increase in the sexual violation of black women during Reconstruction, the act of rape began to reveal its fuller political implications. After emancipation, the rape of black women was a 'message' to black men, which, according to one historian, could be seen as 'a reaction to the effort of the freedman to assume the role of patriarch, able to provide for and protect his family.'[28] Simultaneous with the actual violation of black women, the empty charge of rape hurled at the black man clouded the real issue of black (male) enfranchisement, by creating a smokescreen through the incendiary issue of interracial sexuality. Writing at the turn of the century, black novelist Pauline Hopkins unmasked the alibis for lynching in *Contending Forces*:

> Lynching was instituted to crush the manhood of the enfranchised black. Rape is the crime which appeals most strongly to the heart of the home life ... *The men who created the mulatto race, who recruit its ranks year after year by the very means which they invoked lynch law to suppress,* bewailing the sorrows of violated womanhood![29]

Here is a sexual scenario to rival the Oedipal myth; the black woman sexually violated by the white man, but the fact of her rape repressed and displaced on to the virginal white woman, and thus used symbolically as the justification for the actual castration of the black man. It is against this historical scenario that we should place the symbolic castration that is the penalty of sexual looking – a penalty that must surely diminish in comparison with the very real threat of actual castration that such looking would once have carried with it.

III

Quite simply, then, there are structures relevant to any interpretation of *Mahogany* which override the patriarchal scenario feminists have theorised as formally determining. From Afro-American history, we should recall the white male's appropriation of the black woman's body which weakened the black male and undermined the community. From Afro-American literature, we should also consider the scenario of the talented and beautiful mulatta who 'passes' in white culture, but decides to return to black society.[30] The mulatta suggests the rich possibilities of a theory of black female representation which takes account of 'passing' as an eroticising alternation and a peculiar play on difference, as well as a sign of the double consciousness of those women who can be seen as either black or white at the same time as they may see themselves as both races at once. Further, we need to reconsider the woman's picture narrative convention – the career renounced in favour of the man – in the context of black history. Tracy's choice recapitulates black aspiration and the white middle class model which equates stable family life with respectability, but her decision is significantly different from the white heroine's capitulation since it favours black community cooperation over acceptance by white society. Finally, one of the most difficult questions raised by Afro-American history and literature has to do with inter-racial heterosexuality and sexual 'looking'. *Mahogany* suggests that, since a black male character is not allowed the position of control occupied by a white male character, race could be a factor in the construction of cinematic language. More work on looking and racial taboos might determine whether or not mainstream cinema can offer the male spectator the pleasure of looking at a white female character via the gaze of a black male character. Framing the question of male privilege and viewing pleasure as the 'right to look' may help us to rethink film theory along more materialist lines, considering, for instance, how some groups have historically had the licence to 'look' openly while other groups have 'looked' illicitly.[31] In other words, does the psychoanalytic model allow us to consider the prohibitions against homosexuality and miscegenation?

Feminists who use psychoanalytic theory have been careful to point out that 'looking' positions do not correlate with social groups, and that ideological positioning is placement in a representational system which has no one-to-one correspondence with social experience. This, of course, keeps the levels of the social ensemble hopelessly separate. While I would not want to argue that form is ideologically neutral, I would suggest that we have overemphasised the ideological function of 'signifying practice' at the expense of considering other ideological implications of the conflicting meanings in the text. Or, as Terry Lovell puts it:

> ... while interpretation depends on analysis of the work's signifying practice, assessment of its meanings from the point of view of its validity, or of its ideology, depends on comparison between those structures of meaning and their object of reference, through the mediation of another type of discourse.[32]

The impetus behind Marxist criticism, whether we want to admit it or not, is to make comparisons between social reality as we live it and ideology as it does not correspond to that reality. This we attempt to do knowing full well (having learned from post-structuralism), the futility of looking for real relations which are completely outside ideology in either the present or in history. And we probably need to turn this critique on the emerging notion of the 'days of slavery' as the key to black female sexuality, in order to avoid the temptation of using it as some searing truth which, held up to the bloated discourses of patriarchy, had the power to make them finally groan and shrivel.

Thus, while I am still willing to argue, as I did in the earlier version of this article, that we can see the *Mahogany* narrative as a metaphor of the search for black female sexuality, I see something else in hindsight. I would describe this as the temptation in an emerging black feminist criticism, much like an earlier tendency in lesbian criticism, to place sexuality safely out of patriarchal bounds by declaring it outside culture, by furtively hiding it in subcultural enclaves where it can remain 'its essential self', protected from the meaning-making mainstream culture. *Mahogany*, then, is finally about the mythical existence of something elusive yet potent. We know it through what white men do to secure it, and what black men are without it. It is the ultimate object of desire to the photographer-connoisseur of women who dies trying to record its 'trace' on film. It is known by degree – whatever is most wild and enigmatic, whatever cannot be conquered or subdued – the last frontier of female sexuality. Although it is undetectable to the advertising men who can only analyse physical attributes, it is immediately perceptible to a lesbian (Gavina herself, the owner of the Italian advertising agency), who uses it to promote the most intangible and subjective of commodities – perfume.[33] Contrary to the suggestion that black sexuality might still remain in excess of culture, and hence unfathomed and uncodified, it is worked over again and again in mainstream culture because of its apparent elusiveness, and in this context it is rather like bottled scent which is often thought to convey its essence to everyone but the person wearing it.

To return to my main point, as feminists have theorised women's sexuality, they have universalised from the particular experience of white women, thus effecting what Hortense Spillers has called a 'deadly metonymy'.[34] While white feminists theorise the female image in terms of objectification, fetishisation and symbolic absence, their black counterparts describe the body as the site of symbolic resistance and the 'paradox of non-being', a reference to the period in Afro-American history when black female did not signify 'woman'.[35] What strikes me still in this comparison is the stubbornness of the terms of feminist discourse analysis which has not been able to deal, for instance, with what it has meant historically to be designated as not-human, and how black women, whose bodies were legally not their own, fought against treatment based on this determination. Further, feminist analysis of culture as patriarchal cannot conceive of any connection between the female image and class or racial exploitation which includes the male. Historically, black men and women, although not equally endangered, have been simultaneously implicated in incidents of interracial brutality. During two different periods of Afro-American history, sexual assault, '... symbolic of the effort to conquer the resistance the black woman could unloose', was a warning to the entire black community.[36] If, as feminists have argued, women's sexuality evokes an unconscious terror in men, then black women's sexuality represents a special threat to white patriarchy; the possibility of its eruption stands for the aspirations of the black race as a whole.

My frustration with the feminist voice that insists on change *at the level of language* is that this position can only deal with the historical situation described above by turning it into discourse, and even as I write this, acutely aware as I am of the theoretical prohibitions against mixing representational issues with historical ones, I feel the pressure to transpose people's struggles into more discursively manageable terms. However, a theory of ideology which separates the levels of the social formation, in such a way that it is not only inappropriate but theoretically impossible to introduce the category of history into the analysis, cannot be justified with Marxism. This has been argued elsewhere by others, among them Stuart Hall, who finds the 'universalist tendency' found in both Freud and Lacan responsible for this impossibility. The incompatibility between Marxism and psychoanalytic theory is insurmountable at this time, he argues, because 'the concepts elaborated by Freud (and reworked by Lacan) cannot, *in their in-general and universalist form*, enter the theoretical space of historical materialism'.[37] In discussions within feminist film theory, it has often seemed the other way round – that historical materialism could not enter the space theorised by discourse analysis drawing on psychoanalytic concepts. Sealed off as it is (in theory), this analysis may not comprehend the category of the real historical subject, but its use will always have implications *for* that subject.

NOTES

1. Lucie Arbuthnot and Gail Seneca, 'Pre-Text and Text in "Gentlemen Prefer Blondes"', *Film Reader 5*, Winter 1981, pp. 13–23.
2. Chris Straayer, '"Personal Best": Lesbian/Feminist Audience', *Jump Cut 29*, February 1984, pp. 40–4; Elizabeth Ellsworth, 'Illicit Pleasures: Feminist Spectators and "Personal Best"', *Wide Angle* vol. 8, no. 2, 1986, pp. 46–56.
3. Monique Wittig, 'The Straight Mind', *Feminist Issues*, Summer 1980, pp. 107–11.
4. Gayle Rubin, 'Thinking Sex: Notes for a Radical Theory of the Politics of Sexuality' in Carol Vance (ed.), *Pleasure and Danger*, Boston and London, Routledge & Kegan Paul, 1984, p. 307.
5. Barbara Smith, 'Towards a Black Feminist Criticism', in Elaine Showalter (ed.), *The New Feminist Criticism*, New York, Pantheon, 1985, p. 169.
6. Bonnie Thornton Dill, 'Race, Class, and Gender: Prospects for an All-Inclusive Sisterhood', *Feminist Studies* vol. 9, no. 1, Spring 1983, p. 34; for a slightly different version of this essay see ' "On the Hem of Life": Race, Class, and the Prospects for Sisterhood', in Amy Swerdlow and Hanna Lessinger (eds), *Class, Race, and Sex: The Dynamics of Control*, Boston, Hall, 1983; Margaret Simons, 'Racism and Feminism: A Schism in the Sisterhood', *Feminist Studies* vol. 5, no. 2, Summer 1979, p. 392.
7. Adrienne Rich, in *On Lies, Secrets, and Silence*, New York, Norton, 1979, pp. 302–3, notes that while blacks link their experience of racism with the white woman, this is still patriarchal racism working through her. It is possible, she says, that 'a black first grader, or that child's mother, or a black patient in a hospital, or a family on welfare, may experience racism most directly in the person of a white woman, who stands for those service professions through which white male supremacist society controls the mother, the child, the family, and all of us. It is *her* racism, yes, but a racism learned in the same patriarchal school which taught her that women are unimportant or unequal, not to be trusted with power, where she learned to mistrust and hear her own impulses for rebellion; to become an instrument.'
8. Gloria Joseph, 'The Incompatible Ménage à Trois: Marxism, Feminism and Racism', in Lydia Sargent (ed.), *Women and Revolution*, Boston, South End Press, 1981, p. 96; The Combahee River Collective Statement' in Barbara Smith (ed.), *Home Girls*, New York, Kitchen Table Press, 1983, p. 275, compares their alliance with black men with the negative identification white women have with white men: 'Our situation as Black people necessitates that we have solidarity around the fact of race, which white women of course do not need to have with white men, unless it is their negative solidarity as racial oppressors. We struggle together with Black men against racism, while we struggle with Black men about sexism.'
9. Combahee River Collective, ibid, p. 272
10. Michèle Barrett, *Women's Oppression Today*, London, Verso, 1980, p. 15.
11. For a comparison between radical feminism, liberal feminism, Marxist and socialist feminism, see Alison Jaggar, *Feminist Politics and Human Nature*, Sussex, The Harvester Press, 1983.
12. Sheila Rowbotham, 'The Trouble with Patriarchy', in Raphael Samuel (ed.), *People's History and Socialist Theory*, London and Boston, Routledge & Kegan Paul, 1981, p. 365.

13. Frantz Fanon, *Black Skin, White Masks*, trans Charles Lam Markmann, Paris, 1952; reprinted New York, Grove Press, 1967, p. 161.
14. Margaret Simons, 'Racism and Feminism', p. 387.
15. Barbara Omolade, 'Hearts of Darkness', in Ann Snitow, Christine Stansell, and Sharon Thompson (eds), *Powers of Desire*, New York, Monthly Review Press, 1983, p. 352.
16. Nancy Hall-Duncan, *The History of Fashion Photography*, New York, Alpine Books, 1979, p. 196.
17. Stephen Birmingham *Certain People*, Boston and Toronto, Little, Brown, 1977, pp. 262–3.
18. Manning Marable, in *How Capitalism Underdeveloped Black America*, Boston, South End Press, 1983, p. 157, lists Motown Industries as the largest grossing black-owned corporation in the US which did 64,8 million dollars in business in 1979.
19. Simon Frith, *Sound Effects*, New York Pantheon, 1981, p. 264.
20. Stuart Hall, 'Notes on Deconstructing "The Popular" ', in *People's History and Socialist Theory*, p. 228.
21. 'Spectacular New Film for Diana Ross: "Mahogany" ', *Ebony*, October, 1975, p. 146.
22. Rennie Simpson, 'The Afro-American Female: The Historical Context of the Construction of Sexual Identity', in *Powers of Desire*, p. 230.
23. Angela Davis, 'The Black Woman's Role in the Community of Slaves', *The Black Scholar*, December 1971, pp. 5–6.
24. Barbara Omolade, 'Hearts of Darkness', p. 352.
25. Gloria Joseph, 'The Incompatible Ménage à Trois', p. 99; Audre Lorde, *Sister Outsider*, Trumansburg, New York, The Crossing Press, 1984, p. 119, says: 'Because of the continuous battle against racial erasure that Black women and Black men share, some Black women still refuse to recognize that we are also oppressed as women, and that sexual hostility against Black women is practiced not only by the white racist society, but implemented within our Black communities as well. It is a disease striking the heart of Black nationhood, and silence will not make it disappear.'
26. Hazel Carby, ' "On the Threshold of Woman's Era": Lynching, Empire, and Sexuality in Black Feminist Tehory', *Critical Inquiry* vol. 12. no. 1. Autumn 1985, p. 276; Harriet E. Wilson, *Our Nig*. 1859, reprinted New York, Random House, 1983; Frances E. W. Harper, *Iola Leroy, or Shadows Uplifted*, 1892, reprinted New York, Oxford University Press, 1988; Pauline E. Hopkins, *Contending Forces*, 1900, reprinted Oxford University Press, 1988.
27. Linda Gordon and Ellen DuBois, 'Seeking Ecstasy on the Battlefield: Danger and Pleasure in Nineteenth Century Feminist Sexual Thought', *Feminist Review* 13, Spring 1983, p. 43.
28. Jacquelyn Dowd Hall, ' "The Mind That Burns in Each Body": Women, Rape, and Racial Violence', in *Powers of Desire*, p. 332; see also Jacquelyn Dowd Hall, *The Revolt Against Chivalry*, New York, Columbia University Press, 1979; Angela Davis, *Women, Race and Class*, New York, Random House, 1983, chapter 11.
29. As quoted in Hazel Carby, *Reconstructing Womanhood: The Emergence of the Afro-American Women Novelist*, New York, Oxford University Press, 1987, p. 275.
30. See, for instance, Jessie Fauset, *There is Confusion*, New York, Boni and Liveright, 1924, and *Plum Bun*, 1928, reprinted New York, Routledge & Kegan Paul, 1983; Nella Larsen, *Quicksand*, 1928, and *Passing*, 1929, reprinted New Brunswick, Rutgers University Press, 1936.
31. Fredric Jameson in 'Pleasure: A Political Issue', *Formations of Pleasure*, Boston and London, Routledge & Kegan Paul, 1983, p. 7, interprets Mulvey's connection between viewing pleasure and male power as the conferral of a 'right to look'. He does not take this further, but I find the term suggestive and at the same time potentially volatile.

32. Terry Lovell, *Pictures of Reality*, London, British Film Institute, 1980, p. 90.
33. Richard Dyer, 'Mahogany', in Charlotte Brunsdon (ed.), *Films for Women*, London, British Film Institute, 1986, p. 135, suggested this first about Gavina.
34. Hortense J Spillers, 'Interstices: A Small Drama of Words,' in Carol Vance (ed., *Pleasure and Danger*, p. 78.
35. Ibid, p. 77.
36. Angela Davis, 'The Black Woman's Role in the Community of Slaves', p. 11.
37. Stuart Hall, 'Debate: Psychology, Ideology and the Human Subject', *Ideology and Consciousness*, October 1977, pp. 118–19.

21

'THE OPPOSITIONAL GAZE: BLACK FEMALE SPECTATORS'

bell hooks

When thinking about black female spectators, I remember being punished as a child for staring, for those hard intense direct looks children would give grown-ups, looks that were seen as confrontational, as gestures of resistance, challenges to authority. The 'gaze' has always been political in my life. Imagine the terror felt by the child who has come to understand through repeated punishments that one's gaze can be dangerous. The child who has learned so well to look the other way when necessary. Yet, when punished, the child is told by parents, 'Look at me when I talk to you.' Only, the child is afraid to look. Afraid to look, but fascinated by the gaze. There is power in looking.

Amazed the first time I read in history classes that white slave-owners (men, women, and children) punished enslaved black people for looking, I wondered how this traumatic relationship to the gaze had informed black parenting and black spectatorship. The politics of slavery, of racialized power relations, were such that the slaves were denied their right to gaze. Connecting this strategy of domination to that used by grown folks in southern black rural communities where I grew up, I was pained to think that there was no absolute difference between whites who had oppressed black people and ourselves. Years later, reading Michel Foucault, I thought again about these connections, about the ways power as domination reproduces itself in different locations employing similar apparatuses, strategies, and mechanisms of control. Since I knew as a child that the dominating power adults exercised over me and over my gaze was

* From hooks, b., *Black Looks: Race and Representation*. London: Turnaround, 1992, pp. 115–31.

never so absolute that I did not dare to look, to sneak a peep, to stare dangerously, I knew that the slaves had looked. That all attempts to repress our/ black peoples' right to gaze had produced in us an overwhelming longing to look, a rebellious desire, an oppositional gaze. By courageously looking, we defiantly declared: 'Not only will I stare. I want my look to change reality.' Even in the worse circumstances of domination, the ability to manipulate one's gaze in the face of structures of domination that would contain it, opens up the possibility of agency. In much of his work, Michel Foucault insists on describing domination in terms of 'relations of power' as part of an effort to challenge the assumption that 'power is a system of domination which controls everything and which leaves no room for freedom.' Emphatically stating that in all relations of power 'there is necessarily the possibility of resistance,' he invites the critical thinker to search those margins, gaps, and locations on and through the body where agency can be found.

Stuart Hall calls for recognition of our agency as black spectators in his essay 'Cultural Identity and Cinematic Representation.' Speaking against the construction of white representations of blackness as totalizing, Hall says of white presence: 'The error is not to conceptualize this "presence" in terms of power, but to locate that power as wholly external to us—as extrinsic force, whose influence can be thrown off like the serpent sheds its skin. What Franz Fanon reminds us, in *Black Skin, White Masks*, is how power is inside as well as outside:

> . . . the movements, the attitudes, the glances of the Other fixed me there, in the sense in which a chemical solution is fixed by a dye. I was indignant; I demanded an explanation. Nothing happened. I burst apart. Now the fragments have been put together again by another self. This 'look,' from—so to speak—the place of the Other, fixes us, not only in its violence, hostility and aggression, but in the ambivalence of its desire.

Spaces of agency exist for black people, wherein we can both interrogate the gaze of the Other but also look back, and at one another, naming what we see. The 'gaze' has been and is a site of resistance for colonized black people globally. Subordinates in relations of power learn experientially that there is a critical gaze, one that 'looks' to document, one that is oppositional. In resistance struggle, the power of the dominated to assert agency by claiming and cultivating 'awareness' politicizes 'looking' relations—one learns to look a certain way in order to resist.

When most black people in the United States first had the opportunity to look at film and television, they did so fully aware that mass media was a system of knowledge and power reproducing and maintaining white supremacy. To stare at the television, or mainstream movies, to engage its images, was to engage its negation of black representation. It was the oppositional black gaze that responded to these looking relations by developing independent black cinema. Black viewers of mainstream cinema and television could chart the progress of political movements for racial equality *via* the construction of images, and did so. Within my family's southern black working-class home, located in a racially segregated neighborhood, watching television was one way to develop critical spectatorship. Unless you went to work in the white world, across the tracks, you learned to look at white people by staring at them on the screen. Black looks, as they were constituted in the context of social movements for racial uplift, were interrogating gazes. We laughed at television shows like *Our Gang* and *Amos 'n' Andy*, at these white representations of blackness, but we also looked at them critically. Before racial integration, black viewers of movies and television experienced visual pleasure in a context where looking was also about contestation and confrontation.

Writing about black looking relations in 'Black British Cinema: Spectatorship and Identity Formation in Territories,' Manthia Diawara identifies the power of the spectator: 'Every narration places the spectator in a position of agency; and race, class and sexual relations influence the way in which this subjecthood is filled by the spectator.' Of particular concern for him are moments of 'rupture' when the spectator resists 'complete identification with the film's discourse.' These ruptures define the relation between black spectators and dominant cinema prior to racial integration. Then, one's enjoyment of a film wherein representations of blackness were stereotypically degrading and dehumanizing co-existed with a critical practice that restored presence where it was negated. Critical discussion of the film while it was in progress or at its conclusion maintained the distance between spectator and the image. Black films were also subject to critical interrogation. Since they came into being in part as a response to the failure of white-dominated cinema to represent blackness in a manner that did not reinforce white supremacy, they too were critiqued to see if images were seen as complicit with dominant cinematic practices.

Critical, interrogating black looks were mainly concerned with issues of race and racism, the way racial domination of blacks by whites overdetermined representation. They were rarely concerned with gender. As spectators, black men could repudiate the reproduction of racism in cinema and television, the negation of black presence, even as they could feel as though they were rebelling against white supremacy by daring to look, by engaging phallocentric politics of spectatorship. Given the real life public circumstances wherein black men were murdered/lynched for looking at white womanhood, where the black male gaze was always subject to control and/or punishment by the powerful white Other, the private realm of television screens or dark theaters could unleash the repressed gaze. There they could 'look' at white womanhood without a structure of domination overseeing the gaze, interpreting, and punishing. That white supremacist structure that had murdered Emmet Till after interpreting his look as violation, as 'rape' of white womanhood, could not control black male responses to screen images. In their role as spectators, black men could enter an imaginative space of phallocentric power that mediated racial negation. This gendered relation to looking made the experience of the black male spectator radically different from that of the black female spectator. Major early black male independent filmmakers represented black women in their films as objects of male gaze. Whether looking through the camera or as spectators watching films, whether mainstream cinema or 'race' movies such as those made by Oscar Micheaux, the black male gaze had a different scope from that of the black female.

Black women have written little about black female spectatorship, about our moviegoing practices. A growing body of film theory and criticism by black women has only begun to emerge. The prolonged silence of black women as spectators and critics was a response to absence, to cinematic negation. In 'The Technology of Gender,' Teresa de Lauretis, drawing on the work of Monique Wittig, calls attention to 'the power of discourses to "do violence" to people, a violence which is material and physical, although produced by abstract and scientific discourses as well as the discourses of the mass media.' With the possible exception of early race movies, black female spectators have had to develop looking relations within a cinematic context that constructs our presence as absence, that denies the 'body' of the black female so as to perpetuate white supremacy and with it a phallocentric spectatorship where the woman to be looked at and desired is 'white.' (Recent movies do not conform to this paradigm but I am turning to the past with the intent to chart the development of black female spectatorship.)

Talking with black women of all ages and classes, in different areas of the United States, about their filmic looking relations, I hear again and again ambivalent responses to cinema. Only a few of the black women I talked with remembered the pleasure of race movies, and even those who did, felt that pleasure interrupted and usurped by Hollywood. Most of the black women I talked with were adamant that they never went to movies expecting to see compelling representations of black femaleness. They were all acutely aware of cinematic racism—its violent erasure of black womanhood. In Anne Friedberg's essay 'A Denial of Difference: Theories of Cinematic Identification' she stresses that 'Identification can only be made through recognition, and all recognition is itself an implicit confirmation of the ideology of the status quo.' Even when representations of black women were present in film, our bodies and being were there to serve—to enhance and maintain white womanhood as object of the phallocentric gaze.

Commenting on Hollywood's characterization of black women in *Girls on Film*, Julie Burchill describes this absent presence:

> Black women have been mothers without children (Mammies—who can ever forget the sickening spectacle of Hattie MacDaniels waiting on the simpering Vivien Leigh hand and foot and enquiring like a ninny, 'What's ma lamb gonna wear?') ... Lena Horne, the first black performer signed to a long term contract with a major (MGM), looked gutless but was actually quite spirited. She seethed when Tallulah Bankhead complimented her on the paleness of her skin and the non-Negroidness of her features.

When black women actresses like Lena Horne appeared in mainstream cinema most white viewers were not aware that they were looking at black females unless the film was specifically coded as being about blacks. Burchill is one of the few white women film critics who has dared to examine the intersection of race and gender in relation to the construction of the category 'woman' in film as object of the phallocentric gaze. With characteristic wit she asserts: 'What does it say about racial purity that the best blondes have all been brunettes (Harlow, Monroe, Bardot)? I think it says that we are not as white as we think.' Burchill could easily have said 'we are not as white as we want to be,' for clearly the obsession to have white women film stars be ultra-white was a cinematic practice that sought to maintain a distance, a separation between that image and the black female Other; it was a way to perpetuate white supremacy. Politics of race and gender were inscribed into mainstream cinematic narrative from *Birth of a Nation* on. As a seminal work, this film identified what the place and function of white womanhood would be in cinema. There was clearly no place for black women.

Remembering my past in relation to screen images of black womanhood, I wrote a short essay, 'Do you remember Sapphire?' which explored both the negation of black female representation in cinema and television and our rejection of these images. Identifying the character of 'Sapphire' from *Amos 'n' Andy* as that screen representation of black femaleness I first saw in childhood, I wrote:

> She was even then backdrop, foil. She was bitch—nag. She was there to soften images of black men, to make them seem vulnerable, easygoing, funny, and unthreatening to a white audience. She was there as man in drag, as castrating bitch, as someone to be lied to, someone to be tricked, someone the white and black audience could hate. Scapegoated on all sides. *She was not us.* We laughed with the black men, with the white people. We laughed at this black woman who was not us. And we did not even long to be there on the screen. How could we long to be there when our image, visually constructed, was so ugly. We did not long to be there. We did not long for her. We did not want our construction to be this hated black female thing—foil, backdrop. Her black female image was not the body of desire. There was nothing to see. She was not us.

Grown black women had a different response to Sapphire; they identified with her frustrations and her woes. They resented the way she was mocked. They resented the way these screen images could assault black womanhood, could name us bitches, nags. And in opposition they claimed Sapphire as their own, as the symbol of that angry part of themselves white folks and black men could not even begin to understand.

Conventional representations of black women have done violence to the image. Responding to this assault, many black women spectators shut out the image, looked the other way, accorded cinema no importance in their lives. Then there were those spectators whose gaze was that of desire and complicity. Assuming a posture of subordination, they submitted to cinema's capacity to seduce and betray. They were cinematically 'gaslighted.' Every black woman I spoke with who was/is an ardent moviegoer, a lover of the Hollywood film, testified that to experience fully the pleasure of that cinema they had to close down critique, analysis; they had to forget racism. And mostly they did not think about sexism. What was the nature then of this adoring black female gaze—this look that could bring pleasure in the midst of negation? In her first novel, *The Bluest Eye*, Toni Morrison constructs a portrait of the black female spectator; her gaze is the masochistic look of victimization. Describing her looking relations, Miss Pauline Breedlove, a poor working woman, maid in the house of a prosperous white family, asserts:

> The onliest time I be happy seem like was when I was in the picture show. Every time I got, I went, I'd go early, before the show started. They's cut off the lights, and everything be black. Then the screen would light up, and I's move right on in them picture. White men taking such good care of they women, and they all dressed up in big clean houses with the bath tubs right in the same room with the toilet. Them pictures gave me a lot of pleasure.

To experience pleasure, Miss Pauline sitting in the dark must imagine herself transformed, turned into the white woman portrayed on the screen. After watching movies, feeling the pleasure, she says, 'But it made coming home hard.'

We come home to ourselves. Not all black women spectators submitted to that spectacle of regression through identification. Most of the women I talked with felt that they consciously resisted identification with films—that this tension made moviegoing less than pleasurable; at times it caused pain. As one black woman put, 'I could always get pleasure from movies as long as I did not look too deep.' For black female spectators who have 'looked too deep' the encounter with the screen hurt. That some of us chose to stop looking was a gesture of resistance, turning away was one way to protest, to reject negation. My pleasure in the screen ended abruptly when I and my sisters first watched *Imitation of Life*. Writing about this experience in the 'Sapphire' piece, I addressed the movie directly, confessing:

> I had until now forgotten you, that screen image seen in adolescence, those images that made me stop looking. It was there in *Imitation of Life*, that comfortable mammy image. There was something familiar about this hard-working black woman who loved her daughter so much, loved her in a way that hurt. Indeed, as young southern black girls watching this film, Peola's another reminded us of the hardworking, churchgoing, Big Mamas we knew and loved. Consequently, it was not this image that captured our gaze; we were fascinated by Peola.

Addressing her, I wrote:

You were different. There was something scary in his image of young sexual sensual black beauty betrayed—that daughter who did not want to be confined by blackness, that 'tragic mulatto' who did not want to be negated. 'Just let me escape this image forever,' she could have said. I will always remember that image. I remembered how we cried for her, for our unrealized desiring selves. She was tragic because there was no place in the cinema for her, no loving pictures. She too was absent image. It was better then, that we were absent, for when we were there it was humiliating, strange, sad. We cried all night for you, for the cinema that had no place for you. And like you, we stopped thinking it would one day be different.

When I returned to films as a young woman, after a long period of silence, I had developed an oppositional gaze. Not only would I not be hurt by the absence of black female presence, or the insertion of violating representation, I interrogated the work, cultivated a way to look past race and gender for aspects of content, form, language. Foreign films and US independent cinema were the primary locations of my filmic looking relations, even though I also watched Hollywood films.

From 'jump,' black female spectators have gone to films with awareness of the way in which race and racism determined the visual construction of gender. Whether it was *Birth of a Nation* or Shirley Temple shows, we knew that white womanhood was the racialized sexual difference occupying the place of stardom in mainstream narrative film. We assumed white women knew it too. Reading Laura Mulvey's provocative essay, 'Visual Pleasure and Narrative Cinema,' from a standpoint that acknowledges race, one sees clearly why black women spectators not duped by mainstream cinema would develop an oppositional gaze. Placing ourselves outside that pleasure in looking, Mulvey argues, was determined by a 'split between active/male and passive/female.' Black female spectators actively chose not to identify with the film's imaginary subject because such identification was disenabling.

Looking at films with an oppositional gaze, black women were able to critically assess the cinema's construction of white womanhood as object of phallocentric gaze and choose not to identify with either the victim or the perpetrator. Black female spectators, who refused to identify with white womanhood, who would not take on the phallocentric gaze of desire and possession, created a critical space where the binary opposition Mulvey posits of 'woman as image, man as bearer of the look' was continually deconstructed. As critical spectators, black women looked from a location that disrupted, one akin to that described by Annette Kuhn in *The Power of The Image*:

> ... the acts of analysis, of deconstruction and of reading 'against the grain' offer an additional pleasure—the pleasure of resistance, of saying 'no': not to 'unsophisticated' enjoyment, by ourselves and others, of culturally dominant images, but to the structures of power which ask us to consume them uncritically and in highly circumscribed ways.

Mainstream feminist film criticism in no way acknowledges black female spectatorship. It does not even consider the possibility that women can construct an oppositional gaze via an understanding and awareness of the politics of race and racism. Feminist film theory rooted in an ahistorical psychoanalytic framework that privileges sexual difference actively suppresses recognition of race, reenacting and mirroring the erasure of black womanhood that occurs in films, silencing any discussion of racial difference—of racialized sexual difference. Despite feminist critical interventions aimed at deconstructing the category 'woman' which highlight the significance of race, many feminist film critics continue to structure their discourse as though it speaks about 'women' when in actuality it speaks only about white women. It seems ironic that the cover of the recent anthology *Feminism and Film Theory* edited by Constance Penley has a graphic that is a reproduction of the photo of white actresses Rosalind Russell and Dorothy Arzner on the 1936 set of the film *Craig's Wife* yet there is no acknowledgment in any essay in this collection that the woman 'subject' under discussion is always white. Even though there are photos of black women from films reproduced in the text, there is no acknowledgment of racial difference.

It would be too simplistic to interpret this failure of insight solely as a gesture of racism. Importantly, it also speaks to the problem of structuring feminist film theory around a totalizing narrative of woman as object whose image functions solely to reaffirm and reinscribe patriarchy. Mary Ann Doane addresses this issue in the essay 'Remembering Women: Psychical and Historical Construction in Film Theory':

> This attachment to the figure of a degeneralizible Woman as the product of the apparatus indicates why, for many, feminist film theory seems to have reached an impasse, a certain blockage in its theorization ... in focusing upon the task of delineating in great detail the attributes of woman as effect of the apparatus, feminist film theory participates in the abstraction of women.

The concept 'Woman' effaces the difference between women in specific socio-historical contexts, between women defined precisely as historical subjects rather than as *a* psychic subject (or non-subject). Though Doane does not focus on race, her comments speak directly to the problem of its erasure. For it is only as one imagines 'woman' in the abstract, when woman becomes fiction or fantasy, can race not be seen as significant. Are we really to imagine that feminist theorists writing only about images of white women, who subsume this specific historical subject under the totalizing category 'woman,' do not 'see' the whiteness of the image? It may very well be that they engage in a process of denial that eliminates the necessity of revisioning conventional ways of thinking about psychoanalysis as a paradigm of analysis and the need to rethink a body of feminist film theory that is firmly rooted in a denial of the reality that sex/ sexuality may not be the primary and/or exclusive signifier of difference.

Doane's essay appears in a very recent anthology, *Psychoanalysis and Cinema* edited by E. Ann Kaplan, where, once again, none of the theory presented acknowledges or discusses racial difference, with the exception of one essay, 'Not Speaking with Language, Speaking with No Language,' which problematizes notions of orientalism in its examination of Leslie Thornton's film *Adynata*. Yet in most of the essays, the theories espoused are rendered problematic if one includes race as a category of analysis.

Constructing feminist film theory along these lines enables the production of a discursive practice that need never theorize any aspect of black female representation or spectatorship. Yet the existence of black women within white supremacist culture problematizes, and makes complex, the overall issue of female identity, representation, and spectatorship. If, as Friedberg suggests, 'identification is a process which commands the subject to be displaced by an other; it is a procedure which breeches the separation between self and other, and, in this way, replicates the very structure of patriarchy.' If identification 'demands sameness, necessitates similarity, disallows difference'—must we then surmise that many feminist film critics who are 'over-identified' with the mainstream cinematic apparatus produce theories that replicate its totalizing agenda? Why is it that feminist film criticism, which has most claimed the terrain of woman's identity, representation, and subjectivity as its field of analysis, remains aggressively silent on the subject of blackness and specifically representations of black womanhood? Just as mainstream cinema has historically forced aware black female spectators not to look, much feminist film criticism disallows the possibility of a theoretical dialogue that might include black women's voices. It is difficult to talk when you feel no one is listening, when you feel as though a special jargon or narrative has been created that only the chosen can understand. No wonder then that black women have for the most part confined our critical commentary on film to conversations. And it must be reiterated that this gesture is a strategy that protects us from the violence perpetuated and advocated by discourses of mass media. A new focus on issues of race and representation in the field of film theory could critically intervene on the historical repression reproduced in some arenas of contemporary critical practice, making a discursive space for discussion of black female spectatorship possible.

When I asked a black woman in her twenties, an obsessive moviegoer, why she thought we had not written about black female spectatorship, she commented: 'We are afraid to talk about ourselves as spectators because we have been so abused by "the gaze".' An aspect of that abuse was the imposition of the assumption that black female looking relations were not important enough to theorize. Film theory as a critical 'turf' in the United States has been and continues to be influenced by and reflective of white racial domination. Since feminist film criticism was initially rooted in a women's liberation movement informed by racist practices, it did not open up the discursive terrain and make it more inclusive. Recently, even those white film theorists who include an analysis of race show no interest in black female spectatorship. In her introduction to the collection of essays *Visual and Other Pleasures*, Laura Mulvey describes her initial romantic absorption in Hollywood cinema, stating:

> Although this great, previously unquestioned and unanalyzed love was put in crisis by the impact of feminism on my thought in the early 1970s, it also had an enormous influence on the development of my critical work and ideas and the debate within film culture with which I became preoccupied over the next fifteen years or so. Watched through eyes that were affected by the changing climate of consciousness, the movies lost their magic.

Watching movies from a feminist perspective, Mulvey arrived at that location of disaffection that is the starting point for many black women approaching cinema within the lived harsh reality of racism. Yet her account of being a part of a film culture whose roots rest on a founding relationship of adoration and love indicates how difficult it would have been to enter that world from 'jump' as a critical spectator whose gaze had been formed in opposition.

Given the context of class exploitation, and racist and sexist domination, it has only been through resistance, struggle, reading, and looking 'against the grain,' that black women have been able to value our process of looking enough to publicly name it. Centrally, those black female spectators who attest to the oppositionality of their gaze deconstruct theories of female spectatorship that have relied heavily on the assumption that, as Doane suggests in her essay, 'Woman's Stake: Filming the Female Body,' 'woman can only mimic man's relation to language, that is assume a position defined by the penis-phallus as the supreme arbiter of lack.' Identifying with neither the phallocentric gaze nor the construction of white womanhood as lack, critical black female spectators construct a theory of looking relations where cinematic visual delight is the pleasure of interrogation. Every black woman spectator I talked to, with rare exception, spoke of being 'on guard' at the movies. Talking about the way being a critical spectator of Hollywood films influenced her, black woman filmmaker Julie Dash exclaims, 'I make films because I was such a spectator!' Looking at Hollywood cinema from a distance, from that critical politicized standpoint that did not want to be seduced by narratives reproducing her negation, Dash watched mainstream movies over and over again for the pleasure of deconstructing them. And of course there is that added delight if one happens, in the process of interrogation, to come across a narrative that invites the black female spectator to engage the text with no threat of violation [. . .]

Talking with black female spectators, looking at written discussions either in fiction or academic essays about black women, I noted the connection made between the realm of representation in mass media and the capacity of black women to construct ourselves as subjects in daily life. The extent to which black women feel devalued, objectified, dehumanized in this society determines the scope and texture of their looking relations. Those black women whose identities were constructed in resistance, by practices that oppose the dominant order, were most inclined to develop an oppositional gaze. Now that there is a growing interest in films produced by black women and those films have become more accessible to viewers, it is possible to talk about black female spectatorship in relation to that work. So far, most discussions of black spectatorship that I have come across focus on men. In 'Black Spectatorship: Problems of Identification and Resistance' Manthia Diawara suggests that 'the components of "difference"' among elements of sex, gender, and sexuality give rise to different readings of the same material, adding that these conditions produce a 'resisting' spectator. He focuses his critical discussion on black masculinity.

The recent publication of the anthology *The Female Gaze: Women as Viewers of Popular Culture* excited me, especially as it included an essay, 'Black Looks,' by Jacqui Roach and Petal Felix that attempts to address black female spectatorship. The essay posed provocative questions that were not answered: Is there a black female gaze? How do black women relate to the gender politics of representation? Concluding, the authors assert that black females have 'our own reality, our own history, our own gaze—one which sees the world rather differently from "anyone else."' Yet, they do not name/describe this experience of seeing 'rather differently.' The absence of definition and explanation suggests they are assuming an essentialist stance wherein it is presumed that black women, as victims of race and gender oppression, have an inherently different field of vision. Many black women do not 'see differently' precisely because their perceptions of reality are so profoundly colonized, shaped by dominant ways of knowing. As Trinh T. Minh-ha points out in 'Outside In, Inside Out': 'Subjectivity does not merely consist of talking about oneself . . . be this talking indulgent or critical.'

Critical black female spectatorship emerges as a site of resistance only when individual black women actively resist the imposition of dominant ways of knowing and looking. While every black woman I talked to was aware of racism, that awareness did not automatically correspond with politicization, the development of an oppositional gaze. When it did, individual black women consciously named the process. Manthia Diawara's 'resisting spectatorship' is a term that does not adequately describe the terrain of black female spectatorship. We do more than resist. We create alternative texts that are not solely reactions. As critical spectators, black women participate in a broad range of looking relations, contest, resist, revision, interrogate, and invent on multiple levels. Certainly when I watch the work of black women filmmakers Camille Billops, Kathleen Collins, Julie Dash, Ayoka Chenzira, Zeinabu Davis, I do not need to 'resist' the images even as I still choose to watch their work with a critical eye.

Black female critical thinkers concerned with creating space for the construction of radical black female subjectivity, and the way cultural production informs this possibility, fully acknowledge the importance of mass media, film in particular, as a powerful site for critical intervention. Certainly Julie Dash's film *Illusions* identifies the terrain of Hollywood cinema as a space of knowledge production that has enormous power. Yet, she also creates a filmic narrative wherein the black female protagonist subversively claims that space. Inverting the 'real-life' power structure, she offers the black female spectator representations that challenge stereotypical notions that place us outside the realm of filmic discursive practices. Within the film she uses the strategy of Hollywood suspense films to undermine those cinematic practices that deny black women a place in this structure. Problematizing the question of 'racial' identity by depicting passing, suddenly it is the white male's capacity to gaze, define, and know that is called into question.

When Mary Ann Doane describes in 'Woman's Stake: Filming the Female Body' the way in which feminist filmmaking practice can elaborate 'a special syntax for a different articulation of the female body,' she names a critical process that 'undoes the structure of the classical narrative through an insistence upon its repressions.' An eloquent description, this precisely names Dash's strategy in *Illusions*, even though the film is not unproblematic and works within certain conventions that are not successfully challenged. For example, the film does not indicate whether the character Mignon will make Hollywood films that subvert and transform the genre or whether she will simply assimilate and perpetuate the norm. Still, subversively, *Illusions* problematizes the issue of race and spectatorship. White people in the film are unable to 'see' that race informs their looking relations. Though she is passing to gain access to the machinery of cultural production represented by film, Mignon continually asserts her ties to black community. The bond between her and the young black woman singer Esther Jeeter is affirmed by caring gestures of affirmation, often expressed by eye-to-eye contact, the direct unmediated gaze of recognition. Ironically, it is the desiring objectifying sexualized white male gaze that threatens to penetrate her 'secrets' and disrupt her process. Metaphorically, Dash suggests the power of black women to make films will be threatened and undermined by that white male gaze that seeks to reinscribe the black female body in a narrative of voyeuristic pleasure where the only relevant opposition is male/female, and the only location for the female is as a victim. These tensions are not resolved by the narrative. It is not at all evident that Mignon will triumph over the white supremacist capitalist imperialist dominating 'gaze.'

Throughout *Illusions*, Mignon's power is affirmed by her contact with the younger black woman whom she nurtures and protects. It is this process of mirrored recognition that enables both black women to define their reality, apart from the reality imposed upon them by structures of domination. The shared gaze of the two women reinforces their solidarity. As the younger subject, Esther represents a potential audience for films that Mignon might produce, films wherein black females will be the narrative focus. Julie Dash's recent feature-length film *Daughters of the Dust* dares to place black females at the center of its narrative. This focus caused critics (especially white males) to critique the film negatively or to express many reservations. Clearly, the impact of racism and sexism so over-determine spectatorship—not only what we look at but who we identify with—that viewers who are not black females find it hard to empathize with the central characters in the movie. They are adrift without a white presence in the film.

Another representation of black females nurturing one another *via* recognition of their common struggle for subjectivity is depicted in Sankofa's collective work *Passion of Remembrance*. In the film, two black women friends, Louise and Maggie, are from the onset of the narrative struggling with the issue of subjectivity, of their place in progressive black liberation movements that have been sexist. They challenge old norms and want to replace them with new understandings of the complexity of black identity, and the need for liberation struggles that address that complexity. Dressing to go to a party, Louise and Maggie claim the 'gaze.' Looking at one another, staring in mirrors, they appear completely focused on their encounter with black femaleness. How they see themselves is most important, not how they will be stared at by others. Dancing to the tune 'Let's get Loose,' they display their bodies not for a voyeuristic colonizing gaze but for that look of recognition that affirms their subjectivity—that constitutes them as spectators. Mutually empowered they eagerly leave the privatized domain to confront the public. Disrupting conventional racist and sexist stereotypical representations of black female bodies, these scenes invite the audience to look differently. They act to critically intervene and transform conventional filmic practices, changing notions of spectatorship. *Illusions*, *Daughters of the Dust*, and *A Passion of Remembrance* employ a deconstructive filmic practice to undermine existing grand cinematic narratives even as they retheorize subjectivity in the realm of the visual. Without providing 'realistic' positive representations that emerge only as a response to the totalizing nature of existing narratives, they offer points of radical departure. Opening up a space for the assertion of a critical black female spectatorship, they do not simply offer diverse representations, they imagine new transgressive possibilities for the formulation of identity.

In this sense they make explicit a critical practice that provides us with different ways to think about black female subjectivity and black female spectatorship. Cinematically, they provide new points of recognition, embodying Stuart Hall's vision of a critical practice that acknowledges that identity is constituted 'not outside but within representation,' and invites us to see film 'not as a second-order mirror held up to reflect what already exists, but as that form of representation which is able to constitute us as new kinds of subjects, and thereby enable us to discover who we are.' It is this critical practice that enables production of feminist film theory that theorizes black female spectatorship. Looking and looking back, black women involve ourselves in a process whereby we see our history as counter-memory, using it as a way to know the present and invent the future.

REFERENCES

Burchill, Julie, *Girls on Film* (New York: Pantheon, 1986).
Diawara Manthia, 'Black Spectatorship: Problems of Identification and Resistance'. *Screen*, Vol. 29, No. 4 (1988).

Diawara, Manthia, 'Black British Cinema: Spectatorship and Identity Formation in Territories'. *Public Culture*, Vol. 1, No. 3 (Summer 1989).

Doane, Mary Ann, 'Woman's Stake: Filming the Female Body'. In *Feminism and Film Theory*, edited by Constance Penley (New York: Routledge, 1988).

Doane, Mary Ann, 'Remembering Women: Psychical and Historical Constructions in Film Theory'. In *Psychoanalysis and Cinema*, edited by E. Ann Kaplan (London: Routledge, 1990).

Fanon, Franz, *Black Skin, White Masks* (New York: *Monthly Review*, 1967).

Friedberg, Anne, 'A Denial of Difference: Theories of Cinematic Identification'. In *Psychoanalysis and Cinema*, edited by E. Ann Kaplan (London: Routledge, 1990).

Gamman, Lorraine and Marshment, Margaret (eds), *The Female Gaze: Women as Viewers of Popular Culture* (London: The Women's Press, 1988).

Hall, Stuart, 'Cultural Identity and Diaspora'. In *Identity: Community, Culture, Difference*, edited by Jonathan Rutherford (London: Lawrence & Wishart, 1990).

hooks, bell, 'Do You Remember Sapphire?'. In hooks, *Talking Back: Thinking Feminism, Thinking Black* (Boston: South End Press, 1989).

Kuhn, Annette, *The Power of the Image: Essays on Representation and Sexuality* (New York: Routledge, 1985).

Minh-ha, Trinh T., 'Outside In, Inside Out'. In *Questions of Third Cinema*, edited by Jim Pines (London: British Film Institute, 1989).

Morrison, Toni, *The Bluest Eye* (New York: Holt, Rinehart and Winston, 1970).

Mulvey, Laura, 'Visual Pleasure and Narrative Cinema'. *Screen* Autumn 1975, Vol. 16, No. 3, pp. 6–18.

Mulvey, Laura, *Visual and Other Pleasures* (Bloomington: University of Indiana Press, 1989).

22

'CINEMA AND THE DARK CONTINENT: RACE AND GENDER IN POPULAR FILM'

Tania Modleski

Issues of race, gender, and ethnicity come together in an especially bizarre manner in one of the earliest sound films, *The Jazz Singer*, at the end of which the Jewish son, played by Al Jolson, donning black face for a theatrical perfor-mance, hears 'the call of the ages—the cry of my race,' sings 'Mammy' to his mother, and rushes home to his dying father, promising to take up momentarily the father's role as cantor. Subsequently—and the coda is added to the film version of the stage play—the son returns to his show-business career, thus being permitted the best of both worlds, old and new. Here, of course, are the familiar oedipal themes of Hollywood cinema: the son's accession to the role of the father entails a modification of the stern and unyielding patriarchal attitude, thereby, in the case of *The Jazz Singer*, accommodating the assimilationist ideologies of the period. The mother is a key figure in the process of the hero's growth and acculturation, since in her unconditional love for her child she can serve as the mediating force between father and son, old world and new, the desire for cultural difference and the desire for cultural integration.[1]

But the mother in the film is not the only mediator, not the only person whose sole significance lies in the meaning she holds for the white man and *his* drama; the other such figure is, of course, the black man, metonymically summoned to represent the unalterable fact of 'race,' and thus to form one pole of the assimilationist continuum, at the other end of which stands the Jolson character's *shiksa* girlfriend. It is ironic, if utterly characteristic, that the

* From Modleski, T., *Feminism without Women: Culture and Criticism in a 'Postfeminist' Age*. London: Routledge, 1991, pp. 115–34.

essentialist notion of race the film draws upon is asserted through masquerade and in a space of illusionism, i.e., the theater. That is to say, the jazz singer recognizes his supposed racial *authenticity* as a Semite in the process of *miming* another race—assuming black skin and black voice—so that the film is situated squarely in the realm of the fetish, whereby the notion of ineradicable racial difference (one which defies history and calls out across 'the ages') is simultaneously affirmed and negated.

Recent work by Homi Bhabha has shown how colonialist discourse as a whole involves a process of mimicry that is related psychoanalytically to the mechanism of fetishization, the play of presence and absence. By mimicry, I take Bhabha to be referring to an imposition by one nation of its structures, values, and language upon the colonized nation, an imposition that rather than completely obliterating difference speaks of 'a desire for a subject of a difference that is almost the same, but not quite' and hence is, Bhabha continually emphasizes, *ambivalent*.[2] Although Bhabha's terms of reference concern the British Empire, they apply equally to the American situation, for, as Thomas Cripps points out in his somewhat dated but still useful study of blacks in American film, the position of blacks in relation to the dominant culture and its representations has been an 'ambivalent' one: blacks had 'absorbed American culture but could not expect to be absorbed by it.'[3] Moreover, Cripps himself points out that the British colonial system 'resembled American racial arrangements' in the way 'it encouraged cultural assimilation while denying social integration' (p. 313). One fairly ludicrous result of such 'arrangements' was that, for example, in cinema what used to be called 'race movies' often had to do without white people. 'Without whites, the requirements of dramatic construction created a world in which black characters acceded to the white ideal of segregation, and unreal black cops, crooks, judges, and juries interacted in such a way as to blame black victims for their social plight.' But the lack of versimilitude, which Cripps sees as a problem, can cut two ways: for it is easy to see how how such copies of white cinema could easily reflect back on the model itself, mocking it, defamiliarizing it, casting doubt upon its accuracy as, in the words of one film concerned with the perennial theme of 'passing,' an 'imitation of life' (pp. 322–3) [...]

We need, then, not just to analyze the function of mimicry on the part of the colonized people, but to understand its role in the life and art of the *colonizer*—to understand, that is, the function of minstrelsy. Bhabha writes of the way the 'not quite/not white' element of difference displayed by colonized races is related to the psychoanalytic notion of the fetish: 'black skin splits under the racist gaze, displaced into signs of bestiality, genitalia, grotesquerie, which reveal the phobic myth of the undifferentiated whole white skin.'[4] Minstrelsy would be a method by which the white man may disavow—acknowledge and at the same time deny—difference at the level of the body; as a process of fetishism, it seeks, like all fetishes, to restore the wholeness and unity threatened by the sight of difference, yet because it enters into the game of mimicry it is condemned to keep alive the possibility that there may be 'no presence or identity behind the mask.'[5] The concept of fetishism enables us to understand why minstrelsy has never really died out—why it lives in a different form in the 'trading places' and 'black like me' plots with which Hollywood is enamored [. . .]

Some of Bhabha's discussion covers familiar territory for a feminist reader, since he draws on material elaborated in feminist theory. The problematics of difference and sameness have, for example, been brilliantly analyzed by Luce Irigaray in her readings of Freud's essay 'On Femininity' and Plato's *Republic*. Irigaray shows that for all Western culture's emphasis on the difference between the sexes, there is an underlying negation of the difference—and the threat— posed by the female sex, a negation evidenced for example in Freud's theorizing of the woman as an inferior man, as bearer of the 'lack.'[6] In Freudian theory, of course, the fetish is precisely the means whereby 'lack' and difference are disavowed—accepted and negated simultaneously. It is the means, in other words, whereby 'a multiple belief' may be maintained and hence serves to support the wildly divergent stereotypical associations that accrue around the fetishized body. For it is not just the black who is marked in the dominant discourse as, in Homi Bhabha's words, 'both savage . . . and yet the most obedient and dignified of servants; . . . the embodiment of rampant sexuality and yet innocent as a child; . . . mystical, primitive, simple-minded and yet the most worldly and accomplished liar, and manipulator of social forces.'[7] Much of this description also applies to the representation of woman, who in the male Imaginary undergoes a primal splitting into virgin and whore.

The importance of Bhabha's work, like Fanon's before him, lies partly, for me, in the way it insists on understanding the psychosocial dynamics of colonialism and racism, bringing psychoanalysis to bear on questions that have unfortunately all too often been viewed as not susceptible to a psychoanalytic understanding. Yet, unaccountably, although Bhabha utilizes the very concepts originally developed in the theorization of sexual difference, he almost entirely neglects the issue of gender and slights feminist work. In virtually ignoring the 'woman question,' while retaining the terms in which it has been posed, Bhabha commits the same kind of error for which Freud can be and has been criticized. The latter was undoubtedly being both racist and sexist in designating 'woman' as the dark continent. But the answer is surely not to reverse the proposition and implicitly posit the 'dark continent' as woman—not, at the very least, without carefully theorizing the relation.

Although he does not examine how race and gender intersect, Bhabha nevertheless notes at one point, 'Darkness signifies at once both birth and death; it is in all cases a desire to return to the fullness of the mother, a desire for an unbroken and undifferentiated line of vision and origin.'[8] For the heart of the matter, the heart of darkness, is, after all, 'Mammy'—she who, absent in her own right, is spoken by man as guarantor of his origin and identity. In the face of the male desire to collapse sexual and racial difference into oceanic plenitude, feminism needs to insist on the complex, 'multiple and cross-cutting' nature of identity and to ask: how do we rid ourselves of the desire for a 'line of origin,' how avoid positing either sexuality or race as theoretically primary, while we at the same time undertake to understand the vicious circularity of patriarchal thought whereby darkness signifies femininity and femininity darkness? I would like in this chapter to address this question by examining first the way our culture through its representations explores the highly charged taboo relationships between black men and white women (specifically focusing on *Gorillas in the Mist* and a scene from an early film, *Blonde Venus*) and then to focus on the representations of black women in popular film, looking especially at the ways in which the black woman functions as the site of the displacement of white culture's (including white women's) fears and anxieties.

In *Gorillas in the Mist* the question of origins is posed at the outset by, of course, a white man—in this case the anthropologist Dr Louis Leakey, who is seen in a large hall lecturing about gorillas: 'I want to know who I am, and what it was that made me that way.' As if conjured up by his words, Dian Fossey appears, the woman who will journey alone to the heart of darkest Africa and whose story may be viewed as a phantasmatic answer to the white man's question.

It is an old story, an updated, middlebrow version of the King Kong tale, which itself is part of a tradition of animal movies that have functioned as thinly disguised 'allegories for black brutes.'[9] Of the perennial popularity of the film *King Kong*, for example, X. J. Kennedy wrote:

> A Negro from Atlanta tells me that in movies houses in colored neighborhoods throughout the South, *Kong* does a constant business. They show the thing in Atlanta at least every year, presumably to the same audiences. Perhaps this popularity may simply be due to the fact that *Kong* is one of the most watchable movies ever constructed, but I wonder whether Negro audiences may not find some archetypical appeal in this serio-comic tale of a huge black powerful free spirit whom all the hardworking white policemen are out to kill.[10]

Putting aside the way this passage provides a textbook example of how white racism gets projected into the psyches of the black audience, we may note that Kennedy's remarks are paradoxically couched in a liberal frame which tacitly acknowledges the legitimacy of black political grievances while employing an ahistorical notion of 'archetype,' which would deny the humanity of blacks (imaged as beasts) and so function to prevent them from achieving social and political equality. This is not to say that Kennedy's response is idiosyncratic: on the contrary, films like *King Kong*, made by whites in a racist society, lend themselves to this kind of interpretation, which is situated in the space of disavowal characteristic of colonialist discourse (the fetish indeed being a means by which two apparently opposed beliefs, 'one archaic and one progressive,' may simultaneously be held). This is a space, as we shall see, increasingly occupied in a post feminist, post-civil rights era by a mass culture that must on one level acknowledge the political struggles of the last few decades and on another, deeper level would ward off the threat these struggles pose to the white male power structure.

Thus, for example, *Gorillas in the Mist* seems to respect the notion of a woman sacrificing the opportunity for a husband and family in order to pursue a career, a career that, indeed, involves her living the sort of adventurous and dangerous life usually reserved for men in popular films and that also accords her the kind of single-minded dedication to a cause typically attributed to the *male* scientific investigator. But the film takes it all back, as it were, by 'deprofessionalizing' Fossey, neglecting to mention her growth as a scientist who in the course of her research in the mountains of Rwanda earned a PhD from Harvard. The film further subverts its apparently liberal attitude to woman's independence by suggesting that Dian is merely channeling and sublimating (or should it be *de*sublimating, since she goes 'back' to the apes?) her sexual desires and maternal instincts into her cause. In the last scene, for example, after her death, the image track shows the son of the slaughtered gorilla swinging in the trees—clearly *Fossey's* son, since her tryst with its father, the gorilla Digit (in which the romantic music swells as Dian lies on her back, smiling blissfully when the gorilla slowly takes her hand, leaving a precious little deposit of dirt in her palm) is followed by her coupling with the *National Geographic* photographer. The soundtrack records a conversation between her and Roz Carr, the plantation owner, in which Fossey remarks, 'I expected to get married and have children,' and her friend replies, 'Instead there's a mountain full of gorillas who wouldn't be alive if it weren't for you.' The titles at the end tell us that Fossey's work 'contributed significantly to the survival of the species'—woman's function, after all, even if it isn't quite the right species.

The transfer of Fossey's affection from her fiancé to Digit and his 'group' is visually marked by the film through its replacement of the photo of the fiancé, which we see early in the film placed on a little typing table outside Dian's hut, with photos of the gorillas ('gorilla porn,' as one of my friends remarked) that she passionately kisses right before her murder, while a song of Peggy Lee's ('I'd take a million trips to your lips') plays on the phonograph. But perverse as all this may sound—and in my view *is*—the most remarkable aspect of the film is the way in which it manages to make its psychosexual dynamics seem innocent. Indeed, the very title of the film points to a kind of disavowal, suggesting a tamed, romanticized, 'misty' view of beasts and bestiality: a film whose *own* sublimating efforts work on every level to deny the perversity of the gorilla/woman sexual coupling it continually evokes.

Black skin 'splits' in this film, to recall Homi Bhabha's words, into images of monstrosity and bestiality on the one hand and of nobility and wisdom on the other. Fossey's tracker, Sembagare, represents the latter option; he is presented as a man whose family has been wiped out along with their tribe and thus, having no story or plot of his own, he is free to live a life of self-sacrificing devotion to the white woman. It is impossible to overestimate the importance of this character—a common type in Hollywood cinema—in serving as a guide to the audience's interpretation and judgment of events, and it is interesting to reflect on the fact that such a character's possession of the gaze may be concomitant with a radical *dis*possession in relation to the narrative. Throughout the film, the camera continually cuts to shots of Sembagare, usually gazing approvingly on some action performed by the heroine, but also, occasionally, registering disapproval and dismay. Mostly what Sembagare cares about is that the heroine's sexual and romantic needs be fulfilled, and this is made clear from the very outset when he first sees and comments on the picture of the fiancé. By attributing a kind of maternal concern to the black male as well as granting him a degree of moral authority, the film can appear to be, in liberal fashion, empowering the character while at the same time relieving the audiences' anxieties about the proximity of white womanhood and black manhood.

That fears about the threat posed by the black male to white woman are *not* far beneath the surface can be seen in the film's treatment of all the other black men, who are usually shown in menacing groups, surrounding our heroine, gesturing and muttering in their 'savage' languages, and touching her hair in awe. Early in the film, some black soldiers come to Fossey's hut, destroy her possessions, and evict her from their country. The film treats African civil wars as nothing more than a nuisance impeding Fossey's crusade—a crusade aligned with the film's project of substituting a timeless, pastoral 'gorilla nation' for the eminently less important struggles of emerging black nations. Significantly, as the men attempt to force her to leave, Fossey furiously tells them not to touch her, to get their hands off her. Now, given that the big love scene with the gorilla involves Fossey holding hands with him, and indeed that the love interest is given the name 'Digit' by Fossey because of the webbing of his fingers, and finally that the film is most horrified by the castration of the gorillas' heads and hands, the latter made into curio ashtrays for rich Americans, we might be justified in seeing in this motif of the hand a condensation of the film's basic conflict: a pitting of animals *against* black men, with the former ultimately viewed as less physically and morally repellent than the latter. Here we might note that we come full circle to Griffith's film *Birth of a Nation*, which had intercut shots of Flora being stalked by Gus with ones of squirrels framed in an iris. The black man thus becomes, as Cripps observes, 'a predator about to pounce upon a harmless animal' (p. 48). Thus it is that in *Gorillas in the Mist*, the machete-wielding black men who earn their living destroying gorillas are depicted as *less* truly and movingly human than the tragic and noble gorillas—as was the case in *King Kong*, as well.

Of course, at the level of its script, the film suggests a more complicated view, and at one point the photographer Bob cautions an angry Fossey that the black men are simply pawns in an economic power game that chiefly benefits rich Americans. In this respect too, then, the film operates in the realm of disavowal, verbally disputing its own visual scapegoating of the black men *and*, moreover, projecting the scapegoating onto the character of Fossey, who at one point terrorizes a little black boy by pretending to be a witch and at another point conducts a mock lynching of a black male poacher.

It is the white man, then, who in the end seems to be the most fully human character, while the black men are either self-sacrificing servants or threatening monsters, and the white woman is at the same time both a noble savior of innocent creatures and a witch whose unholy alliance with the beasts of the forests turns her into a raving monomaniac. In other words, into the space hollowed out by the film's fetishistic splittings steps the white man, equipped with the photographic apparatus which apparently enables him to establish the proper voyeuristic distance from the perversity that surrounds him. Interestingly, since this is Dian Fossey's story, and most of the film is from her point of view, the film gives the point of view over to Bob on several occasions. I have already referred to one instance—when Bob stares in fascination at Dian's 'mating' with Digit, the camera cutting to tight close-ups of him as he crouches near his photographic equipment and stares intently at the coming together of woman and ape. Another such moment occurs when he first arrives on the scene, and we see Dian squatting on the floor, imitating the gorillas' movements and noises. So vertiginous does the film's play with mimicry become that the woman is constantly shown copying the gorillas, aping the anthropomorphized apes; like the blacks, she seems to occupy a position one step below the animals, to be not quite capable of achieving the same degree of humanity attained by the beasts.

But while an analysis of the point-of-view structure of *Gorillas in the Mist* suggests that, like most Hollywood films, and despite its biographical claims, this one is largely concerned with white male fears and fantasies and seems designed to assure the white man of his full humanity in relation to the animals, the female sex, and other races, it is important to understand that the voyeuristic distance between the white male and his 'others' ultimately collapses. Bob, it turns out, is drawn to gorillas too, and he gets to act out his bestial lusts vicariously when he and Dian become lovers after he sees her with Digit and during an elaborate verbal play in which references to the beauty of the animals serve as double entendres applying to Fossey herself. Here we encounter the perennial thematics of homosocial desire, according to which the woman functions in a triangular relationship between two males, the woman becoming attractive to the second male as a result of being sought after or possessed by the first: a matter of, in René Girard's words, *mimetic* desire—of, in the film's case, man imitating beast.[11] Thus, we might say, by the end of the twentieth century, homosocial desire, long the cornerstone of patriarchal society, has expanded to include the entire order of Primates.

In *Gorillas in the Mist*, then, woman serves to initiate man into the secrets of his origin, whereupon he goes off to a new job in the wider world, escaping the carnage and destruction visited on the other players. Such violence is made to seem an appropriate ending to a film that touches on so many taboo areas, situating itself at the shifting borders between man and woman, whites and blacks, humans and animals, nature and society. One might expect that because of its unsettling obsession with these taboos, its nearly uncontrollable play of iteration, audiences would be troubled by the film's perversity. Seldom, however, did reviewers even mention the film's bizarre psychosocial dynamics; instead, the main 'controversy' surrounding *Gorillas in the Mist* had to do with its accuracy as representation of Fossey's life—a question, once again, of mimicry, or mimesis. It is tempting to speculate that this question arises as a response to the disturbances created *by* the film at a phantasmatic level, instilling in us a longing for an authentic human life to serve as ground and source of the film's meaning, just as the film itself attempts to foreclose the historical process and establish a natural, pastoral space which would pre-exist the struggles of feminists and black nationalists. Such a question would take on a special urgency precisely because the lines toed by the film are so thin that it comes perilously close to mocking its own quest, making monkeys of us all.

In his book, *The Signifying Monkey: A Theory of Afro-American Literary Criticism*, Henry Louis Gates praises Jean Renoir's silent film *Sur un air de Charleston* for its parody of the literature of discovery popular in Renaissance and Enlightenment Europe. In the film, a black man in blackface discovers a post-holocaust Europe and its only survivors, 'a scantily clad white Wild Woman . . . and her lascivious companion, an ape.' Gates sees in this scenario a 'master trope of irony,' which operates a 'fairly straightforward . . . reversal . . . of common European allegations of the propensity of African women to prefer the company of male apes.' That Gates can see nothing dubious in Renoir's 'surrealistic critique of . . . fundamental conventions of Western discourse on the black' and can entirely neglect to consider the potency of myths like *King Kong* (which long precede the 1933 film) suggests a very large blind spot indeed—blind, that is, to the way the female Other, regardless of race, has been frequently consigned to categories that put her outside the pale of the fully human.[12] (Why, we might inquire, did it not occur to the 'master' ironist to depict a scantily clad white man lewdly gyrating with his pet ape?)

Most pertinently we need to ask if, given the fetishistic nature of discourses on race and gender, a politically effective representational strategy can ever operate via 'reversal.' Gates's own lucid discussion of the complexity of black American 'signifying,' which he argues both participates in and subtly undermines white discourse, implicitly repudiates the viability of 'straightforward reversal' as political critique. If, as Gates argues, blacks have developed a double-edged discourse capable of responding to what W. E. B. DuBois called the 'twoness' of their existence in American culture, how much more pertinent is the theorization of such a discourse for anyone concerned with understanding the complex articulations of race *and* gender in American life and with avoiding the 'reversals' that keep us continually veering between the Scylla of racism and the Charybdis of sexism.

To illustrate this point, I want to return to a scene in a film by a director whose presence is strongly felt at the 'originary' moment of feminist psychoanalytic film theory: namely, Josef von Sternberg, the auteur who was the focus of Laura Mulvey's comments on the way popular narrative cinema tends to fetishize the female body.[13] The film—*Blonde Venus*—has been as riveting to contemporary theorists of cinema as the sight of Dian Fossey lying among the apes was to the character Bob in *Gorillas in the Mist*.[14] A still from the scene to which I am referring graces the cover of an issue of *Cinema Journal* which includes an article about the subversiveness of the film's treatment of female sexuality.[15] In the plot leading up to this scene, the heroine Helen, played by Marlene Dietrich, has recently left her humble home and her husband and son to return to a career on the stage; in the still, she has just emerged from an ape costume, although hairy bits of the costume remain around her genital area, her shoulders, and her derrière, and she is about to sing 'Hot Voodoo.' On her head is a blonde Afro wig and behind her stand a group of women in blackface holding spears and giant masks painted with large mouths and teeth.

Nowhere does Sternberg more forcefully reveal himself to be the master fetishist of the female body than in this scene, which for an adequate reading requires us to apply the insights of *both* a Homi Bhabha and a Laura Mulvey. Too often feminist film critics have alluded only parenthetically to the film's racism while devoting themselves chiefly to considering whether the film is 'progressive' in its emphasis on performance and spectacle, its subtle visual undermining of the domestic ideal that the narrative purports to uphold. Yet the racism is not an incidental, 'odd' moment to be bracketed off in order to pursue more pressing concerns, but is, in fact, central to the evocation and manipulation of desire that begins with the Hot Voodoo number and continues up to and beyond Helen's flight south to increasingly exotic locales, the last of which is a Louisiana boarding house run by a black woman.

In the Hot Voodoo sequence, the fetishistic working of presence and absence, difference and sameness, depends, as it does in *Gorillas in the Mist*, on the interplay of the elements of white woman, ape, and blacks. If it can be said that the film draws on the stereotypical association, referred to by Gates, of apes and black women, it can also be that said the white woman *is* the ape. But then again, of course, she is not the ape. Part of the sexual charge of the spectacle derives from the disavowal, the doubleness, the contradictory belief structure whereby she is posited as *simultaneously* animal and human, as well as simultaneously white and not white (suggested by the blonde Afro wig). Similarly, the white women in blackface and black Afro wigs who stand behind Dietrich are also affirmed and denied as African 'savages' (and are fetishized further in that the war-paint on their faces resembles the painting on the masks they carry in front of the lower halves of their bodies—the teeth on these masks clearly symbolizing the *vagina dentata*). I think we can take this fully theatricalized image as emblematic of some of the complex interrelations of gender and race in popular representation.[16]

In doing so, however, we are forced to recognize that while everyone in this scenario (except for the white male, played by Cary Grant, who is looking on) is relegated to 'the ideologically appointed place of the stereotype'[17]), the black women in the film are in the *most* marginalized position. If it is true, to cite Claire Johnston's famous formulation, woman as woman has largely been absent from patriarchal cinema, this has obviously been much more literally the case for black women than for whites.[18] And if the white woman has usually served as the signifier of male desire (which is what Johnston meant when she spoke of the absence of woman *as* woman), the black woman, when present at all, has served as a signifier of (white) female sexuality or of the maternal ('Mammy'). In the last part of this essay I would like to explore the way in which black women in contemporary popular film are reduced to being the signifiers of signifiers.

The use of the black woman to signify sexuality is vividly illustrated in one of the most recent films in the tradition of *The Jazz Singer*. In this case, however, the protagonist is a *woman* who finds herself going back to her Jewish roots. In *Crossing Delancey*, directed by Joan Micklin Silver, Amy Irving plays Izzy, a thirty-three year-old white woman who lives alone in Manhattan, works in a prestigious bookstore organizing readings by the literati, and, vehement disclaimers to the contrary notwithstanding, is clearly desperate to find a man. Indeed, she is so desperate that after ridding herself of an infatuation with a self-absorbed and pretentious writer, she overcomes a strong distaste for a Jewish pickle salesman, who has been chosen for her by a marriage-broker in collusion with Izzy's grandmother. In a brief scene occurring rather early in the film, Izzy is trying to decide whether or not to call the writer to ask him out, and she asks the advice of a friend as the two relax in the sauna after a workout in the gym. While the women recline in their towels, the camera pans down to reveal two black women, one of whom, a very large woman whose ample flesh spills out of a tight bathing-suit, loudly recounts to her friend an anecdote about love making in which while performing fellatio ('I'm licking it, I'm kissing it, he's moaning') she discovers a long—'I mean long'—blonde hair, which the man rather lamely tries to explain away. The camera tilts back up, as Izzy, having listened intently to the conversation, thoughtfully remarks, 'Maybe I *will* call him.'

Clearly the black woman, small as her role is, represents sexuality and 'embodiment' in a film that never mentions sex at any other time (to be sure, the fact of sex is hinted at when Izzy spends an occasional night with a married male friend, but it is never shown or discussed). Even the framing of the scene we have been discussing suggests in amazingly exemplary fashion the hierarchical division between black and white women, with the uptown Manhattanite princess-'on-her-high-horse' (to quote the grandmother), who will be forced to accept as a lover a Jewish man from lower Manhattan, placed in the upper part of the frame and the sexualized black females situated, as always, on the bottom (a spatial metaphor with both social and psychic dimensions). The black woman's story not only hints at the threat of miscegenation for, just as this woman's lover has strayed, so too is Izzy straying from her roots—but represents directly all those desires that this postfeminist film is disavowing: both a voracious sexuality and a voracious hunger in general, resulting from the deprivations suffered by single middle-class white women in the modern world. Thus the fact that the one sexual act mentioned in the film (which is about a woman's love for a pickle salesman, no less) is the act of fellatio is not surprising given the ubiquitous presence of food in the film (scenes of Izzy and her friend eating hotdogs on Izzy's birthday after she lies to her boss about going to a fancy restaurant [obviously women cannot nurture themselves or each other]; of lonely women picking at food in salad bars and eating Chinese takeout while watching television; of a baby nursing at his mother's breast while the heroine looks on in envy—envy *not*, it is quite clear, of the mother but of the suckling child; and finally, of the [as the film portrays her] obnoxiously loud female marriage broker continually gobbling down other people's food, eating with greasy fingers and talking with her mouth crammed full).

Elsewhere I talked about the horror of the body expressed in contemporary culture, the anorexic mentality to which this horror gives rise, and the tendency on the part of men to deal with these fears by displacing them onto the body of the female;[19] what we need to note here is the special role played by the woman of color as receptacle of these fears. The function of the fat, sexually voracious black woman in *Crossing Delancey*, is to enable the white Jewish subculture, through its heterosexual love story, to represent itself in a highly sentimentalized, romanticized, and sublimated light, while disavowing the desires and discontents underlying the civilisation it is promoting. (Once again, then, we see the need for feminist analysis to consider the ways in which ethnic and racial groups are played off against—and play themselves off against—one another.[20])

If in *Crossing Delancey*—a film written and directed by *women*—the black female body is the sexualized body, in other films the black woman functions not only as the sexual other, but as the maternal body, as psychic surrogate for the white mother—in short, as 'Mammy.' Recent feminist theory has shown that the nursery maid in Freud's own time played an important, although largely unacknowledged, role in initiating the child into sexual knowledge.[21] In America, as black feminists have pointed out, the black woman has more often than not served a similar function in the acculturation of white children. *Clara's Heart*, starring Whoopi Goldberg, provides an unusually stark illustration of the process whereby the young white male achieves maturity through penetrating the mystery of the black woman—'her wisdom, her warmth, her secret,' as the poster proclaims. That (returning to the metaphor of the dark continent) we are dealing here almost literally with the 'heart of darkness' is suggested by Clara's last name, which *is* 'Heart'—an organ that turns out to be a euphemism for a more libidinally cathected body part.

For Clara's secret, which her young charge David, suffering from neglect at the hands of his narcissistic parents, attempts to discover, is that she has been raped by her own son. The horror, the horror, indeed. The black male thus literalizes the psychic reality of the bourgeois male, for the rape is in fact the logical result of the *white* boy's—and the narrative's—probing. At one point, for example,

David sits at Clara's knee and begins slowly and sensually to feel her leg, moving inexorably upward until Clara screams at him—an 'overreaction' explained when we learn of the son's rape. Moreover, David not only continually badgers Clara to reveal her story but reads in secret the letters he finds in a suitcase under her bed. Again, Clara reacts furiously, saying he has ruined their friendship, although at other times she says he can never do anything to destroy her affection. The intense aggression aroused by the promise and withholding of unconditional love ultimately finds expression in the revelation of incest and rape—a rape that is enacted by the sexually monstrous black male, who is presumably incapable of sublimating such feelings and thus destined to remain forever a casualty of Oedipus, while the recognition of his own desires in the mirror provided by the black male enables the white boy to rechannel his hostilities and become a man: previously unathletic, we now see him win a swimming championship under the approving eye of his father! Thus the black man comes to serve as as the white male's oedipal scapegoat, and the black woman is positioned, as in so many popular representations (like Spielberg's *The Color Purple*), as sexual victim—not of the white man, of course, the historical record notwithstanding—but of black men, including even their own sons.[22] And black people in general are once again consigned to the level of bestiality.

A more recent, enormously popular film in which Whoopi Goldberg again has a major role shows yet another way the black woman serves the function of embodiment. In *Ghost*, Whoopi Goldberg plays a spiritual medium, Oda Mae Brown, who stands in for the body of the white *male*, Sam, played by Patrick Swayze. Sam has died as a result of a mugging, which turns out to have been engineered by a coworker embezzling funds. When he learns of the plot and of his wife's danger at the hands of the mugger, he seeks out Oda Mae to help him communicate to his wife. After a great deal of mutual mistrust between the wife and Oda Mae, climaxed by a scene in which Oda Mae stands outside the door trying to convince the wife of her 'authenticity,' as it were, she is allowed inside the house, and the wife expresses a great longing to be able to touch her husband one last time. Oda Mae offers up her body up for the purpose, and Sam enters into it. The camera shows a close-up of the black woman's hands as they reach out to take those of the white woman, and then it cuts to a shot not of Oda Mae but of Sam, who in taking over her body has obliterated her presence entirely.

This sequence, in which Goldberg turns *into* a man may be seen as a kind of logical extension of all her comedic roles, for she is always coded in the comedies as more masculine than feminine. For example, there is a scene in *Jumping Jack Flash* in which she dresses up in a sexy evening dress that nearly gets chewed up by a shredding machine, and, as she climbs the stairs to her apartment at the end of the evening, she is heard muttering in anger because the taxi cab driver mistook her for a male transvestite. In *Fatal Beauty*, too, Goldberg's donning of women's clothes is seen to be a form of drag—of black female mimicry of (white) femininity, and when she dresses in such clothes she walks in an exaggeratedly awkward fashion like a man unaccustomed to female accoutrements.

Two important points need to be made here. First, the kind of 'gender trouble' advocated by Judith Butler and others in which gender, anatomy, and perform-ance are at odds with one another does not necessarily result in the subversive effects often claimed for it [. . .]; on the contrary, in certain cases, such as those involving the woman of color who has often been considered, in Bhabha's words, 'not quite' a woman, this kind of 'play' may have extremely conservative implications. Second, when both extremes of the Whoopi Goldberg persona are considered together—those in which she represents the maternal/female body (as in *Clara's Heart*) and those in which she is coded as more or less male—we see that we are not all that far from the situation addressed by Sojourner Truth[23] [. . .] The black woman is seen either as too literally a woman (reduced to her biology and her biological functions) or in crucial ways not really a woman at all.

I must acknowledge, however, although it places me in an uncomfortable position, that I personally find the Goldberg character in the comedies both attractive and empowering (and I know some young white girls who have made Goldberg a kind of cult heroine), and that part of this attraction for me lies in the way she represents a liberating departure from the stifling conventions of femininity. Yet I have to recognize as a white woman the extent to which these images are at least in part the creation of a racist mentality and to acknowledge how such images and my own reaction to them may serve to keep me and black women at odds (although I would also argue strongly that Goldberg's powerful acting allows her frequently to transcend some of the limitations of her material or else to bring out the subversive potential buried within the text).

It is urgent that white women come to understand the ways in which they themselves participate in racist structures not only of patriarchal cinema—as in *Crossing Delancey*—but also of contemporary criticism and theory. In an important article surveying the work of white women newly addressing issues of race, Valerie Smith points out that some white feminist theorists may be participating in an old tradition of forcing the black woman to serve the function of embodiment:

> [It] is striking that at precisely the moment when Anglo-American feminists and male Afro-Americanists begin to reconsider the material ground of their enterprise, they demonstrate their return to earth, as it were, by invoking the specific experiences of black women and the writings of black women. This association of black women with reembo-diment resembles rather closely the association, in classic Western philosophy and in nineteenth-century cultural constructions of woman-hood, of women of color with the body and therefore with animal passions and slave labor.[24]

What Smith's remarks clearly suggest is the black woman's need to refuse to function as either the man's *or* the white woman's bodily scapegoat, just as some white women are refusing any longer to function this way in male discourse.

I would like to end, however, with a fantasy, which involves reading the scene

I have discussed in *Ghost* against the grain. This may be a fantasy that for many reasons black women will not fully share, since it points in a utopian direction and wishes away some of the contradictions I have been analyzing. Without for a moment *forgetting* these contradictions, without denying the force of Hazel Carby's observation that feminist criticism (to say nothing of a 'woman's film' like *Crossing Delancey*) has too often ignored 'the hierarchical structuring of the relations between black and white women and often takes the concerns of middle-class, articulate white women as the norm,' I nevertheless want to point to an alternative to the dominant fantasy expressed in *Ghost*.[25] If in the film the black woman exists solely to facilitate the white heterosexual romance, there is a sense in which we can shift our focus to read the white male as, precisely, the obstacle to the union of the two women, a union tentatively suggested in the image of the black and white hands as they reach toward one another. I like to think that despite the disturbing contradictions I have pointed out in this chapter, a time will come when we eliminate the locked door (to recall an image from *Ghost*) that separates women (a door, as we see in the film, easily penetrated by the white man), a time when we may join together to overthrow the ideology that, after all, primarily serves the interests of white heterosexual masculinity and is *ultimately* responsible for the persecutions suffered by people on account of their race, class, and gender. But since it is white women who in many cases have locked the door, it is their responsibility to open it up.

NOTES

1. See the discussion of the film in Patricia Erens, *The Jew in American Cinema* (Bloomington: Indiana University Press, 1984), pp. 101–6.
2. Homi K. Bhabha, 'Of Mimicry and Man: The Ambivalence of Colonial Discourse,' *October* 28 (Spring 1984): 131. Other texts by Bhabha that I draw on here include: 'The Other Question: Difference, Discrimination and the Discourse of Colonialism,' in *Literature, Politics and Theory: Papers from the Essex Conference 1976–84*, ed. Francis Barker, Peter Hulme, Margaret Iversen, and Diana Loxley (London: Methuen, 1986), pp. 148–72; 'The Commitment to Theory,' *New Formations* 5 (Summer 1988): 5–24; 'Signs Taken for Wonders: Questions of Ambivalence and Authority under a Tree Outside Delhi, May 1817,' in *'Race,' Writing, and Difference*, ed., Henry Louis Gates, Jr. (Chicago: University of Chicago Press, 1985), pp. 163–84.
3. Thomas Cripps, *Slow Fade to Black: The Negro in American Film, 1900–1942* (New York: Oxford University Press, 1977), p. 37.
4. Bhabha, 'Of Mimicry and Man,' p. 132. For other articles discussing the ambivalent nature of minstrelsy, see Sylvia Wynter, 'Sambos and Minstrels,' *Social Text* 1 (1979): 149–56; and Susan Willis 'I Shop Therefore I Am: Is There a Place for Afro-American Culture in American Commodity Culture,' in *Changing Our Own Words: Essays on Criticism, Theory, and Writing by Black Women*, ed. Cheryl Wall (New Brunswick, N.J.: Rutgers University Press, 1989), pp. 173–95.
5. Ibid., p. 128.
6. See Luce Irigaray, *Speculum of the Other Woman*, trans. Gillian C. Gill (Ithaca, N.Y.: Cornell University Press, 1985).
7. Bhabha, 'The Other Question,' p. 179.
8. Ibid., p. 170.
9. Cripps, *Slow Fade to Black*, p. 155.

10. X. J. Kennedy, 'Who Killed King Kong?,' in *Focus on the Horror Film*, ed. Roy Huss and T. J. Ross (Englewood Cliffs, N. J.: Prentice Hall, 1972), p. 109.

11. See René Girard, *Deceit, Desire, and the Novel: Self and Other in Literary Structure*, trans. Yvonne Freccero (Baltimore, Md.: Johns Hopkins University Press, 1972), and Eve Kosofsky Sedgwick's discussion of Girard's work in terms of 'homosocial desire,' in her *Between Men: English Literature and Male Homosocial Desire* (New York: Columbia University Press, 1985), pp. 21–5.

12. Henry Louis Gates, *The Signifying Monkey: A Theory of Afro-American Literary Criticism* (New York: Oxford University Press, 1988), pp. 108–9.

13. Laura Mulvey, 'Visual Pleasure and Narrative Cinema,' *Screen* 16, no. 3 (Autumn 1975): 6–18.

14. For examples, see Patricia Mellencamp, 'Made in the Fade,' *Ciné-Tracts* 3, no. 3 (Fall 1980): 13; Bill Nichols, *Ideology and the Image* (Bloomington: Indiana University Press, 1981), pp. 104–32; and E. Ann Kaplan, *Women and Film: Both Sides of the Camera* (New York and London: Methuen, 1983, pp. 49–59.

15. Lea Jacobs, 'The Censorship of *Blonde Venus*: Textual Analysis and Historical Methods,' *Cinema Journal* 27, no. 3 (Spring 1988): 21–31.

16. For a controversial discussion of race, gender and spectacle, see Sander L. Gilman, 'The Hottentot and the Prostitute: Toward an Iconography of Female Sexuality,' in *Difference and Pathology: Stereotypes of Sexuality, Race, and Madness* (Ithaca, N. Y.: Cornell University Press, 1985), pp. 76–108.

17. Isaac Julien and Kobena Mercer, 'De Margin and De centre,' *Screen* 29, no. 4 (Autumn 1988): 5.

18. Claire Johnston, 'Women's Cinema as Counter-Cinema,' in *Sexual Strategems: The World of Women in Film*, ed. Patricia Erens (New York: Horizon Press, 1979), p. 136.

19. ' "When the direction of the force acting on the body is changed": The Moving Image,' in Mary Ann Doane, *Femmes Fatales: Feminism, Film Theory, Psycho-analysis* (London: Routledge, 1991) pp. 188–206.

20. For a discussion of the complex relations between racism and anti-Semitism, see Elly Bulkin, Minnie Bruce Pratt, and Barbara Smith, *Yours in Struggle: Three Feminist Perspectives on Anti-Semitism and Racism* (New York: Long Haul Press, 1984).

21. For an interesting discussion of this, see Peter Stallybrass and Allon White, 'Below Stairs: the Maid and the Family Romance,' in their *The Politics and Poetics of Transgression* (Ithaca, N. Y.: Cornell University Press, 1986), pp. 149–70.

22. Jane Gaines, 'White Privilege and Looking Relations—Race and Gender in Feminist Film Theory,' *Screen* 29, no. 4 (Autumn 1988): 12–27. In this article, which has a strong ideological axe to grind, since Gaines is attacking psychoanalytic film theory, Gaines tries to prove that psychoanalysis cannot be of use in discussing the issue of race. I hope I have shown that this is not necessarily the case, even though people who have *used* psychoanalysis may be racially biased: such bias is hardly sufficient to discredit the entire discipline.

23. Sojourner Truth's speech 'A'n't I a woman' is reprinted in Beverly Guy-Sheftall (ed.), *Words of Fire* (New York: The New Press, 1995) pp. 35–8. For further discussion of this speech, see T. Modleski, 'Postmortem on Postfeminism,' in *Feminism without Women* (New York and London: Routledge, 1991) pp. 3–22.

24. Valerie Smith, 'Black Feminist Theory and the Representation of the "Other",' in *Changing Our Own Words: Essays on Criticism, Theory, and Writing by Black Women*, ed. Cheryl A. Wall (New Brunswick, N. J.: Rutgers University Press, 1989), p. 45.

25. Hazel Carby, *Reconstructing Womanhood: The Emergence of the Afro-American Woman Novelist* (New York: Oxford University Press, 1987), p. 17.

23

'GENDER IS BURNING: QUESTIONS OF APPROPRIATION AND SUBVERSION'

Judith Butler

We all have friends who, when they knock on the door and we ask, through the door, the question, 'Who's there?,' answer (since 'it's obvious') 'It's me.' And we recognize that *'it is him,' or 'her'* [my emphasis].
    – Louis Althusser, 'Ideology and Ideological State Apparatuses'

The purpose of 'law' is absolutely the last thing to employ in the history of the origin of law: on the contrary, . . . the cause of the origin of a thing and its eventual utility, its actual employment and place in a system of purposes, lie worlds apart; whatever exists, having somehow come into being, is again and again reinterpreted to new ends, taken over, transformed, and redirected.
    – Friedrich Nietzsche, *On the Genealogy of Morals*

In Althusser's notion of interpellation, it is the police who initiate the call or address by which a subject becomes socially constituted. There is the policeman, the one who not only represents the law but whose address 'Hey you!' has the effect of binding the law to the one who is hailed. This 'one' who appears not to be in a condition of trespass prior to the call (for whom the call establishes a given practice as a trespass) is not fully a social subject, is not fully subjectivated, for he or she is not yet reprimanded. The reprimand does not merely repress or control the subject, but forms a crucial part of the juridical and social *formation* of the subject. The call is formative, if not *performative*,

* From Butler, J., *Bodies that Matter: On the Discursive Limits of 'Sex'*. London: Routledge, 1993, pp. 121–40.

precisely because it initiates the individual into the subjected status of the subject.

Althusser conjectures this 'hailing' or 'interpellation' as a unilateral act, as the power and force of the law to compel fear at the same time that it offers recognition at an expense. In the reprimand the subject not only receives recognition, but attains as well a certain order of social existence, in being transferred from an outer region of indifferent, questionable, or impossible being to the discursive or social domain of the subject. But does this subjectivation take place as a direct effect of the reprimanding utterance or must the utterance wield the power to compel the fear of punishment and, from that compulsion, to produce a compliance and obedience to the law? Are there other ways of being addressed and constituted by the law, ways of being occupied and occupying the law, that disarticulate the power of punishment from the power of recognition?

Althusser underscores the Lacanian contribution to a structural analysis of this kind, and argues that a relation of misrecognition persists between the law and the subject it compels.[1] Although he refers to the possibility of 'bad subjects,' he does not consider the range of *disobedience* that such an interpellating law might produce. The law might not only be refused, but it might also be ruptured, forced into a rearticulation that calls into question the monotheistic force of its own unilateral operation. Where the uniformity of the subject is expected, where the behavioral conformity of the subject is commanded, there might be produced the refusal of the law in the form of the parodic inhabiting of conformity that subtly calls into question the legitimacy of the command, a repetition of the law into hyperbole, a rearticulation of the law against the authority of the one who delivers it. Here the performative, the call by the law which seeks to produce a lawful subject, produces a set of consequences that exceed and confound what appears to be the disciplining intention motivating the law. Interpellation thus loses its status as a simple performative, an act of discourse with the power to create that to which it refers, and creates more than it ever meant to, signifying in excess of any intended referent.

It is this constitutive failure of the performative, this slippage between discursive command and its appropriated effect, which provides the linguistic occasion and index for a consequential disobedience [...]

It is in this sense that Irigaray's critical mime of Plato, the fiction of the lesbian phallus, and the rearticulation of kinship in *Paris Is Burning* might be understood as repetitions of hegemonic forms of power which fail to repeat loyally and, in that failure, open possibilities for resignifying the terms of violation against their violating aims. Cather's occupation of the paternal name, Larsen's inquiry into the painful and fatal mime that is passing for white, and the reworking of 'queer' from abjection to politicized affiliation will interrogate similar sites of ambivalence produced at the limits of discursive legitimacy.

The temporal structure of such a subject is chiasmic in this sense: in the place

337

of a substantial or self-determining 'subject,' this juncture of discursive demands is something like a 'crossroads,' to use Gloria Anzaldúa's phrase, a crossroads of cultural and political discursive forces, which she herself claims cannot be understood through the notion of the 'subject.'[2] There is no subject prior to its constructions, and neither is the subject determined by those constructions; it is always the nexus, the non-space of cultural collision, in which the demand to resignify or repeat the very terms which constitute the 'we' cannot be summarily refused, but neither can they be followed in strict obedience. It is the space of this ambivalence which opens up the possibility of a reworking of the very terms by which subjectivation proceeds—and fails to proceed.

AMBIVALENT DRAG

From this formulation, then, I would like to move to a consideration of the film *Paris Is Burning*, to what it suggests about the simultaneous production and subjugation of subjects in a culture which appears to arrange always and in every way for the annihilation of queers, but which nevertheless produces occasional spaces in which those annihilating norms, those killing ideals of gender and race, are mimed, reworked, resignified. As much as there is defiance and affirmation, the creation of kinship and of glory in that film, there is also the kind of reiteration of norms which cannot be called subversive, but which lead to the death of Venus Xtravaganza, a Latina/preoperative transsexual, cross-dresser, prostitute, and member of the 'House of Xtravanganza.' To what set of interpellating calls does Venus respond, and how is the reiteration of the law to be read in the manner of her response?

Venus, and *Paris Is Burning* more generally, calls into question whether parodying the dominant norms is enough to displace them; indeed, whether the denaturalization of gender cannot be the very vehicle for a reconsolidation of hegemonic norms. Although many readers understood *Gender Trouble* to be arguing for the proliferation of drag performances as a way of subverting dominant gender norms, I want to underscore that there is no necessary relation between drag and subversion, and that drag may well be used in the service of both the denaturalization and reidealization of hyperbolic heterosexual gender norms. At best, it seems, drag is a site of a certain ambivalence, one which reflects the more general situation of being implicated in the regimes of power by which one is constituted and, hence, of being implicated in the very regimes of power that one opposes.

To claim that all gender is like drag, or is drag, is to suggest that 'imitation' is at the heart of the *heterosexual* project and its gender binarisms, that drag is not a secondary imitation that presupposes a prior and original gender, but that hegemonic heterosexuality is itself a constant and repeated effort to imitate its own idealizations. That it must repeat this imitation, that it sets up pathologizing practices and normalizing sciences in order to produce and consecrate its own claim on originality and propriety, suggests that heterosexual performativity is beset by an anxiety that it can never be finally or fully achieved, and that it is consistently haunted by that domain of sexual possibility that must be excluded for heterosexualized gender to produce itself. In this sense, then, drag is subversive to the extent that it reflects on the imitative structure by which hegemonic gender is itself produced and disputes heterosexuality's claim on naturalness and originality.

But here it seems that I am obliged to add an important qualification: heterosexual privilege operates in many ways, and two ways in which it operates include naturalizing itself and rendering itself as the original and the norm. But these are not the only ways in which it works, for it is clear that there are domains in which heterosexuality can concede its lack of originality and naturalness but still hold on to its power. Thus, there are forms of drag that heterosexual culture produces for itself—we might think of Julie Andrews in *Victor, Victoria* or Dustin Hoffmann in *Tootsie* or Jack Lemmon in *Some Like It Hot* where the anxiety over a possible homosexual consequence is both produced and deflected within the narrative trajectory of the films. These are films which produce and contain the homosexual excess of any given drag performance, the fear that an apparently heterosexual contact might be made before the discovery of a nonapparent homosexuality. This is drag as high het entertainment, and though these films are surely important to read as cultural texts in which homophobia and homosexual panic are negotiated,[3] I would be reticent to call them subversive. Indeed, one might argue that such films are functional in providing a ritualistic release for a heterosexual economy that must constantly police its own boundaries against the invasion of queerness, and that this displaced production and resolution of homosexual panic actually fortifies the heterosexual regime in its self-perpetuating task.

In her provocative review of *Paris Is Burning*, bell hooks criticized some productions of gay male drag as misogynist, and here she allied herself in part with feminist theorists such as Marilyn Frye and Janice Raymond.[4] This tradition within feminist thought has argued that drag is offensive to women and that it is an imitation based in ridicule and degradation. Raymond, in particular, places drag on a continuum with cross-dressing and transsexualism, ignoring the important differences between them, maintaining that in each practice women are the object of hatred and appropriation, and that there is nothing in the identification that is respectful or elevating. As a rejoinder, one might consider that identification is always an ambivalent process. Identifying with a gender under contemporary regimes of power involves identifying with a set of norms that are and are not realizable, and whose power and status precede the identifications by which they are insistently approximated. This 'being a man' and this 'being a woman' are internally unstable affairs. They are always beset by ambivalence precisely because there is a cost in every identification, the loss of some other set of identifications, the forcible approximation of a norm one never chooses, a norm that chooses us, but which we occupy, reverse, resignify to the extent that the norm fails to determine us completely.

The problem with the analysis of drag as only misogyny is, of course, that it figures male-to-female transsexuality, cross-dressing, and drag as male homo-sexual activities—which they are not always—and it further diagnoses male homosexuality as rooted in misogyny. The feminist analysis thus makes male homosexuality *about* women, and one might argue that at its extreme, this kind of analysis is in fact a colonization in reverse, a way for feminist women to make themselves into the center of male homosexual activity (and thus to reinscribe the heterosexual matrix, paradoxically, at the heart of the radical feminist position). Such an accusation follows the same kind of logic as those homophobic remarks that often follow upon the discovery that one is a lesbian: a lesbian is one who must have had a bad experience with men, or who has not yet found the right one. These diagnoses presume that lesbianism is acquired by virtue of some failure in the heterosexual machinery, thereby continuing to install heterosexuality as the 'cause' of lesbian desire; lesbian desire is figured as the fatal effect of a derailed heterosexual causality. In this framework, hetero-sexual desire is always true, and lesbian desire is always and only a mask and forever false. In the radical feminist argument against drag, the displacement of women is figured as the aim and effect of male-to-female drag; in the homo-phobic dismissal of lesbian desire, the disappointment with and displacement of men is understood as the cause and final truth of lesbian desire. According to these views, drag is nothing but the displacement and appropriation of 'women,' and hence fundamentally based in a misogyny, a hatred of women; and lesbianism is nothing but the displacement and appropriation of men, and so fundamentally a matter of hating men—misandry.

These explanations of displacement can only proceed by accomplishing yet another set of displacements: of desire, of phantasmatic pleasures, and of forms of love that are not reducible to a heterosexual matrix and the logic of repudiation. Indeed, the only place love is to be found is *for* the ostensibly repudiated object, where love is understood to be strictly produced through a logic of repudiation; hence, drag is nothing but the effect of a love embittered by disappointment or rejection, the incorporation of the Other whom one originally desired, but now hates. And lesbianism is nothing other than the effect of a love embittered by disappointment or rejection, and of a recoil from that love, a defense against it or, in the case of butchness, the appropriation of the masculine position that one originally loved.

This logic of repudiation installs heterosexual love as the origin and truth of both drag and lesbianism, and it interprets both practices as symptoms of thwarted love. But what is displaced in this explanation of displacement is the notion that there might be pleasure, desire, and love that is not solely determined by what it repudiates.[5] Now it may seem at first that the way to oppose these reductions and degradations of queer practices is to assert their radical specificity, to claim that there is a lesbian desire radically different from a heterosexual one, with *no* relation to it, that is neither the repudiation nor the appropriation of heterosexuality, and that has radically other origins than those which sustain heterosexuality. Or one might be tempted to argue that drag is not related to the ridicule or degradation or appropriation of women: when it is men in drag as women, what we have is the destabilization of gender itself, a destabilization that is denaturalizing and that calls into question the claims of normativity and originality by which gender and sexual oppression sometimes operate. But what if the situation is neither exclusively one nor the other; certainly, some lesbians have wanted to retain the notion that their sexual practice is rooted in part in a repudiation of heterosexuality, but also to claim that this repudiation does not account for lesbian desire, and cannot therefore be identified as the hidden or original 'truth' of lesbian desire. And the case of drag is difficult in yet another way, for it seems clear to me that there is both a sense of defeat and a sense of insurrection to be had from the drag pageantry in *Paris Is Burning*, that the drag we see, the drag which is after all framed for us, filmed for us, is one which both appropriates and subverts racist, misogynist, and homophobic norms of oppression. How are we to account for this ambivalence? This is not first an appropriation and then a subversion. Sometimes it is both at once; sometimes it remains caught in an irresolvable tension, and sometimes a fatally unsubversive appropriation takes place.

Paris Is Burning (1991) is a film produced and directed by Jennie Livingston about drag balls in New York City, in Harlem, attended by, performed by 'men' who are either African-American or Latino. The balls are contests in which the contestants compete under a variety of categories. The categories include a variety of social norms, many of which are established in white culture as signs of class, like that of the 'executive' and the Ivy League student; some of which are marked as feminine, ranging from high drag to butch queen; and some of them, like that of the 'bangie,' are taken from straight black masculine street culture. Not all of the categories, then, are taken from white culture; some of them are replications of a straightness which is not white, and some of them are focused on class, especially those which almost require that expensive women's clothing be 'mopped' or stolen for the occasion. The competition in military garb shifts to yet another register of legitimacy, which enacts the performative and gestural conformity to a masculinity which parallels the performative or reiterative production of femininity in other categories. 'Realness' is not exactly a category in which one competes; it is a standard that is used to judge any given performance within the established categories. And yet what determines the effect of realness is the ability to compel belief, to produce the naturalized effect. This effect is itself the result of an embodiment of norms, a reiteration of norms, an impersonation of a racial and class norm, a norm which is at once a figure, a figure of a body, which is no particular body, but a morphological ideal that remains the standard which regulates the performance, but which no performance fully approximates.

Significantly, this is a performance that works, that effects realness, to the extent that it *cannot* be read. For 'reading' means taking someone down, exposing what fails to work at the level of appearance, insulting or deriding someone. For a performance to work, then, means that a reading is no longer possible, or that a reading, an interpretation, appears to be a kind of transparent seeing, where what appears and what it means coincide. On the contrary, when what appears and how it is 'read' diverge, the artifice of the performance can be read as artifice; the ideal splits off from its appropriation. But the impossibility of reading means that the artifice works, the approximation of realness appears to be achieved, the body performing and the ideal performed appear indistinguishable.

But what is the status of this ideal? Of what is it composed? What reading does the film encourage, and what does the film conceal? Does the denaturalization of the norm succeed in subverting the norm, or is this a denaturalization in the service of a perpetual reidealization, one that can only oppress, even as, or precisely when, it is embodied most effectively? Consider the different fates of Venus Xtravaganza. She 'passes' as a light-skinned woman, but is—by virtue of a certain failure to pass completely—clearly vulnerable to homophobic violence; ultimately, her life is taken presumably by a client who, upon the discovery of what she calls her 'little secret,' mutilates her for having seduced him. On the other hand, Willi Ninja can pass as straight; his voguing becomes foregrounded in het video productions with Madonna et al., and he achieves post-legendary status on an international scale. There is passing and then there is passing, and it is—as we used to say—'no accident' that Willi Ninja ascends and Venus Xtravaganza dies.

Now Venus, Venus Xtravaganza, she seeks a certain transubstantiation of gender in order to find an imaginary man who will designate a class and race privilege that promises a permanent shelter from racism, homophobia, and poverty. And it would not be enough to claim that for Venus gender is *marked by* race and class, for gender is not the substance or primary substrate and race and class the qualifying attributes. In this instance, gender is the vehicle for the phantasmatic transformation of that nexus of race and class, the site of its articulation. Indeed, in *Paris Is Burning*, becoming real, becoming a real woman, although not everyone's desire (some children want merely to 'do' realness, and that, only within the confines of the ball), constitutes the site of the phantasmatic promise of a rescue from poverty, homophobia, and racist delegitimation.

The contest (which we might read as a 'contesting of realness') involves the phantasmatic attempt to approximate realness, but it also exposes the norms that regulate realness as *themselves* phantasmatically instituted and sustained. The rules that regulate and legitimate realness (shall we call them symbolic?) constitute the mechanism by which certain sanctioned fantasies, sanctioned imaginaries, are insidiously elevated as the parameters of realness. We could, within conventional Lacanian parlance, call this the ruling of the symbolic, except that the symbolic assumes the primacy of sexual difference in the constitution of the subject. What *Paris Is Burning* suggests, however, is that the order of sexual difference is not prior to that of race or class in the constitution of the subject; indeed, that the symbolic is also and at once a racializing set of norms, and that norms of realness by which the subject is produced are racially informed conceptions of 'sex' (this underscores the importance of subjecting the entire psychoanalytic paradigm to this insight).[6]

This double movement of approximating and exposing the phantasmatic status of the realness norm, the symbolic norm, is reinforced by the diagetic movement of the film in which clips of so-called 'real' people moving in and out of expensive stores are juxtaposed against the ballroom drag scenes.

In the drag ball productions of realness, we witness and produce the phantasmatic constitution of a subject, a subject who repeats and mimes the legitimating norms by which it itself has been degraded, a subject founded in the project of mastery that compels and disrupts its own repetitions. This is not a subject who stands back from its identifications and decides instrumentally how or whether to work each of them today; on the contrary, the subject is the incoherent and mobilized imbrication of identifications; it is constituted in and through the iterability of its performance, a repetition which works at once to legitimate and delegitimate the realness norms by which it is produced.

In the pursuit of realness this subject is produced, a phantasmatic pursuit that mobilizes identifications, underscoring the phantasmatic promise that constitutes any identificatory move—a promise which, taken too seriously, can culminate only in disappointment and disidentification. A fantasy that for Venus, because she dies—killed apparently by one of her clients, perhaps after the discovery of those remaining organs—cannot be translated into the symbolic. This is a killing that is performed by a symbolic that would eradicate those phenomena that require an opening up of the possibilities for the resignification of sex. If Venus wants to become a woman, and cannot overcome being a Latina, then Venus is treated by the symbolic in precisely the ways in which women of color are treated. Her death thus testifies to a tragic misreading of the social map of power, a misreading orchestrated by that very map according to which the sites for a phantasmatic self-overcoming are constantly resolved into disappointment. If the signifiers of whiteness and femaleness—as well as some forms of hegemonic maleness constructed through class privilege—are sites of phantasmatic promise, then it is clear that women of color and lesbians are not only everywhere excluded from this scene, but constitute a site of identification that is consistently refused and abjected in the collective phantasmatic pursuit of a transubstantiation into various forms of drag, transsexualism, and uncritical miming of the hegemonic. That this fantasy involves becoming in part like women and, for some of the children, becoming like black women, falsely constitutes black women as a site of privilege; they can catch a man and be protected by him, an impossible idealization which of course works to deny the situation of the great numbers of poor black women who are single mothers without the support of men. In this sense, the 'identification' is composed of a denial, an envy, which is the envy of a phantasm of black women, an idealization that produces a denial. On the other hand, insofar as black men who are queer can become feminized by hegemonic straight culture, there is in the performative dimension of the ball a significant *reworking* of that feminization, an occupation of the identification that is, as it were, *already* made between faggots and women, the feminization of the faggot, the feminization of the black faggot, which is the black feminization of the faggot.

The performance is thus a kind of talking back, one that remains largely constrained by the terms of the original assailment: If a white homophobic hegemony considers the black drag ball queen to be a woman, that woman, constituted already by that hegemony, will become the occasion for the rearticulation of its terms; embodying the excess of that production, the queen will out-woman women, and in the process confuse and seduce an audience whose gaze must to some degree be structured through those hegemonies, an audience who, through the hyperbolic staging of the scene, will be drawn into the abjection it wants both to resist and to overcome. The phantasmatic excess of this production constitutes the site of women not only as marketable goods within an erotic economy of exchange,[7] but as goods which, as it were, are also privileged consumers with access to wealth and social privilege and protection. This is a full-scale phantasmatic transfiguration not only of the plight of poor black and Latino gay men, but of poor black women and Latinas, who are the figures for the abjection that the drag ball scene elevates as a site of idealized identification. It would, I think, be too simple to reduce this identificatory move to black male misogyny, as if that were a discrete typology, for the feminization of the poor black man and, most trenchantly, of the poor, black, gay man, is a strategy of abjection that is already underway, originating in the complex of racist, homophobic, misogynist, and classist constructions that belong to larger hegemonies of oppression.

These hegemonies operate, as Gramsci insisted, through *rearticulation*, but here is where the accumulated force of a historically entrenched and entrenching rearticulation overwhelms the more fragile effort to build an alternative cultural configuration from or against that more powerful regime. Importantly, however, that prior hegemony also works through and as its 'resistance' so that the relation between the marginalized community and the dominative is not, strictly speaking, oppositional. The citing of the dominant norm does not, in this instance, displace that norm; rather, it becomes the means by which that dominant norm is most painfully reiterated as the very desire and the performance of those it subjects.

Clearly, the denaturalization of sex, in its multiple senses, does not imply a liberation from hegemonic constraint: when Venus speaks her desire to become a whole woman, to find a man and have a house in the suburbs with a washing machine, we may well question whether the denaturalization of gender and sexuality that she performs, and performs well, culminates in a reworking of the normative framework of heterosexuality. The painfulness of her death at the end of the film suggests as well that there are cruel and fatal social constraints on denaturalization. As much as she crosses gender, sexuality, and race performatively, the hegemony that reinscribes the privileges of normative feminity and whiteness wields the final power to *renaturalize* Venus's body and cross out that prior crossing, an erasure that is her death. Of course, the film brings Venus back, as it were, into visibility, although not to life, and thus constitutes a kind of cinematic performativity. Paradoxically, the film brings fame and recognition not only to Venus but also to the other drag ball children who are depicted in the film as able only to attain local legendary status while longing for wider recognition.

The camera, of course, plays precisely to this desire, and so is implicitly installed in the film as the promise of legendary status. And yet, is there a filmic effort to take stock of the place of the camera in the trajectory of desire that it not only records, but also incites? In her critical review of the film, bell hooks raises the question not only of the place of the camera, but also that of the filmmaker, Jennie Livingston, a white lesbian (in other contexts called 'a white Jewish lesbian from Yale,' an interpellation which also implicates this author in its sweep), in relation to the drag ball community that she entered and filmed. hooks remarks that,

> Jennie Livingston approaches her subject matter as an outsider looking in. Since her presence as white woman/lesbian filmmaker is 'absent' from *Paris Is Burning*, it is easy for viewers to imagine that they are watching an ethnographic film documenting the life of black gay 'natives' and not recognize that they are watching a work shaped and formed from a perspective and standpoint specific to Livingston. By cinematically masking this reality (we hear her ask questions but never see her) Livingston does not oppose the way hegemonic whiteness 'represents' blackness, but rather assumes an imperial overseeing position that is in no way progressive or counterhegemonic.

Later in the same essay, hooks raises the question of not merely whether or not the cultural location of the filmmaker is absent from the film, but whether this absence operates to form tacitly the focus and effect of the film, exploiting the colonialist trope of an 'innocent' ethnographic gaze: 'Too many critics and interviewers,' hooks argues, '. . . act as though she somehow did this marginalized black gay subculture a favor by bringing their experience to a wider public. Such a stance obscures the substantial rewards she has received for this work. Since so many of the black gay men in the film express the desire to be big stars, it is easy to place Livingston in the role of benefactor, offering these "poor black souls" a way to realize their dreams' (63).

Although hooks restricts her remarks to black men in the film, most of the members of the House of Xtravaganza, who are Latino, some of whom are light-skinned, some of whom engage in crossing and passing, some of who only do the ball, some who are engaged in life projects to effect a full transubstantiation into femininity and/or into whiteness. The 'houses' are organized in part along ethnic lines. This seems crucial to underscore precisely because neither Livingston nor hooks considers the place and force of ethnicity in the articulation of kinship relations.

To the extent that a transubstantiation into legendary status, into an idealized domain of gender and race, structures the phantasmatic trajectory of the drag ball culture, Livingston's camera enters this world as the promise of phantasmatic fulfillment: a wider audience, national and international fame. If Livingston is the white girl with the camera, she is both the object and vehicle of desire; and yet, as a lesbian, she apparently maintains some kind of identificatory bond with the gay men in the film and also, it seems, with the kinship system, replete with 'houses,' 'mothers,' and 'children,' that sustains the drag ball scene and is itself organized by it. The one instance where Livingston's body might be said to appear allegorically on camera is when Octavia St Laurent is posing for the camera, as a moving model would for a photographer. We hear a voice tell her that she's terrific, and it is unclear whether it is a man shooting the film as a proxy for Livingston, or Livingston herself. What is suggested by this sudden intrusion of the camera into the film is something of the camera's desire, the desire that motivates the camera, in which a white lesbian phallically organized by the use of the camera (elevated to the status of disembodied gaze, holding out the promise of erotic recognition) eroticizes a black male-to-female transsexual—presumably preoperative—who 'works' perceptually as a woman.

What would it mean to say that Octavia is Jennie Livingston's kind of girl? Is the category or, indeed, 'the position' of white lesbian disrupted by such a claim? If this is the production of the black transsexual for an exoticizing white gaze, is it not also the transsexualization of lesbian desire? Livingston incites Octavia to become a woman for Livingston's own camera and Livingston thereby assumes the power of 'having the phallus,' i.e., the ability to confer that femininity, to anoint Octavia as model woman. But to the extent that Octavia receives and is produced by that recognition, the camera itself is empowered as phallic instrument. Moreover, the camera acts as surgical instrument and operation, the vehicle through which the transubstantiation occurs. Livingston thus becomes the one with the power to turn men into women who, then, depend on the power of her gaze to become and remain women. Having asked about the transsexualization of lesbian desire, then, it follows that we might ask more particularly: what is the status of the desire to feminize black and Latino men that the film enacts? Does this not serve the purpose, among others, of a visual pacification of subjects by whom white women are imagined to be socially endangered?

Does the camera promise a transubstantiation of sorts? Is it the token of that promise to deliver economic privilege and the transcendence of social abjection? What does it mean to eroticize the holding out of that promise, as hooks asks, when the film will do well, but the lives that they record will remain substantially unaltered? And if the camera is the vehicle for that transubstantiation, what is the power assumed by the one who wields the camera, drawing on that desire and exploiting it? Is this not its own fantasy, one in which the filmmaker wields the power to transform what she records? And is this fantasy of the camera's power not directly counter to the ethnographic conceit that structures the film?

hooks is right to argue that within this culture the ethnographic conceit of a neutral gaze will always be a white gaze, an unmarked white gaze, one which passes its own perspective off as the omniscient, one which presumes upon and enacts its own perspective as if it were no perspective at all. But what does it mean to think about this camera as an instrument and effect of lesbian desire? I would have liked to have seen the question of Livingston's cinematic desire reflexively thematized in the film itself, her intrusions into the frame as 'intrusions,' the camera *implicated* in the trajectory of desire that it seems compelled to incite. To the extent that the camera figures tacitly as the instrument of transubstantiation, it assumes the place of the phallus, as that which controls the field of signification. The camera thus trades on the masculine privilege of the disembodied gaze, the gaze that has the power to produce bodies, but which is itself no body.

But is this cinematic gaze only white and phallic, or is there in this film a decentered place for the camera as well? hooks points to two competing narrative trajectories in the film, one that focuses on the pageantry of the balls and another that focuses on the lives of the participants. She argues that the spectacle of the pageantry arrives to quell the portraits of suffering that these men relate about their lives outside the ball. And in her rendition, the pageantry represents a life of pleasurable fantasy, and the lives outside the drag ball are the painful 'reality' that the pageantry seeks phantasmatically to overcome. hooks claims that 'at no point in Livingston's film are the men asked to speak about their connections to a world of family and community beyond the drag ball. The cinematic narrative makes the ball the center of their lives. And yet who determines this? Is this the way the black men view their reality or is this the reality that Livingston constructs?'

Clearly, this *is* the way that Livingston constructs their 'reality,' and the insights into their lives that we do get are still tied in to the ball. We hear about the ways in which the various houses prepare for the ball, we see 'mopping;' and we see the differences among those who walk in the ball as men, those who do drag inside the parameters of the ball, those who cross-dress all the time in the ball and on the street and, among the cross-dressers, those who resist transsexuality, and those who are transsexual in varying degrees. What becomes clear in the enumeration of the kinship system that surrounds the ball is not only that the 'houses' and the 'mothers' and the 'children' sustain the ball, but that the ball is itself an occasion for the building of a set of kinship relations that manage and sustain those who belong to the houses in the face of dislocation, poverty, homelessness. These men 'mother' one another, 'house' one another, 'rear' one another, and the resignification of the family through these terms is not a vain or useless imitation, but the social and discursive building of community, a community that binds, cares, and teaches, that shelters and enables. This is doubtless a cultural reelaboration of kinship that anyone outside of the privilege of heterosexual family (and those within those 'privileges' who suffer there) needs to see, to know, and to learn from, a task that makes none of us who are outside of heterosexual 'family' into absolute outsiders to this film. Significantly, it is in the elaboration of kinship forged through a resignification of the very terms which effect our exclusion and abjection that such a resignification creates the discursive and social space for community, that we see an appropriation of the terms of domination that turns them toward a more enabling future.

In these senses, then, *Paris Is Burning* documents neither an efficacious insurrection nor a painful resubordination, but an unstable coexistence of both. The film attests to the painful pleasures of eroticizing and miming the very norms that wield their power by foreclosing the very reverse-occupations that the children nevertheless perform.

This is not an appropriation of dominant culture in order to remain subordinated by its terms, but an appropriation that seeks to make over the terms of domination, a making over which is itself a kind of agency, a power in and as discourse, in and as performance, which repeats in order to remake—and sometimes succeeds. But this is a film that cannot achieve this effect without implicating its spectators in the act; to watch this film means to enter into a logic of fetishization which installs the ambivalence of that 'performance' as related to our own. If the ethnographic conceit allows the performance to become an exotic fetish, one from which the audience absents itself, the commodification of heterosexual gender ideals will be, in that instance, complete. But if the film establishes the ambivalence of embodying—and failing to embody—that which one sees, then a distance will be opened up *between* that hegemonic call to normativizing gender and its critical appropriation.

NOTES

1. Louis Althusser, 'Ideology and Ideological State Apparatuses,' pp. 170–7; see also 'Freud and Lacan,' pp. 189–220 in *Lenin and Philosophy and Other Essays* (New York: Monthly Review Press, 1971).
2. Gloria Anzaldúa writes, 'that focal point or fulcrum, that juncture where the mestiza stands, is where phenomena tend to collide' (p. 79) and, later, 'the work of *mestiza* consciousness is to break down the subject-object duality that keeps her a prisoner,' 'La conciencia de la mestiza,' *Borderlands/La Frontera*, (San Francisco: Spinsters, Aunt Lute, 1987), p. 80.
3. See Marjorie Garber, *Vested Interests: Cross-Dressing and Cultural Anxiety* (New York: Routledge, 1992), p. 40.
4. bell hooks, 'Is Paris Burning?' Z, Sisters of the Yam column (June 1991): p. 61.
5. Whereas I accept the psychoanalytic formulation that both the object and aim of love are formed *in part* by those objects and aims that are repudiated, I consider it a cynical and homophobic use of that insight to claim that homosexuality is nothing other than repudiated heterosexuality. Given the culturally repudiated status of homosexuality as a form of love, the argument that seeks to reduce homosexuality to the inversion or deflection of heterosexuality functions to reconsolidate heterosexual hegemony. This is also why the analysis of homosexual melancholy cannot be

regarded as symmetrical to the analysis of heterosexual melancholy. The latter is culturally enforced in a way that the former clearly is not, except within separatist communities which cannot wield the same power of prohibition as communities of compulsory heterosexism.

6. Kobena Mercer has offered rich work on this question and its relation to a psychoanalytic notion of 'ambivalence.' See 'Looking for Trouble,' reprinted in Henry Abelove, Michèle Barale, and David M. Halperin, eds, *The Lesbian and Gay Studies Reader* (New York: Routledge, 1993), pp. 350–9. Originally published in *Transition* 51 (1991); 'Skin Head Sex Thing: Racial Difference and the Homoerotic Imaginary' in Bad Object-Choices, ed, *How Do I Look? Queer Film and Video* (Seattle: Bay Press, 1991), pp. 169–210; 'Engendered Species,' *Artforum* vol. 30, no. 10 (Summer 1992): pp. 74–78. See also Bhabha, 'Of Mimicry and Man: The Ambivalence of Colonial Discourse' in *October* 28 (Spring 1984): pp. 125–33.

7. See Linda Singer, *Erotic Welfare: Sexual Theory and Politics in the Age of Epidemic* (New York: Routledge, 1992).

PART VI
FURTHER READING

Bhabha, Homi K. 1983: The Other Question, the Stereotype and Colonial Discourse. In *Screen*, 24, 6, pp. 18–36.

Bobo, Jacqueline 1995: *Black Women as Cultural Readers*. New York: Columbia University Press.

Bobo, Jacqueline and Seiter, Ellen 1991: Black Feminism and Media Criticism. In *Screen* 32, 3, pp. 286–302.

Butler, Judith 1990: *Gender Trouble: Feminism and the Subversion of Identity*. New York and London: Routledge.

Butler, Judith 1991: Imitation and Gender Insubordination. In Fuss, D. (ed.), *Inside/Out: Lesbian Theories, Gay Theories*. New York and London: Routledge, pp. 13–31.

Butler, Judith 1993: *Bodies That Matter: On the Discursive Limits of 'Sex'*. New York and London: Routledge.

Carby, Hazel 1982: White woman listen! Black feminism and the boundaries of sisterhood. In Centre for Contemporary Cultural Studies, *The Empire Strikes Back: Race and Racism in 70s Britain*. London: Hutchinson, pp. 212–35.

Collins, Patricia Hill 1990: *Black Feminist Thought*. New York and London: Routledge.

Cook, Pam and Dodd, Philip (ed.) 1993: *Women and Film: A Sight and Sound Reader*. London: Scarlett Press.

De Lauretis, Teresa 1994: *The Practice of Love: Lesbian Sexuality and Perverse Desire*. Bloomington and Indianapolis: Indiana University Press.

Doane, Mary Ann 1991: Dark Continents: Epistemologies of Racial and Sexual Difference in Psychoanalysis and the Cinema. In *Femmes Fatales: Feminism, Film Theory, Psychoanalysis*. New York and London: Routledge, pp. 209–248.

Dyer, Richard 1997: *White*. London and New York: Routledge.

Fanon, Frantz 1986 (1952): *Black Skin, White Masks*. London: Pluto.

Fischer, Lucy 1989: *Shot/Countershot: Film Tradition and Women's Cinema*. London: Macmillan/BFI.

Fuss, Diana (ed.) 1991: *Inside/Out: Lesbian Theories, Gay Theories*. New York and London: Routledge.

Gever, Martha, Greyson, John and Parmar, Pratibha (eds), *Queer Looks: Perspectives on Lesbian and Gay Film and Video*. New York and London: Routledge.

Gilman, Sander L. 1985: *Difference and Pathology: Stereotypes of Sexuality, Race, and Madness*. Ithaca and London: Cornell University Press.

Grosz, Elizabeth 1995: *Space, Time, and Perversion*. New York and London: Routledge.

Grosz, Elizabeth and Probyn, Elspeth (eds) 1995: *Sexy Bodies: The Strange Carnalities of Feminism*. London and New York: Routledge.

hooks bell 1984: *Feminist Theory: from margin to centre*. Boston, MA.: South End Press.

hooks, bell 1992: *Black Looks: Race and Representation*. London: Turnaround.

Mayne, Judith 1995: A Parallax View of Lesbian Authorship. In Pietropaolo, L. and Testaferri, A. (eds), *Feminisms in the Cinema*. Bloomington and Indianapolis: Indiana University Press, pp. 195–205.

Minh-Ha, Trinh T. 1989: *Woman, Native, Other*. Bloomington and Indianapolis: Indiana University Press.

Modleski, Tania 1991: *Feminism Without Women: Culture and Criticism in a 'Postfeminist' Age*. New York and London: Routledge.

Nicholoson, Linda J. (ed.) 1990: *Feminism/Postmodernism*. New York and London: Routledge.

Pietropaolo, Laura and Testaferri, Ada (ed.) 1995: *Feminisms in the Cinema*. Bloomington and Indianapolis: Indiana University Press.

Shohat, Ella 1991: Gender and the Culture of Empire: Toward a Feminist Ethnography of the Cinema. In *Quarterly Review of Film and Video*, 13 (1–3), pp. 45–84.

Smith, Barbara 1986 (1977): Toward a Black Feminist Criticism. In Showalter, E. (ed.), *The New Feminist Criticism: Essays on Women, Literature, and Theory*. London: Virago, pp. 168–85.

Spivak, Gayatri Chakravorty 1990: *The Post-Colonial Critic: Interviews, Strategies, Dialogues*, Sarah Harasym (ed.). New York and London: Routledge.

Thornham, Sue 1997: Chapters Six and Seven. In *Passionate Detachments: An Introduction to Feminist Film Theory*. London: Arnold, pp. 117–57.

Weiss, Andrea 1991: *Vampires and Violets: Lesbians in the Cinema*. London: Unwin Hyman.

Wilton, Tamsin (ed.) 1995: *Immortal, Invisible: Lesbians and the Moving Image*. London and New York: Routledge.

Young, Lola 1996: *Fear of the Dark: 'Race', Gender and Sexuality in the Cinema*. London and New York: Routledge.

COPYRIGHT ACKNOWLEDGEMENTS

Grateful acknowledgement is made to the following sources for permission to reproduce material in this book previously published elsewhere. Every effort has been made to trace copyright holders, but if any have been inadvertently overlooked the publisher will be pleased to make the necessary arrangement at the first opportunity.

1. Sharon Smith, 'The Image of Women in Film: Some Suggestions for Future Research', from *Women and Film*, No. 1, Berkeley: University of California Press, 1972.
2. Molly Haskell, 'The Woman's Film', from *From Reverence to Rape: the Treatment of Women in the Movies* (second edition), Chicago: University of Chicago Press, 1974; 1987, Molly Haskell, c/o Georges Borchardt, Inc., New York.
3. Claire Johnston, 'Women's Cinema as Counter-Cinema', from *Notes on Women's Cinema* by C. Johnston (ed.), London: Society for Education in Film and Television, 1973.
4. B. Ruby Rich, 'The Crisis of Naming in Feminist Film Criticism' from *Jump Cut – A Review of Contemporary Media*, Number 19, 1978.
5. Laura Mulvey, 'Visual Pleasure and Narrative Cinema', from *Visual and Other Pleasures* by Laura Mulvey, from *Screen*, Glasgow: John Logie Baird Centre, University of Glasgow, 1975.
6. Mary Ann Doane, '*Caught* and *Rebecca*: the Inscription of Femininity as Absence', from *Enclitic*, 5:2, 1981.
7. Teresa de Lauretis, 'Oedipus Interruptus', from 'Desire in Narrative' from *Alice Doesn't: Feminism, Semiotics, Cinema* by Teresa de Lauretis, London: Macmillan, 1984.
8. Kaja Silverman, 'Lost Objects and Mistaken Subjects', from *The Acoustic Mirror: the Female Voice in Psychoanalysis and Cinema* by Kaja Silverman, Bloomington and Indianapolis: Indiana University Press, 1988.
9. Michelle Citron, Julia Lesage, Judith Mayne, B. Ruby Rich, Anna Marie Taylor, and the editors of *New German Critique*, 'Women and Film: a Discussion of Feminist Aesthetics', from *New German Critique*, 13, New York: Telos Press, 1978.
10. Laura Mulvey, Afterthoughts on Visual Pleasure and Narrative Cinema (inspired by King Vidor's *Duel in the Sun* (1946)', from *Framework* 15–16–17, summer 1981.
11. Mary Ann Doane, 'Film and the Masquerade: Theorising the Female Spectator', from *Screen*, 23, Glasgow: John Logie Baird Centre, University of Glasgow, 1982.
12. Annette Kuhn, 'Women's Genres: Melodrama, Soap Opera and Theory', from *Screen*, 25:1, Glasgow: John Logie Baird Centre, University of Glasgow, 1984.
13. Christine Gledhill, 'Pleasurable Negotiations', from E. D. Pribham (ed.), *Female Spectators: Looking at Film and Television*, London and New York: Verso, 1988.
14. Valerie Walkerdine, 'Video Replay: Families, Films and Fantasy', from V. Burgin et al (eds), *Formations of Fantasy*, London: Routledge, 1986.
15. Jackie Stacey, 'Feminine Fascinations: Forms of Identification in Star-Audience

Relations', from C. Gledhill (ed.), *Stardom: Industry of Desire*, London: Routledge, 1991.

16. Janet Staiger, 'Taboos and Totems: Cultural Meanings of the *Silence of the Lambs*', from J. Collins, H. Radner and A. P. Collins (eds), *Film Theory Goes to the Movies*, London: Routledge, 1993

17. Carol J. Clover, 'Her Body, Himself: Gender in the Slasher Film', from J. Donald (ed.), *Fantasy and the Cinema*, London: British Film Institute Publishing, 1989.

18. Barbara Creed, 'Horror and the Monstrous Feminine: an Imaginary Abjection', from *Screen* 27:1, Glasgow: John Logie Baird Centre, University of Glasgow, 1986.

19. Linda Williams, 'Film Bodies: Gender, Genre and Excess', from *Film Quarterly*, Vol. 44, No. 4, Berkeley: University of California Press, 1991.

20. Jane Gaines, 'White Privilege and Looking Relations: Race and Gender in Feminist Film Theory', from *Screen* 29:4, Glasgow: John Logie Baird Centre, University of Glasgow, 1988.

21. bell hooks: 'The Oppositional Gaze: Black Female Spectators' from *Black Looks: Race and Representation*, London: Turnaround, 1992.

22. Tania Modleski, 'Cinema and the Dark Continent: Race and Gender in Popular Film' from *Feminism without Women: Culture and Criticism in a 'Post-Feminist' Age*' by Tania Modleski, London: Routledge, 1991.

23. Judith Butler, 'Gender is Burning: Questions of Appropriation and Subversion' from *Bodies that Matter: On the Discursive Limits of 'Sex'* by Judith Butler, London: Routledge, 1993.

INDEX

INDEX

and desire, 2
negotiation, 170, 173
Negulesco, Jean, 140
Newman, Paul, 30
Newton, Helmut, 296
Niagara, 206
Nietzsche, Fredrich, 336
Night of the Living Dead, The, 253
Nightmare on Elm Street, 267
Ninotchka, 17
No Sad Songs For Me, 21
Nolte, Nick, 120
Norris Kathleen, 23
Not A Love Story, 83
Not Wanted, 38
Notes, on Women's Cinema, 11
Now Voyager, 133–4, 139

O'Hara, Scarlett, 23, 26
object, 9, 18, 99, 115
    of desire, 2
    of narrative punishment, 2
    person as, 61
objectification *see* Woman as Object
Oedipus complex, 44, 83, 85, 88, 90, 93, 112, 117,
    118, 123, 125–9, 149, 167, 184, 187, 214, 215,
    218, 240, 263
    Oedipal fantasy, 34, 98, 103
    Oedipal transference, 25
Of Mice and Men, 16
Old Aquaintance, 25
Old Maid, The, 24, 27, 28
Old Man and the Sea, The, 14
Olivier, Laurence, 74
Omen, The, 253
Only Angels Have Wings, 64
Only Yesterday, 27
Ophuls, Max, 27, 29, 70
oppression of women, 9
Ordinary People, 276
otherness, 34, 61, 84, 91, 98, 100, 102, 104, 119, 167,
    173, 188, 257, 265, 308, 340
Our Gang, 309

Panofsky, Erwin, 31, 32, 38
Paris is Burning, 4, 290, 291, 337, 338, 339, 341, 342,
    348
Paris Match, 32
Passion of Anna, The, 21
Passion of Remembrance, 319
patriarchy, 4, 13, 45, 46, 59, 60, 68, 70, 115, 116, 117,
    118, 123, 149, 162, 168, 173, 176, 209, 220, 258,
    259, 269, 274, 295, 299, 302, 321
Peckinpah, Sam, 11
Peeping Tom, 140
penis envy, 25
Penley, Constance, 2, 314
Penny Serenade, 27
Perils of Pauline, 234
Perkins, Anthony, 295
Personal Best, 293
perversion, 61
Petulia, 21
phallic replacement, 34, 77, 89
phallocentrism, 34, 58, 59, 251, 289, 310, 311, 313
phallus, 33, 58, 101, 103, 116, 120, 123, 124, 127,
    128, 215, 238, 240, 254, 255, 260, 263, 264, 273,
    275, 316, 317, 346

Pink Flamingo, 244
pleasure, 87
    destruction of, 59
    in film, 2
politics, 181
Pollock, Griselda, 185
Poltergeist, 261
pornography, 3, 17, 84, 118, 232, 268, 269, 270, 271,
    273, 275, 276, 274, 278
Portrait of Jason, 37
post-colonial theory, 2, 4
postmodernism, 2
Powell, William, 30
pre-Oedipal, 112, 123, 231, 258, 261, 263
primal scene, 229, 231, 232, 258, 259, 260
Propp, Vladimir, 126
Psycho, 83, 140, 239, 241, 242, 243, 253, 254, 265,
    271, 275, 297
psychoanalysis, 2, 25, 58, 59, 97, 112, 136, 147, 162,
    163, 167, 176, 181, 184, 191, 196, 197, 215, 272,
    288, 293, 314
    psychoanalytic feminist theory, 3, 328
    psychoanalytic theory, 3, 4, 12, 58, 64, 68, 74, 76,
        89, 91, 111, 113, 118, 169, 287, 302
Punishment of Anne, The, 275
Pygmalion, 26

queer theory, 2, 4

race, 120, 289, 291, 292, 297, 299, 303, 321–34, 342
Radway, Janice, 172, 173, 187, 192
rape, 26, 271, 294, 300, 309
Raymond, Janice, 339
realism, 36, 37, 143
    social, 29
Rear Window, 66, 140
Rebecca, 70–81, 92, 93
Reckless Moment, The, 27
redemption
    of the mother, 27
Redford, Robert, 30
Redgrave, Vanessa, 119
Reflection of Fear, 253
Renoir, Jean, 328
repression, 167
    of woman, 34
resistance, 33, 198
Reynolds, Burt, 117
Rich, Adrienne, 41, 43, 46
Rich, B. Ruby, 2, 12, 13, 111
Riddles of the Sphinx, The, 46, 116, 118
River of No Return, The, 63
Riviere, Joan, 113, 138
Rocky Horror Picture Show, The, 244
Rocky II, 162, 163, 180–93
roles
    female, 32
    male, 32
romance, 173
    romantic idols, 29
    Stendhalian, 23
Room of One's Own, A, 14
Rose, Jacqueline, 71
Rosemary's Baby, 253
Rosen, Marjorie, 42
Ross, Diana, 288, 295, 296, 298, 299
Rothman, Stephanie, 33
Rowbotham, Sheila, 46, 116, 295